Luminos is the Open Access monograph publishing program from UC Press. Luminos provides a framework for preserving and reinvigorating monograph publishing for the future and increases the reach and visibility of important scholarly work. Titles published in the UC Press Luminos model are published with the same high standards for selection, peer review, production, and marketing as those in our traditional program. www.luminosoa.org

Awarded the

Joseph W. Elder Prize in the Indian Social Sciences

by the American Institute of Indian Studies and published with the Institute's generous support

Merchants of Virtue

South Asia Across the Disciplines

SOUTH ASIA ACROSS THE DISCIPLINES

Edited by Muzaffar Alam, Robert Goldman, and Gauri Viswanathan

Dipesh Chakrabarty, Sheldon Pollock, and Sanjay Subrahmanyam, Founding Editors

Funded by a grant from the Andrew W. Mellon Foundation and jointly published by the University of California Press, the University of Chicago Press, and Columbia University Press.

For a list of books in the series, see pages 257–258.

Merchants of Virtue

Hindus, Muslims, and Untouchables in Eighteenth-Century South Asia

Divya Cherian

UNIVERSITY OF CALIFORNIA PRESS

University of California Press
Oakland, California

Suggested citation: Cherian, D. *Merchants of Virtue: Hindus, Muslims, and Untouchables in Eighteenth-Century South Asia*. Oakland: University of California Press, 2023. DOI: https://doi.org/10.1525/luminos.139

Cataloging-in-Publication Data is on file at the Library of Congress.
ISBN 978-0-520-39005-8 (pbk.)
ISBN 978-0-520-39006-5 (ebook)

28 27 26 25 24 23
10 9 8 7 6 5 4 3 2 1

CONTENTS

LIST OF ILLUSTRATIONS

MAPS

FIGURES

NOTE ON TRANSLITERATIONS AND CITATIONS

I have used diacritics and italics for all non-English words, except for the following: personal and place names; "brahman," "rajput," and "mahajan," which occur often in the text; and words like "bazaar" and "avatar" that have made their way into the English language. If a personal name includes a caste title for which I otherwise use diacritics, I have dropped the diacritics. For Marwari words, I have followed the conventions of R. S. McGregor's *Oxford Hindi-English Dictionary*, with the exception of using "ch" and not "c" to transliterate "*ch*" as in "*chandan*" (sandalwood; pronounced as the "ch" in "lunch") and "chh" instead of "ch" for "*chh*" as in "*chhatrī*" (umbrella). This is in keeping with common practice in English-language writing outside of academia in India today. I have not capitalized "brahman," which is conventionally capitalized in English. This is, following Nandita Prasad Sahai, to avoid conferring a sort of distinction upon brahmans through the capitalization of this word.

I have rendered Marwari terms without adapting them to their Persian forms. For instance, I have retained "*kānuṅgo*" instead of adapting it to the more familiar Persian "*qānūngo*." When quoting from the original, I have transliterated words as they were written in the original, leading to nonstandardized transliterations of Marwari words that are inconsistently spelled in the documents. This is in order to avoid imposing my own standardization upon the historical materials. For Persian words, I have followed F. J. Steingass, with the exception of diacritics for the letters "*tā*" and "*zād*," which I have left out. I have rendered Sanskrit words into English using scholarly conventions standardized for this language. For words that have become common in their Sanskritic form in English scholarly writing about South Asia, I retain these now familiar spellings, as for instance with *dharma*. In pluralizing South Asian language words, I follow the English-language pattern of adding an “s” at the end of the word.

This book relies on an examination of more than seventy volumes of the *Jodhpur Sanad Parwāna Bahīs* (discussed in the introduction and chapter 1), annualized compilations of the orders and decrees of the Rathor crown in Jodhpur to its district officers. When citing these records, I have abbreviated them to “JSPB” followed by the *bahī* or register number (as assigned by the Rajasthan State Archives and written on the cover of each register), the year of inscription by the Vikram Samvat (VS) calendar and the Gregorian calendar, and the folio number (f) and side (a or b) on which the information cited is written. For calendric conversion, I have deducted fifty-seven years from the Vikram Samvat year, as is established practice in the study of Rajasthan broadly and Marwar in particular.

Introduction

"To put it simply: People who touch things that we do not touch *become* untouchable."[1]

How significant is the history of untouchability for an understanding of South Asia's early modern past? Studies that approach early modern caste as a whole tend to represent the "untouchable" castes as being at the bottom-most rung of a graded order and untouchability as part of the larger complex of caste practices. But the exclusion and discrimination that those deemed "Untouchable" experienced was not merely a degree removed from the castes just above them. To the contrary, a chasm separated the "untouchable" castes from "caste society," a chasm that extends into the ritual domain to the present day, with *bhaṅgīs* and *halālkhors*—groups associated in the caste imagination with clearing human waste—having their own religious practices that have little or nothing to do with those of "caste" Hindus and Muslims.[2] Nor do they capture how central the specter of the Untouchable was to the operation of caste. There is then a need to pay attention to untouchability in distinction from the larger caste order in early modern South Asia.[3] This book offers a history of the reconstitution of the "Untouchable" in the precolonial, early modern period, a process that I argue was intertwined with the reconfiguration in this same period of the "Hindu."

Aniket Jaaware argues, in contradistinction to sociological and anthropological approaches that privilege marriage and inter-dining in their study of caste, that the practices of touchability and untouchability operate at a deeper, more foundational level to be the markers of caste.[4] Traces of "untouchable" things, Jaaware tells us, carry the potential to be identified with the whole of the persons who touch those "untouchable" things.[5] This is certainly reflected in the eighteenth-century archives on which this book is based. These archives, which among other things record the experience of castes engaged in clearing human waste and working with carcasses and hides, can be observed to have played a unique and constitutive role in the creation and renewal of caste consciousness. At the same time, despite the discursive configuration of untouchability as bodily pollution, land, labor, and debt relations too played a significant role in placing particular castes outside the pale of the social.[6]

Generations of historical research have firmly laid to rest for scholars of South Asia the conception of a timeless India lacking in history produced and nurtured by colonial administrators and historians, of which an unchanging, hereditary caste order was a key pillar.[7] Nicholas Dirks and Sumit Guha have shown that in precolonial South Asia, kings were integral to caste politics and hierarchies, that caste orders changed over time and were not anchored in brahmanical scripture and ideals alone, and that caste was only one of many loci of identity.[8] The picture of a timeless caste "system," however, persists in popular discourse, albeit reborn among some quarters as a relatively benign order of occupational and "worth"-based stratification.[9] Yet, this book argues, there was a limit to the fluidity or negotiability of caste and that limit stood at the boundary that separated the *bhaṅgī* (or *halālkhor*)—the remover of household and bodily waste—from all others and which served to anchor the precolonial conception of the Untouchable. The figure of the *bhaṅgī* embodied in elite minds the specter of Untouchability, a living and tangible vector of it that lived and worked within caste society. The *bhaṅgī*, as the Untouchable par excellence, could be amalgamated with other castes deemed "proximate," as I will show, to draw a line separating caste from outcaste. In the eyes of caste elites, this line was not fixed and, depending on context, could shift so far as to include almost everyone but the rajputs (landed warrior elites), brahmans (priests, scholars, and scribes), and merchants. The *bhaṅgī*, however, was indisputably and always "untouchable."

The margins of caste society then faded from fullest inclusion to total exclusion, with the *bhaṅgī* marking the core of the always excluded. Proximity to the *bhaṅgī*, whether real or imagined, placed others at risk of being rendered beyond the pale of social inclusion. This perhaps also explains what Ramnarayan Rawat and K. Satyanarayana have called the "Gandhian Harijan ideology," which represented Dalits through "the stereotype of the *bhaṅgī* (scavenger) figure and stigmatized victim in need of reform from above."[10] M. K. Gandhi, as a merchant-caste man who came of age in western India about a century after the period about which I write here came to a close, likely inherited the perspective on untouchability and its embodiment in the *bhaṅgī* that the records of the Rathor state reflect. There was, it appears, a deeper history to the reading of the *bhaṅgī* as the emblem of untouchability. This in turn makes clear that among the merchant, brahman, and other elite-caste actors who petitioned the state, concerns with ritual purity and pollution, though certainly not the only and "encompassing" principles ordering caste society and life within it,[11] did guide behavior and priorities. These ideas of purity and pollution were centered on the body, generating particular forms of exclusion in which touch, bodily substances, descent, and other corporeal aspects of personhood were central.

While historians have written about "untouchable" communities in the colonial and postcolonial periods, the focus of their analysis remains on the transformations wrought by modernity upon the history of these groups. Still, these studies have made preliminary efforts to understand the precolonial context preceding the changes they trace, and I build in this book on their efforts.[12] Discussions of untouchability through precolonial, early modern South Asian sources have been limited to studies of poetry composed in the voice of "untouchable" poet-saints such as Ravidas (also known as Raidas), born to a leatherworking family in Varanasi and thought to have lived in the fifteenth or sixteenth century. These studies make clear the limits of extrapolating historical information about interfaith or caste-centered conflict from poetry and literature.[13] My reliance on state orders responding to subjects' petitions and localized disputes allows me to offer a more granular, everyday account of the construction and practice of untouchability in the early modern period. It also makes possible a better understanding of the role of state power in caste orders in precolonial South Asia than has so far been possible by scholars working with literary, devotional, or philosophical texts.

At the same time, I do not try to recuperate the "voice" of the castes deemed untouchable or lowly, recognizing the mediation of scribal renderings and truncations upon petitions and testimonies. I do, however, seek to represent the historical experiences of eighteenth-century actors even as filtered through the "scripts of power" that are the Rathor archives. I also excavate the particular ways in which lowliness, marginality, and exclusion were engineered through law and administration in this historical setting. Understanding Hindu-ness and caste in precolonial South Asia requires a close engagement with the history of the construction and practice through law of untouchability. The state, its law, and its administrative machinery were integral to the operation of caste, not just through the distribution of honors and kingly substance as gifts,[14] but also through direct interventions in favor of local elites. In this history, it was not an already-defined, textually derived set of brahmanical values that formed the axis along which localized caste orders and their exclusions occurred in the eighteenth century.[15] Instead, the ideals and practices of other, nonbrahman caste groups could play a role in shaping the ethical, social, and bodily requirements of elite caste rank and in constructing ideological notions of purity in precolonial South Asia.

This discussion of elites brings me to the other central concern of this book: Where is the merchant in early modern South Asian history? And where is the merchant in histories of caste? While there are many studies of mercantile activity in the domain of trade and to a lesser extent politics, merchants remain peripheral to ideas about social change in early modern South Asia. This book suggests that the eighteenth century saw South Asian merchants make the leap from participants in state machinery to leaders of political change. Joining hands with others with more tenuous claims to courtly leadership, such as brahmans, the merchants of Marwar were catalysts in the crafting through state power of a new elite identity—

the "Hindu." When operationalized on the ground, it was defined not against the Muslim as such but rather in caste terms, against the specter of the Untouchable. The "Otherness" of the Muslim too was rendered legible through caste, with an emphasis on embodied difference. The "Untouchable," in turn, was a social body named in these records as "*achhep*," a term that translates to "untouchable."

"Hindu" was a transcaste, umbrella category defined against the Untouchable. But the "Untouchable" also included the Muslim (*turak*), who in turn was collapsed into the same category as leatherworkers, landless vagrants, and castes engaged in clearing waste. Nowhere is this more clear than in the following command:

> [1785] *Kāgad do koṭvālī chauntrā ūpar doḍhī rā: aprañch uṭhai saihar maiṁ sārā ī nu kaih deṇo su pohar rāt bājyā pachhai doy ghaḍī tāīṁ śrī parameśvar rā nāṁv rojīnai līyaṁ karai su hinduvāṁ nu kehjo nai turak ḍheḍh chamār thorī bāvrī halālkhor achhep jāt huvai jīnāṁ nu nahī kehṇo nai pher chauntrā rā ādmī rojīnai saihar mai phir nai kayāṁ karai su pohar rāt bājyā pachhai doy ghaḍī tāīṃ sadāī nāṁv levo karai śrī hajūr ro hukam chhai.*

1 nāgaur	*kāsīd chalāyo huvā dai*
1 meḍtai	*kāsīdāṁ rī ḍāk maiṁ dīyo*
2	*duvāyatī pañcholī nandrām nu phurmāyo*[16]

> [1785] Two documents for the front room at the magistracy: Instruct everyone in these towns to recite the name of Śri Parameśvar (the Supreme Lord) two *ghaḍīs* into the night *pahar* (or, about a quarter of an hour past sunset) every evening. Relay this to Hindus (*hinduvāṃ*) but not to the *achhep* ("untouchable") castes, these being *turaks*, *chamārs*, *ḍheḍhs*, *thorīs*, *bāvrīs*, and *halālkhors*. By the order of His Highness, men from the magistracy should roam through the town daily, announcing that the name must always be recited two *ghaḍīs* into the night *pahar*.

1 to Nagaur	a mail carrier has been dispatched
1 to Merta	has been sent with the mail carriers' post
2	issued by Pañcholī Nandram to whom it was told

The office of the Maharaja Vijai Singh (r. 1752–93) dispatched this order to two of its provincial capitals, the towns of Nagaur and Merta, in 1785. These towns were administrative headquarters for two of the most populous of the sixteen provinces that made up Vijai Singh's kingdom of Marwar, situated in the southern and central parts of the modern-day state of Rajasthan in western India and sometimes also known by the name of its capital, Jodhpur. Both of the towns at the heart of the order were also regional centers of trade, and Nagaur had the added trait of being a busy center of Sufi pilgrimage due to the presence there of the shrine of Saint Hamiduddin Chishti. The order states quite plainly that all the Hindus (*hinduvāṁ*) in these two towns should recite the holy name of *Śrī Parameśvar* (literally, "Supreme Lord") at a fixed time of evening each day.[17] The wording of the order suggests that "Hindu" was an umbrella term that subsumed within it a number of castes. At the same time, the order makes amply clear that "Hindus" did not include members of another transcaste body—the Untouchable (*achhep*, literally "untouchable"[18]). While leaving the constitution of "Hindu" vague, this state command defined clearly who exactly counted as Untouchable: Muslims (*turaks*),[19] skinners and leatherworkers (*ḍheḍhs* and *chamārs*, who also worked as agricultural laborers in the countryside), vagrant hunters (*thorīs* and *bāvrīs*),[20] and removers of human waste (*halālkhors*, also called *bhaṅgīs* elsewhere in these records).[21]

This imagination of the local caste order can be discerned in a large number of petitions and commands inscribed in the Rathor records, making clear that this order, even if it articulated this vision in the starkest terms, was not an isolated one in terms of its import. In tracing this push for a clearer demarcation of caste boundaries in this region in eighteenth-century South Asia, I make three interventions. First, I argue that a heightened polarization of the caste order in some parts of South Asia was due to the local effects of economic shifts occurring at transregional and global scales. Second, I suggest that this emergent Hinduness was defined in caste terms, with the Muslim and the Untouchable reinforcing each other to make legible what the limits of Hindu-ness were. Third, I submit that the association between elite caste status and vegetarian diet on the one hand and between lowliness and eating meat on the other owes much to this chapter in South Asian history and to the rise of merchants to localized power in the early modern period. Gopal Guru and Sundar Sarukkai have called for a re-centering of the body and of everyday sensory experience in the conception of the social.[22] In this book, I offer such a history of everyday and localized encounters between different sensory-ethical regimes focused on remaking social bodies. This fusing of lowliness and eating meat with being outsiders to the "Hindu" fold as defined in eighteenth-century, precolonial South Asia continues to be of significance to caste politics and everyday life in India and in the South Asian diaspora today.

CASTE AND CAPITAL

So what was it about the eighteenth century that fueled the rise of a state like that of the Rathors in Marwar, one that did not hesitate to intervene in localized patterns and caste customs in order to impose a particular vision of an ideal caste body upon its subjects? Answering this question entails attention to changes that occurred at not only the regional and subcontinental levels but also at transregional and global scales. Drawing on recent turns in global history, I suggest that shifts beyond and seemingly outside the region help explain changes that otherwise appear to be purely local in origin.[23] Transformations at multiple scales—regional, subcontinental, and global—and along different timelines then worked to generate particular changes legible in the locality. This is a particularly fruitful approach for Marwar, since the eighteenth century was one that brought an extraordinary transformation in the fortunes of merchant-moneylenders from the region who had spread out across the Indian subcontinent.

Perhaps due to their proximity to Gujarat, a coastal region with a deep history of participation in Indian Ocean trade, merchant castes from Marwar were among a slew of western Indian mercantile castes well acquainted with sophisticated accounting and banking skills that took advantage of the peace and territorial consolidation made possible by the Mughal Empire from the mid-sixteenth century onward. Mughal revenue demand in cash, the greater standardization of weights and measures, the administrative need for men trained in accounts, for credit, and for the transfer of large amounts of money from one part of the empire to another, were among the factors that benefitted western Indian merchants both as traders and as employees of the expanding Mughal state. The hereditary mercantile castes of Gujarat and Rajasthan were able to deploy networks of caste and kinship to quickly funnel funds and business intelligence across vast distances in the seventeenth and eighteenth centuries. The line between statecraft and trade became blurred, with political functionaries, nobles, and even kings participating in trade on the one hand and merchants thriving in administrative departments on the other.[24] While such a close connection between trade and politics may have existed in coastal polities from the medieval period onward, the sixteenth century saw a deepening of this relationship inland as well.

As a number of historians have argued, the period encompassing the sixteenth to eighteenth centuries was an age that saw the emergence of new kinds and organizations of production in South Asia that may be characterized as early, commercial, or mercantile capitalism.[25] The era of commercial capital was a global one, unfolding coevally across the world from the medieval period and intensifying from the sixteenth to eighteenth centuries. It differed among other ways from its successor, industrial capitalism, by the constant circulation and high fluidity of capital rather than its investment into fixed assets.[26] Frank Perlin has shown the many ways in which South Asia as a region became deeply interlinked in the course of the seventeenth and eighteenth centuries—even prior to colonial conquest by the English East India Company—with the rest of the world. For instance, Indian textiles and cowrie shells were carried to Africa by European traders and exchanged for slaves to be traded across the Atlantic.[27] Over time, the strong control that merchants began to exercise over commercial manufacturing led to a drain of resources from regions and populations specializing in production and to the concentration of wealth not only in the hands of particular groups in South Asia but, with the involvement of European traders, in metropolitan centers in western Europe. Areas that flourished as centers of commercial manufacture were not in fact necessarily poised to make a transition to industrial capitalism.[28] Instead, the webs that tied them to transregional exchange made these regions of commercial manufacturing essential contributors to organizational change, capital accumulation, and reinvestment in world regions.[29]

So interwoven were nodes of economic activity around the world in the early modern age that economic forms and changes in some (though not all) parts of

historiography of premodern South Asia more generally. In the pages that follow, I show the localized and everyday nature of the construction of a self-conscious and self-naming Hindu community. I argue that the struggles to carve out this community played out in small, tight-knit urban neighborhoods and in the provincial courts of eighteenth-century Marwar.

This is also a history of law and legal culture in precolonial South Asia, with the book offering a history of the practice of law in India on the eve of colonial conquest. In approaching the Rathor state as a legal order, I find an unselfconsciously Persianate lexicon at its heart, even in its pursuit of new "Hindu" publics. Alongside, while historians of western India have pointed to the significance of variable and malleable custom as a guide for kings and their delegates in the administration of social life, I show here that these customary regimes coexisted with efforts, even contradictory ones, that sought to impose more generalized laws upon all subjects. Even so, there are plenty of hints in this state archive of a thriving, legal pluralism, with references to *qāẓīs* (Islamic jurists) and localized caste *pañchs* (councils). Still, legal adjudication, including the maintenance of a documentary body of past legal pronouncements, emerged in the eighteenth century in Marwar as a central element of state formation.

It is important to clarify here that these efforts to harden boundaries through state intervention were not all-encompassing in the way that colonial historians and some postcolonial ones have sought to represent precolonial interfaith relations. The drive to craft a singular Hindu community was cross-cut by a range of forces, not least among which was the weight of customary practice. The Rathor court continued its patronage of Sufi shrines and maintained diplomatic ties with Muslim-ruled polities. Branches within the Rathor family, including the nineteenth-century Maharaja Man Singh (r. 1803–43), chose to affiliate with Nath Yogis rather than the Vaishnav sects that were central to the ritual life of eighteenth-century Hindus in Marwar.[56] At the popular level, a diversity of practices, including ones that occupied an overlapping space between Muslim and Hindu, thrived.[57]

Groups at the receiving end of the Rathor state's drive to cast a new body of subjects did not simply resign themselves to these changes. The resistance of "low" castes, landless communities, and Muslims—the "Untouchables" described in the command with which I began this introduction—is inscribed in these records in the form of petitions and protests as well as through the continuing of the dietary, ritual, and occupational practices that Rathor administrators sought to condemn. Yet, the persistence of these continuities, of diversity, and of resistance does not make the drive to carve out a singular, self-conscious Hindu community in a precolonial setting any less of a departure nor soften the breaks in local orders and regional culture that this entailed. "Popular" and non-Vaishnav practice did not remain unaffected by the efforts to reformulate elite identity in the eighteenth century.

It is also necessary to establish that this book does not see the decades under study as being the first point of departure in the construction of Hindu-ness nor does it argue for the birth, fully formed, of the modern Hindu community. "Hindu," as it was imagined in Marwar on the cusp of colonial conquest, differed from the meanings the category took on in the colonial era in several key ways. First, the eighteenth-century, precolonial Hindu community was an exclusive one, quite unlike its quest for demographic inclusivity from the colonial era onward. Another significant way in which the premodern Hindu community differed from its modern counterpart, as already emphasized, was the centrality of caste and of the imagined Untouchable to the construction of both the Hindu and the Muslim, a centrality that was "forgotten" in the course of the nineteenth and early twentieth centuries by mainstream discourse on Hinduism. In these ways then I recognize the significant transformations that colonialism and modernity did unleash upon the diversity of practices and beliefs that became united under the banner of "Hinduism," upon Hindu-ness, and upon Hindu-Muslim interaction. While recognizing early modern South Asia as fostering pluralism, tolerance, and inclusivity, I turn attention toward the hardening and enforcement of difference that could and did simultaneously thrive in pockets of it.

ETHICS, VIOLENCE, AND PURITY

Walking around the streets of north India, it is not uncommon to come across a "*Shuddh Shakahari Vaishno Dhaba*," or "Pure Vegetarian Vaishnav Food Kiosk." While these roadside eateries have been around for decades, the ethical pressure across India to be vegetarian appears to have reached a fever pitch only in recent years. The expansion of vegetarian residential complexes, vegetarian cafeterias at workplaces and schools, and government-supported bans on animal slaughter during Jain holy days have generalized the expectation of adherence to a vegetarian diet even to those whose religious and caste codes or personal convictions do not prescribe it. As commentators and scholars of contemporary South Asia have emphasized, vegetarianism in India is loaded with association to caste, that is, to "high" caste. It is also associated with the rise to power of dominant strands within Hindu nationalism. In regions where political Hinduism is dominant, such as Gujarat, with a long and deep history of Jainism and Vaishnavism, meat eating is not only a major component of the radical otherness of Muslims but also a justification for the violence Muslims have suffered during recent pogroms.[58] Vegetarianism is associated with cleanliness; it symbolizes "purity" both literal and ritual. Eating meat, conversely, is dirty. How did this come to be?

An important but neglected part of the answer to this question lies in the early modern past. Values and ethical cultures of the body emerged in parts of early modern South Asia, such as Marwar in the eighteenth century, as central axes for the formulation of an elite caste, Hindu identity, and for the expression of its distinction from the Untouchable. The book shows how the virtues associated with some—nonharm and vegetarianism along with chastity, temperance, and purity—were elevated to the status of laws applicable to all across the Rathor kingdom. In Marwar by the eighteenth century, it was merchants and to a lesser extent brahmans who, as a caste, combined regional political authority with subcontinental fiscal power to muscle their way into the top of the region's social order. Some brahman communities in Marwar such as the Palliwals and Nandwana Bohras were successful traders and moneylenders.

Brahmans in Marwar had occupied an ambivalent social location. Their own claims to high social rank found ample justification in brahmanical textual tradition as well as claims grounded in ritual, priestly, and scholarly functions. Yet, brahmans in north India, including Marwar, had not acquired the kind of political and economic standing that brahmans in peninsular India had achieved through their command of landed temple estates.[59] Brahmans' literacy facilitated their absorption into the expanding Rathor state as administrators. This, along with their leadership of Vaishnav sects whose presence and power in Rajasthan increased during the eighteenth century, improved the political position of brahmans. At the same time, brahmans had nowhere near the command over money and administrative offices that the merchant castes enjoyed.

This was indeed a novel situation, for rajputs had until then exercised blood- and land-based claims to the pinnacle of political and social orders.[60] The many different castes associated with trade and moneylending had consolidated in Rajasthan by the eighteenth century into an umbrella caste category called "mahajan."[61] Mahajans, with much of their power rooted in the indebtedness of others and in the circulation of money, could not draw upon existing cultural resources to justify their claims upon high social rank. Instead, they justified their rise to inclusion among the region's most elite through a turn to virtue. They adopted a righteous stance, expressed through the protection of nonhuman life, an adherence to an ascetic code of bodily restraint, and the valorization of these caste codes through their elevation into law. Rather than merely living by such ethical codes, they used their influence upon the region's state to impose this moral order upon all in the kingdom of Marwar.

Could it be that in this moment of transition globally from the old regime to one in which status derived not from land but from money, moral reform was a necessary component of efforts to challenge the status quo? In particular, the arrogation of the voice of the "voiceless"—whether the distant slave in a North American plantation in the case of English abolitionists or the nonhuman animal in the case of the Vaishnav-Jain merchants of Marwar—appears to have been the preferred mode of making a moral intervention in the politics of the day. The eighteenth century was a time also in Europe of the rise of early humanitarianism, which included a growing concern for preserving animal life or at least minimizing "needless" animal suffering.[62] In the case of Marwar, the pursuit of this righteous agenda underwrote the rise of a new elite that derived its status not from land but from capital.

In the process, the Rathor state in Marwar emerges as one that intervened widely in the lives of its subjects, particularly its upwardly mobile and aspirant elite ones, in order to produce ethical subjects. Bans on injury to nonhuman beings, and by extension on eating meat, on abortion, gambling, and drinking, as well as the enforcement of chastity and efforts to separate "high" from "low" and "Hindu" from "Untouchable," are reminiscent in part of the picture we have of the Peshwa state in the Deccan. But the Peshwa state can easily be explained as an aberration—its policies attributed to brahmans being rulers and therefore putting into practice brahmanical ideals. Marwar, however, continued to be ruled by an active and capable rajput king with the aid of a merchant-dominated administration. Brahmans too took on the role of administrators but they remained in a minority when compared with merchants. Like Marwar and the Deccan, Jaipur too was witness to the emergence of a similarly active state, governing the moral lives of its subjects. It appears then that the eighteenth century, with the rapid collapse of the Mughal state, generated a new state form, one that drew in a wider ambit of participants as bureaucrats and petitioners but which extended the remit of state power into the moral lives of its subjects. In Marwar this process entailed the discursive reconstitution of what it meant to be "high" caste or "Hindu" alongside a heightened rhetoric around the "Untouchable." As I show in the pages to come, the Rathor state, with a Vaishnav king at its helm, carried this imagination into practice, deploying its punitive and surveillance capabilities toward normalizing the newly imagined Hindu body.

Norbert Peabody and Madhu Tandon Sethia's respective studies of Kota, in southeastern Rajasthan today, have highlighted the role of merchants in shaping this polity. These studies have focused on the changing nature of kingship and on courtiers. They also have unearthed the growing penetration of rural trade and agrarian relations as well as of the state by merchants, though they do not venture into the effects of this mercantile influence on the administration of social life.[63] I depart from the focus on kings, landlords, and courtly texts on the one hand and on specific subsets of the population, such as artisans and mobile communities, on the other that have dominated the study of Rajasthan and turn attention instead to a particular regime's administration of everyday life and the micropolitics of localized social orders as a whole.[64] Where Nandita Sahai has traced in these same sources from eighteenth-century Marwar a story of artisanal resistance to unjust extractions and departures from custom through petitioning and protest, I focus instead on political realignments and efforts to establish new regimes of dominance that were simultaneously unfolding in eighteenth-century Marwar. In narrating this history, I have often retained a number of "small" details, rather than reducing every document to its "essence." I have done so in order to retain the texture, color, and variety of everyday life and to convey a more immersive sense of eighteenth-century life and lifeworlds in South Asia. I have also retained this texture to make clear how the drive to rework the region's caste order played out through micropolitics.

I tell this history in two parts, preceded by a chapter that explains the historical shifts in state form, kingship, and economy that made possible the effort to reshape the regional caste order and its basis that the rest of the book discusses. Part I lays out the axes along which the Rathor state's orders articulated an effort to express distinction and difference from those deemed lowly in caste terms. Chapter 2 discusses the explicit use of the category "Untouchable" in the Rathor record. This chapter examines the investment of the Rathor crown and its officers in policing the boundary between Hindu and Muslim, between Hindu and Untouchable, and sometimes even between Hindu and everyone else. In chapter 3 I consider the interest that Maharaja Vijai Singh and the Rathor state took in fostering Vaishnav devotion. I show the convergence of elite patronage with localized struggles in temple communities in Marwar, resulting in the emergence of a less inclusive Vaishnav devotional public. I also trace the fissures and struggles that developed in response to efforts to create and police boundaries with Muslims. Chapter 4 argues that a campaign to protect nonhuman life, in pursuit of the Vaishnav-Jain ethic of nonharm, translated into a regime of surveillance, banishments, economic dispossession, and marginalization for members of particular castes—armed, landless vagrants (*thorīs* and *bāvrīs*) and Muslims—explicitly identified as "Untouchable" in the 1764 order that I discussed earlier. Leatherworkers, also "Untouchable," were yet another group that suffered harsher punishment for the "crime" of killing animals than members of other castes.

Part II centers the recasting of elite identity through the elevation of merchant ethics, which aligned in many ways with brahman mores, into kingdom-wide law. Collectively, the chapters in this part of the book point to the role of the state, staffed as it was by merchant and brahman administrators, toward enforcing consistency in adherence to mercantile values from members of merchant and brahman communities. A vegetarian diet and a lack of moral "contamination" from causing bodily harm to living beings (chapter 5), bodily austerity, temperance, and sobriety (chapter 6), and chastity (chapter 7) were among the virtues the pursuit of which caused the Rathor state to outlaw injury to animals and animal slaughter, abortion, drinking, and gambling in its domain. These imperatives were imposed through a concerted effort at enforcement, even if merchants and brahmans appeared to be at the receiving end of the Rathor state's punitive drives on most of these fronts. The exception to this pattern was the effort to protect animals from violence and death: toward this goal, the Rathor state made no exceptions. Everyone was to toe the line. The epilogue traces the afterlives of these shifts, carried beyond Marwar and into the colonial era through the circulation of Marwari merchants across South Asia.

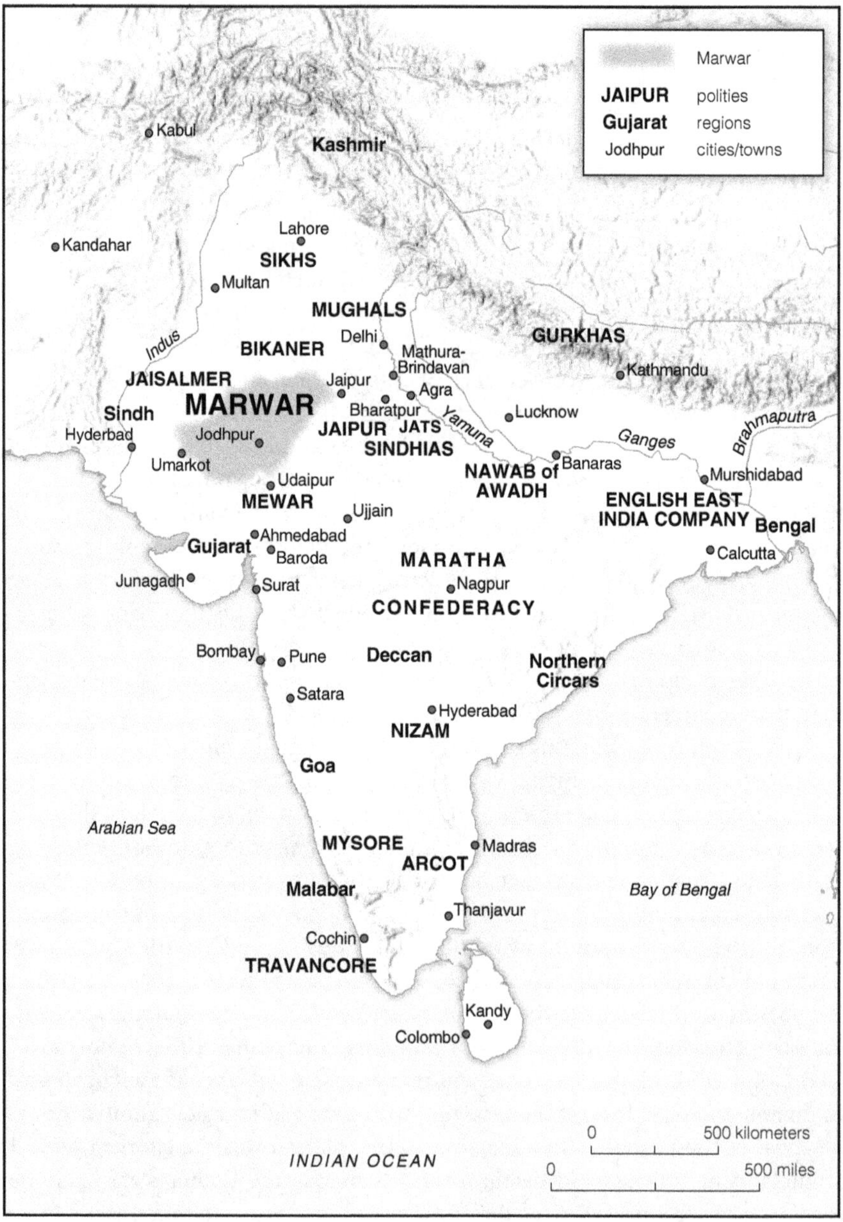
Marwar
JAIPUR polities
Gujarat regions
Jodhpur cities/towns
Kabul
Kashmir
Kandahar
Lahore
SIKHS
Multan
MUGHALS
Indus
BIKANER
Delhi
Mathura-Brindavan
GURKHAS
Kathmandu
JAISALMER
Jaipur
Agra
MARWAR
Bharatpur
Lucknow
Sindh
Yamuna
Brahmaputra
Hyderbad
Jodhpur
JAIPUR
JATS
Ganges
SINDHIAS
Umarkot
Banaras
NAWAB of AWADH
Murshidabad
Udaipur
MEWAR
Ujjain
ENGLISH EAST INDIA COMPANY
Bengal
Ahmedabad
Gujarat
Baroda
MARATHA
Calcutta
Junagadh
Surat
Nagpur
CONFEDERACY
Bombay
Pune
Deccan
Northern Circars
Satara
Hyderabad
NIZAM
Goa
Arabian Sea
MYSORE
Madras
ARCOT
Malabar
Bay of Bengal
Thanjavur
Cochin
TRAVANCORE
Kandy
Colombo
0
500 kilometers
INDIAN OCEAN
0
500 miles

MAP 1. Marwar in South Asia, c. 1780.

1

Power

In the South Asian popular imagination today, Marwar is most closely identified with the Marwari, the astute businessman and moneylender found in parts of India far removed from his homeland in the dusty towns and villages on the eastern edge of the Thar Desert. When viewed as a part of the wider region that is today known as Rajasthan, the other figure that the idea of Marwar conjures is that of the princely rajput, known for his martial ethos, opulent *havelī* (mansion), "secluded" womenfolk, and vast lands. But Marwar is home, as it has been for centuries, to a diverse population immersed in an array of trades and activities. Before the separations introduced by national borders, the region was interwoven through webs of migration, conquest, and pilgrimage not only with more accessible territories such as the Gangetic Plains, Gujarat, and Punjab but also with areas across the sands of the Thar, such as Sindh, Multan, and Balochistan. These vectors, along with trade, expanded the reach of this seemingly landlocked region into parts of the world much farther afield. This chapter traces the shifts in social, political, and economic life in Marwar that emerged from the fifteenth century onward and intersected to create the conditions necessary for the transformations in "Hindu" identity and caste that unfolded in the eighteenth century.

KINGSHIP RECAST

Studies of the Mughal state on the ground have made clear that key operations of government, such as tax collection and the legal resolution of disputes, depended on the cooperation of local notables.[1] As Rathor kings too sought to strengthen their monarchical claims over other rajputs, they built out a bureaucracy to better know and more directly interface with their subjects. From the early eighteenth century, the Rathor kings of Marwar no longer had a strong Mughal state to lean on in order to prop up their monarchical assertions above the kinship- and brotherhood-based (*bhāībāṇṭ*) claims of their Rathor kin in Marwar.[2] Even as they built upon the move toward monarchy set in motion by their predecessors in a century or so of stable Mughal rule, the Rathor kings of Marwar from Ajit Singh (r. 1707–24) onward worked to craft their authority in alliance with groups other than rajputs. They sought junior allies who could not articulate the blood- and caste-based claims to a share in kingship and land that all rajputs, particularly those of the Rathor clan, asserting fraternal bonds or *bhāībandh*, could.[3] In the search for a counterweight to rajput claims as they shaped their monarchical order, it was the mercantile and moneylending castes of Marwar—the mahajans—to whom the Rathor kings of Marwar turned to the greatest degree.

When the Mughal state began to crumble after the death of Aurangzeb in 1707, the Rathors faced a new set of challenges as well as possibilities. The greatest challenge before the Rathors was the rise of the Marathas from the middle of the eighteenth century.[4] Mahadji Sindhia (1730–1794, alternative spelling "Scindia"), the general who managed the Maratha Empire's efforts at expansion in north India, loomed large over the rajput polities of Rajasthan.[5] The rajput states, individually and in alliance, were simply no match for Sindhia's forces. Starting in 1756, Sindhia repeatedly routed Rathor armies. The vanquished Rathors were forced to cede formal control of the high-revenue district of Ajmer to the Marathas and to agree to the payment of large sums as war indemnity and as tribute.[6] Over the years, Marwar paid upward of two and a half million rupees to Mahadji Sindhia, even as it managed to reassert at least a degree of administrative control over Ajmer.[7]

At the same time, for the Rathors as for all dynasts in the subcontinent, the void left behind by the much-reduced Mughal state also offered opportunity for growth.[8] By 1740, the weakened Mughal state stopped asking the Rathor kings of Jodhpur to perform service for it outside of their home territory.[9] For Vijai Singh, king from 1752 to 1793, this permitted more time in Marwar and allowed him to invest greater energy toward reshaping his polity and meeting internal challenges. He was an able strategist, waging a multiyear war against a rival and cousin, Ram Singh, who had used the help of the Marathas to capture half of Marwar between 1754 and 1756. Vijai Singh emerged victorious in this struggle in 1761,[10] despite many of Marwar's rajput nobles supporting his rival. After 1761, Vijai Singh mixed incentives with harsh reprisals to subdue those rajput nobles who had continued to resist his authority even after he defeated his princely rival.[11]

Working within the constraints posed by Maratha demands and internal rebellion, Vijai Singh crafted for himself a new model of kingship. Through a mix of imitation and innovation, he departed from his Rathor predecessors in a number of significant ways. Most importantly for this book, it was in Vijai Singh's reign that the Rathor chancery began to systematically order its records. A number of important record series, each bound together in *bahīs* or registers, in the Rathor kingdom began to be kept during the years immediately following Vijai Singh's accession to the Rathor throne. Vijai Singh also began to maintain a standing army, a departure from his predecessors who had relied largely on troop levies from subordinate rajput lords. The army consisted of bands of soldiers recruited from Sindh as well as from the Vaishnav and Shiva-worshipping, militarized ascetic orders such as the Nagas and the Vishnuswamis. Historians of the eighteenth century in South Asia have focused on the rise of military fiscalism—the crafting of a centralizing state taxation system to streamline finances and to develop a more disciplined and tightly controlled army—as a new development triggered by the dynamism and multipolarity of this period.[12] Certainly, Vijai Singh's Marwar experienced elements of such an effort.

Under him, the Rathors began to mint their own coins in 1780, albeit with the permission and in the name of the reigning Mughal emperor, Shah Alam II. Mints in Jodhpur, Merta, Nagaur, and Sojhat produced these coins.[13] The Rathor crown relied on a range of taxes: land revenue (*bhog*); taxes on wells, plows, houses, grazing animals, and hearths; dues in kind from artisanal producers; and *corvée* (unremunerated labor known as *begār*). By the eighteenth century, the Rathor state had also started farming out land revenue assignments under the fixed-rate *muqātī* tenure, which was given on contract.[14] In addition, fines on subjects for violating customary or ethical codes were a steady source of income for the Rathor crown, as the chapters ahead will show. With the acquisition of the fertile region of Godwad in the southeast through a diplomatic arrangement with Udaipur and the conquest of the Umarkot region on the west in Sindh, Vijai Singh managed to rebuild the royal treasury despite the drain caused by war against the Marathas and the cost of keeping his fractious rajput nobles in place. This enabled him to meet the many internal and external challenges that marked his reign. Vijai Singh's refashioning of Rathor kingship through new patronage practices, architectural works, and reforms were made possible, in a time of Maratha fiscal demands, by these fresh sources of income that he managed to carve out.

THE "SERVANT" KING

In his reconstitution of Rathor kingship, Vijai Singh's efforts went beyond administrative, military, and fiscal reform. Drawing perhaps upon models from neighboring rajput polities such as Kota and Kishangarh, Vijai Singh fashioned for himself the public image of a *bhakt* or devotee par excellence. He took initiation in 1765 into the Vallabh *sampradāy*, among the more popular and influential of the many *sampradāys* or sects centered on devotion toward Krishna, an avatar of the god Vishnu.[15] The Vallabh sect, also known as the Pushtimarg (or "Way of Grace"), coalesced around the memory of a brahman teacher, Vallabhacharya (c. 1478–1530), from the Telangana region in peninsular India as its founder.[16] Sectarian narratives assert that Vallabhacharya traveled widely across north India in the fifteenth century, preaching a message of pure and unmediated devotion or *bhakti* to Krishna.

It is worth pausing here to note that South Asianist scholars have discussed the problems generated by the terms "sect" and "sectarianism." "Sect," deriving from the Christian context, assumes a branching off from an original body or a mainstream.[17] For South Asia, this language generated in the nineteenth century the ahistorical idea of a unified and preexisting brahmanical religion under threat from dissident splinter groups, thereby painting sectarianism as an attack on the unity of brahmanism.[18] In South Asia, on the other hand, "sects" often emerged independently and only later came to be organized in relation to each other, whether externally or among themselves by consensus, into an overarching category. Historians of Hinduism have pointed to this problem and use the terms "sect" and "sectarian" only after making clear the distinct meanings of these terms in the South Asian context.[19] Elaine Fisher argues that sectarianism in early modern South Asia was a mode of religious engagement that, rather than generating fragmentation, in fact facilitated some of the earliest articulations of a unified religion while still asserting distinction. My usage of "sect" and "sectarian" in this book draws on this reflexive deployment of these terms among historians of South Asian religion and philosophy.

Returning to Vijai Singh's formal initiation into the strictly vegetarian, animal sacrifice–eschewing Vaishnav community of the Vallabhite sect, this generated a significant new locus of elite rajput and kingly religiosity in Marwar, one that cut against older ritual expressions of rajput status. Vijai Singh was not the first rajput king to adopt the stance of a Krishna devotee. Nor was the rajput kings' embrace of Krishna devotion unrelated to its rise to subcontinental prominence. The history of Vaishnav devotionalism is fundamentally intertwined with that of the Mughal state and its rajput vassals, some of whom were also related by marriage to the Mughals.[20] The familial relationship that emerged between particular rajput clans from Rajasthan, including the Rathors of Marwar, and the Mughal royal family shaped not only Vaishnav devotion but also the social and political worlds of the Mughals as well as the rajputs.[21] The patronage of successive Mughal emperors, particularly Akbar (r. 1556–1605) and Jahangir (r. 1605–27), and of their rajput nobles and kin played a central role in elevating Krishna devotion to a position of prestige and prominence. Brindavan, not far from the Mughal capitals of Agra and Delhi, emerged in the mid-sixteenth century as the center of devotional activity for the Vallabhite order as well as another prominent Vaishnav order, the Gaudiya sect.[22]

An embrace of Vaishnav religiosity, of which Krishna devotion was part, became in these centuries an articulation of cosmopolitan kingship among rajput lords.[23] In addition to the Kachhwahas of Jaipur, the Bundela rajput king, Madhukar Shah (r. 1552–92) of Orchha in central India also embraced Krishna devotion.[24] By the eighteenth century, the Sisodiyas of Udaipur, the Rathor ruling lineages in Bikaner and Kishangarh, the Hadas of Kota, and a number of smaller principalities in Rajasthan had become patrons and members of Vaishnav orders centered on Krishna. Krishna-centered Vaishnav devotionalism's association with the highest echelons of rajputs and its evocation of cosmopolitanism, prestige, and power attracted a growing number of kings and chiefs. Upstart ruling lineages, such as the Malla kings of Bengal, spent large sums on displaying their commitment to Vaishnavism.[25]

Some of these princely devotees were moved to compose devotional poetry. The sixteenth-century prince Prithviraj of Bikaner composed an ode to the romance of Krishna and his consort, Rukmini, *Velī Krisan Rukmanī Rī*.[26] In Vijai Singh's own lifetime, the Rathor prince of the neighboring principality of Kishangarh, Savant Singh (1699–1764), composed verses steeped in Krishna devotion, celebrating the love of Krishna and Radha under the pen name Nagaridas.[27] Bhim Singh, Hada rajput king of Kota (r. 1707–20), was so deeply devoted to the Vallabhite icon of Krishna in his possession that he dedicated his entire kingdom to the deity and referred to himself as merely the *dīvān* or prime minister of the Lord's domain.[28] Some sought to rebuild their capitals in the image of Braj, the area between Delhi and Agra, in which Krishna's idealized mythical childhood and youth is believed to have unfolded. Rup Singh (r. 1643–48) of Kishangarh strove to transform his new capital, Rupnagar, into a Braj-like pastoral idyll and Bhim Singh of Kota renamed his capital Nandgaon after Krishna's childhood village.[29]

From the last quarter of the seventeenth century, the connection between rajput courts and Vaishnav sects was further strengthened when brahman leaders of these orders decided to escort key icons out of the Braj region and settle down in the rajput kingdoms of western India. Bearing the most important icons of their respective sects, the leaders of both the Gaudiya and Vallabhite orders approached rajput courts for shelter from the instability caused in the Delhi region by *jāṭ* rebels against the Mughal Empire.[30] Sectarian accounts reflect that divisions and tensions within the orders were also a significant reason why the caretakers of different icons decided to leave Braj.[31] New centers of Vaishnav worship and pilgrimage thus sprouted in such rajput kingdoms as Udaipur and Jaipur that offered residence to the Krishna idols and their brahman caretakers.[32]

Once key Krishnaite icons became unmoored from Braj and mobile, Norbert Peabody has argued, any site in which they settled became associated, in the eyes of Krishna devotees, with ritual and affective power. By taking on the posture of a devotee-protector to a Vallabhite icon, a king communicated his possession of the tutelary and protective powers as well as the blessings of the deity immanent in the icon. The departure of the deity in turn signaled the loss of divine support. The efforts of *bhakt*-kings to communicate their close association with Vallabhite icons then had political currency in a milieu in which Vaishnav devotion held sway. Finally, the residence of a Vallabhite icon within a king's domain attracted pilgrims and their monetary donations, drew business to bazaars that enriched the kingdom's merchants, and boosted tax revenues.[33]

By Vijai Singh's reign then there already were a few precedents in the kingdoms around Marwar of the devotee king. In crafting his own authority, Vijai Singh likely drew upon these examples. He took initiation into the Vallabhite order in 1765, during a trip to their ritual center in Nathdwara in the adjacent kingdom of Udaipur.[34] A history of Vijai Singh's reign, *Mahārājā Śrī Vijai Siṅghjī rī Khyāt* (Chronicle of Maharaja Vijaisingh, henceforth "*MVSK*"), written at the Jodhpur court in the early nineteenth century under Maharaja Man Singh (r. 1803–48), records this development as "*mhārāj gusāyāṁ nai mānīyā* (the Maharaja acceded to the Gusains)."[35] Among the Vallabhites, Gusain (*gusāīṁ*) was a title held by descendants of Vallabhacharya, the order's founder.[36] They held positions of leadership in the devotional order and were treated with reverence.

The *MVSK* notes that the unnamed Gusains prevented Vijai Singh from visiting the *samādhi* (place of cremation or entombment) of Guru Atmaram, a preceptor of unknown spiritual affiliation of whom Vijai Singh had been a follower prior to his shift to the Vallabhite order. The Gusains are said to have called the *samādhi* a *masāṇ* (cremation site), a less respectful term, and to have told the Maharaja that if kings went there, they would be ritually polluted ("*mhārāj hajūr ātmārāmjī ra darsaṇ karaṇ nu padhāre tare gusāīṁjī kayo: mhārāj abe u to masāṇ chhe. Su the rājā lok jāvo su chhot lāgai*").[37]

In this early nineteenth-century court history, the episode was a mark of the growing influence of Vallabh sectarian leaders upon Vijai Singh, who heeded Krishnaite Gusains' advice and did not visit the teacher he had earlier so revered (*jaṭhā pachhe samād ro darsaṇ karṇo mokub kīyo nai gusāyāṁ ro idhkār vadhīyo*). Later, this same text describes the successes of Vijai Singh's reign in words attributed to a contemporary observer, Singhvi Khubji, a courtier of a merchant caste:

> A lion and a goat can be drinking water from the same bank without the lion harassing the goat. [Vijai Singh] is the crown jewel of all Hindustan (*hindusathān*). Fifty-one minor kings are in his service. The *vakīls* (intercessors) of the emperor (*pātsyāh*) of Ghazni, of the emperor of Sindh, of [the Nawab of Awadh] Shuja-ud-daulah, and of Hyderabad in the Deccan, along with 105 *vakīls* representing the Hindu and Muslim houses (*turkāṁ-hinduvāṁ rā ghar 105 ek sau pāñch*), all write reports to him of the goings-on in their masters' domains. The Lord's temples (*prabhu rā mandir*) are everywhere; their bells ring. The Lord grants a glimpse of himself at regular intervals. People discuss episodes from the Lord's life (*prabhu-kathā*). If a gold rupee falls on the ground, no one but its owner picks it up.[38]

Written only a few decades after the end of Vijai Singh's reign, this passage represents the king's success in terms that emphasize not only his attainments in the world of politics and as the upholder of justice but also his achievements in furthering the Vaishnav faith in Marwar. The measure of his success is also material and moral: the passage has an allusion to the profusion of money, both in the form of currency and as wealth, in Vijai Singh's Marwar.[39] Was gold so plentiful that its falling on the ground would not entice onlookers to grab it? Or had Vijai Singh managed to cultivate such contentment and virtue among his subjects that theft had no place in his kingdom? Perhaps this representation of his reign evoked all of these ideas.

Prominent in the passage is the celebration of Vijai Singh's Marwar as a land pervaded with holiness. *Prabhu* or "the Lord" spoken of here is likely Krishna. A play on words is also possible with a secondary but only suggested allusion to the king himself as "the Lord."[40] And indeed, Vijai Singh did build a number of new temples dedicated to Krishna. Records from his reign attest that he lavished as grants thousands of rupees upon Vaishnav temples and sectarian leaders and supported many Vaishnav devotees in Brindavan.[41] He sponsored the construction of new Vaishnav temples in Marwar, including a Vallabhite shrine to Krishna (Murlimanoharji) inside the Mehrangarh Fort in Jodhpur in 1759.[42] He commissioned, for the first time in Marwar, beautifully illustrated manuscripts of the *Bhāgavata Purāṇa*, an account of Krishna, and of the *Rāmcharitmānas*, a Hindi telling of the *Rāmāyaṇa* or the epic of the Ram avatar of Vishnu.[43] The *Rāmcharitmānas* told the story of Ram in a devotional mode, originally composed more than a century earlier by the poet Tulsidas. Vijai Singh also commissioned illustrated manuscripts of the *Gajendra Mokśa* (The Prayer of the Elephant King) and the *Durgā Charit*, also known as the *Devī Mahātmya* (recounting the victories of the Goddess). The continuing significance of the Goddess in a set of otherwise Vaishnav texts points to the persistence of other loci of devotion even after Vijai Singh's initiation into and elevation of the Vallabhite order.

Still, the image of devotee par excellence was prominent in his self-fashioning. Around 1770, Vijai Singh commissioned at least three different portraits depicting him in prayer before Vallabhite icons of Krishna as "Shri Nathji."[44] In all the paintings, Vijai Singh stands in a devout posture to the right of the Vallabhite Krishna icon while a brahman priest performs *sevā* or service to the deity by ringing a small hand-held bell and rocking the icon or waving a set of lamps before it. According to Debra Diamond, the priest in one of the 1770 paintings (fig. 1) is Gusain Giridharji,[45] who served at the Vallabhite temple at Chaupasni, near Jodhpur.[46] Since his portraiture remains remarkably stable through all three paintings, it is likely that the brahman priest in the other two paintings is also Gusain Giridharji.

In each of figures 1 and 2, the painter Udairam Bhatti aligns all the figures either to the left or the right sides of the painting, creating a central axis. This leads the viewer's eye to the Krishna icon, the only figure whose eyes look back at the viewer. Despite being almost tiny in relation to the figures of the Maharaja and the priests, the icon, through the device of the engaging eyes, draws the viewer's attention. Such a visual construction, with devotees clustered either to the right or left of the icon when they would in practice have also clustered in front of it, was a typical feature of *chitra darśan* paintings.[47] In Vallabh practice, *chitra darśan* (audience through a picture) and *chitra sevā* (service to a picture) are important devotional acts. Vallabhites believe that Krishna manifests himself in his painted and sculptural representations.[48] Viewing these paintings of Vijai Singh worshipping Krishna as Shri Nathji then was in itself an act of devotion. By placing himself prominently

FIGURE 1. Maharaja Vijai Singh worshipping Krishna, by Udairam Bhatti, Jodhpur, c. 1770, 55 x 8 cm, Mehrangarh Museum Trust, RJS 2049. ©Mehrangarh Museum Trust, Jodhpur, Rajasthan, India, and His Highness Maharaja Gaj Singh of Jodhpur. Do not reuse or reproduce image without permission from the Mehrangarh Museum Trust.

in these paintings that also were ritual objects, Vijai Singh not only built the reputation of a dedicated devotee but also elevated himself to the divine plane.

Peabody and Nandita Sahai see rajput kings' embrace and performance of Vallabhite devotion as significant for a number of reasons. Peabody notes this to be a transition from one ethic to another in the rajput courtly milieu, from that of *chākarī* or loyal service to an earthly lord to one of *sevā* or service more in the nature of devotion. In the context of eighteenth-century Kota, he sees the infantilization

FIGURE 2. Maharaja Vijai Singh worshipping Krishna, by Udairam Bhatti, Jodhpur, c. 1770, 34.7 x 30.6 cm), Mehrangarh Museum Trust, RJS 4267. ©Mehrangarh Museum Trust, Jodhpur, Rajasthan, India, and His Highness Maharaja Gaj Singh of Jodhpur. Do not reuse or reproduce image without permission from the Mehrangarh Museum Trust.

of the object of devotion as a powerful metaphor for the reduction of the Kota king to a puppet in the hands of his prime minister.[49] Sahai, on the other hand, sees in Vijai Singh's performance of maternal care of the Krishna icon an effort to recast his relationship with his subjects in the image of a parent-child relationship.[50] He sought to project maternalism, evoking a stance of nurturing and care toward his subjects. This image of caregiving did not displace the projection of martial valor that had been central to rajput warrior identity. To memorialize his successes on the battlefield, Vijai Singh is said to have commissioned the *Vijay Vilās*.[51] This text is focused on Vijai Singh's martial valor and does not offer insight into the changes afoot in his life or kingdom.

Vijai Singh's crafting of this kingly image was a departure in numerous ways from his Rathor predecessors. His was a formal adherence to a single devotional order as opposed to worship of a mix of deities and an emphasis on Goddess worship that prior Rathor sovereigns had adhered to. This is not to say that Vijai Singh cut off court patronage to all other deities, sects, or religious communities. Older patterns, of widely distributing patronage to a range of holy men, religious sites, and communities, mostly continued through Vijai Singh's reign.[52] Yet, his formal initiation into the Vallabhite sect and his fashioning through practice and patronage of the image of a Krishna devotee belonging to the Vallabhite sect also marked an elevation of Krishna devotion in general and Vallabhite affiliation in particular to a higher plane among the plethora of religious paths that flourished in Marwar. This was an enduring model of self-presentation, for both of Vijay Singh's immediate successors to the throne, Bhim Singh and Man Singh, commissioned strikingly similar portraits of themselves. There is at least one painting with a similar composition depicting Bhim Singh bowing before Krishna and one of Man Singh bowing before the Yogi Jalandarnath (fig. 7).[53]

There were other innovations in Vijai Singh's reign. A concubine or *pāsvān* named Gulab Rai, despite her marginal origin as an enslaved performer, charted an unparalleled path in Marwari history for herself.[54] From the 1770s, she played an active role in administration, having her favorites such as Singhvi Bhimraj and his son Akhairaj, both of a merchant caste, appointed to high offices such as *hākim* (governor) of various *parganās* (districts) and the head of military affairs, *bakhśī*. She was active in political matters for more than twenty years and, toward the end of Vijai Singh's reign, received an unprecedented honor for a concubine—a *jāgīr* (revenue assignment) of an entire district, Jalor.[55] She was a patron of Vaishnav devotion and of public works.[56] She carved out a public profile for herself not only through the marks she left on the built landscape and through her charity but also by embarking on pilgrimages outside the kingdom in which she was accompanied by grand processions of men and animals.[57]

Modern histories of Vijai Singh's reign usually gloss over Gulab Rai, though recent scholarship has begun to address this lacuna.[58] Only stray references to her activities survive in the chronicles and records of the Rathor state and these are heavily inflected by how loaded her memory was to nineteenth-century memorialists of the Rathor past. Still, it is clear even from these bits of information that we cannot fully understand Vijai Singh's reign without recognizing Gulab Rai's influence upon his court. She was his beloved consort for more than twenty years and his attachment to her spanned a large chunk of his reign.[59] While we do not yet know the precise measures and administrative appointments Gulab Rai was responsible for, statements about her growing influence at court, her active role in strategizing Marwar's resistance to the Marathas prior to the Battle of Merta in 1790, and her hand in the appointment of key administrators are discussed in early nineteenth-century Rathor court chronicles.[60] Her interventions were sufficiently "out of place" for her to be assassinated in 1792. Alas, it is difficult from the available source materials to trace her precise interventions in the administration of social life that are the subject of this book. Yet, one way in which Gulab Rai surely did shape the policies and the everyday administration of the types of petitions addressed in the *Jodhpur Sanad Parwāna Bahīs* is the hand she had in appointing particular men of merchant caste to high offices that issued commands and adjudicated disputes.

Vijai Singh then was willing to break with Rathor tradition in significant ways, whether through his cultivation of the public persona of a Krishna devotee or his willingness to allow his concubine to advise on and participate in matters at court. Under his leadership, despite a constant onslaught by Maratha forces, Marwar experienced a measure of internal stability. Vijai Singh's grandson and successor, Bhim Singh (r. 1793–1803), appears to largely have followed precedents set by Vijai Singh.[61] For instance, he too projected the image of a Krishna devotee and commissioned at least one painting that recorded his public participation in Vallabhite ritual.[62] His reign was too short, lasting only a decade, and too interrupted by internal rebellions and external threats to introduce significant policy changes. Modern historians have cast him in a negative light, likely reproducing the bias against him in accounts composed in the reign of his rival and successor, Man Singh, that are major sources of Marwar's political history.[63]

Vijai Singh's embrace of the Vallabh order, a Krishnaite devotional community that was already immensely popular among western Indian merchants, generated a bond, in addition to the growing dependence on merchants as administrators, that brought Vijai Singh into the same spiritual and moral community as many merchants of Marwar.[64] As in eighteenth-century Kota, the entry of the rajput rulers into the Vallabhite order helped forge a king-merchant intimacy. The bonds of shared religion were also nurtured, as Peabody shows for Kota, by the role that the merchants' earnings from trade could play in providing to the kings an income source, whether through tax or credit, that offset their dependence on prebendal revenues controlled by rajput chiefs.[65] In Marwar as well devotion and debt brought the king into a closer alliance with merchants.

MERCHANT AND BRAHMAN BUREAUCRATS

Discussions of the state in early modern South Asia tend to center heavily on kings, their courts, and the nobility. By the eighteenth century, however, there were plenty of polities in early modern South Asia that were large and complex enough to have bureaucracies. Histories of politics and statecraft in early modern South Asia then need to widen the conception of "state" to include the many offices and officers that constituted it. To an extent, this has been achieved through attention to scribes in early modern South Asia.[66] By the eighteenth century, the Rathors had developed an elaborate bureaucracy to aid the monarch in administering his territory. Alas, we do not have unbroken records with the kind of comprehensiveness that the court narratives like the *Khyāt* and *Vigat* provide for the late seventeenth and early eighteenth centuries in Marwar. Decades of tumult, caused by the war of succession following the death of Emperor Shahjahan in 1658 and then by the new Emperor Aurangzeb's intervention in succession within Marwar, could explain why there is a thinner source base for this period. Instead, it is from the middle of the eighteenth century that Rathor recordkeeping picks up in density and volume. From the proliferation of offices as well as the records generated by the functioning of these offices, it becomes clear that the Rathor state had expanded and changed in the hundred years since the composition of the *Khyāt* and *Vigat*. It also becomes clear that the drive toward documentation and toward the elaboration of a complex state bureaucracy intensified in the course of Vijai Singh's reign, that is, in the latter half of the eighteenth century.

As the state expanded, it was merchant castes and, to a lesser extent, brahmans who benefitted from the new opportunities available in administration. Among merchants, likely because of shared ritual and cultural practices, economic function, professional practice, and political interest, the many different caste groups involved in trade, moneylending, and, increasingly, bureaucracy had drawn together into a cohesive social unit by the eighteenth century. They adopted the title "mahajan," literally "great man," and this is how the state's orders and decrees referred to them.

There is much that is noteworthy about this. First, it suggests that the merchant castes had sufficiently consolidated to act and be perceived as a single body. Second, it indicates that boundaries like those marked by spiritual affiliation to Jain, Vaishnav, or Shaiva orders, or those created by caste-conditioned social and kinship behavior, could be set aside in contexts that demanded unified action toward common goals. Third, it demonstrates the formation of a trans- or supra-caste identity that functioned, in relation to the state and other social groups, as a large, singular caste category akin to "brahman" or "rajput." Participation at court and in state bureaucracy no doubt became an important vector for the solidification of a larger "merchant" or mahajan caste category.[67] At the same time, the emergence of a transcaste locus of unification such as "mahajan" did not completely override distinctions of caste and faith. There were occasional instances, for example, of conflict, even violence, between merchant-caste men of different castes (such as Khandelwal and Agarwal) and different faiths (such as Vaishnav, Jain, and subgroups within the Jains).[68]

The dominance of merchants in high offices at the capital, Jodhpur, is discernible. The administrative office of *dīvān* was of such great significance by the eighteenth century in Marwar that it can be translated to "prime minister." Its primary function was oversight of the kingdom's finances, but in practice it appears to have extended also into a crucial advisory role to the king and wider administrative authority over the kingdom. The king usually appointed a *dīvān* in consultation with trusted and influential allies. For instance, as noted earlier in this chapter, Vijai Singh offered the position of *dīvān* to Singhvi Bhimraj, a favorite of Gulab Rai's.[69]

It was not only in Vijai Singh's reign that the position of *dīvān* was assigned to men largely of a mahajan background. From the early seventeenth century—that is, almost since the introduction of this office in Rathor administration, beginning with Rao Maldev (r. 1532–62) and through successive kings thereafter—it was given largely to men from the Osvāl Jain mercantile community, usually from the Bhandari, Singhvi, or Muhnot clans. From the mid-eighteenth century, these included Singhvi Fatehchand, Bhandari Bhagvandas, also known as Bhavanidas (1790–95), Bhandari Shivchand (1795–96), Singhvi Jodhraj (1796–98), Muhnot Savairam (1798–1802), Singhvi Vijairaj (1802), Bhandari Gangaram (1803), Muhnot Gynanmal (1803–5), Bhandari Gangaram (1805), Singhvi Indraraj (1805–15), Singhvi Fatehraj (1815), and Singhvi Likhmichand (1817). Jain and Vaishnav merchants monopolized other key offices at the center as well. The office of *bakhśī*, in charge of military affairs, whose work included keeping rebellious rajput feudatories under control, was held since the seventeenth century by Jain and Vaishnav mahajans such as Bhandaris and Singhvis. Another indicator of the swelling ranks of nonrajput officers in the Rathor capital is the creation of a new office, the *pyād bakhśī*, in the brief reign of Maharaja Bakhat Singh (r. 1751–52). This office specialized in matters pertaining to nonrajput officers of the state and it too was held largely by mahajans.[70] The line between Osvāl Jain and Vaishnav was a blurred one due to the cross-cutting ties of caste and marriage. To that extent, these mahajan officers were from a shared Jain-Vaishnav milieu.

To offset the growing concentration of power in mahajan hands, key offices such as *dīvān* and *bakhśī* would occasionally be handed out to *pañcholīs*, a *kāyasth* or scribal group.[71] Even as *pañcholīs* do show up in Rathor records as authors of commands and holders of high administrative office, they were eclipsed in sheer numbers by men of mercantile castes in terms of both their total population and their participation in administration. *Pañcholīs*, unlike mahajans, did not participate in trade and remained limited to administrative functions.[72] They also did not share, at least as observed in the late nineteenth century, in the ethical and somatic approaches of mahajans and brahmans in that they did not disapprove of the men of their caste eating meat and drinking liquor.[73] Their relative inactivity in the records of the Rathor state in comparison to brahmans and merchants may have been due to their comparatively small demographic presence in Marwar. What really did set them apart was their dependence, unlike brahmans and mahajans, on state employment and revenue assignments. While *pañcholīs* emerge as issuers of commands under Vijai Singh and Bhim Singh, they appeared to have acted largely as agents of the Maharaja.

Under the direct supervision of the *dīvān* was the royal chancery, or the *śrī hajūr rā daftar* (with "*śrī hajūr*" referring to the king). Situated at the Fatehpol Gate in Mehrangarh Fort, this office issued and maintained royal orders in consultation with the *dīvān* and the king. The sources upon which this study relies, the *Jodhpur Sanad Parwāna Bahīs*, were written in this office. The superintendent or *darogā* of the royal chancery was more than just a scribe. According to an eighteenth-century description of the office, the head of the chancery was expected to be well acquainted with the customs of the many places and peoples of Marwar, to keep abreast of the latest developments across the kingdom, and to exercise sound judgment on which disputes ought to be placed before the king for resolution.[74] This suggests that the head of the chancery played a significant role in the adjudication of disputes and in the shaping of the state's response to petitions, appeals, and complaints. This office was assigned through the latter half of the eighteenth century and the early nineteenth century largely to a mix of brahmans, Osvāls, and other mercantile castes and to the occasional *pañcholī*.[75]

While some orders issued by this office, which are copied and compiled in the *Jodhpur Sanad Parwāna Bahīs*, do not name any individual or office as the issuing authority, others do. These latter orders use "with the permission of" or "*duvāyatī*" followed by a name, usually merchant, brahman, or *pañcholī*. When the orders name issuing officers, they do not specify which office they held. Sometimes, the authorizing officers can be cross-checked against other records, particularly the Rathors' officer lists compiled in *Ohdā Bahīs*, to be identified as the *dīvān*, the superintendent of the chancery, or a district governor.[76] For instance, a high-ranking member of Gulab Rai's faction, Singhvi Bhimraj, comes up as the issuing authority on an order issued in 1786, when he was serving as head of military affairs in the kingdom.[77]

It appears then that the orders compiled in the *Jodhpur Sanad Parwāna Bahīs* were largely issued not by the Maharaja himself but rather by officers representing him. While the orders were dispatched, likely bearing the relevant seals, to the district officers that they address, these same orders were copied at the chancery into a running ledger, a *bahī*. The orders were organized into *bahīs* by year, with commands from each year being bound into a single volume, sometimes two. Internally, each *bahī* is ordered by district. The *bahīs* are long and narrow, approximately three feet in length and a foot wide. They are bound at the top with a thick string. The pages of the *bahīs* are made of plain but strong paper, with standardized writing in Old Marwari in a neat hand and black ink. A feature of Rathor documentary culture in the eighteenth century is embodied in the form of the *bahīs*. This is the Rathor state's shift in the course of the eighteenth century to a heavy reliance on Old Marwari language and script, at the expense of Persian, for its commands, decrees, and other administrative documents.[78] This was a change from its late sixteenth- and seventeenth-century practices, and it is for this reason that my engagement with Rathor administration of political and social life relies exclusively on Marwari-language materials.

The formal qualities of the *bahī* are noteworthy. First, *bahīs* as a form were commonly associated with merchants and moneylenders who recorded their transactions in *bahīs* of their own. This innovation in Rathor recordkeeping is perhaps yet another indicator of the penetration of the state and its operation by merchant castes. Second, the plain, unadorned, standardized form of the records and their addressing of their recipients by title (*hākim*, *koṭvāl*) or office (*kachaiḍī*, *chauntrā*) rather than by name indicates a turn to a more bureaucratized and impersonal administration. Third, the keeping of copies of key orders in a central repository, the chancery, allowed for consultation in case of later disputes over those same issues. This too was an important departure and it occurred in 1765, when these records began to be maintained. This is noteworthy in comparison with the records of the Peshwa state or of the Kachhwaha kingdom of Jaipur in this same century whose orders in response to subjects' petitions consist of loose papers tied together with string or in cloth bundles. Unlike loose sheets of paper, individual entries into bound volumes could not easily be reordered or removed. The very turn to maintaining these records then marked a departure in the history of recordkeeping and administration in Marwar. Alongside, it was a departure in legal practice, for claims and counterclaims based on prior government rulings could now be tested against a centralized record ordered by date and district. This built upon the growing importance of paper in the early modern period in South Asia.[79] By the eighteenth century, in polities like Marwar, the turn to paper documentation that had occurred in prior centuries developed into centralized recordkeeping.

It was not just for writing and accounts, as a *potdār* (treasurer, vernacularization of *fotedār*) or a *muśraf* (accountant, vernacularization of *mushrif*), that Rathor kings hired merchant groups.[80] They also held most of the highest offices in the districts of the Rathor kingdom, called *parganās*, such as that of governor (*hākim*) and the many accountant, treasurer, and scribal positions in both central and district bureaucracies.[81] The *hākim* was responsible for maintaining law and order within the district, which included preventing and punishing crime and banditry as well as dispensing justice in response to social or economic disputes. The governor was to keep the rajput lords in his domain obedient to the king, making sure they fulfilled their military obligations, passed on the state's share of the revenues they collected, and did not collect unjust amounts from the peasants in their estates. The *hākim*'s office was called the *kachaiḍī*, a Marwari vernacularization of *kachahrī*.[82] The officers who held positions such as treasurer and newswriter in this office too were largely drawn from brahman, mercantile, or scribal communities.[83] Also under the district governor was the *sāyar*, the office in charge of nonagrarian levies. It was staffed with a superintendent (*darogā*), an *amīn* who helped assess revenue demands from the land assignments (*paṭṭās*) in the district, accountants (*mushrafs*), and treasurers (*potdārs*). Revenue officials called *kānuṅgos* were responsible for gathering on-the-ground statistics on yield and collections as well as for collecting land revenue for clusters of villages. Most of these officers in the *sāyars* were either Jain or Vaishnav merchants or brahmans.[84]

Yet another important district office, albeit one directly appointed by the court in Jodhpur and not under the supervision of the district governor, was that of the magistrate of the district capital, the *koṭvāl*. The *koṭvāl* was in charge of the district capital's defense and the maintenance of law and order within it. His office was called the *koṭvālī chauntrā*.[85] While in some districts like Nagaur the position was set aside for rajputs, in other districts like Merta, it too could be held by mahajans.[86]

Even as men from mahajan families dominated the administration, their proximity to political power was fraught with risk, at least until the early eighteenth century. There are several instances of mahajan *dīvāns* and governors being summarily fired from their posts and imprisoned on charges of graft or conspiracy. These imprisoned former ministers were only able to secure their release on the payment of huge sums of money, ranging from twenty-five thousand to several lakhs of rupees.[87] A notable and early example of this phenomenon was Mumhta Nainsi himself, the author of the mid-seventeenth-century *Khyāt* and the *Vigat* mentioned earlier in this chapter. When Nainsi fell from political favor, the Maharaja accused him of graft and threw him behind bars. Nainsi refused to accept guilt and pay the fine asked of him and eventually committed suicide in prison.[88] Some high-ranking mahajan administrators accused of conspiracy were given the death penalty while others, like Nainsi, preferred to commit suicide in prison than bear the humiliation of a large bail payment.[89] The practice of imprisoning and imposing heavy fines upon merchant bureaucrats on charges of graft or conspiracy appears to have largely disappeared by the mid-eighteenth century.[90] This may have been due to the growing dependence of the kings of Marwar upon this group.

Brahmans were perceived in this caste order as disinclined to deceit and theft. For this reason, some positions requiring the highest levels of honesty and fealty were reserved for brahmans. Superintendents of the royal treasury (*khāsā khajānā ra darogā*) and newswriters from the women's quarter (*janānī dyoḍhī uvākā naves*) were overwhelmingly brahmans.[91] This was in addition to positions specifically created for brahmans due to their priestly and scholarly status, such as *rājguru* (also known as *purohit*, or the head priest in charge of performing the royal family's brahmanical rituals) and *vyās* (tutor and advisor to the king).[92] The state also passed on certain collections, such as dues paid by the bride's family at the time of marriage (*chaṃvarī*) and octroi (*chūṅgī*), to designated brahman families in each locality.[93] This was in addition to the granting of tax-free lands, *ḍohlī* and *sāsaṇ*, to brahmans and other ritualists. There was then a material dimension to the rise of brahmans in Marwar, one that lay in favor shown by the state.

The Rathor kings tried to maintain a balance of power among these influential demographic groups in their domain. Toward this end, one significant post at court remained reserved for rajputs, that of *pradhān*. The *pradhān* (loosely, "chief") was the head and spokesperson of the body of leading rajput lords within the kingdom. He advised the king on policy in consultation with other leading rajput chiefs in

Marwar. This office dated back to the earliest years of Rathor rule, to a more fraternal order, and the later establishment of the office of *dīvān* cut into the powers and functions of the *pradhān*. Rajputs of course continued to exercise control over a share of the revenues of the vast tracts of land that were their hereditary estates and maintained their own armed retinues. What they lacked in bureaucratic power was compensated to some extent by their command over land-based wealth, arms-based power, and blood-based prestige. Still, as this section has shown, the majority of posts in the larger emergent structure of Rathor administration were in the hands of Vaishnav-Jain mahajans and, to a lesser extent, brahmans.

MERCHANTS AND STATES IN EARLY MODERN SOUTH ASIA

The growing intermixture of trade and statecraft was not unique to Marwar. In other eighteenth-century polities, both in Rajasthan and beyond, merchants had begun to participate to varying degrees in state machinery as courtiers, bureaucrats, and scribes. They purchased temporary revenue assignments, *ijāras*, and in that way became involved in the administration of land revenue.[94] It was not only land revenue but also a number of other income-generating offices that were let out on *ijāra* contracts by eighteenth-century regimes. In Marwar, Vijai Singh ran his mints by farming out their operation and revenues on *ijāra* to the highest bidder. In one such example, a man of the mercantile community of Agrawals won a year-long contract for the mints of Jodhpur and Pali by paying 2,901 rupees to the state in 1771.[95] Merchants also formed associations that acted collectively as pressure groups upon local and regional officers. Evidence for this sort of interface between merchants and the state dates back to the late medieval period in South Asia, such as the merchant-warrior Vastupāla at the Vaghela court in thirteenth-century Gujarat. The Jain Vastupāla became deeply influential at this court and there is evidence of a Jain orientation at certain late medieval courts in Gujarat.[96] Medieval Malabar too witnessed the agency of merchants in forging Islamic practice and authority in a multifaith setting in which there was no Islamic state to appoint *qāẓīs*.[97]

This medieval legacy was foundational for the expansion of mercantile engagement with the state. Rich evidence of collective action survives from Mughal Gujarat and nineteenth-century Awadh.[98] Evidence for the type of formalized collective association with a designated name ("*mahājan*") in seventeenth-century Gujarati towns is absent from eighteenth-century Marwar. Still, there are plenty of episodes described in Rathor records of merchants coming together despite their internal caste barriers to lobby the Rathor government and to push for localized change collectively.

The rise of merchants to influential positions in state and local politics was a product of a number of historical processes. First, the Mughal Empire, established in 1526, integrated into a single political unit a vast expanse of South Asia. It spanned all of the northern half of India for two centuries and subsumed most of the subcontinent for a few decades at its territorial peak in the late seventeenth century.[99] The Mughal Empire stabilized and standardized currencies, weights, and measures. Mughal demand for and success in extracting the payment of land revenues in cash as well as their incentivization of the cultivation of cash crops fueled the growth of a money economy in rural areas.[100] Landholders (*zamīndārs*) and revenue assignment holders (*jāgīrdārs*) frequently borrowed from money-lenders in order to meet the state's land revenue demand in years when they had overspent or not yet collected the revenue.[101] Men of merchant castes, particularly those who moved in from western India, played a central role in the Mughal fiscal system as operators of mints, as creditors, and in the remittance of money.[102] They also took employment in the Mughal bureaucracy, working as accountants, agents, and recordkeepers.[103]

The period saw the rise of a new type of political entrepreneur, the "portfolio capitalist." The portfolio capitalist combined official functions such as command over military resources and a role in administration with more entrepreneurial ones such as investments in revenue farms, participation in local agricultural trade, and dabbling in long-distance, particularly Indian Ocean, trade. What distinguished portfolio capitalists in north India was their dependence on large moneylending firms, dominated by western Indian Vaishnav-Jain families, for the capital outlay they needed to manage and expand their portfolios.[104]

The Mughal aristocracy also became an important clientele for moneylenders, and its members took loans to meet personal, military, or official expenses. Scribal and military elites in the state's employ, who held land-based revenue assignments (*jāgīrs*), frequently diversified their operations into trade. Mughal Emperors, members of the royal family, and nobles participated in the Indian Ocean trade, channeling state power to protect and promote their enterprise.[105] This imperial involvement in overseas trade may have peaked in Emperor Shahjahan's reign (1628–58).[106] To Mughal princes and other royalty raising money for such expensive undertakings as wars of succession, moneylenders would charge very high interest rates.[107] In the seventeenth century, these wealthy bankers had the clout to refuse to lend to Emperor Aurangzeb when he demanded a large interest-free loan to fund his expansionary campaign in peninsular India.[108]

The significance of merchant castes, particularly those from Gujarat, in the operation of Mughal finance, imperial and local, was so great that historian Karen Leonard explains Mughal decline as rooted in a withdrawal of credit by the great banking houses of Gujarat in the late seventeenth century.[109] John F. Richards and, more recently, Sudev Sheth have challenged this argument on the grounds that the Mughal state was fiscally healthy and politically strong enough to not be as dependent on mercantile credit as Leonard suggests through the seventeenth century. That said, Richards notes that the eighteenth-century decline of the Mughal state did indeed allow bankers and moneylenders to emerge as a political class.[110]

The second important process fueling the blurring of the line between mercantile and state activity was the increased integration of hinterland South Asia into expanding global trade networks and new geographies of capital. This was combined with a positive balance of trade. As a result, large sums of bullion and traders from all over the world circulated through the region.[111] Moneychangers (*sarrāfs*, often Anglicized as "shroff"), brokers (*dallāls*), and bankers (*sāhukārs*, *seṭhs*, and mahajans) who loaned money and transmitted it over long distances using letters of exchange (*huṇḍīs*) grew in number and wealth. These men were overwhelmingly drawn from the demographic pool of Vaishnav and Jain mercantile castes.

European trading companies too relied on a network of agents and brokers, frequently drawn from Hindu and Jain trading communities, in order to do business. They also borrowed heavily from bankers in market towns such as those in Gujarat, particularly in Surat.[112] As New World silver flowed into India and the export trade expanded, merchants channeled their profits from trade and credit services into moneylending. Deposit banking, insurance, and bottomry were other revenue streams in the banking business in seventeenth-century Gujarat.[113]

The merchants of western India, particularly Gujarat but also southern Rajasthan, acquired both the capital and skills needed to become bankers across South Asia in the early modern period. Origins in Gujarat, with its centuries of flourishing, transregional oceanic trade, gave merchants from the region a head-start in taking command of early modern fiscal networks across the Mughal Empire. During the heyday of Mughal rule, western Indian merchants, including those from Marwar, branched out to all the important trading marts and political centers across north India, reaching as far east as Bengal.[114] They were able to very quickly transmit not just money but also crucial information and market intelligence across vast distances, giving them a business advantage over other mercantile groups. Men from Marwar were an important segment among the Vaishnav and Jain merchants who scattered and set up banking and other businesses across north India. Some went farther out, making inroads into peninsular India in the south and the southern fringes of the Russian Empire in the north.[115] In the west, they ventured as far as Sindh and occasionally beyond to Iran and Central Asia.[116]

The third historical process fueling the fusion of mercantile and state power in Marwar was the intensification of trading activity, particularly in this region. Webs of commercial capital in the early modern age not only boosted the banking business but also linked Marwari consumers and producers with the wider world. This expansion in Marwar was due to its location on an arterial trade route connecting the booming ports of Gujarat, such as Surat, with inland depots such as Delhi, Agra, Burhanpur, Patna, and Lahore. One of the routes most favored by merchant caravans wound its way through the towns of Jalor and Merta in Marwar.[117] Merchants imported horses, dried fruit, tobacco, lac, asafetida, and perfumes from Multan and Kabul; betel-nut, turmeric, rice, coconuts, and antimony from Sindh; cloth, black pepper, silk, spices, dates, sandalwood, pearls, dyes, and camphor from Gujarat; silks, other fine cloths, sugar, elephants, and paper from the east; opium, tobacco, Chanderi cloth, sulphur, and sugar from Malwa in central India; and fine woolen fabrics and shawls from Kashmir. Marwar exported iron tools, wool, woven and printed cloth, indigo, salt, bullocks, camels, and horses.[118] This thriving exchange within Marwar offered increased business opportunities to the region's merchants.

Fourth, the collapse of the Mughal Empire, rather than ushering in an era of decline for moneylenders, only boosted moneylenders' businesses. During the eighteenth century, merchants from Marwar were able to build on their subcontinental networks to further consolidate their hold over credit and commodity markets far beyond their homeland. In Punjab, Marwari firms were active in the local wool trade. They set up businesses (*koṭhīs*) in political and economic centers across most of India, including places like Lahore, Delhi, Banaras, Patna, Dhaka, Pune, and Hyderabad.[119] They had deeply penetrated aspects of state functioning such as revenue collection, money changing, and minting, and they only strengthened that control to become indispensable intermediaries between landowners and peasants on the one hand and the state on the other.[120] The banking firm of merchants Fatehchand and Manekchand in Dhaka, whose ancestor Hiranand Sahu migrated from the town of Nagaur in Marwar, had such a large financial outlay that the Mughal ruler Muhammad Shah bestowed upon them the title of Jagat Seth or "Banker of the World" in 1723.[121]

Marwari merchants also sought to profit from the growing market for opium created by the British trade in this commodity in China. In the latter half of the eighteenth century, the English East India Company decided to use its newly acquired territories in India to cultivate opium at lesser cost, which it would then use to fuel demand in China, a market that it was keen to penetrate. Merchants from Marwar invested in opium cultivation in central India, making neat profits by meeting the growing export demand for opium.[122]

As the decline of the Mughal Empire gave rise to smaller polities, new processes of state formation, and fresh attempts at empire, Marwari merchants were able to leverage their hold over capital and credit to extend their activities from finance to gain a greater hold upon the state and political authority. They lent money to the many rulers in need of funds to finance the ceaseless demands of war and administration, as well as to European traders moving goods across the globe. The *hunḍī* (bill of exchange) networks of large banking firms continued to play a significant role in remitting money—profits, loans, revenues—across long distances in the eighteenth century.[123] Rather than weakening them, the collapse of Mughal authority strengthened the hand of merchants involved in moneylending. Men of trade rose to center-stage in the regional polities that mushroomed after the weakening of Mughal central authority during the eighteenth century. As the European companies became military and political players in the Indian subcontinent, Marwari merchants lent money to them as well.

The rise and, even more so, the decline of Mughal authority, the corresponding growth of regional polities, and European trading and political activity in the Indian subcontinent were extremely lucrative for merchants and moneylenders, and it was the merchants of Marwar, as noted by numerous historians, who seized a generous share of the generated profits. The merchants of the region retained strong familial ties with it, the women of the household remaining back home in Marwar and the men often retiring there after long careers elsewhere.[124]

Within Marwar, merchants occupied a place of prominence and prosperity in the major towns of the kingdom by the mid-seventeenth century, as is indicated by a study of Muhnot Nainsi's state-commissioned survey of the region.[125] By Nainsi's reckoning, mahajans constituted roughly 30 to 40 percent of the population of three major towns of the kingdom (Sojhat, Jaitaran, and Merta).[126] In eastern Rajasthan, merchants penetrated the countryside, becoming indispensable intermediaries in the state's relationship with peasants. They were providers of agricultural loans, directly as well as through the state, to peasants.[127] By the seventeenth century, merchants were crucial buyers of the grain that the state collected as tax and commuted into cash through sale. So indispensable was their role in the local grain trade of eastern Rajasthan that it placed a limit upon the power that the state could exercise upon them.[128] G. S. L. Devra has shown the growing investment in agrarian land by merchants in the small market towns of northwestern Rajasthan by the end of the seventeenth century.[129] As Denis Vidal has pointed out, the extent of mercantile influence over the early modern economy cannot be understood with reference only to the merchants' involvement in the state's fiscal arrangements. Rather, a whole domain of mercantile moneylending activity existed outside of the state.[130] They were not just indispensable as creditors but also as important buyers of grain and manufactures from villages.[131]

MERCHANTS IN MARWAR

Merchants began to play an active role in local administration in Marwar, as discussed in the previous section. In addition to the many offices I have already discussed that merchants began to hold, revenue administration in Rajasthan also slipped into mahajan hands.[132] In the early eighteenth century, they stood as surety for revenue farmers (*ijāradārs*) and, in the second half of the eighteenth century, began to bid for revenue farms themselves.[133] As in eastern Rajasthan, merchants in Marwar expanded their sphere of activity from trade to revenue farming in the eighteenth century.[134] Merchant moneylenders became deeply influential in local politics and economics.[135] Indebtedness to merchant moneylenders became widespread in the course of the eighteenth century not only among ruling elites but also more widely in rural Rajasthan among peasants.[136] In urban areas, mercantile castes were prominent among the ranks of property holders.[137] As merchant moneylenders, they were able to channel the Rathor court's dependence upon them for credit to extract concessional terms to conduct trade.[138] The Rathor court allowed many a trader to conduct his business at a reduced tax rate and provided security and infrastructure to boost trade in the kingdom.[139]

Artisans too borrowed from local moneylenders and small merchants in order to fund life-cycle rituals and to finance subsistence agriculture.[140] Textile manufacture, a sector that saw rapid growth in the eighteenth century, became subject to the growing role of the merchant-middleman.[141] In the latter half of the eighteenth century, the artisans of Marwar found themselves "caught in the quicksand of indebtedness," even if most artisanal manufacture did not fall under the control of merchant capital as it had in coastal India in the same decades.[142] It was not just peasants and landlords in the countryside and artisans in the towns but the king himself who borrowed large sums of money from the merchants, men who had the outlay to loan the sums needed and the good credit required to make large fiscal transfers to overlords.[143] Ties of kinship, business, and, increasingly, shared religious activity lent cohesiveness to localized communities of merchants.

Claude Markovits has linked the Marwari merchants' rise to subcontinental dominance over money markets, since at least the sixteenth century, with their holding high office in the Rathor state. Some merchant clans commanded political authority and access to the crown as well as to rajput nobility.[144] The aridness of the region and its location between the Gangetic Plains on the one hand and West and Central Asia on the other may indeed, as Markovits suggests, explain the rise of a thriving mercantile community in Marwar. Given the simultaneity of the two processes—the growing political role of Marwari merchants and their rise as bankers in and outside Marwar—it is hard to say which caused the other. And yet, for all the reasons listed above, local, subcontinental, and global, there is no doubt that by the middle of the eighteenth century, the Jain and Vaishnav merchants of Marwar formed a diasporic community that commanded a large share of the banking business in South Asia.

When Vijai Singh ascended to the Rathor throne in 1752, he inherited a polity markedly different from the mobile world of his pre-Mughal ancestors. Since the sixteenth century, Marwar had experienced the slow assertion of monarchical command over an order that valorized blood-based claims to fraternal shares in political power and land; the turn to nonrajput groups, particularly merchant castes, to build out a bureaucracy to counter the kinship- and land-based power of the internal rajput rivals of the Rathor monarchy; the rise to subcontinental dominance of merchants originally from Marwar in businesses of trade and moneylending; the immense inflow of silver into South Asia due to a thriving export trade through the early modern period; and the increasing blurring of boundaries between trade, investment, and statecraft in the course of the early modern period. Marwar, like many other parts of early modern South Asia, was a node in an interlinked web of changes that drew upon shifts in and connections with

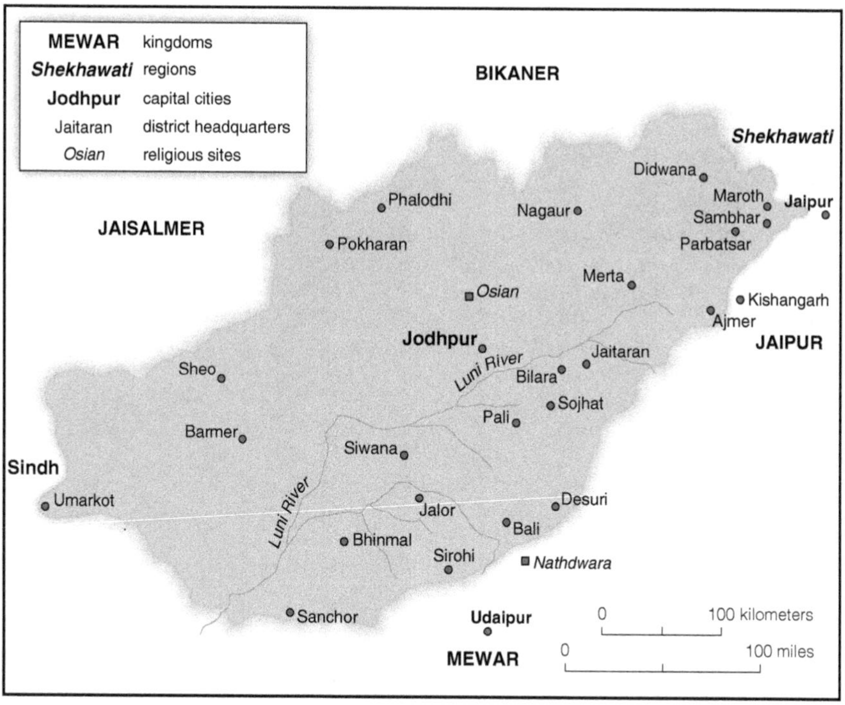

MAP 2. Marwar, c. 1780.

places near and far, local and global. By the mid-eighteenth century, merchants in Marwar, along with brahmans, wielded far more political power—localized as well as at court—than they ever had before. The geographies of commercial capital and the ebbs and flows of empire generated long-term streams of historical change, flowing at the local, subcontinental, and global scales, that converged in the latter half of the eighteenth century to produce a new elite identity.

PART ONE

Other

2

Purity

> [To the Pali governor, 1785] And the merchants of Pali came here and made their appeal known. The order is as follows: "At ponds and stepwells, all the people draw water from the same bank. If they draw water from another bank, then our dignity (*marjād*) will be preserved." From now, the brahmans, mahajans, and other high castes should draw water from one side and the Untouchable castes from another.[1]

Year after year in Vijai Singh's reign, members of the mercantile and priestly castes brought petitions before the Rathor state, objecting to proximity with "low" castes and Untouchables. It is worth noting that rajputs, a caste of lordly warriors and landholders, did not petition the Rathor state for such interventions, which indicates that rajputs were secure in their position at the top of the regional social order. There was no need for them to channel state authority to underscore social and spatial distance from the "lowly" and the untouchable. Merchants and brahmans, on the other hand, petitioned the state, objecting to the spatial or social proximity of "low" castes and seeking a departure from existing patterns. These petitions were not framed in the language of custom nor presented in any way as a continuation or revival of past practice. Instead, they legitimized their claims by appealing to the king's duty to maintain *dharma* or moral order.[2] These elite groups asked the state to intervene in favor of their demand for a change in established spatial or social patterns in order to create a more segregated society.

CUSTOM AND LAW

The petitions by merchants and brahmans were a departure from the deference toward custom as the basis for legal claims that held such value for large areas of Rathor jurisprudence, as Nandita Sahai has shown, even in these same decades.[3] As Sahai has argued for eighteenth-century Marwar and Sumit Guha for the Maratha-ruled Deccan in the same century, custom was being constantly reshaped by localized struggles and negotiations among ordinary actors, and this placed the customary firmly in the domain of political life.[4] This was much like directly administered Mughal territories, in which *dastūr* (custom) had an important place in Mughal law.[5] In Marwar, disputes, whether social or economic in nature, were resolved with reference to custom. In the course of the seventeenth century, as the Rathor state transitioned toward a monarchy, successive Rathor kings also expanded and centralized an administrative structure for revenue, military purposes, and law. District administration, the details of which I discussed in the last chapter, served as an intermediary layer in legal matters between the crown and its subjects. A vigorous culture of petitioning flourished in Marwar. It was not just well-to-do folk such as merchants and landlords but also artisans and poor service groups that approached the crown with petitions (*araj*, a vernacularization of *arzī*). The petitions that are available to us from the mid-eighteenth century offer a glimpse into the application of law and legal culture in a late precolonial South Asian polity. This aspect of legal history is particularly important as a counterpoint to the study of law codes and normative texts as a means of understanding the history of law in South Asia prior to colonial conquest.

There are hundreds of orders in the *Jodhpur Sanad Parwāna Bahīs*, in which the crown orders disputes resolved through a return to or continuation of past practice. Nandita Sahai has identified the term *uvājabī* (also transliterated as *uwājabī*) as central to Rathor jurisprudence, a term she translates as representing that which is legitimate. This word was derived from the Arabic *wājib*, which connotes acts that are enjoined upon a person as duties or ethical imperatives. As Sahai notes, the Rathor state's commands to its officers to do what is *uvājabī* in turn suggest that in practice this meant an upholding of that which was customary.[6]

In many other cases, the Rathor crown directly invoked the past in its response to quarrels among its subjects. *Sadāmand suṁ*, *sadāmand māfak*, and *theṭ suṁ* (all three of which translate to "as always") and *rīt* (custom) are phrases that the Rathor crown often used to enjoin its district-level officers to uphold existing patterns. For instance, in 1768:

> [To the Nagaur governor's office]: Teli (oilpresser) Dola, a *mehtar* [headman of the local caste group] came here and submitted a petition: "We have always (*sadāmand suṁ*) observed the mahajans' days of prayer and rest (*agatāṁ*) and whenever they host a feast (*jīmaṇ*), they have always (*sadāmand*) given us a serving (*kāṁso*) from it. Now, they have stopped giving us a share of their feasts." The order is (*hukam huvo hai*): Tell the mahajans to continue serving a share as they always have (*sadāmand kāṁso pūrastā huvai jīṇ māphak pūras dīyā karai*).[7]

This command displays a mutually recognized arrangement between the oilpressers and merchants of Nagaur in which the merchants gave the oilpressers a portion from their communal feasts on certain holy days, an act not just of providing food but also one that built a social bond between the two caste groups. In return, the oilpressers observed the merchants' holy days. The mahajans' seemingly unprovoked withdrawal from their end of the arrangement disrupted the ties that wove the two groups into a relation that transcended a purely market-based exchange. The oilpressers' petition to the crown then was less about a share from communal feasts held occasionally through the year and more about restoring the symbolic tie that undergirded their relationship to the merchants of Nagaur. The merchants' own attempt to break this reciprocal tie can in turn be read as an effort to rewrite the terms of their relationship with the oilpressers, effecting a demotion in status for the oilpressers by no longer considering them worthy of a share of the merchants' communal feasts. It was a move that communicated a disregard for the oilpressers' standing and is one of many indicators in the eighteenth-century records of the Rathor state of an underlying change in the socioeconomic position of the merchants, the roots of which I laid out in the previous chapter. The important feature of this record for the discussion here is the emphasis placed upon past practice or custom by both the petitioning oilpressers and the adjudicators working on behalf of the Rathor crown in Jodhpur.

The undesirable opposite of *uvājabī* or "legitimate" then was the condition of being *beuvājabī* or *gair uvājabī*, meaning roughly "unsuitable" or "illegitimate." In deeming a situation to be worth rectifying, Rathor officers would describe it as being *sadāmand sivāy* (in departure from past practice), *berīt* (violating custom), or *navāsīr suṁ* (establishing a new precedent). The invocation of the past, even an ancient or timeless past as the use of the terms *sadāmand* and *theṭ* suggests, became a powerful plank upon which shared notions of righteous order and justice rested in the Marwar polity. Both the state's judgments and subjects' petitions emphasized the illegitimacy of a departure from custom. State power then drew sustenance and renewal from the defense of that which could be established as customary.

This seeming defense of past practice, however, did not mean that local society was trapped in a recursive loop of historical stasis. As several historians have noted, custom was malleable, transmitted as it was by popular memory and notions of moral economy instead of being written down and cast in stone.[8] When cited, custom carried the aura of immutability and this aura was the foundation of its authority. In practice, however, the customary was an arena of constant negotiation and modification, adapting to changes in the context within which it was set. Custom was the site of politics, redefined and reshaped in response to changing power relations among constituents.

The persistence of custom in guiding political and adjudicatory action stands at odds with the historical processes that I show in this book that were unfolding in the same decades of the eighteenth century. That is, in these same decades, merchants working in alliance and through the Rathor state introduced new laws, practices, and patterns of everyday life. They did so without bothering to turn to the authority of custom, even in name and even though custom had the malleability to accommodate departures disguised as past practice. Instead, it was ethics and the pursuit of virtue that were implicitly the legal reasoning behind merchants' and brahmans' petitions and which justified state decrees concerning elite exclusivity and its cultural markers. These ethics upheld austerity and the protection of nonhuman life and appended vegetarianism to preexisting conceptions of the "purity" that defined elite caste status. Merchants legitimized their petitions demanding policies of segregation, discrimination, and marginalization in spatial, social, economic, and ritual domains by invoking ethics and not custom. This perhaps is the other part of a shift traced by Sahai: the emergence of a gap after 1780 between the Rathor state's reading of what was customary and that of the artisanal communities she studies.[9] Social life in precolonial South Asia was not only governed by law but also by the overlapping domain of locally variable and negotiated custom. Even so, the latter half of the eighteenth century saw an erosion of the power of custom as a "weapon of the weak," alongside a turn to other discourses of law.

SOCIAL DISTANCE

Purity and caste have frequently gone together in scholarly and popular thinking about caste. The purity in question in those conversations is ritual in nature; that is, it evokes a set of embodied practices centered on avoiding the contagion of ritual pollution. These practices and ideas about what constitutes ritual pollution are thought to derive from textual prescriptions and commentaries that brahmans have composed since ancient times. Historical research has made clear that brahmanical notions of purity and pollution were not the only determinant of caste in practice, particularly prior to colonial rule.[10] When I bring up purity here then, it is not ritual but demographic purity I refer to. In the petitions and local politics of eighteenth-century Marwar, I see a drive toward "purifying" such social bodies as caste groups or an imagined "Hindu" community through an expulsion of persons and practices now deemed extrinsic. In this chapter, I will show that this drive played out in sites as varied as residential space, drinking water, social bodies, and economic life. All of these domains came "under the knife," so to speak, as the merchant and brahman subjects and functionaries of the Rathor state sought to carve out a subject body that was in line with their vision.

In the effort to purify an elite domain, sometimes named Hindu and other times not, merchants often acted collectively or teamed up with other "high" castes such as brahmans and, in villages, peasants of the *jāṭ* caste. Collective merchant-brahman and merchant-*jāṭ* actions are recorded in 1775[11] and 1787[12] in Merta, in 1789 in Nagaur,[13] and in 1779[14] and 1803[15] in Sojhat. These actors justified to the state their refusal to live close to a leatherworker (*chamār*) or other "low" caste by asserting it was contrary to their *dharma*, that is, to their moral duty (for instance, "*bhāmbhī rai pākhtī rahyā mhāro dharam nahī*," or "living next to a leatherworker violates my *dharma*,"[16] and "*jaṭhai vai pāṇī pivai to mhāro dharam rahai*," or "if they drink water there [or away from 'us'], my *dharma* will remain intact").[17] Singhvi Tilokmal, a mahajan himself, responded to this reasoning on behalf of the crown in both of these cases in which elite-caste *dharma* undergirded demands for social distance. He ruled in the former case that the leatherworker should be allotted another place to live, and in the latter that leatherworkers should draw water from different wells than Shrimali merchants.

Research on other parts of seventeenth- and eighteenth-century South Asia indicates that merchants were able to organize into corporate bodies and this contributed to their success as pressure groups upon local governments. Writing about seventeenth-century Gujarat, a society in which merchants formed a wealthy and influential segment that was well incorporated into systems of rule, Farhat Hasan notes merchants' protests were not in defense of customs or privileges but rather increasingly "more productive," or working to change the "systems of rule" to suit their interests.[18] In late eighteenth- and early nineteenth-century Awadh as well, as Christopher Bayly has shown, merchants organized into transcaste corporate bodies and began to act as a check upon kingly authority.[19]

In Marwar, this "civic" activism of mahajan groups was directed toward moving merchants squarely into the domain of other, more established elite castes—primarily rajputs and brahmans—and connectedly, toward increasing social distance from all social "inferiors." The role that state authority played, the discussion below will argue, in the success of mahajans' campaign to reorder social and spatial patterns was crucial. That the Rathor state, as I showed before, was manned by mahajans and in key offices, brahmans, aided the mahajans' efforts to create a new elite identity of which they were a part. Having their caste fellows in positions of authority both at the district level and in the capital helped them win sympathetic judgments and allowed the implementation of new policies, openly departing from custom, that might otherwise have had to contend with insurmountable resistance.

THE HOLY AND THE LOWLY

There are several appeals from merchants in the historical record that testify to an urge to socially distance themselves from *all* artisanal and service castes, including but not limited to those practicing ritually defiling occupations such as skinning, leatherwork, and sweeping. Groups that traditionally earned an income from artisanal and service work were called the *chhattīs pāvan jāt* (literally, "the thirty-six receiving castes") or colloquially, *pūṇ jāt*. The practitioners of these trades tended to range from economically middling to poor and usually occupied the middle to lower segments of local caste hierarchies.[20] The number thirty-six was notional and the actual number of communities in this demographic could vary from locality to locality. Pointing out that the term *pūṇ* meant "three-quarters," Nandita Sahai suggests that members of these castes were considered "three-fourth persons" and thus inferior to full persons.[21] Despite being ambiguous in its constitution, this class of people was internally stratified. Another inexact term, but one with a derogatory connotation, *kamīṇ* or *kamīṇā*, which translates to "lowly," could collectively address those at the lower end among the *pūṇ jāts*.[22] In various records, the castes described as *kamīṇ* include washermen (*dhobī*), barbers (*nāī*), potters (*kumbhār*), and carpenters (*khātī*).[23]

Merchants took the lead in pushing to eliminate these "lowly" castes from communal as well as public life. For instance, it was customary for district crown officials to be invited to wedding feasts hosted by the merchant community. In 1784, the mahajans of Sojhat protested to the crown when these district officers, like the governor, treasurer, magistrate, accountant, and superintendent, began to bring as part of their retinue men of such *kamīṇ* ("lowly") castes as washermen and barbers.[24] They were happy to continue hosting the officers but not their "low" caste hangers-on. It was not just the addition of extra mouths to feed but also the status of these new guests that the mahajans were objecting to. Agreeing with the mahajans, the crown ordered its district officers in Sojhat to explain this abuse of their authority.[25]

In another episode centered on access to water, merchants asked for and won segregation from the broad swath of the "lowly." This played out in the hot summer month of July in 1788, as is visible from the following order:

> [To the Pali governor's office] The merchants of Pali submitted an appeal to Śrī Hajūr: "There is drought here in the summers. The people get very restless. A stepwell, Ganga Bav, has been dug earlier but it remains to be built. It will cost between one and two thousand rupees to build it. If Śrī Hajūr permits and we receive the order from the governor, we can collect around two and a half rupees from each merchant home and build this stepwell. Please send a written order to the governor if you approve of this. There is now another stepwell (*jhālrā*) from which the thirty-six *pūṇ* castes draw water. We lose all our dignity (*marjād koī reh nahīṁ*). If Ganga Bav is built then all the people can fill water there while brahmans and mahajans draw water from the old stepwell. Then our dignity will remain intact." The order is: Take two and a half rupees from each home in the town and have Ganga Bav completed from which other people will draw water while brahmans and mahajans will fill water at the old stepwell.
>
> In the margin: Write "due to the mahajans' petition"—By the order of the Superintendent of Messengers, Rupram.[26]

In this petition, the mahajans of Pali expressed their willingness to channel their own resources toward completing the construction of a stepwell to ease the water scarcity in the bustling urban center that year. They offered to pay a small levy to the state to collect the sum needed to pay for the stepwell's construction. The offer, however, was not as altruistic as it appears, for the mahajans appended a condition to it. In exchange for footing the bill for the construction of the new stepwell, they requested that the state support their efforts to segregate the town's water supply. They demanded that the new stepwell would be set aside for the use of all members of the artisanal and "low" service castes (*pūṇ jātis*). The existing water source, also a stepwell (*jhālrā*), would then be reserved for Pali's mahajans and brahmans alone.

In their appeal, the mahajans complained that the existing situation, which had them drawing water at the same source as the artisans and "low" service castes (*chhatīs pūṇ*), was totally undignified (*marjād koī rahai nahī*). Responding favorably to this petition and without questioning the logic undergirding it, the state ordered the district administration of Pali to collect a small cess from Pali's mahajan households in order to support the construction of a new stepwell. It made clear that once the new well was ready, the governor should direct everyone other than mahajans and brahmans to draw water from it.

Taken together, these petitions indicate that the artisanal castes held a "lowly" place in local social orders and their representation as such could constitute a sound legal basis—overriding custom—for merchants' claims to create greater social distance from them. This, combined with the ability of new elites like merchants to finance the social distance they sought, along with the influence they had within and over the state, allowed these aspirations to be implemented into practice. Other cases in the Rathor archive show that artisans were at risk in these decades of being collapsed with those even further below them, that is, the Untouchables. But who were the Untouchables?

LEATHERWORKERS, SPACE, AND WATER

Leatherworkers—known by the caste names *chamār, bhāmbhī, ḍheḍh, meghvāl,* and *jaṭīyā*—became an important focus of mahajans' efforts to reshape social geography. Along with merchants, brahmans too attempted to distance themselves from any group that was deemed "untouchable." Merchants would often ally with brahmans in these efforts. The Rathor crown responded unequivocally in favor of all of the merchants' and brahmans' recorded demands to introduce as much distance from the leatherworking castes as possible. Leatherwork, which involved skinning carcasses and treating hides, was deemed ritually defiling due to its contact with death. The "impurity" of leatherworkers was not rooted entirely in their association with hides and skins. It also had its foundations in labor and land relations. In rural areas, leatherworkers directed much of their labor toward agricultural work as tenant farmers and farmhands.[27] Most leatherworkers were landless, although some did hold small plots.[28]

In their quest to make ends meet, leatherworkers often became trapped in debt and were at risk of being reduced to bonded labor (*vasīpaṇā*) controlled by rajput landholders.[29] Landlessness and debt bondage then were important elements of the leatherworkers' low caste status. Leatherworkers used petitions, protest, flight, and rarely, violence to resist efforts by landed elites and occasionally merchants to reduce them to bonded labor.[30] *Vasīpaṇā*—from being a bond of loyalty tying dependents of a range of castes and professions to a mobile rajput in the medieval period—had changed in the course of the early modern period into bonded labor. Rather than ties of *naukarī* or service, which too were interwoven with dependence and hierarchy, now it was the far more impersonal relation caused by debt, whether of cash loans or loans of desperately needed food, that tied agrarian workers to rural landlords and moneylenders.

At the same time, social proximity to leatherworkers could be read as a sign of lowliness by association. In the more polarized caste order of the eighteenth century, such "mixing" became undesirable. So, in 1764, the state acceded to the demand of a brahman from the village Pipad to be rehabilitated to a brahman neighborhood since there was a leatherworkers' quarter close to his current home.[31] In 1775, the state forcibly resettled the leatherworking *jaṭīyās* of Merta far from brahman and merchant quarters when the latter groups demanded this change.[32] In both cases, the brahmans and merchants who objected to the proximity of a 'low"-caste home to their own had until this point been neighbors with the "low"-caste communities. What these groups asked for and won from the state was a departure from existing patterns. As for the leatherworkers, apart from the dislocation and financial loss caused by enforced relocation, they also had to wage a battle to receive the rehabilitation that was promised to them.

In Merta district, the merchants and upper *jāṭ* peasantry channeled their superior wealth to have the leatherworkers (*meghvāls*) of their village evicted. The merchants and *jāṭs* paid the state (*darbār*) five rupees and won a favorable ruling. It was the leatherworkers who then turned to the crown in Jodhpur for help, pointing out that their residential settlement had been encompassed in prior years by the expanding village.[33] All they got from the crown was a guaranteed reimbursement of the assessed value of their homes and a reprieve of a couple of months until the monsoon rains subsided. After that, they were to be shown a piece of land outside the village to build new huts on (*dūjī jāygā batāso jaṭhāṁ tāprāṁ kar jāy rehsī*).[34] In Nagaur district, the *jāgīrdār* of Phasan village began to use his authority to harass a brahman resident.[35] Apart from confiscating some of the brahman's property, he also settled a leatherworker close to the brahman's home, knowing that this would bother the brahman.[36] The brahman petitioned the crown for help, winning an order for the *balāī* leatherworker to be immediately moved far from the brahman's home.[37]

Similar struggles ensued elsewhere. In 1782, the leatherworking *jaṭīyās* of Nagaur appealed to the state for help when they were thrown out of their homes in the town to make way for a new public works project but never received new plots of land on which to rebuild their lives.[38] Almost twenty years later, in 1801, the same community, but this time in Sojhat, found itself facing eviction not only from their homes but from the town. In order to raise money, the crown had ordered that the leatherworkers' plots be immediately confiscated and sold in order to generate five rupees per plot as revenue.[39] The leatherworkers put up a fight for two years.[40] In 1803, facing the crown's pressure to leave, they protested that they had nowhere to go since the promised settlement that was meant to accommodate them outside the town was still incomplete.[41] Ignoring their protests and insisting that the new settlement was ready, the crown ordered the governor of Sojhat to immediately resettle them outside the town and to discipline them if they continued to protest.[42]

In large parts of the Marwar kingdom, groundwater was hard to reach and rainfall scanty. Situated on the edge of the Thar Desert in western India, the people of this region had adapted their lives and livelihoods to the scarcity of water. Famine occurred every few years. Differential access to water resources served as an additional and cruel marker of social inequality. In 1765, the merchants, brahmans, *jāṭ* farmers, and others of Mahevra village in Merta district joined forces to prevent the leatherworking *balāīs* of their village from drawing water from a well, even though the well had earlier been demarcated for the exclusive use of the leatherworking castes.[43] This suggests that this village had already seen an aligning of the local caste order in a manner that permitted the exclusion of leatherworkers from the public water supply. Doubling down on this exclusion, caste elites of this village now worked to expel the *balāīs* even from the segregated water access they had. The leatherworkers appealed to the state for help and the state ruled in their favor, citing custom and decreeing that the *balāīs* should continue to draw water from the well that had been allocated to their use.[44]

While in this case pressure from local elites did not yield the desired result, most subsequent attempts at such segregation were received favorably by state officers. Ten years later, in 1775, a group of Shrimali merchants of Samdadi village in Siwana district could not accept that leatherworkers such as *balāīs* and *jaṭīyās* were drawing water from a well that the Shrimalis considered exclusively theirs,[45] even though it was only after their own well dried up that the leatherworkers had turned to the Shrimali-controlled well for water supply. The Shrimalis petitioned the state, asking that the leatherworkers turn to other, smaller wells in the area for their water needs. The state complied with the Shrimalis' demand, ordering that the leatherworkers be forced to refrain from drawing water from the same well as the Shrimalis and that they be directed to alternative water sources.[46]

Similarly, a merchant from Merta complained to the crown in 1780 when the *chamārs* and *balāīs*, both leatherworking castes, began to fill water at a public water source instead of sticking to a small waterhole that had customarily been reserved only for them. The mahajan petitioned the state to direct the leatherworking groups to draw water at a designated tank, the Naval Sagar, instead of filling their vessels where the mahajans did. The crown assented and ordered its district officers in Merta to ensure that the leatherworkers drew water only from the designated tank.

From the perspective of mahajans and brahmans, then, sharing space and water supply with the loosely defined "lowly" might have been undesirable but also largely unavoidable. But sharing space and water supply with leatherworkers was even less acceptable. In fact, it was unacceptable enough to provide a strong case for state intervention. As clearly stated in the command I presented in the introduction to this book, leatherworkers were squarely in the category "Untouchable." The maintenance of the purity of the elite social body demanded insulation from the Untouchable. The latter half of the eighteenth century in Marwar provided suitable conditions to make this ideal a reality.

In a region such as Marwar, with arid, semi-arid, and rainfall-dependent ecologies, water was a source of power. In these ecological conditions, access to water resources was prized and control over these could be a source of economic prosperity and local dominance.[47] The building of public tanks, stepwells, and lakes was expensive and it was the region's kings, rajput lords, and merchants who took the lead in sponsoring their construction and maintenance.[48] Rulers also offered loans or concessional land revenue rates as incentives to peasants to dig new wells.[49] Building water bodies, with the donor's name often installed nearby on a stone inscription, created a legacy for the donor or king and generated goodwill and spiritual merit. Water bodies were in that sense political resources. But, as the cases discussed in the section show, they also could be political resources in local struggles to demarcate elite status and the caste order. The desert ecology of Marwar intensified the politics of water access.

UNTOUCHABLES PAR EXCELLENCE

There are probably only a handful of cases where castes associated with removing waste—largely *bhaṅgīs* and *halālkhors* in Marwar—even show up in the administrative and judicial decrees of the Jodhpur crown. This is unlike those other castes that were also considered quite lowly and whose work was deemed polluting such as the leatherworkers discussed above. Even within the broad rubric of the "untouchable" then, there were distinctions and degrees of untouchability, with the sweepers being so far removed from the social domain that their disputes, petitions, and even crimes were not of concern to the state. Quite as likely, the state was not of concern to *bhaṅgīs*, at least in their social life. As the silence of the archive suggests, they likely resolved their own disputes largely among themselves. The state's legal apparatus was not the means through which to challenge punishments, violations of customary rights, or other injustices. In the rare occasions that *bhaṅgīs* do appear in the orders, judgments, and decrees of the Rathor state, it is not as petitioners for justice but mostly as nebulous figures that are occasionally referred to but whose own concerns remain unstated.

I will begin by sharing the few references to *bhaṅgīs* that I could find in the Rathor archive. In one judgment, reflecting their reduction to a condition of inescapable and inherent defilement, the *bhaṅgīs* were forced into being the instruments of rough justice at the hands of local elites. In 1785, Mahajan Rajiye of a village in Parbatsar district appealed to the crown for help when he was punished for a crime that he claimed he did not commit.[50] He was accused by another mahajan of stealing grain and, acting upon this complaint, the village's scribe slapped Mahajan Rajiye with a series of punishments, among which was tying him amid *bhaṅgīs* and ordering the *bhangīs* to spit onto his face.[51] The mere company of *bhaṅgīs* and contact with their bodily fluids were considered so offensive that they were forms of penalty. While petitioning the crown for justice, Mahajan Rajiye was careful to include in his petition a clarification that those *bhaṅgīs* did not actually go through with spitting on him.[52] Crown officer Purohit Kesorai, a brahman, agreed with the merchant that this was an excessive punishment, and one without judicial precedent (*bedastūr*). It ordered an official inquiry into how such a resolution could have been arrived at, as seen in the order reproduced as figure 3 in this book.[53]

That said, contrary to the crown's claims, this punishment of forced bodily contact with *bhaṅgīs* was not entirely without precedent. In 1782, only three years earlier, the crown had sentenced two of its subjects to being tied up in a public square and beaten with *bhaṅgīs'* shoes for ten to twelve days.[54] This earlier precedent was different from the later case in that here the crown, not its junior functionaries, exercised the prerogative of handing out such a punishment. In addition to these examples of the *bhaṅgī* body being an instrument of justice, another kind of reference to the sweeper castes is the order from 1785 with which I began this history. In it, the state defines what the category "*achhep*" or "Untouchable" consists of—listed along with the leatherworkers, vagrant castes, and Muslims are the sweepers.[55]

In these sources, we have an unequivocal expression of not just the marginalization of sweeper castes but also of the existence, and further, the inscription into law of a category called "*achhep*." *Achhep* appears to be a variation of *achhop*, a term found in at least one verse composed by an early-modern bhakti *sant* poet, the Muslim cotton-carder Dadu Dayal.[56] The verse, which has been found in manuscript copies dated to the seventeenth century, says, "*sevā sañjam kar jap pūjā, sabad na tinko sunāvai / maiṁ achhop hīn mati merī, dādū ko dikhlāvai*" (You won't speak to those who perform service, austerities, recitation, or prayer / But you show yourself to me, Dadu, an *achhop* dimwit).[57] Ramnarayan Rawat has pointed to the use of the term *chhūt* (meaning "touch"), which in turn derived from the Sanskrit *chupa* or "touch," to name the practice of caste-based untouchability in early modern north Indian *bhakti* poetry.[58] I suggest that the term *achhop* and its variants *āchhop* and *achhep* also derived from this same Sanskrit root, *chupa*, and therefore they mean that which cannot be touched.[59]

Denoting "untouchable" in Marwari, the precolonial use of this term that I have shown here lays to rest the idea that the naming in everyday practice and in state law, and not just in normative brahmanical texts, of the Untouchable as such was a product of colonial modernity. The language and content of the Rathor state's commands make untenable the argument that the word "Untouchable" did not

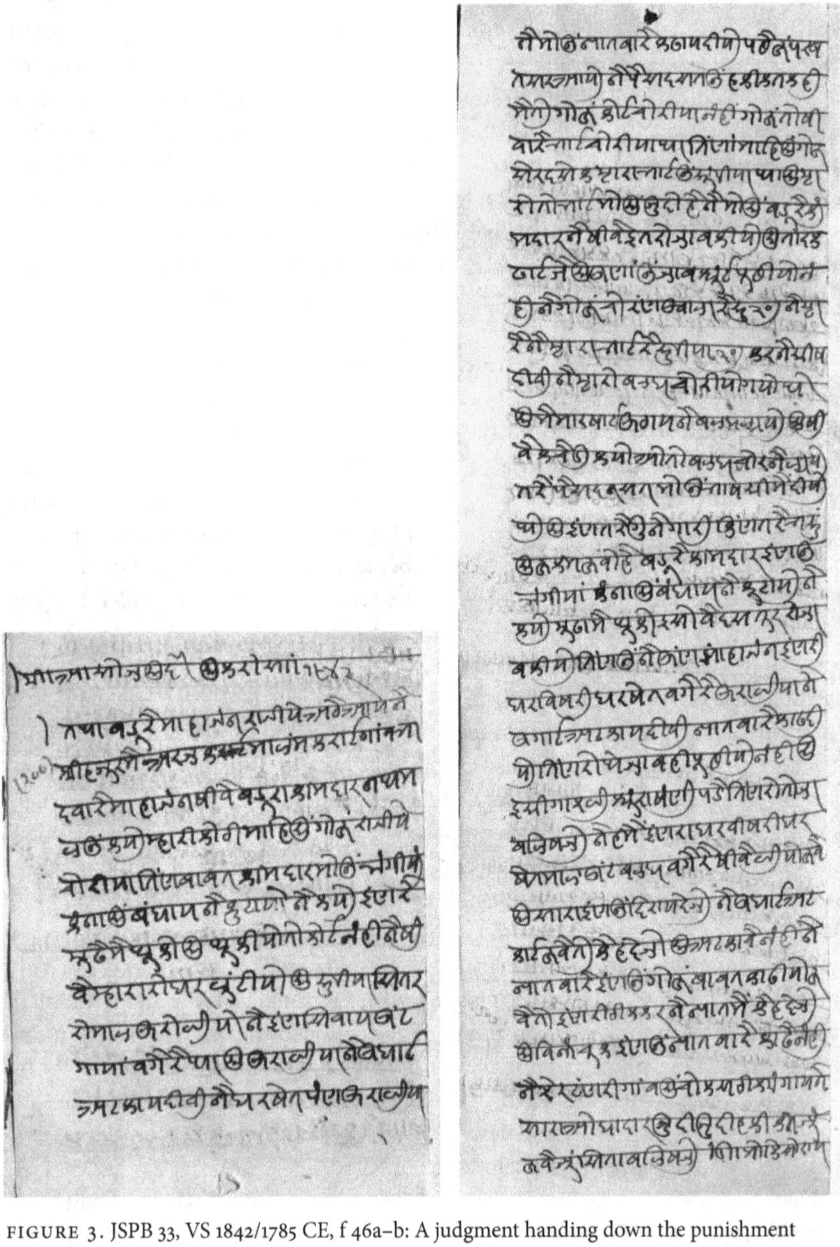

FIGURE 3. JSPB 33, VS 1842/1785 CE, f 46a–b: A judgment handing down the punishment of being beaten with *bhaṅgīs*' shoes. Image courtesy of the Rajasthan State Archives, Bikaner (RSAB). Do not reuse or reproduce without permission from the RSAB.

exist as a social category outside of brahmanical texts before colonialism. Simon Charsley, in particular, has articulated this view most clearly, citing the role of the colonial census in the naming of the bottom-most rung of the caste order as "Untouchable." Charsley argues that this, combined with the efforts of nationalist reformers like Gandhi and the anticaste leader B. R. Ambedkar, led to a naturalization of the idea of a multicaste identity with all-India salience imagined in dichotomous opposition to the "caste Hindu" or the Hindu.[60] Charsley's view continues to be cited in recent anthropological studies on caste as an overview of the history of the category "Untouchable."[61] Rupa Viswanath has pushed back against Charsley's view using colonial sources.[62] Joining her, I show through these precolonial sources that both the category "Untouchable" and its positing in opposition to the "Hindu" were already in place in at least this one regional order by the eighteenth century, prior to colonialism. Also, Charsley sees the implications of his findings as showing that the consolidation of a transcaste, flattening "Untouchable" identity only worked to consolidate caste hierarchy and discrimination.[63] To the contrary, the imagination of the "Untouchable" precisely in these terms, in opposition to Hindu-ness, was already essential to the working of the caste order before colonialism. It cannot be held as either a solely modern innovation or a cause for the modern consolidation of caste. It also ought to be noted that the existence of an overarching "Untouchable" category could coincide, as I show, with internal differentiation and power asymmetries within the members deemed to be in this group and contestation and variation in the precise constitution of this group.

Rawat's engagement with the significance of the history of the category "Untouchable" for the mobilization of Dalit political identity in colonial India shows that the term "*achhūt*" (literally "untouchable" in Hindi today) until the 1920s meant "untouched" in the sense of being pure and unsullied. It was used not as a noun but as an adjective. Rawat notes, through a reliance on nineteenth-century sources, that the physical touch (*chhūt*) of the lowest castes was stigmatized and that Untouchables may have been known by other overarching adjectives such as *aspriśya*.[64] The references to *aspriśya* (literally, "untouchable") that he cites are all from the early twentieth century and are presented as revivals of ancient Sanskrit usage.[65] What is new, argues Rawat, is the use of *achhūt* as a noun. Working with Rawat's framework, the deployment of a new term (*achhūt*) to name the lowest castes does not negate the possibility of the use of a term like *achhep* for the same task in eighteenth-century Marwar. Rawat's is an important intervention, particularly in showing that the transformation of the term *achhut* played a role in the earliest mobilizations of Dalit politics in north India. By showing that a change of name could be significant for political mobilization, Rawat's work points to the potential for social and political change that the naming, in precolonial state records, of a transcaste community of Untouchables could have possessed.

THE UNTOUCHABLE IN LAW

The contours of the Untouchable domain were never entirely fixed. Rather, certain caste groups stood in for the core of the Untouchable while others could slip in and out of the category. For a better sense of what constituted the "Untouchable" in elite eyes in precolonial Marwar, it is necessary to go over all the uses of the term in petitions and decrees that survive in the Rathor archive. Among other points, what is clear from this survey, I will show, is that the use of the term in state orders imparted to it the force of law, and fueled an effort to mobilize this category as the basis for demanding changed patterns of everyday life.

In 1785, the mahajans of Pali requested the crown's help in putting to an end the existing practice of all the townspeople drawing water from the same tanks and stepwells (*talāb bāvḍī sārā hī lok ekaṇ ghāṭ bharai hai*). Instead, they requested segregation in water access. Acceding to this demand, the Rathor crown ordered the governor of Pali to ensure that the "superior castes," defined as brahman, mahajan, "and others," filled water from one bank and the Untouchable castes from another (*āgāṁ sū brāmaṇ mahājan vagairai ūtam jāt to ekai ghāt bharīyā karai nai achhep jāt dūjai ghāṭ pāṇī bharīyā karai*).[66] It is noteworthy that the mahajans banded together to make this appeal and that, in its response, the state included them in an imagined collective of *ūtam jātis* or "superior castes."

The generalized and intentionally vague usage here of the label "Untouchable" to encompass everyone but brahmans, mahajans and "other" (though unnamed) elite castes was different from the narrower and much more precise listing of particular castes in the 1785 state order pertaining to the public performance of Vaishnav identity discussed in the introduction. This suggests that "untouchable" could sometimes be deployed as a broad rubric that rhetorically subsumed everyone other than a handful of the most elite and the precise application of this category in practice could have shifting contours. In encompassing all but the most elite, it is also reminiscent of terms like *strīśūdrādika* (literally, "women, lower castes, and others") that were used in early modern Marathi devotional literature.[67] An obvious difference, however, is that *achhep*, unlike *strīśūdrādika*, does not seem to encompass all women.

Despite the shifting contours of the category, the meaning of *achhep* remained consistent across its usages. It designated that group of castes with whom contact was considered socially and physically degrading by groups that had escaped this classification.[68] The label was perhaps intentionally vague, more a placeholder to mark a community from whom a loud proclamation of distance was essential to eliding an underlying relationship of inextricable entanglement. The naming of this community was necessarily at the hands of those who were not its members and, as a result, it was open to contention and variation. From the perspective of the social elite, it could be so expansive as to encompass almost everyone who was not a merchant, brahman, rajput, charan, or *jāṭ* peasant. The "Untouchable" so imagined could include all artisans such as cloth printers, dyers, weavers, blacksmiths, and potters, and service providers too. More commonly in state orders, however, it was a much narrower category, with leatherworkers, Muslims, vagrant hunters, and most essentially, sweepers at its core.

Leatherworking castes, namely the *chamārs*, *bhāmbhīs*, *meghvāls*, *ḍheḍhs*, and *balāīs* and landless vagrant hunters such as *bāvrīs* and *thorīs*, all appear to have been more clearly *achhep*. This is expressed most unequivocally in the 1785 state command presented in the introduction that lists these groups, along with sweepers and Muslims, as *achhep* castes. There are other instances as well of members of these caste communities being labeled "Untouchable." In 1801, the state's newswriters informed officers in Jodhpur that a man in charge of taxing the sale of clarified butter (ghee) in Sojhat district, a certain Ghadvai Savai, had not just taken a bribe of one rupee from a ghee seller named Bhambhi Udiyo, of a leatherworking caste, but had also taken one and a half *sers* of ghee in the *bhāmbhī*'s own plate to keep for future sale.[69] It was not the taking of the bribe that offended the crown's officers. Instead, they were horrified that the man took the ghee in the leatherworker's vessel into his own home with the intention of selling it later. This created the risk of buyers purchasing the ghee without knowing its origins. "*Achhep jāt rā vāsaṇ ro ghīrat kāḍh dūjā ro dharam sābat kīṇ tarai rahai*," or "How does one's *dharma* remain intact after taking ghee from an Untouchable's vessel?" asked the order.[70]

It is clear then that Rathor officers were invested in the regulation of the boundary between the Untouchable and the rest of the population. In 1782, the crown received news of a group of girls who the Merta city magistrate's office had gathered.[71] While it is unclear how these girls had been separated from their families, it is likely that their guardians had sold them due to economic distress. The crown commanded the district magistrate of Merta to dispatch to the capital city a list that enumerated the caste origins of each girl.[72] Pancholi Nathuram declared on behalf of the crown, in an order copied twice in the record: "*uṇā chhorīyāṁ meṁ khātaṇ luhārī sunārī nāyaṇ turakaṇī tathā aur hī achhep itrī jāt vinā chhorīyāṁ huvai jikai kisī kisī jāt rī hai nai kitrī jaṇyāṁ hai . . . aṭhai likhjo*." That is, it said to send to Jodhpur details about all the girls from this group who were not of carpenter, blacksmith, goldsmith, barber, and Muslim families or of any other untouchable (*achhep*) castes.[73] In another instance, when a female slave (*baḍāraṇ*) ran away with a servant, their master, rajput Jodha Bhopat Singh, tried to recoup the cost of the runaway girl from the trader who had sold her by claiming that the trader had withheld the girl's "Untouchable" identity at the time of sale.[74] "*Ā baḍāraṇ to achhep jāt thī*" or "that female slave was of an untouchable caste," Bhopat Singh said. These two examples illustrate that, at least in principle, a woman of "Untouchable" status was not considered fit to be even a household slave. If slavery was a form of social death, in the caste imagination, this death still could not erase the social attribution of untouchability upon a body.

This segregation between elite groups and Untouchables was enforced in prisons as well. In Jalor, the magistrate objected when the governor began to house untouchable and elite castes in the same cells of the town's fort. The magistrate complained to the crown and asked, "How can you house rajputs, mahajans, et cetera, together with Untouchables (*rājpūt mahājan vagairai nu achhep bhelā kīṇ tarai rakhnī āvai*)?" Purohit Kesodas, a brahman, commanded on behalf of the crown that Untouchables, here specified as *meṇā* (known today as "Meenas") and *bhīls* (hill-dwelling and armed communities that controlled lands), should be jailed separately from *bhomīās* (rajput landholders), mahajans, and other elite castes going forward.[75]

Mahajan Rukma of village Agolai in Phalodhi complained to the state in 1788 when his pregnant daughter died. The woman's husband, he said, had kicked her, causing her to go into labor. Right after the child was born, Rukma's daughter breathed her last. As Rukma's daughter's body lay on a funeral pyre, her husband got a *thorī* ascetic (a *jogī*) to slit her womb open.[76] This may have been to ensure that no unborn child remained in her womb. *Thorīs*, as was explicitly stated in the 1785 command with which this book began and which was issued three years before this episode, were Untouchable (and explicitly listed as *achhep*).[77] As a result, the crown ruled that the mahajan was guilty not only of the crime of kicking and killing his wife but also of having a mahajan woman's corpse slit by an Untouchable (*īṇ tarai mahājan rī beṭī rī lāt rī dai nai mārī nai achhep jāt kanai peṭ kyūṁ phaḍāvaṇo paḍai*). If these allegations were proven true, Jodhpur officers Mahajan Singhvi Motichand and Pancholi Fatehkaran commanded the Pali magistrate to fine Rukma's son-in-law.[78]

Every once in a while, there were occasions when the castes broadly classed under the rubric "Untouchable" defied the segregation imposed upon them. In 1797, the *meghvāls* (leatherworkers) refused to restrict their celebration of the spring Holi festival to their own quarters in the town of Bilada.[79] While every other caste was said to have celebrated in their respective quarters, the town's *meghvāls* chose to hold their festivities in the town bazaar's main square. This disrupted the free movement of elite women that otherwise transited through the area. Citing the merchant and priestly women's suffering, caused by their inability to fetch water due to the "polluting" presence (*bhīṇṭā chuṭī had sudhī rahai* or "they remain within the limits [of their quarters] for fear of ritual pollution") of the leatherworkers, mahajan Muhnot Sibhukaran decreed on behalf of the crown that the governor of Bilada should threaten the *meghvāls* with punishment if they did not contain their festive celebrations to their own quarters in future.[80]

So, what do we make of these references to the practice of untouchability in eighteenth-century Marwar? First, these orders and petitions are a unique vantage point into the history of the practice of untouchability in the precolonial past. Most studies of untouchability in the precolonial period are based on the study of literary texts, whether prescriptive codes, brahmanical commentaries, didactic tales, hagiographies, or devotional poetry. There is a large body of writing on caste and untouchability in ancient and medieval South Asia tracing the origins of and changes in both phenomena.[81] For the early modern period, scholars of *bhakti* literature—poetry in the voice of such "untouchable" *sant*-poets such as Ravidas and Chokhamela as well as hagiographies and sectarian literature—have built up a picture of untouchability as an idea and a discourse.[82] These sources, however, leave open-ended the question of how untouchability was practiced in everyday life, which authorities enforced it and to what extent, and what its relationship was to historical changes particularly in early modern South Asia.

What the Rathor records that I examine here can offer us, foremost, is a history of the implementation of untouchability through state law and local politics in precolonial South Asia. Steps in this direction have been taken for Maratha territories and the Rajasthani kingdom of Kota in eighteenth-century South Asia.[83] These studies show that some eighteenth-century regimes intervened in localized caste orders and that these interventions extended to keeping Untouchables "in their place." Other studies tell us about the place of such "untouchable" groups as *chamārs* and *bhuīṁyās* in regimes of land and labor, revealing the role of early modern political expansion, conquest, and the introduction of new agrarian and land revenue arrangements in inscribing the location of these castes in local power structures.[84] The orders that I have gathered from eighteenth-century Marwar show that the mediations of eighteenth-century states could extend beyond policing the place of the Untouchable and into redefining who was Untouchable. Who was Untouchable, what defined untouchability, and how it was imposed was due to the play of historical forces. The changing contours of the Untouchable domain, in turn, shaped social and political orders. The outcaste, far from being outside society and therefore history, was right at the center of it.

What then is this history of untouchability in precolonial India? The use of *achhep* in administrative documents demonstrates that the conception of a category of people—of multiple castes, united by the characteristic of being so ritually impure that they were not to be touched—was not limited to normative brahmanical prescriptions. Even in normative brahmanical prescriptions, the category that we today translate as "Untouchable" was denoted through Sanskrit terms like *caṇḍāla*, *bāhya*, and *antyaja* that are not focused on physical touch. The term *aspṛśya*, literally "untouchable," does occur in ancient Sanskrit texts but its use is rare. Further, as Ambedkar cautions, scholars must be careful not to equate references to ritual impurity in brahmanical texts with the practice of hereditary and permanent untouchability.[85] Even as the emergence of the idea and practice of untouchability as permanent and hereditary in some texts occurred at some point well before the eighteenth century, the records of the Rathor state in Marwar show that in parts of eighteenth-century, precolonial South Asia the idea of the "Untouchable" existed as such and was put into practice through state law.

This history of untouchability tells us that there are limits to the fluidity, mobility, and fuzziness attributed by some to precolonial caste.[86] These limits were etched upon the Untouchable body—which was the material, tangible, and physical manifestation of that against which the Hindu social defined itself. While the exact contours of the "Untouchable" category could indeed be shifting in precolonial Marwar, one caste group upon whom the application of this label was placed beyond dispute was that of sweepers. The *bhaṅgī* (or the *halālkhor*) was the tangible reality and a living reminder visible to all others of the otherwise shifting, shadowy state of untouchability. Fear of contact with the *bhaṅgī*'s spit and the *bhaṅgī*'s shoes derived from the emanation of these materials from or their association with the *bhaṅgī*'s body. The *bhaṅgī* body represented the possibility of contagion, even if temporary and treatable through expiation, for the "clean" castes, offering to mahajan administrators a tool in their disciplinary arsenal. The sweeper was the embodiment of untouchability.

Second, while the fixity of being Untouchable was borne by some, the very slipperiness of it for others was essential to the practice of power. Fear of slipping into this category could produce compliance to the behavioral expectations of local elites, and aspirations to rise out of it could similarly encourage conformity with the ethical codes and prescriptions of locally powerful groups. In all of this, the *bhaṅgī* body served as the necessary index of a state of unsociality and a constant, physical reminder of the essence of untouchability.

Finally, the ability of the category to theoretically encompass all but the very elite made it a site for political struggle. Changes in social, economic, and political circumstances could generate different and shifting outcomes in terms of who exactly was Untouchable and who was not. There certainly was a core to the category, constituted by leatherworkers, sweepers, and vagrant hunters, but there was room for others to be added to it. It was this potential for expansion that drew untouchability into the orbit of history, leading to changes over time in terms of both its criteria and those who constituted it.

THE OUTCASTE MUSLIM

Muslims, at least from the perspective of the Jodhpur crown and its elite subjects, were also Untouchables. So it was that it forbade, as mentioned above, the sale of any girls on the slave market to buyers of "carpenter, blacksmith, goldsmith, barber, Muslim, and of any other Untouchable (*achhep*) caste (*khātaṇ luhārī sunārī nāyaṇ turakaṇī tathā aur hī achhep itrī jāt*)."[87] Tracing yet another thread back to the 1785 order at the start of this book and reproduced in this chapter as Figure 4, there too Muslims (*turak*) are classed among those "Untouchable" castes (*turak ḍheḍh chamār thorī bāvrī halālkhor achhep jāt huvai*, or "Muslims, leatherworkers, vagrant castes and sweepers are Untouchable castes") that were to be forbidden from participating in a ritual whose performance was compulsory for all "Hindus" (*hinduvāṁ*).[88] Another crown decree from 1785, figure 5 in this book, sees Muslims in caste terms, prohibiting "Muslims and other low castes" (*musalmān vagairai nīch jāt*) from keeping herds of goats or sheep.[89] These orders placed Muslims explicitly in the same category as Untouchables and the lowly (*nīch*).

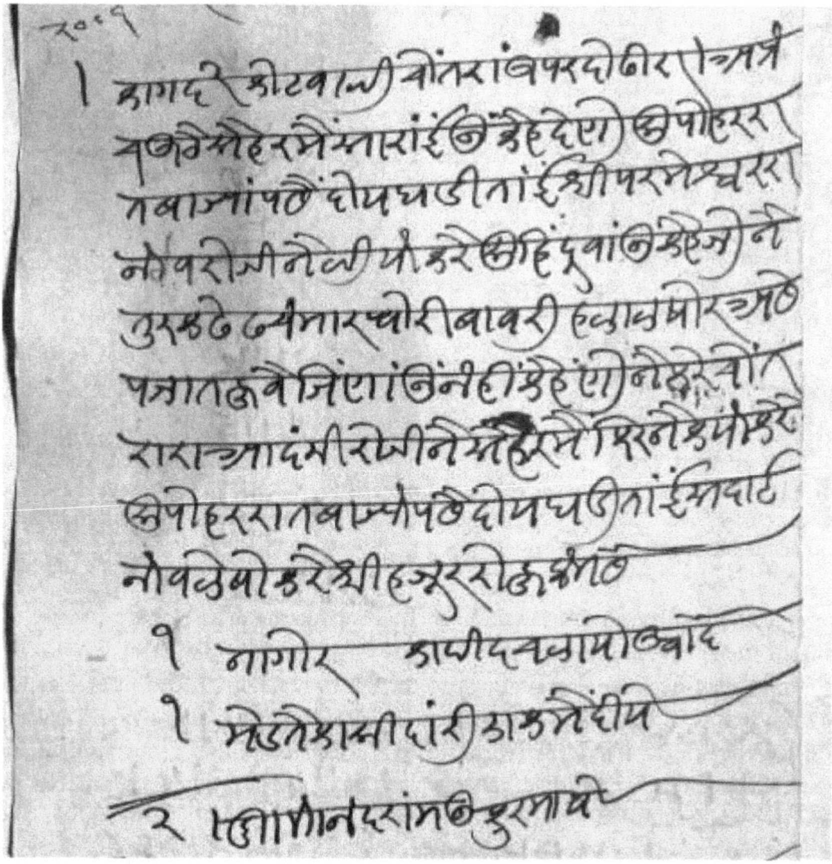

FIGURE 4. JSPB 32, VS 1842/1785 CE, f 293b: A command defining "*achhep*" and separating it from "Hindu." Image courtesy of the Rajasthan State Archives, Bikaner (RSAB). Do not reuse or reproduce without permission from the RSAB.

Lowly enough, in this political and legal imagination, to sometimes be classed as Untouchable, Muslims too suffered from efforts at segregation at the hands of merchants and brahmans. These efforts were similar to those endured by leatherworkers. So, in 1765, the Shrimali merchants of Sojhat complained that a spinner (*pīñjārā*) lived too close to their neighborhood. The Rathor crown responded sympathetically and ordered the governor of Sojhat to have the *pīñjārā*, a caste that we know was Muslim in Marwar, to move.[90] In another instance, the state agreed with a *jāṭ* woman's contention that such castes as *jāṭs* and mahajans would be hesitant to buy her plot of land because it was adjacent to a Muslim quarter.[91] In 1778, in Nagaur town, brahman Gordhan petitioned the crown in 1778 for help when a Muslim tailor bought the plot right next to his home.[92] He pleaded, "*mhāre pākhtī turak ro khaṭāv nahī huvai*," or "having a Muslim neighbor is unbearable." Heeding

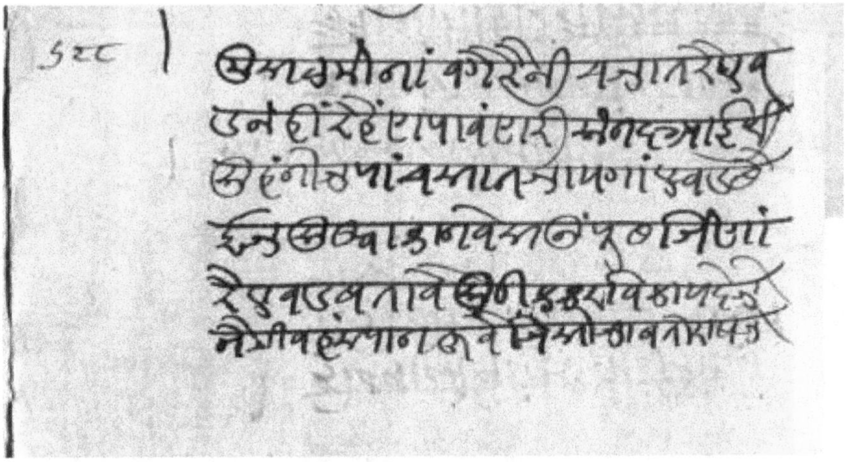

FIGURE 5. JSPB 32, VS 1842/1785 CE, f 293b: Order classing Muslims with other "low" castes. Image courtesy of the Rajasthan State Archives, Bikaner (RSAB). Do not reuse or reproduce without permission from the RSAB.

his appeal, Bhandari Savantram and Pancholi Fatehkaran ordered the governor of Nagaur to help the brahman with buying the plot from the Muslim tailor.[93]

There were occasional exceptions to the state's inclination to support spatial segregation. In 1773, some *khatrīs* (a caste of petty traders) in the town of Nagaur resisted the efforts of *julāvās* (weavers) to reclaim residential property in their neighborhood on grounds that the weavers were Muslim. The *julāvās* countered by asserting that Hindus and Muslims had lived together peacefully as neighbors for generations in that neighborhood. Perhaps because the *khatrīs* lacked the clout of merchants (mahajans) and brahmans, in this case they were unable to win a favorable order that could keep the weavers out.[94] Even as in this case the drive toward segregation was effectively countered with reference to custom, in the larger set of appeals seeking distance from Muslims, this was an exception. The case still shows that the *khatrīs* chose to frame their appeal for distance on grounds of the Muslim identity of the weavers, suggesting either that they thought this would be an effective strategy or that this is how they felt. It also is worth noting that I did not come across a single command in which a Muslim family or caste group appealed for distance from a neighbor due to their "Hindu" identity.

The Rathor state supported several other petitions seeking to enforce the physical segregation of elite castes from Muslims in the late eighteenth century. Take the case of *jāṭ* farmer Gidha's wife, likely a widow, who appealed to the crown in 1787 for help with selling her land. She had earlier pawned the plot of land, which bordered a *qāẓī* quarter, to Qazi Sher Ali of her village in Nagaur district and now she wished to sell it. She explained that selling the plot to this *qāẓī* was not an option since that would be a violation of the local prohibition on the sale of land to Muslims (*musalmān nai zamīn nā deṇī*). Finding no other buyers, she petitioned the crown for guidance on what to do with her land. The crown's response was that she should try to sell it to a person of a caste such as *jāṭ* and mahajan. Only if such people refused to buy it due to its proximity to the *qāẓīs'* lands, could she then sell it to the *qāẓī* with the crown's special permission.[95] This prohibition upon the sale of land to Muslims, even if localized, suggests that the drive toward the exclusion of those deemed "Untouchable" could extend into measures intended to shut off access to avenues of economic prosperity. Land ownership was a marker of status, apart from being an economic resource generating income. We do not know to what extent and for how long the order to not sell land to Muslims was implemented in late eighteenth-century Nagaur, but this petition suggests that Rathor policy could formalize and implement discrimination on the basis of faith.

The effort to draw spatial boundaries on the ground unfolded elsewhere too. In Merta, a temple functionary (*bhagat*) protested in 1788 that the door from a Muslim oilpresser's home might open onto the *bhagats'* quarter.[96] The issue had already snowballed into a confrontation since many other town residents, likely all of artisanal castes, had threatened to march *en masse* to the capital, Jodhpur, in support of the Muslim oilpresser. Yet, Pancholi Fatehkaran, ruling on behalf of the crown, favored the *bhagat's* petition and decreed that the *bhagat's* Muslim neighbor should build his front door to lead onto a public street and not into the *bhagat* quarter.[97] A Muslim oilpresser, combining "low" caste and an adherence to Islam, passing through the *bhagats'* quarter was unacceptable then not only to the *bhagat* but also to state officers.

That same year, in the winter of 1788, Pancholi Fatehkaran and the *pyād bakhśī* Mumhta Gopaldas, a mahajan in the office in charge of nonrajput personnel, decreed from Jodhpur that the until-then prevalent practice of Hindus and Muslims drawing water together and from the same wells (*hindu nai musalmān sel bhel pāṇī bharai hai*) in Didwana town was to be discontinued. Going forward, "Hindus and Muslims" were to fill water from separate and designated wells.[98] This order does not elaborate who was Hindu, but its construction of the two communities in binary terms, alongside its introduction of a new practice of social distance, illustrates once more the role of the state in the consolidation of a Hindu social body against an Other, here Muslim.

The logic of caste—centered on bodily qualities and interactions—underpinned the types of actions that were implemented by Rathor officers to mark off the contours of this new Hindu community in eighteenth-century Marwar. The imagined Otherness of Muslims was part of the construction of the Hindu body, whether social, political, or corporeal, and should be read as interwoven with the processes of separating from an "Untouchable Other" described in the earlier sections of this chapter. The Hindu Self was constituted in caste terms. The reconfiguration of elite identity to also include merchants and brahmans entailed greater caste-based polarization in everyday life and the micropolitics of the region. Mahajans and brahmans used the Rathor state to engineer new segregations in residential patterns and water access, segregations that separated Hindus from "Untouchables" such as leatherworkers and landless vagrant castes of *thorīs* and *bāvrīs*. The category "Untouchable," in the orders of the Rathor state and in the imaginations of their elite-caste Hindu officers and petitioners, was one that also included Muslims. Later in the book, I will show that this process was concurrently intensified by the fusing together of Muslims with vagrant, landless castes stigmatized on the charge of being irremediably mired in the habit of hurting animals. The processes underway in Marwar were an effort to reconstitute what it meant to be Untouchable. The boundaries built and adjudicated through the Rathor state in these decades helped define the contours of a new Hindu community in caste terms. Even as merchants, in alliance with brahmans and in rural areas also with *jāṭ* peasants, were at the forefront of localized struggles to create social distance from the "lowly," none of this could have been possible, as the next chapter will show, without Maharaja Vijai Singh's quest to be an ideal Krishna devotee.

3

Hierarchy

The political self-fashioning of Hindu subjects in Marwar was not without precedent. The early modern period saw the articulation of what Peabody has called "Hindu kingship." By the eighteenth century this effort, as it unfolded in such royal settings as the Sisodiya and Kachhwaha courts of Rajasthan, emphasized a degree of uniformity within the imagined "Hindu" community that in turn prioritized the expulsion of "impure" elements. The eighteenth-century summoning of an imagined Hindu community shorn of and sometimes also standing against extraneous elements played out in terrains such as language, devotion, and caste. I will begin this chapter with a short, preliminary, and by no means complete history of how kings and courts participated in shaping religious practice and communities and, in the process, reshaped "Hindu" religion in medieval and early modern South Asia. This is a history that no doubt proceeded along multiple avenues, sometimes intersecting and at other times flowing in parallel across the vast region and its many social worlds. I will then discuss shifts in Vaishnav devotional practice pertaining to "low"-caste communities and Muslims that occurred in the eighteenth century. With this discussion as context for the use of the term "Hindu" in eighteenth-century Rathor court records, I will turn to how the constitution of the categories "Hindu," "Muslim," and "Untouchable" played out beyond courtly patronage practices, in terms of carving out the devotional domain, urban and rural residential space, water bodies, and the contours of caste groups.

IMAGINING THE "HINDU"

The origin of the term "Hindu" dates back to early Arab encounters with the region around the river Indus (known as "Sindhu" in local languages). As Islamicate polities took root in many different parts of South Asia, the twelfth and thirteenth centuries saw a wider association of the non-Muslim inhabitants of the region with the term "Hindu." Arabic and Persian literature, however, continued until the thirteenth century to use "Hindu" as a broad category denoting geographical origin.[1] Sanskrit texts, on the other hand, express from the twelfth century onward a recognition of the political, religious, demographic, and cultural changes that the establishment of the Delhi Sultanate and other Turkic polities introduced at that historical juncture in South Asia. Sheldon Pollock argues that early efforts toward conceptualizing a singular "Hindu" identity—albeit not named as such—developed in response to the rise of Muslim polities in South Asia. Patron kings began to be identified with the divine King Ram, and Turkic opponents with the demons Ram had slain in the battles of the *Rāmāyaṇa* epic.[2] The *Rāmāyaṇa*, with its binary "Othering" of the *asuras* as demons, provided the right vehicle for vilifying the Muslim kings who presented a grave new challenge to the authority of non-Muslim kings.

Basile Leclère suggests that Jain- and brahman-authored Sanskrit plays in the twelfth and thirteenth centuries depicted Muslims as "Others" by using literary and linguistic conventions that encoded Muslims not only as foreigners but also as lowly and demonic.[3] As Leclère points out, however, such efforts at demonization through literary representations were also channeled by brahmin and Jain authors against members of non-Muslim orders that they viewed as rivals. Contests between followers of Vishnu, Shiva, or among different schisms of the Jain community could inspire the same kind of demonization in Sanskrit literature. Sanskrit authors in later centuries also composed texts in praise of Muslims kings, having them speak Sanskrit (a marker of high social rank) in plays or describing them as avatars of Hindu deities.[4]

Andrew Nicholson, in his study of thirteenth-century philosophy, notes the beginnings of the effort to craft a more unified identity for the many diverse and competing schools of brahmanical philosophy at this time.[5] Still, it was not until the fourteenth century—that is, around the same time as the widespread usage of the term in Persian and Arabic writing—that local communities began to adopt the term "Hindu" to denote themselves. Cynthia Talbot has shown what may be the earliest known application in an Indic language of the label. This occurred in fourteenth-century Andhra in peninsular India, in Telugu inscriptions that described Vijayanagara kings as "sultans among Hindu kings" (*hindu-rāya-suratrāḷa* or *hindu-rāya-suratrāna*).[6] Yet, in inscriptions such as these two, Hindu, defined in opposition to the Turk, remained an ethnic category, denoting differences in dress, language, food, and cultural norms.[7] And, as André Wink argues, the Vijayanagara conception of "Hindu" was in any case borrowed from Muslim observers.[8]

From the fifteenth centuries onward, certain courts—particularly Vijayanagara under Krishnadevaraya in the fifteenth century and the courts of the Marathas and Jai Singh II in the early eighteenth century—emerged as powerful patrons of change in the crafting of a trans-sectarian unity among Vaishnav sects and the invention of new brahmanical rituals of kingly legitimation that were presented as revivals of ancient forms. The eighteenth-century Maratha court and Jai Singh II of Jaipur made departures in the projection of a king as a virtuous defender against demonized and flattened Muslim enemies, and the shift among Vaishnav orders toward a greater acceptance of caste hierarchy.[9] These shifts occurred in courts and under kings who continued to foster cosmopolitan and pluralistic polities.[10]

Yet, in the departures that kings like Krishnadevaraya, the Marathas, and Jai Singh II made, new precedents were set that acquired accretive force with each succeeding generation. The Vijayanagara model of kingship left a mark so deep that it was emulated centuries later by Tipu Sultan as he asserted his own claims to sovereign power.[11] Still, the forging of this umbrella "Hindu" category occurred in connection with the efforts of imaginative sovereigns who broke from established patterns around them to articulate new types of kingly authority. Their efforts were crucial to the real-world activation of brahmanical ideas, albeit steeped in and modified by centuries of participation in a Persianate milieu, about social order and ritual life.

These monarchs adopted rituals of kingship that self-consciously drew on "Vedic" forms. At the same time, these "revivals" often really were inventions of new traditions, especially by the eighteenth century, in which Vaishnav ideals and rhetoric were merged with current trends in brahmanical orthodoxy. Their efforts translated into a unification of a trans-sectarian Vaishnav identity, a Hindu-ness, even if only at the level of courtly discourse and elite religiosity. Proximity to these kings also shepherded Vaishnavism toward a more brahmanical orientation, one that upheld caste-based hierarchy.[12] By the latter half of the seventeenth century, brahmans favoring a more orthodox reading of scripture began to assert their hold upon the recitation and performance that undergirded the ritual life of Vaishnav *bhakti* communities in north India.[13]

LORDLINESS AND HINDU-NESS IN MARWAR

Since the late medieval period, a key locus of the ritual practices of the landed and warrior rajput communities in western India, as is also legible in the mid-seventeenth-century Rathor court chronicle, the *Vigat*, was reverence for the agency exercised by the Goddess. The Goddess could be an abstract "Devi" (literally, "Goddess") or a particular deity associated with the region or the clan, such as Nagnechi Mata (clan goddess to all Rathors), Karni Mata (an additional clan goddess to the Rathor kings of Bikaner), and Hinglaj Mata (clan goddess to whole caste groups such as the charans of western India). In the *Vigat*, the Devi appears in dreams, bestows her blessings if pleased and withdraws them if not, and takes earthly form to slay mortal enemies and defeat demons. The autumn festival of Dussehra, which celebrates both the Goddess Durga's defeat of the demon Mahishasura as well as the divine king Ram's defeat of the demon Rāvaṇ as recounted in the *Rāmāyaṇa*, held special significance in the ritual calendar of rajput kings and warriors. Prayers to the Devi on this day, one whose public performance was associated with the annual renewal of kingly status, included the dedication of rajput arms to the Goddess for her blessings and the ritual sacrifice of a live animal, preferably a buffalo, to her.[14] Each of the goddesses conjured a sacred geography of her own and was associated with a particular site. For instance, Nagnechi Mata was rooted in the village of Nagana on the outskirts of Jodhpur and Karni Mata in Deshnok near Bikaner. This ritual order gave special significance to charans, a caste of poets that were generally associated with patron families of rajputs for whom they maintained genealogies and about whose heroic deeds they composed and sang ballads. Charans were closely associated with the worship of the Goddess. Charans could also be ritualists and were considered to wield sacerdotal power. In keeping with the significance of charans to the goddess-centered ritual world of rajputs, many of the goddesses that rajputs revered were considered to have been born into a charan family.

The rajput world from the thirteenth to the fifteenth centuries was akin to the frontier society that existed in other parts of Eurasia, for instance in medieval Anatolia: characterized by shifting alliances, respect for a code of honor and etiquette, a constant quest for booty and followers, strategic marriages into families of more powerful or wealthy chiefs, and openness and fluidity in identities and alliances.[15] As Shahid Amin has noted, north India in the fourteenth century nurtured localized cults of equestrian heroes martyred in the act of protecting cows from raiders.[16] Oral epics about them, such as that of the rajput Pabuji in Rajasthan, enjoyed popularity and sites associated with these legendary figures became centers of worship and pilgrimage. Amin notes the overlapping motifs between the legends of certain *ghāzīs*, or holy warriors, revered as saints across north India and those of cow-protecting heroes such as Pabuji. Other elements of the Rajasthani "folk-hero" cult also make more sense when seen in the context of this shifting world of martial men and their mobile followers. So it is that these cattle-protecting folk deities of Marwar are still known as the *pāñch pīr* or "five [Sufi] saints" and worship at their principal shrines is aniconic.[17] The openness of rajput status also translated, until the sixteenth century at least, into its full inclusion of Muslims. As numerous historians have shown, being Muslim, whether by birth or conversion, was not a disqualification for rajput status.[18] Marriages of rajputs into nonrajput families of Muslim chiefs and warlords who did not claim rajput status were common.[19] Many rajput clans had branches that were Muslim.[20]

By the seventeenth century, stray references from Marwari court chronicles betray the emergence of complexity in attitudes toward Muslims. This can be seen, for instance, in Nainsi's retelling in the *Khyāt* of the tale of Kanhadde, the fourteenth-century Songara Chauhan chief of Jalor in Marwar, which Rathor Maldev annexed in 1561. The *Khyāt* notes that after defeating "*Pātsāh*"[21] Alauddin Khilji at Somnath, Kanhadde reinstated the *śivliṅg* (Shiva icon) there and built a temple.[22]

Alauddin Khilji did indeed conquer Jalor in 1311, but Persian sources do not offer much detail about this episode. Regional rajput and Jain memories, however, nurtured narratives centered on this confrontation at Jalor. Commenting on Kanhadde's purported defeat of Alauddin and his supposed reinstatement of the Shiva icon at the Somnath temple in Gujarat, the *Khyāt* says, "Kanhadde upheld the dignity of *hindusthān* (*kānhaḍde hindusthān rī baḍī marjād rākhī*). Then, the Patsah's men [now integrated into Kanhadde's polity] killed cows, which was unacceptable to Hindus (*piṇ pātsāhī rā raihaṇhārā su gāyāṁ mārai, su hinduvāṁ rai khaṭāvai nahīṁ*)."[23] As Ramya Sreenivasan has argued in her comparison of Nainsi's version of the Kanhadde story with another one composed by brahmans and dated to mid-fifteenth-century Gujarat, this emphasis on cow killing as a violation of moral order was in keeping with a widespread strategy in texts sponsored by kings who faced a military threat from expanding Muslim polities.[24] Such representations drew, as Cynthia Talbot has argued, upon a longer tradition in brahmanical writing of portraying threats from "foreign" groups.[25]

Still, as Sreenivasan notes about Nainsi's version of the Kanhadde tale, this mid-seventeenth-century Rathor account depicts the successful, even if posthumous, marriage of Kanhadde's son with the Sultan's daughter, who in turn commits *sati* (ritual suicide through self-immolation) upon the son's funeral pyre just as a dutiful rajput wife would do.[26] This was among a few key departures through which Nainsi's account dissolved some of the imagined boundaries between "Hindu" and Muslim that the earlier, mid-fifteenth-century, brahman-composed version had inscribed. Sreenivasan notes the composition of the earlier account against the backdrop of ongoing conflict with an expanding Islamicate polity, whereas that of Nainsi was the product of a time when the sponsoring court was in a relationship of mutual benefit with the dominant power of the day. To that extent, in situations of territorial conflict and rivalry, Muslim foes could be encoded as radically "Other"—enemies of a righteous moral order, killers of cows and brahmins, destroyers of temples, and bearers of embodied impurity. That said, through the seventeenth century, Rathor rhetoric depicting the Mughals or other contemporary Muslim powers in this manner was uncommon in comparison with the wealth of evidence for mingling and mutual respect.

MUSLIMS IN EARLY-MODERN RAJPUT COURTLY IMAGINATION

In other rajput courts as well, particularly Udaipur, changes were afoot in attitudes to Muslim political authority. Cynthia Talbot's history of the transformation over the centuries of the legend of the rajput hero, Prithviraj Chauhan, is instructive. Prithviraj Chauhan was a twelfth-century rajput king whom the Afghan warrior Shihabuddin Muhammad Ghuri defeated in 1192. In the late seventeenth century, the Sisodiya rajput rulers of Udaipur emphasized a familial connection to Prithviraj, asserting that an ancestor of theirs had married Prithviraj's sister and had been a loyal ally in Prithviraj's battles against Ghuri.[27] The Sisodiya court commissioned literary compositions commemorating Prithviraj's heroism, adding new elements such as a prominent role played by their ancestor in Prithviraj's struggle against Ghuri and turning the story into one about resistance to a Muslim enemy.[28]

These seventeenth-century Sisodiya-sponsored retellings of the Prithviraj story, in comparison to earlier versions, amplified the threat that Ghuri represented in the tale. They also heightened the antagonism between rajputs and Muslims.[29] This shift in the Prithviraj story under the patronage of the Udaipur court was part of a wider political program geared toward regaining for the kingdom preeminence among all the rajput principalities of Rajasthan. This wider program included patronage of the arts and religion and the projection of a history of resistance to Muslim conquerors. From the mid-seventeenth century, only decades after accepting Mughal suzerainty, the Sisodiyas began to display their opposition militarily and culturally to the Mughals even as they collaborated with them outside Rajasthan. They presented their anti-Mughal politics as resistance on the part of a besieged "hindu *dharma*" against Muslim aggression.[30] A Sisodiya court poet produced a narrative of the war of succession between Shahjahan's sons, the *Rājvilās* (c. 1680), which presents Aurangzeb in a negative light, as a killer of kin, and which speaks of Hindu *dharma* and Muslim *asuras* (demons) as being in eternal conflict.[31] It is worth noting, however, that in these same decades, other texts produced by the Sisodiyas represented Aurangzeb positively.[32]

The Sisodiyas' sponsorship of literary narratives that cast Muslim political adversaries as enemies of a "Hindu *dharma*" can also be seen in the recasting of the Padmini legend at the Udaipur court in the late seventeenth century. Originally a fifteenth-century Sufi tale composed in the Awadh region near Agra, the allegorical tale played off the historical capture of the rajput fortress of Chittor by the Delhi sultan Alauddin Khilji. The tale, however, adapts the barest details of the siege toward its own didactic ends, providing guidance on the discarding of one's ego and worldly attachments in order to make possible the soul's metaphysical union with God. Versions produced for the Udaipur court for the first time cast the Sultan Alauddin as an alien "Other," on a quest to besmirch Hindu *dharma* through the taking of the rajput queen Padmini. Padmini became a symbol not only of the honor of her clan but also of a singular Hindu community.[33] To drive home the embodied "impurity," the danger of pollution posed by the Muslim antagonist, a court-commissioned, late seventeenth-century Padmini tale has Alauddin spitting at everything he sees as he walks through the Chittor fort and its lakes, gardens, and temples. In this account, "the spittle of the Musalman" drove off the blessings of Hindu gods, paving the way for the eventual fall of the fortress.[34] This is reminiscent of the pollution borne by the *bhaṅgī's* spit and its use as a type of punishment for "high"-caste subjects in Rathor-ruled Marwar in the eighteenth century.

BEYOND KINGS AND BRAHMANS

What is missing from this history of Hindu-ness in precolonial South Asia is the role of other social actors, beyond kings and brahmans. How do we link this history of kings and intellectuals with everyday life in South Asia that goes beyond the descriptions of elite literati? In the case of Marwar, the changes underway in Vaishnav sectarian orientations toward each other and toward brahmanical "orthodoxy" would quickly have traveled to the Vaishnav communities located in the Rathor domain. With Jaipur and Jodhpur kingdoms sharing a fluid and porous border, crossed frequently by mobile and interconnected communities, especially those of merchants, the shift in Vaishnav practice toward a greater concern with caste would surely have touched the everyday lives and ritual practices of these sects' adherents in Marwar. For those like the upwardly mobile mercantile groups that were seeking to cement their status as an elite caste, an enthusiastic embrace of brahmanical orthodoxy—even as they remade it—was a necessary ingredient for success.

Another facet that remains concealed if one does not look beyond kings and brahmanical texts is the extent and manner of the enactment of Hindu-ness outside political rhetoric and theological debate. For this was a history that also played out in everyday life in the towns and villages of places like eighteenth-century Marwar. And on the ground, it took on a different color. The "Other" was not the Muslim as Muslim but rather the "Untouchable" of which the Muslim was a part in this worldview. In the imagination of local elites, particularly merchants and brahmans, the more tangible danger to their purity, and therefore their status, was the "low"-caste body. On the ground, the Rathor state defined "Hindu" as that sphere which could never include Untouchables, and Muslims *as* Untouchables, and which at its core was an exclusive community of caste elites.

Turning attention to the thick description of everyday life and conflict in eighteenth-century Marwar makes possible the excavation of how "Hindu" translated into lived experiences and into law. This "Hindu" identity was not merely a precolonial mirror image of its colonial counterpart. Rather than being expansive and inclusive as was the colonial construction of a "Hindu" community, the precolonial Hindu domain was an exclusive one, limited as much as possible to the most elite of local castes. Further, on the ground, it was imagined not against the Muslim as such, as became the case in the colonial era, but against the Untouchable. This finding pushes against the dominant frame that historians espouse when debating the early modern antecedents of the Hindu community; that is, a conceptualization of "Hindu" in a binary relationship with "Muslim."

In Marwar, localized Krishna-centered Vaishnav communities, themselves in the process of reconstitution into a more elite group, formed an important locus in the formation of this new Hindu identity. The Rathor crown under Vijai Singh ensured that Vaishnav temples were well maintained, remained in active use, and were serviced by a ritual functionary. Officers ensured that disrespect toward Krishna temples was punished. If one of the key traits of *bhakti* is its public nature, this was a public in which "low" castes were welcome but only if they remained at the peripheries of devotional life. From early in the record series, a remarkable if succinct order centers on a charismatic leatherworker named Balāī Nanag, who drew around him a community of followers of different castes. These included four Maheshwari merchants, two clothprinters (*chhīṁpās*), one brahman, and one *bhojag* (a caste of temple servants). These men would listen to the sermons (*sabad*) of Balāī Nanag, much to the chagrin of a Vaishnav *bhagat* who reported them to the crown for this. Crown officer Dodhidar Anadu ordered the governor of Merta to discipline the ten men and warn them to never go to the leatherworker again.[35] In the eyes of state officers, a leatherworker, considered "untouchable," had no place as a preacher, let alone to a mixed-caste flock that included merchants and brahmans.

The Rathor state also supported the efforts of subjects, particularly merchants who had the outlay and drive, to build new Vaishnav temples.[36] It ensured that Vaishnav temples were sites of dignified behavior. Temple-centric Vaishnav communities became, in the decades under study, sites of struggle between elite and "low"-caste subjects such as shoemakers and tailors who found themselves forbidden from participating as fully as they previously had in shared rituals of the temple and the sect. This included orders to not touch ritual offerings and to pay obeisance from a set distance if not from outside the temple.[37] These artisanal communities pushed back, petitioning Vijai Singh's state repeatedly to challenge these efforts at marginalization that local authorities seemed unable or unwilling to impede.[38]

In some cases, the delineation of Vaishnav spaces and rituals as exclusive to elite-caste "Hindus" was a top-down effort, with functionaries of the Rathor state issuing commands toward this end. For instance, a Rathor officer commanded administrators in Bilada district to stop using leather bags (*chaḍas ro pakhāl masak*) to water rose bushes whose petals were to be dried to make a red pigment (*kumkum*) for ritual use. Those hired for the care of the rose bushes and the production of the pigment were to be "Hindu and excellent" (*hindu nai utam*) workers and were to use metal buckets or earthen pots, instead of leather bags, for watering the bushes.[39] Leather, in this perspective, was a ritually polluting material that had no place in sanctified spaces. In the state's eyes, the removal of "impure" leather was of a piece with the admission only of "excellent and Hindu" workers for the production of this ingredient for ritual use. Similarly, in a series of commands pertaining to the safe transport of sacred Yamuna water (*jamnājal*) through the districts of Marwar, crown officers commanded the employment of workers (*majūr*) or footsoldiers (*pālāṁ*) who were "Hindu and excellent" (*hindu nai ūtam*), "Hindu of caste" (*jāt rā hindu*), or of Hindu brotherhoods (*hindu bīrādarīyāṁ rā*).[40] In another order, Purohit Kesorai and Chhangani Nathu instructed the Nagaur magistrate to have cotton yarn and string woven, likely for ritual use, by Hindu artisans in a "good and neat place" (*āchhī suthrī jāygā hindu kārīgar kanai*).[41] Materials meant for the royal worship of gods were to be protected from contact with "untouchable" things (leather) and people.

When a respected brahman, Bhat Shrikrishanji, wanted to make a pilgrimage to the holy town of Dwarka in Gujarat, the merchant-administrator Muhnot Gyanmal ordered on behalf of the crown that Muslims were to be hired to work as footsoldiers for his party only if the requisite number of Hindus could not be found.[42] In working to meet Vijai Singh's commitment of sending soldiers to keep a watch on three Krishna temples in Jaipur, Muhnot Gyanmal issued an order instructing the governor of Sambhar district to send along twelve excellent Hindu (*hindu aval kāmūṁ*) footsoldiers.[43] As Vijai Singh sought to articulate the identity of an ardent Vaishnav and a leading member of the royal brotherhood of Vaishnav kings, he ensured through his mahajan ministers that ideally only Hindu footsoldiers represented him outside his kingdom.

Muslims too found themselves unwelcome in Vaishnav spaces, as made clear by their inclusion among the "*achhep*" who were barred from reciting the name of the Lord in the order discussed in the introduction. More diffuse incidents attest to the unwelcome stance toward Muslims being practiced in eighteenth-century Marwar. For instance, the Rathor state ordered its officers in Merta to find a plot of land in a mahajan-brahman neighborhood that was in the crown's control and devoid of Muslim *sipāhīs'* presence and to allot it to a Vaishnav devotee looking to build a Krishna temple.[44]

Almost two decades later, administrator Asopa Surajmal, a brahman, heard through Rathor newswriters that two Muslims (*musalmān*) had sat on the parapet of a Krishna temple. "*Musalmān nu ṭhākurdvārai kyūṁ āvaṇo paḍai?* (Why does a Muslim have to come to a temple?)," he asked, ordering that the soldiers of the magistracy who were supposed to have investigated this matter ought to suffer a pay cut for their incompetence in punishing the guilty.[45] Similarly, crown officer Pancholi Gulalchand upheld the expulsion of a *bairāgaṇ* (woman ascetic) named Tulchhi from a temple community in Merta when "her caste was revealed to be Muslim" (*jāt rī turakṇī huī nīsrī*).[46] A *jāṭ* farmer complained in 1787 that "*musalmān sipāhī vagairai*" or men of the Muslim rajput Sipāhī community and (unspecified) others would come to the Krishna temple (*ṭhākurdvārā*) that was recently made in his village in Parbatsar district. This was not right (*su ṭhīk nahīṁ*), the *jāṭ* argued. Three crown officers, Brahman Asopa Fatehram, Pancholi Fatehkaran, and Mahajan Singhvi Motichand, agreed and ordered the governor of Parbatsar to prevent the Muslim rajputs from coming to the temple.[47] That same year, Purohit Kesorai ruled from Jodhpur that a plot of land next to a Krishna temple in Merta should be taken from the Muslim who owned it and allotted instead to a Vaishnav devotee, Bhagat Girdhari Das. The Muslim was to be given another plot in exchange, he commanded.[48]

In 1789, an order issued by Singhvi Akhairaj, son of the influential merchant officer Bhimraj, working with Dodhidar Khinvo, noted that the bricks of a Sufi hospice (*turak ro takīyo*) in Sojhat had been used some years ago to build the town's fort. Now, they approved a request by a Shrimali merchant asking that the plot, due to its location at the gate of his own caste's residential quarter, should be allotted for the construction of a Vaishnav temple that he wanted to build.[49] Looking at all of these scattered episodes, what emerges is the picture of an expanding Vaishnav public: a site for the coming together *ostensibly* of all devotees of Vishnu, irrespective of caste, gender, or class. This public domain, however, debarred the participation of Muslims: disallowing them entry, creating spatial distance from them, and dislocating them from the vicinity of the Vaishnavs' growing presence. Once more, the exclusion of Muslims from a "Hindu" sphere dovetailed with the exclusion from this same sphere of oppressed castes.

Vaishnav communities had not always been unwelcoming to Muslims in the manner witnessed on the ground in eighteenth-century Marwar. In preceding centuries, there had been many crossovers between Vaishnavs and Muslims. Devotional poets Kabir and Dadu, whose verses became foundational for many Vaishnav communities, were born in Muslim families. Muslim poets Raskhan and Rahim (or Abdul Rahim Khan-i-Khanan, who was a high-ranking Mughal official) were among the most prominent composers of Krishnaite poetry in Brajbhasha in the sixteenth century.

There also was considerable exchange between practitioners of Sufism and Vaishnavism. The Sufi poetic genre of *premākhyān* drew heavily, among other influences, from forms and idioms native to India. In 1540, the Avadhi poet Malik Muhammad Jayasi wrote a romance, *Kanhāvat*, in the Sufi *masnavī* genre, narrating the story of Krishna. Francesca Orsini has suggested that Jayasi used "coded religious vocabulary" in a manner that would have allowed his multireligious audience to receive it as both a Krishna tale and a Sufi one.[50] In eastern Rajasthan, a poet of the devotional Dadupanthi sect, Sundardas (1596–1689), composed verses that drew upon Sufi concepts, reflecting the multiplicity of religious practices that enjoyed a following in the region.[51] Musical traditions, literary genres, and people moved between and dwelt simultaneously in Vaishnav and Muslim milieus throughout the early modern period.

And yet, by the latter half of the seventeenth century, it is possible to discern a discomfort in certain Vaishnav quarters associated with acknowledging any contact with Muslims. For instance, as Jack Hawley has shown, the late seventeenth-century brahman composers of the *Bhāgavat Mahātmya* choose to completely omit any reference to Muslims while narrating the history of *bhakti*.[52] A similar unease with Muslim contact can be traced in the Vallabhite order's didactic body of hagiographic literature. Shandip Saha points out that Muslim government officials whose generous patronage the sect's leadership happily accepted are revealed in this hagiographic literature to have been brahmans or *daivī jīvas* (spiritual souls) in past lives whose inadvertent transgression of a ritual prescription caused them to be reborn as Muslims. For instance, the late seventeenth-century *Chaurāsī Vaiṣnavāṁ ki Vārtā* discloses that Akbar had been a brahman in a past birth but had unwittingly swallowed a piece of cow hair while drinking milk. This inadvertent consumption of a cow's hair caused him to be reborn as a Muslim.[53]

In the *Chaurāsī Vaiṣṇavāṁ kī Vārtā*, or Account of Eighty-Four Vaishnavs, which is a hagiographical compendium of the first followers of the Vallabhite sect, *anya* ("other") is a term frequently used to denote other religious groups and figures of religious authority. Vasudha Dalmia points out that in the episodes compiled in this text, *anyāśraya* (seeking refuge in another) and *anyamārgīya* (being a follower of another path) are undesirable states, although attitudes toward the "Other" vary from an assertion of equality with a rival to complete rejection.[54] The *Chaurāsī Vaiṣṇavāṁ kī Vārtā* was compiled in 1696, though it is thought to have consisted of tales orally circulating since the late sixteenth century. The tales warn against keeping the company of members of other religious communities, worshipping any deity other than Shri Nathji (the Vallabhite order's primary Krishna idol), or discussing Vallabhite sectarian beliefs and practices with those of other communities. In their capacity as didactic tales, these episodes imparted to Vallabhite devotees the importance of maintaining the exclusivity of their order. They instructed Vallabhites to cut off all contact from not just Islam but folk traditions, Shiva worship, even the Krishna deities of other Vaishnav sects, and brahmans who refused to surrender to Vallabhite devotion were to be kept at a distance.[55]

The *Do Sau Bāvan Vaiṣṇavāṁ kī Vārtā*, or Account of Two Hundred and Fifty-Two Vaishnavs, whose earliest manuscript copy dates to the late eighteenth century, reflects the clearer enunciation of a harsher attitude toward Muslims, with several episodes about particular devotees reflecting the importance of staying away from Muslims due to their inferior, *mleccha* (barbarian) status.[56] Recognizing the practical difficulties of mobile merchants avoiding all contact with Muslims, Vallabhite hagiographical literature advised them to diligently continue practicing Vallabhite ritual toward Krishna and to create a tight network with other Vaishnavs in distant lands.[57] In the few positive references to Muslims in the late eighteenth-century *Do Sau Bāvan Vaiṣṇavāṁ kī Vārtā*, a complete immersion of even the most ardent of Muslim Krishna devotees into the Vallabhite community is avoided. In one instance, a Muslim vegetable seller is rewarded for her persistent devotion to Krishna by finally being initiated into the Vallabhite community, but only on her deathbed. In another instance, an insistent Muslim woodcutter is allowed to join the community only if he sits at a distance from Guru Viṭṭhalnāth and his followers.[58]

This shift in attitudes toward Muslims was perhaps a wider phenomenon in eighteenth-century South Asia. Purnima Dhavan points to hardening attitudes toward Muslims, accompanied by an increasing acceptance of caste, in the Sikh community in the eighteenth century.[59] Brendan LaRocque shows that the heterodox teachings of the seventeenth-century founder of the central Indian Prannami sect, many of whose followers were merchants, underwent revision in the hands of his eighteenth- and nineteenth-century memorialists, who sought to recast him as a holy warrior fighting to protect Hindu *dharma* from Muslim oppressors.[60] The emphasis upon exclusiveness with respect to all other religious practices and, as the eighteenth century progressed, the heightened disdain for Muslims in Vallabhite sectarian literature, compiled as it was in Rajasthan, reflected the efforts at social reorganization engineered by its chief patrons in the region, the merchants. Merchants and brahmans petitioned Jodhpur as they sought to reorder residential patterns to bring them in line with their efforts to create an exclusive, elite domain.

The process of the delineation of the eighteenth-century Hindu community was an aggregate of localized struggles for political domination and social ascendance, expressed through the very public creation of exclusive spaces, rituals, and activities that were inaccessible to those deemed "Untouchable." In this, the merchants of the kingdom played an important part as holders of governmental office in the capital, Jodhpur, and in the districts and as wealthy, upwardly mobile new elites in the kingdom. They were able to channel state authority and judicial processes toward the localized reorganization of social hierarchies in order to construct this new, transcaste Hindu community in Marwar.

STATUS AND BOUNDARIES

The forging of the new Hindu community necessitated the identification and exclusion of "Untouchables." The involvement of the state, manned by mahajan and brahman officers, allowed this segregation to span the spatial and economic, as well as social, domains. In order to cordon off the nascent Hindu community, state power was instrumental in the effort to police the boundary between Hindus on the one hand and "low" castes and Muslims on the other. Apart from introducing these segregations in terms of residential patterns and access to water, the state also played a role in hardening caste bodies to keep Muslim or "low"-caste elements out.

The manner in which the Rathor crown dealt with several cases of this nature testifies to this quest. For a period of almost twenty years, from 1770 to 1789, and probably beyond, barber[61] (*nāī*) Kana and his son Mayala found themselves in the eye of a storm that split the barbers of the town of Maroth into two factions. Some years before the dispute, Kana had sold his son, in a period of famine, to a band of Muslim *bañjārās* (an itinerant community that transported goods across vast distances in South Asia and beyond).[62] Living among the *bañjārās*, Kana's son Mayala had become Muslim, getting circumcised (*sunat kīvī*) in the process.[63] Four years later, Mayala managed to escape the *bañjārās* and return home. His family was delighted to have him back.[64] But when news of Mayala's conversion began to spread among the barbers of the area, caste (*nyāt*) leaders deemed it unacceptable to include a Muslim and decided to expel Kana's family from their caste if they did not disown the boy.

There clearly was no easy answer in Marwar to the question of whether a barber could be Muslim. A faction of the *nyāt* challenged the decision to expel Kana's family and banded together in support of reintegrating them into the caste. They approached the governor's office for help, winning a written order (*likhat*) that permitted the convert Mayala's inclusion into the *nyāt*. Unwilling to back down, the opposing faction refused to budge on its stand, and three years later petitioned the crown for intervention. The crown supported the pro-expulsion faction, issuing a written order (now a *kāgad*) that stated that no convert to Islam would be allowed to rejoin the barber community.[65]

The pro-inclusion barbers did not give up, even in the face of a government order. Seven years after the crown's order, in 1780, "Śrī Hajūr received a petition about this and Singhvi Bhimraj sent a written order (*kāgad*) for Surana Chainmal saying, 'Those who are trying to take him into the *nyāt* despite his being a *musalmān* (Muslim) should be disciplined'."[66] Singhvi Bhimraj, as discussed in chapter 1, was immensely powerful at court in the 1770s and 1780s. When these barbers refused to back down, the crown once again sided with the anti-inclusion barbers. Rajput Parihar Manrup and brahman Acharya Fatehram issued an order making clear to the pro-inclusion barbers that the crown's earlier decision was just and therefore final. This faction was to stop trying to reintegrate a Muslim convert into their caste.[67] Even as the crown reiterated its quest to restore harmony among the barbers, clearly this harmony was conditional on the Muslim convert's expulsion from the caste.

Seven years later, in 1787, the fight was still on. The pro-inclusion faction of barbers was showing complete disregard for the orders of the crown and, in complete defiance, were considering Kana and his son, Mayala, caste fellows.[68] By this stage, the matter became one in which it was not just local precedent or caste custom that was at stake. Rather, the resistant barbers were challenging the crown's own authority as well. Those barbers refused to back down. Now, a brahman officer named Purohit Kesoram sent an order (*hukam*) on behalf of Jodhpur to the governor of Maroth bearing instructions to warn the pro-inclusion barbers of the not customary (*gair dastūr*) and therefore unacceptable nature of their actions. Years into this conflict, mahajan and brahman officers remained unmoved, reiterating that reintegrating a Muslim convert into the barber caste was not permissible.[69] After that point, the archival trail runs cold, leaving it unclear how the matter was resolved. A similar disagreement, but without as much to and fro with the crown, occurred between the shoemakers (*mochīs*) of the adjacent kingdom of Jaipur and those of the Marwari town of Merta. While the former did not consider conversion to Islam enough reason to expel a member from their midst, at least some shoemakers in Merta did.[70]

In both these cases of attempted reinclusion after conversion to Islam, involving barbers and shoemakers, the caste groups involved held low positions in the local social hierarchies of Marwar. It is noteworthy that in the sole instance of the conversion of an elite-caste individual, a brahman, to Islam, there was no question of considering his inclusion within his caste's fold.[71] It appears then that among non-elite castes the relationship between caste membership and religious affiliation was open to negotiation. That is, among artisanal and other non-elite castes at the time, whether conversion to Islam was equivalent to becoming outcaste was still up for debate. Members of these not very prosperous castes spent multiple decades pursuing their cases, convening caste councils, shuttling between district and crown authorities, and sometimes approaching superior bodies within their caste. This suggests that many among artisanal and service castes believed that religious affiliation ought not to supersede kinship and caste ties. At the same time, others in the same caste felt differently, holding that conversion to Islam merited expulsion from the caste and a denial of all the social ties and professional entitlements that caste membership entailed. When seen in the context of the coexistence of Muslim segments in the artisanal and service groups, perhaps the need to lay down a clear line of separation became linked up with questions of social status in the increasingly polarized eighteenth-century Vaishnav milieu.

The anxiety of the Rathor crown and of certain sections of Marwari society about the policing of the boundary between what they saw as Hindu and Muslim, is also evident in the case of a *jāṭni* (a peasant woman) who was allegedly "made Muslim" (*turakṇī kīvī*) after she began to live with a Muslim lac bangle maker (*lakhārā*).[72] For living out of wedlock with a woman, the crown fined the bangle maker nine rupees and threw him in jail for a few days. When the authorities discovered he had also supposedly converted the *jāṭ* woman to Islam, it ordered that he be placed under arrest once again and fined a greater amount, in proportion to his means. In Marwar, *jāṭs* generally were not Muslim. As a result, the crown saw the woman's conversion, forced or not, as sufficient cause to punish the man with whom she was living at the time she became Muslim.

Even slaves were ideally to be segregated by faith. When discussing the traffic in children within the kingdom, the state decreed in two different orders, forty-three years apart, to multiple districts that the local authorities should ensure that "*hindu ro chhorā-chhorī kīṇī musalmān nu bechaṇ nā pāvai*," that is, the sale of Hindu children to Muslims should be forbidden.[73] The drawing of this boundary was driven as much by caste as a sense of faith-based difference. The overlap between low castes and Muslims as unwelcome elements from a Hindu perspective was stated plainly in the latter of the two orders, issued by the *dīvān* in 1811, in which the Rathor state also forbade the sale of children of elite Hindu castes to "lower"-caste buyers (*hindu ūtam jāt rī huvai su to chhoṭī jāt leṇ nā pāvai*).[74]

The anxiety of Rathor officers in Jodhpur to police the boundary between Hindus on the one hand and Muslims "and other low castes" on the other was part of the larger shift toward a more polarized social order observable in other arenas of local life in Marwar. The use in Rathor rulings and legal decrees of the term "Hindu" points to the shifting contours of this social and legal category, echoing the slipperiness of its polar opposite, the "Untouchable." While in some decrees, such as the many discussed in this chapter, Hindu is sharply defined against the Muslim, in others, as also discussed in the previous chapter, it is defined against the Untouchable or the lowly. Just as with Untouchable, certain castes were without dispute "Hindu"—brahmans, mahajans, rajputs, and *jāṭs*. Others had a more tenuous location and could potentially slip from being Hindu into being "lowly" (*nīch*, *kamīṇ*) or "Untouchable" (*achhep*).

ISLAMIC LAW AND HINDU KINGSHIP

The demarcation and elevation of a distinct Hindu sphere also entailed forms of economic discrimination against Muslims, in addition to the new spatial segregations discussed in the previous chapter. Some Muslims, unlike artisanal and service caste groups, wielded wealth, military power, command over land, or a steady income. In that sense, their discursive construction as "lowly" or "Untouchable" was anomalous with their economic and military standing. The encoding of Muslims as outcastes, as it unfolded in eighteenth-century Marwar, then could spill over into policies meant to keep them out of positions that generated wealth and power. This dynamic can be seen in an episode spelled out in a crown order from 1789:

> [To the Nagaur magistracy] Pancholis Dhanrupram, Vagasva, and Hadarmal [all members of an elite scribal caste] submitted an appeal to Śrī Hajūr: "A member of our paternal grandmother's extended family (*vaḍero*), Manordas who had two sons, Harsingh and Hirdairam, held the hereditary position of revenue recordkeeper and collector (*kānuṅgo*) at the Ajmeri Gate in Nagaur. We are descended from Hirdairam. Harsingh was expelled from the local caste group, after which he became Muslim (*nyāt su ṭāl dīyo su ṭālīyoḍo tho īj nai pachhai musalmān huvo*). In VS 1736 [1679 CE] when Aurangzeb was the emperor and Muslims were dominant (*jad pātsyāh noraṅgjeb rī pātsyāhī thī su musalmānāṁ ro joro tho*), Harsingh took the office of *kānuṅgo* from Hirdairam. Harsingh had a son Khuspal who had a son Habib. Habib died and many years after him, some months ago, his wife died too. Habib had no sons or daughters and passed away without an heir. Now, justice (*insāf*) demands that the office, the *kānuṅgoī*, returns to us." But since Habib's wife has died, his sister-in-law's sons Khokhar, Jivan, and Hisam have also come here and submitted: "Habib's wife gave the office to us so you should give it to us." We have now learned the details from both sides. The order is: Harsingh's line has run out. Now the office of *kānuṅgo* is not given to Muslims (*hamai turkāṁ nu kānuṅgoī koī āvai nahī*). The heirs to the office are the *kāyasths* (the larger caste group to which *pañcholīs* belong). Give it to them. The office of revenue collector of Ajmeri Gate has been granted to Pancholis Dhanrupram, Vagasva, and Hadarmal, sons and descendants of Hirdairam. Hand it to them. By the order of Śrī Hajūr, they will do the work of revenue recordkeeping and collection that is needed at the Gate. In the margin: Copy this order in the chancery and hand it to them.
>
> —By the order of Pancholi Fatehkaran and the Pyād Bakhśī.[75]

As the three *pañcholī* petitioners presented it, Hirdairam's conversion to Islam supposedly at the time of Aurangzeb facilitated his takeover of the office of *kānungo* of the Ajmeri Gate in 1679. This depiction of Mughal emperor Aurangzeb (r. 1658–1707) as a king who had treated Hindu subjects unfairly is echoed elsewhere in precolonial, eighteenth-century north Indian texts.[76] These hostile representations, however, could occur in texts which elsewhere lauded the emperor, demonstrating that no simple conclusions can be drawn about popular and collective memories of Aurangzeb, which in turn were multiple and not singular. After Aurangzeb's death, several communities nurtured memories of him that ranged from ambivalent to positive.[77]

For the three petitioners in this case in Marwar, the evocation of the memory of a purported time of Muslim dominance, alongside the marshaling of kinship claims, turned out to be a successful strategy. The crown officer who decided their case was a caste fellow, Pancholi Fatehkaran, who reasoned that Muslims no longer received the office of revenue collector.[78] When read alongside the prevention of the sale of land to Muslims in a rural part of Nagaur district in the previous year, this tussle over the revenue collector's office in Nagaur suggests that the Rathor state in Marwar had instituted specific policies—even if unevenly followed—meant to exclude Muslims from such sources of power and wealth as the acquisition of land and of hereditary revenue offices.

At the same time, the fact that both these orders were in place in the Nagaur region may point to unique dynamics within this district. Through the heyday of Mughal rule, Nagaur had remained within the territories directly administered by the Mughals, although in practice they assigned its administration to a cadet line of the Rathors. It was not a part of the *waṯan jāgīr*, or hereditary revenue estate, granted to the Marwar kings. On the ground then, for almost a century since the 1630s, a Rathor clan that was related to the main ruling line in Jodhpur but autonomous from it had controlled Nagaur. In the early eighteenth century, Maharaja Ajit Singh conquered Nagaur district and his son, Bakhat Singh, further strengthened the royal Rathor hold over it after 1724. Maharaja Vijai Singh was the son of Bakhat Singh and it was in this district that he came of age and learned the ropes, so to speak. When he eventually became king of Marwar in 1752, he was able to completely integrate Nagaur into the Rathor principality.[79] As a result of this relatively late incorporation into the Rathor kingdom, Nagaur was a kind of frontier territory in the eighteenth-century transition from Mughal to Rathor rule. The restriction there of Muslims' economic options then may have been part of the wider set of political changes that Vijai Singh and his merchant-manned state introduced on the ground to remake Nagaur's administrative elite in their own favor.

This entry in the *Jodhpur Sanad Parwāna Bahīs* tells us also about legal authority and the practice of law in post-Mughal Marwar. Nandini Chatterjee has reflected deeply on the question of what law in Mughal India was like in practice and makes a case for the emergence of a "Mughal law" over the course of the seventeenth century. This was experienced by each subject as a systematic body of rules that together constituted "law" and not as an eclectic mix of different sources of law, such as the brahmanical *dharmaśāstras*, local customary practice, and Islamic law. Even so, this law was in practice variable from subject to subject based on social and geographic location.[80] Law in Mughal India, Chatterjee argues, derived from a sense of "right"—both as "what ought to be" and as "entitlement." The word that corresponded closest with "law" in Mughal India was *dastūr*, a term that is also commonly translated today to "custom." Second, Chatterjee traces a field of legal power playing out among three sources of legal authority: royal grace; locally rooted, land-based power (the zamindars); and jurisprudential authority (*qāẓīs*). This picture does not quite align with post-Mughal, Rathor-ruled Marwar. For one, it is hard to gauge precisely how subjects perceived "law," whether as a single but variable set of rules or as multiple traditions and sources, each with its own set of experts, that they could turn to for justice. In addition, as chapter 1 showed, the discourse of custom, and the local variability it permitted, began to be challenged in the eighteenth century by a turn to ethics—in principle, applicable to all—as the foundation for legal judgments.

Chatterjee calls for relinquishing the vision of a Mughal legal archive that derives, she argues, from the Ottoman context, one in which *qāẓīs* copied out their rulings in running registers called *sijills*. Instead, Chatterjee argues that in most parts of the Islamic world, including Mughal India, *qāẓīs* did not "find it necessary to create and maintain registers, whether recording the adjudication of disputes or the activities of many other branches of government." Instead, she speculates that the onus may have been on the people—the recipients of legal decisions or transfers of rights—to maintain records of entitlements, transactions, and judgments.[81] Indeed, the absence of *sijills* or bound registers of *qāẓīs'* decisions and authorizations before the Ottomans or outside of Ottoman lands has been noted by historians, leading some to argue that these were a decidedly Ottoman form. Wael Hallaq has countered this to argue that in fact volumes of *qāẓīs'* key decisions, known not as *sijills* but rather as *dīwān-i qāẓīs* (within which the *sijill* was one among numerous kinds of documentary forms and information recorded), did in fact exist in pre-Ottoman and non-Ottoman Islamic societies. He suggests that these collections may have been loosely gathered sheaves of paper, which most *qāẓīs* did not bind together or have copied into registers, and which after a few generations were discarded by descendants since they did not have much literary or other value.[82]

Where do Rathor sources fit in to this history of law and documentary cultures? The *Jodhpur Sanad Parwāna Bahīs* are, as the name suggests, bound volumes (*bahīs*) containing copies of *sanads* (confirmatory orders) and *parwānas* (orders issued by subroyal nobles and representatives of the sovereign) issued in the Rathor kingdom of Marwar. Their contents certainly fall within the purview of "law," in that the commands recorded within them adjudicated allegations of murder, theft, and other wrongs, separated "just" from "unjust," and took steps to restore a righteous order or provide redress to aggrieved parties. But here we have a body of sources that look very much like *sijills*, including Ottoman ones, in that they are bound registers of legal decisions and entitlements. To that extent, there does appear to be in Marwar something akin to a state archive of legal decisions, which could have been one of many, including household ones. Just as Chatterjee finds for Mughal-ruled Malwa, there is no explicit reference in these records to a jurisprudential authority such as a *muftī* or a brahman expert in dharmashastric laws.

At the same time, a significant difference of course is that Rathor rulings in the eighteenth century were not issued or authorized by *qāẓīs* or even by brahman experts in dharmashastric texts and commentaries but rather by state functionaries, sometimes identified and sometimes not. These state functionaries were ruling on behalf of the Rathor king, referred to in these orders as Śrī Hajūr, but it was under their own names that each command was issued. Another difference from Malwa is that unlike *sijills*, which usually were accompanied by detailed *mahzars* (containing claims and counterclaims of the people involved and signed by witnesses),[83] the *Jodhpur Sanad Parwāna Bahīs* have only a perfunctory statement of the issue at hand, a terse summary of the petitioner or defendant's testimony and a short declaration of the state officer's command to resolve the matter, as made clear in the command above and in all the others that I have translated in this book.

Wael Hallaq suggests that the *sijill*, that component of what later became the *dīwān-i qāẓī* that summarized the *qāẓī's* judgment, may have been the earliest of the subparts of the *dīwān-i qāẓī* to emerge. This happened in the first century of Islam, and may indeed have originated in pre-Islamic practices in the broader region that is today called the Middle East.[84] In the first century of Islam, Hallaq argues, *sijills* consisted of a brief summary of the case and the judgment issued, very much like the Rathor *Sanad Parwāna Bahīs*.[85] Was the instinct to record, compile, and bind written judgments an impulse that emerged in diffuse ways across different political orders at different times? Or were the *Jodhpur Sanad Parwāna Bahīs* Islamicate in form—inspired by the idealized or prescribed practice of the *qāẓī's* office, even though, as Chatterjee shows, the practice of maintaining a register of rulings does not appear to have been common in Mughal India? That said, even as the *bahīs* in their form owed a lot to the role of the merchant-caste men who staffed Rathor administration, including its highest ranks, this body of records could also be an example of the Islamicate nature of this eighteenth-century kingdom, one that was simultaneously the site of the emergence of this new Hindu identity.

It is no surprise to see the imprint of Islamic law on the Rathor kingdom. The region that is Marwar had been part of the Mughal Empire since the late sixteenth century. Going back further still, the Rathor ruling family had since Delhi Sultanate times gladly made marital alliances with rulers of Muslim polities. The Rathor kingdom included or abutted late medieval centers of Sufi pilgrimage and learning such as Ajmer (also part of the Rathor domain briefly in the eighteenth century) and Nagaur. Marwar was separated from Sindh, with its long history of rule by Muslim kings, by the Thar Desert, which was no barrier to human migration and exchange.[86] What emerges through an examination of the *Jodhpur Sanad Parwāna Bahīs*, of the type of command translated above, is a deep and layered history of Islam and Islamic legal practice and the emergence over many centuries of a shared culture, a culture that included the practice of law. This brings findings about Mughal law, including its Rathor cousin, well within the ambit also of the Persianate as Mana Kia theorizes it. Kia argues that Persian and the Persianate were a product of the permeation of Islam in the being of the category of people she identifies as "Persian," who may be neither Muslim nor from regions we today call Iran.[87] Was law yet another trajectory of cosmopolitanism in the broader Persianate or Islamicate sphere? Certainly, in Marwar, what we may have is a way of being "Persian" with only traces of the language itself and a way of being Hindu with traces of an aspect of Islam, forms of law and legal practice. Given how central the maintenance of law and justice was to Persianate kingly ideals, particularly as they emerged in Mughal imperial discourse, no doubt law-giving and the preservation of justice would have been significant to the post-Mughal Rathor rajput fashioning of new kingly forms. In the language and legal practices visible in Rathor rulings, it is possible to discern that traces of Islamic forms and Persianate terms were not only top-down impositions or aspirations; rather, there were multiple channels, old and new, through which ethical and legal modes of the Persianate were already within Marwar prior to the Mughals.

NEW BOUNDARIES

Commands ordering new segregations between Hindus and Muslims, conceptualized as such, were then issued within a legal culture steeped in Islamic legal practice and concepts. Another site in which the Rathor state introduced separations between Hindus and Muslims was that of food. For instance, the administrators of Didwana regularly distributed porridge (*gūdhrīyāṁ*) to the poor and the needy.[88] The cooks of this community kitchen happened to be Muslim until 1771, when Bhaiya Sivdan, a merchant of the Maheshwari subcaste, commanded from Jodhpur that this assignment should be handed over to Hindus because food cooked by Muslims was not of use to Hindus (*su gudhrīyāṁ turak kanai raṇdhāvo su hinduvāṁ rai kām āvai nahī*).[89] In another instance of drawing boundaries between Hindus and Muslims, in 1785, Brahman Vyas Sadasiv ordered the governor of Nagaur on behalf of the crown to ensure that Muslim rajputs, called Sipahis, refrained from collecting levies in the form of utensils from Hindu households (*hukam huvo hai musalmān hindu ra ghar thālī vāṭko koī leṇ nā pāvai*).[90] The order notes that these Muslim rajputs had been exercising this prerogative in defiance of a recent order that they not do so. It is noteworthy that the state officer expressed his command in terms of Muslims "taking" without justification from Hindu homes.

In drawing these boundaries that placed Hindus on one side and Muslims on the other, the Rathor crown not only introduced separations but also flattened, at least for the purposes at hand, a complex and overlapping set of social groups. Muslims in Marwar were a diverse group, spanning a range of class locations and faith practices. Some sections among the region's native rajputs had converted to Islam during the Delhi Sultanate era. They were called Desvali Musalmans.[91] Another group, the Kyamkhanis, a Muslim branch of the Chauhan clan, had migrated from northern Rajasthan into Marwar and lived in some of its eastern districts such as Didwana, Merta, and Nagaur.[92] More recent, and much poorer, Muslim rajput migrants into Marwar were known as Sindhis.[93] As their name suggests, they likely came from Sindh, from across the Thar Desert that lay on the western fringes of Marwar. These Sindhis tended to lead a pastoral existence. All three castes of Muslim rajputs were also called Sipahis (literally, soldiers).[94]

These Muslim rajputs, particularly the Kyamkhanis, were closely integrated with their Hindu peers, and observers noted in the late nineteenth century that theirs was a Hindu-Muslim set of faith practices and beliefs. The Islam practiced by most Muslim rajputs in Marwar adhered most closely to the observation of Islamic life-cycle rituals and shared much with the religious practices of other local communities. The Kyamkhanis had done well in the Mughal era and their high, martial status, combined with their interpretation of Islam which shared much with local non-Muslims, meant that the more numerous Hindu rajputs did not exclude their Kyamkhani caste fellows from their social exchanges.[95] The Desvali Muslims on the other hand, at least by the late nineteenth century—that is, a century after the changes under study here—were considered "outsiders" by the Hindu rajputs of the more populous eastern districts of Marwar.[96] There also were nonrajput Muslims in Marwar. Stray references in the Rathor record suggest that Nagaur district, likely due to its closer integration since the thirteenth century with the Delhi Sultanate and then the Mughals, had small settlements of *qāẓīs*. It is unclear if these families only retained the "*qāẓī*" title as descendants of practicing jurists or if they continued their juridical work for clusters of Muslims in Marwar. Finally, Sufi shrines such as that in Nagaur were centers of pilgrimage and piety that attracted a diverse following and were interconnected with other Sufi sites in the region such as that of Muinuddin Chishti in Ajmer.[97]

At a lower social location were a range of other adherents to Islam. Some were artisans, with segments of groups such as barbers, ironsmiths, lac bangle makers, tailors, cloth printers, weavers, brewers, oilpressers, stonemasons, potters, and gram roasters being Muslim.[98] Among merchants, perhaps only a very small number of itinerant traders may have been Muslim.[99] It is likely that the elite, rajput Muslims of Marwar maintained caste-like social distance from the Muslims of artisanal caste. There is little to suggest that the Muslims of Marwar were united into a singular, cohesive social unit.

Given this diversity among Muslims in Marwar, the Rathor crown's usage in its commands and rulings of "*musalmān*" and "*turak*" as a monolithic category in the administration of social life was then an important step toward the projection of a unified Muslim community in precolonial Marwar. Even as "Hindu" was set in opposition to "Muslim" or to "Muslim" as part of the "Untouchable" in these commands, this is not a precolonial precedent to the "communal" conflict between Hindus and Muslims as monolithic religious blocs that emerged in the colonial context. Instead, many of the Rathor orders discussed above described Muslims being as among the "low" castes or as among the Untouchables. Many others, even if ostensibly articulating difference from Muslims as such, tended to object to proximity with Muslims of artisanal, or non-elite, castes. I argue then that it was the logic of caste that undergirded the imagination of the Muslim as belonging to the Other against whom the Hindu Self defined itself.

Recent scholarship has highlighted the roles of kings, court-sponsored texts, and brahman scholars in expressing, often in periods of political conflict with Muslim kings, a hardened and more strident stance toward an imagined Muslim "Other." Other studies, particularly those centered on Rajasthan, have emphasized the growing influence of Vaishnav sects on regional potentates and a kingly performance of devotional service to Krishna and his image. With or without the use of the term "Hindu" in these representations and texts, the slow congealing of a type of kingship that projected the stance of a devout defender of symbols of brahmanical practice such as the cow or a temple icon or of Hindus as a community is discernible in the early modern period. Maharaja Vijai Singh's brand of devotee-kingship then drew upon a deeper and longer history of "Hindu kingship." What the administrative records from his reign make clear, however, is that at least in Vijai Singh's case, the posture of the *bhakt*-king went beyond words into the domain of action. With Vijai Singh at the helm and a body of mahajan and brahman administrators who shared an investment in a meaning of "Hindu" that centered bodily ethics with implications for caste rank, the Rathor state worked to draw a harder line separating Hindus from Muslims and Untouchables than had existed before. On the ground, this tore the fabric of local caste groups and temple-centered Vaishnav communities and dislocated people from their homes. Its longest-lasting impact, through the accumulated effect of diffuse and seemingly unrelated decrees and rulings, was the normalization through law and administrative practice of the understanding of Hindu as that which was not Untouchable, with the inadmissibility of the Muslim and the Untouchable mutually reinforcing each other.

4

Discipline

In 1799, the mahajans of Pali paid the local butchers five rupees in exchange for the butchers' promise to refrain from slaughtering animals.[1] When the Rathor crown in Jodhpur heard of this, the *dīvān*, at the time an Osvāl merchant-administrator named Mumhta Sardar Mal, ordered the governor of Pali to provide the mahajans with a copy of the crown's order banning violence against animals, probably in order to lend weight to their efforts to get the butchers to abandon their trade.[2] Why did the merchants try to stop butchery in their town? Why did the state support this effort? This episode and the documentary trace it left on the Rathor archive was a product of a kingdom-wide campaign that engulfed all of Marwar in the latter half of the eighteenth century, which this chapter and the next one will discuss. Such a campaign to enforce vegetarianism upon an entire body of subjects using the punitive and surveillance capabilities of the state is without precedent in Indian history, raising the question of why the eighteenth-century Rathor state channeled its resources into the policing of its subjects' dietary choices. I show in this chapter that this campaign in pursuit of a kingdom-wide law against animal slaughter came down much harder on certain groups that, not coincidentally, were among those explicitly demarcated as "*achhep*" in Rathor court orders.

The encoding of the "Hindu" and the "Untouchable" rested not only on ideas of embodied pollution and uncleanliness. A central element of the redefinition of the Untouchable in Marwar was the elevation of nonharm to living beings as the ethical practice of elite, Hindu identity. The "innate" tendency to take animal lives, whether for ritual, sport, or consumption, then was deemed not only unethical but also a trait of the Untouchable. The quest for a vegetarian body politic served as a powerful plank for the demarcation of "low" castes and Muslims as inherently different. The Rathor state introduced a set of laws enforcing noninjury toward its nonhuman subjects in the late eighteenth century, which I will discuss in greater detail in the next chapter. These were not just goals the failure of whose implementation relegated them to the realm of ideals. Rather, Vijai Singh and his merchant and brahman functionaries zealously pursued the implementation of these regulations across the towns and villages of late eighteenth-century Marwar. The crown used its administrative apparatus to hound the practitioners of violence against animals, apprehending anyone who was accused of the crime in all its myriad manifestations. The majority of those accused, however, were involved in meat eating since this was the most common reason for taking animal lives.

The political campaign against nonvegetarianism and other sources of violence against animals created a fissure in Marwari society between meat-eaters and vegetarians. Vijai Singh and his merchant bureaucrats sought to universalize their own ethics throughout the entirety of their domain. It is noteworthy that of all the ethical precepts that the Rathor state enshrined in law—temperance, chastity, a disavowal of gambling, and nonharm—only the last one was rigorously pursued by the Rathor state by active and unrelenting enforcement throughout its territory and across all castes. This is in line with observations of the Jain attitude toward ethical codes in twentieth-century Rajasthan and Gujarat. That is, *ahiṃsā* or nonharm is the only ethical precept that Jains do not see as applicable only to their own path, but rather as one that it is their duty to promote among all. Still, while in twentieth-century contexts this promotion of nonharm by non-Jains was especially to be pursued during the holy days of Paryūśaṇ, in the eighteenth-century Rathor context we see this effort underway all through the year.[3]

Through a circumscription of alimentary alternatives grounded in an appeal to ethical precepts, the Rathor state sought to create moral subjects. The pursuit of an ethical, and in this case, vegetarian body politic was accompanied by the simultaneous delineation of peoples whose bodies irremediably were the domain of the unethical and the criminal. State functionaries singled out butchers (*kasāīs* and *khaṭīks*), vagrant hunters (*thorīs* and *bāvrīs*), and Muslims in particular, for campaigns of arrest, dispossession, and surveillance. It is in this punitive campaign that we gain a glimpse of the anxiety generated among the region's ruling elite by those deemed "Untouchable." The overlap between those most suspect as animal killers and those explicitly deemed "Untouchable" in other Rathor state orders is remarkable. What also stands out is the betrayal in state orders of anxiety toward the ability of *thorīs* and *bāvrīs* to wield arms. With respect to these two communities, the campaign for the protection of animal lives also served the dual purpose of legitimizing the disarming of "low"-caste subaltern groups that could and did rebel against the Rathor government.

THE UNTOUCHABLE AS CRIMINAL

Bāvrīs and *thorīs* were castes that dwelt on the margins of villages and in scrubby tracts. *Bāvrīs* lived at a remove from settled society and were largely landless. They used their ability to recede into uninhabited lands to carry out small-scale theft, usually by breaking into homes. Late nineteenth-century observers noted that *bāvrīs*, like *sāṃsīs* (often spelt "Sansi"), were willing to eat a range of wild animals that most other groups did not consider food. Foxes, spiny-tailed lizards (*sāṇḍā*), monitor lizards (*goh*), and migratory demoiselle cranes (*kuraj*) are a few examples of the animals they were thought to eat, at least in the late nineteenth century.[4] *Thorīs* were a landless caste, marked by their poverty and their reduction to begging and wage labor for survival. What all these castes had in common was a willingness to use arms, sometimes just sticks and knives, to rob others. The *sāṃsīs*, though they occur rarely in the commands of the Rathor state, were also a vagrant and landless caste and were associated with petty crime in other parts of north India.[5]

The material I discuss in this chapter on *thorīs* and *bāvrīs* in the Rathor archive is yet another set of shifts that can be fully understood only with reference to the Rathor command separating Hindus from Untouchables, which the introduction presents. As a reminder, in that command, *thorīs* and *bāvrīs* were among the castes explicitly named as not belonging to the domain of the Hindu and as belonging to the "*achhep*" or Untouchable.[6] From the perspective of the Rathor state, *thorīs* and *bāvrīs* were not just Untouchable—as also made clear by other commands presented in chapter 2—but along with butchers and Muslims, were irredeemably steeped in habitual animal slaughter. In fact, as will become clear in the pages to come, the irremediable tendency to take animal lives and eat meat may indeed have been articulated through these policies as a marker of being Untouchable. It is noteworthy that in the campaign to protect animal lives, the Rathor state also treated with greater suspicion and singled out for harsher treatment than others nearly all the castes that were explicitly named as "Untouchable" in the 1785 order cited in the introduction—Muslims, leatherworkers, *thorīs*, and *bāvrīs*.

State punishments for animal slaughter differed for different sections of its populace. This differential treatment may have arisen from the everyday, on-the-ground operation of the state. But about midway through the decades-long campaign, in 1779, two Rathor orders broadcast to each district these differential punishments, varying by caste and status, for the crime of *jīv haṃsyā* ("injury to living beings").[7] If members of the wealthy, landowning communities slew an animal, whether on a hunt or otherwise, their lands were to be confiscated. The crown instructed all of its district authorities to gain the acquiescence of the landed elite, mostly rajputs, for the new policy through this punishment.[8] For the rest of the subject body, anyone guilty of involvement in the killing of animals was to be detained and only released after the imposition of as heavy a fine as the person could bear.[9] Other orders, also dispatched to all the kingdom's districts over the years, were more specific about the punishments for different kinds of violence upon different kinds of beings. For the "crime" of castrating bulls, the punishment was to be imprisonment for a few days in the course of which the violator was to be terrorized into agreeing to never commit this deed again.[10] Laxity in covering the flames of lamps, which imperiled the lives of winged insects, was to be punished with a fine of one *paisā*.[11] This set of punishments for elite or middling groups stands in contrast with how the Rathor state responded to allegations of animal slaughter at the hands of butchers, *thorīs* and *bāvrīs*, and Muslims, as the following sections will show.

BUTCHERS

As early as 1764, that is, around the time of Vijai Singh's formal initiation in 1765 into the Vallabhite sect, an unidentified officer issued a command on behalf of the crown to the *jāgīrdār's* men, peasant headmen (*chaudharīs*), and the people of a village called Palyasani: "The court (*darbār*) has forbidden butchery (*kasāb karaṇo*) and yet it continues to occur in Palyasani. This is not all right. Do not permit butchery going forward. If it happens again then the butchers' hands will be cut off (*pher huvai to kasāyāṁ rā hāth vaḍhsī*) and they will be punished (*sajhāvār husī*)."[12] Again, in 1775, the crown dispatched an order to Sambhar district in which it observed that the *kasāīs* (a Muslim caste of butchers) were continuing with their trade and urged the local authorities to put an end to the practice. Interestingly, the crown invoked the authority of the neighboring Jaipur kingdom when commanding the butchers to refrain from animal slaughter, stating that if they refused to comply, they would be presented with a written order from Jaipur.[13] The ban on animal slaughter was evidently incompatible with the butchers' trade and an assault on their livelihood.

The state then escalated its efforts against the butchers. In 1784, it rounded up and jailed all the butchers of Nagaur, among the largest towns in the kingdom. Muhnot Gyanmal, an Osvāl mahajan, and Pancholi Parsadiram then issued an order directing the magistrate of Nagaur on what to do next:

> [To the Nagaur magistracy, 1784] And the butchers are under arrest there. An order to release them will be written. You release them but make the following efforts: Release them on the bail condition (*jāmaṇ*) that they not hurt animals again. Replace four members of the magistracy's troops with two butchers and two brahman administrators. Tell the butchers who are hired in the magistracy to keep a watch to prevent animal slaughter and that if it happens, they have to solve the case. Tell the brahman officers to keep an eye on the butchers and to inspect their houses to make sure that the butchers do not keep any goats or sheep. The main goal is to make sure that there is no animal slaughter. There should be no negligence in this . . .
>
> —By the permission of Muhnot Gyanmal and Pancholi Parsadiram[14]

Faced with the persistence of animal slaughter and meat eating, as also with their own continuing anxieties about these practices, the two crown officers devised the solution of offering two members of the local butcher caste steady employment in exchange for their surveillance over their own community. But this was not enough. As a check on the butcher footsoldiers, the crown ordered the governor of Nagaur to employ two brahmans as officers in the same department. The brahmans' work also was to keep an eye on the butchers of the town and they were to do so by regularly roaming through the butcher quarter to ensure that butchers did not even possess animals, let alone kill them. The crown officers made it clear that no negligence in the execution of these commands would be tolerated.

Soon after, perhaps realizing just how difficult these measures were to sustain, the merchant-administrator Muhnot Gyanmal sent an order on behalf of the crown to the magistrate of Nagaur to expel all the butchers who were imprisoned there from the kingdom. To make sure that the command was executed, the magistrate was to send an escort (*tathā kasāī jīv haṃsyā bābat uṭhai kaid mai hai tiṇā nu mulak bārai kāḍh deṇ ro hukam huvo hai su uṇā kasāyāṁ nu sāthai ādmī de nai mulak bārai kaḍhāy dejo śrī hajūr ro hukam chhai*).[15] We do not know of course if all the butchers of Nagaur were indeed thrown out of Marwar, but given how widespread and sustained the campaign against animal slaughter in Marwar was during these decades, it is possible.

In 1795, in Bhim Singh's reign, the Rathor state was still pursuing this agenda. Dodhidar Khivkaran and Joshi Balu, a brahman, ordered all the governors of Marwar to shut down any butcher shops that may be functioning and to make sure the work did not resume.[16] In 1797, a Muhnot merchant-caste officer in Jodhpur ordered that the magistrate in Didwana should go ahead with the fine of seventy rupees that he had assessed upon butchers for killing animals.[17] In 1803, Prime Minister Bhandari Gangaram, an Osvāl mahajan, sent out an order on behalf of the king to all the districts underscoring the need to shut down all slaughterhouses (*kasāīkhāno huṇ mat dejo śrī hajūr ro hukam chhai*).[18]

Another community that was hit hard by the ban on animal slaughter was that of birdcatchers. While the Rathor state did not issue kingdom-wide commands about birdcatchers, this community too found its occupation becoming a hazardous one. In 1776, some birdcatchers (*chiḍīmār*) were caught in Nagaur for capturing birds and other creatures. Bhandari Chaitram Kusalchand, a mahajan, ordered on behalf of the crown that their nets be burned (*tathā samāchār śrī hajūr mālam huvā chīḍīmāryāṁ jāl nākh nai jīnāvar chīḍī kabūtar vagairai nag pakaḍīyā . . . chīḍīmārāṁ rai jāl hai su balāy dejo*). The birdcatchers were too broke (*nādār*) to pay a fine, but the three cloth-printers who bought the birds from them were to be fined, the mahajan's order stated.[19] A month later, the birdcatchers' wives formed a delegation and appealed to the crown in Jodhpur, pointing to their poverty and the hardship they were suffering due to their husbands' imprisonment. The merchant-administrator Singhvi Tilokmal then ordered the Nagaur magistrate to fine the birdcatchers in proportion to their means and to release them.[20]

THORĪS AND *BĀVRĪS*

Tracing the evolution of the Rathor state's attitude toward *thorīs* and *bāvrīs*, as with the butchers, also reveals intensified persecution. In 1768, the merchant-caste officer Muhnot Suratram dispatched a decree to all of its constituents in which it blamed the *thorīs* and *bāvrīs* who dwelt in the countryside for routinely killing animals. Reiterating the ban on hurting nonhumans, the crown ordered its district governors to fine them. Underscoring the predilection of *bāvrīs* and *thorīs* toward hunting, Muhnot Suratram warned district administrators to stop them from taking animal lives and to keep an extra watch on them (*tathā praganā ra gāṃvā mai thorī bāvrī gāṃv rī nīṃv mai jīv jināvar mārai chhai su sārā gāṃvā mai kuhāḍ deṇo koī jīv jināvar māraṇ pāvai nahī kiṇī mārīyo to nukhsāṇ husī īṇ bāt ro visekh tākīd rākhṇī*).[21] Some years later, in 1775, the Rathor state's response to a large number of reports of animal slaughter from some villages in Merta district was to pin the blame on yet another "Untouchable" vagrant community, the *sāṃsīs*.[22] Just as with *thorīs* and *bāvrīs*, the Rathor state saw these landless, mobile people as regular slayers of animals. It directed the governor of Merta to make special arrangements to prevent animal deaths at the hands of itinerant *sāṃsīs* (*parganā mai sāṃsī phīrtā jīv hatai su visekh tākīd karāy deṇī su jīv hatai nahī* or "*sāṃsīs* roam the districts killing animals, make special arrangements to make sure they do not kill animals").[23]

By 1779, this suspicion of *thorīs*, *bāvrīs*, and to a lesser extent, other armed vagrants like *sāṃsīs* had developed into a policy of social surveillance. In an order from that year addressed to each of its district headquarters, the crown laid down the punishment for those found guilty of animal slaughter. Unlike the temporary confiscation of land grants that the crown prescribed as punishment for *jāgīrdārs* and the fines upon all others, the Rathor state developed a different approach for the *thorīs* and *bāvrīs*. Since these groups could get away with hunting without being spotted by the state's officers, the crown ordered that it was ordinary crown subjects who would also watch *thorīs* and *bāvrīs*.[24] The state ordered all of its district governors to get a written commitment from the peasants and their representatives (*chaudharīs*) to assume collective responsibility for making sure that the *thorīs* and *bāvrīs* no longer killed animals. If the body of villagers collectively failed to prevent animal slaughter, it was they who would be slapped with a fine for the crime.[25]

With this administrative measure, the crown drew a clear line of separation between armed vagrants such as the *thorīs* and *bāvrīs* on the one hand and its body of settled, agriculturist subjects on the other. The latter were now mandated with the task of keeping a watchful eye, on behalf of the crown, upon the *thorīs* and *bāvrīs* who were their neighbors. Already the objects of mistrust and suspicion, the *thorīs* and *bāvrīs* would now also become the recipients of social hostility. The residence of *thorīs* and *bāvrīs* in or near a villages would now become an onerous burden upon the residents, since they were forced by the crown to shoulder the blame and the fines for any incidence of animal slaughter committed by these groups.

After three years, the Rathor state further escalated its policy of persecuting *thorīs* and *bāvrīs*. The *dīvān*'s office in Jodhpur now directed each of its district governors to expel the *thorīs* and *bāvrīs* from every village in which they dwelt and throw them out of the kingdom.[26] The *dīvān*'s office was held in that year, according to the officer lists of the Rathors, in *khālisā*; that is, it was reserved by the Maharaja. In practice, however, it is more likely that specific mahajan officers were informally performing its functions. This order from the *dīvān* commanded that not a single *thorī* or *bāvrī* was to remain in the kingdom. The effort to expel these two groups was still on two years later, in 1784, when an officer named Pancholi Nandram disapprovingly observed the continuing residence of *bāvrīs* in the countryside, accusing them of theft and injury to animals (*aur gāṃv mai bāvrī hai su kujamānā nai rāh chorī chakhārī karai nai jīv haṃsyā karai*).[27] It instructed the magistracies of Nagaur, Merta, Sojhat, Jaitaran, Parbatsar, Phalodhi, Maroth, Siwana, Daulatpura, and Koliya districts to immediately expel them from each village and out of the kingdom (*tiṇā nu mulak bārai kāḍh deṇā kiṇī gāṃv mai bāvrī raiṇ nahī pāvai śrī hajūr ro hukam chhai*). The command was reiterated in 1798, when the state noted that despite a round or two of expulsion, the *bāvrīs* had started to reappear in the villages of Marwar. It reiterated that all *bāvrīs* were to be banished from the kingdom. Local authorities were to report any *jāgīrdār* who failed to execute this order and, at the crown's command, revoke the *jāgīrdār*'s revenue assignment.[28]

These directives had the intended effect. For instance, the charans, a respected community of litterateurs, ritualists, and genealogists, of Panchetiya village in Sojhat district rounded up all the *thorīs* and *bāvrīs* who dwelt in their village and presented them before the local authorities.[29] Complaining that these *thorīs* and *bāvrīs* had repeatedly indulged in animal slaughter, the charans advised the local authorities to pay special attention to these people. They warned that if the *thorīs* and *bāvrīs* got away, they would certainly descend into criminal activity again. Despite the words of warning by the charans, district authorities released the *thorīs* and *bāvrīs* without any punishment. When the crown got wind of this, it commanded the district authorities in Sojhat to round up these groups again and to punish them suitably to guarantee that they never hurt an animal again.[30] For individuals from these blacklisted communities, punishment for animal slaughter was much harsher than for others. For instance, the crown ordered district authorities to fine Thori Padmiya and his nephew on charges of slaying many animals. The authorities were to then expel them from the village in which they lived. If they had already been expelled, the fine was to be borne by the village's *jāgīrdār*.[31] Banishment from one's village or town or worse, from the kingdom, were harsh punishments in a penal regime that preferred to exact fines for the vast majority of crimes.

Some of the state's rulings against the *thorīs* and *bāvrīs* provide a sense of its rationale for targeting these groups for harsher treatment in the campaign against animal slaughter. In a ruling from 1779, an unidentified officer described the *thorīs* and *bāvrīs* as "thieving castes" (*chor jāt*) who secretly killed animals in the scrub (*thorī bāvrī chor jāt hai su rohī meṁ chhāṁnai chhurkai sikār bījī jīv haṃsyā karai*).[32] Referring to the *thorīs'* and *bāvrīs'* use of guns while hunting deer in the brambly thickets on the edges of deserts, audible to villagers dwelling nearby, Pancholi Nandram announced on behalf of the crown that these groups had no need for guns (*aur uṭhā keik gāṃv meṁ thorī bāvrī rahai chhai su īṇ jāt rīt rahai rohī mai kaḍmādai jiṇ mai hiraṇ āy paḍai nai bandūk ro bhaḍko huvai to pākhtī ra hā suṇai su īṇ maiṃ bandūk ro kām hī paḍai nahī*).[33] Clearly, from the perspective of the Rathor state's administrators, perhaps a reflection of wider societal perspective, there were legitimate and illegitimate bearers of arms. Landless Untouchables were not, in this view, among the "legitimate" bearers of arms. As noted above, the Rathor state observed that the *thorīs* and *bāvrīs* regularly committed theft, especially during times of unrest in the kingdom (*kujamānā* or "bad times").[34] While most of the Rathor state's orders for disciplining or even expelling *thorīs* and *bāvrīs* only mentioned a concern for the protection of animal lives, occasional orders such as these revealed an added, and perhaps underlying, reason for why the *thorīs* and *bāvrīs* were particularly targeted by the Rathor state's quest to end animal slaughter within its territories.

As ecologically "marginal" people, by which I mean people who could recede into fastnesses and scrub, *thorīs* and *bāvrīs* were a challenge to the state and a nuisance to administrators of settled villages. The *thorīs* and *bāvrīs* were much weaker than other groups that also navigated the margins of settled cultivation, hill-dwelling communities such as the *meṇas* (today, *mīṇās* or Meenas), *mers*, and *bhīls*, both in terms of their martial resources and their socioeconomic standing. The *meṇās*, *mers*, and *bhīls* did not receive anything near the kind of treatment that *thorīs* and *bāvrīs* did from Rathor state or society. Some *meṇās*, *mers*, and *bhīls* were organized into well-armed bands led by chieftains, bands that could raid settled villages in broad daylight without the state's *jāgīrdārs* and other agents being able to resist them. Rajput chiefs too engaged in raiding. Tanuja Kothiyal discusses this blurriness between the *meṇās*, *bhīls*, and *mers* on the one hand and rajputs on the other, suggesting that Rathor court sources from the early modern period are invested in the representations of rajputs as kings and these other communities as bandits ineligible for kingship precisely due to overlap between lordliness and banditry that continued to exist in the more arid as well as hilly parts of Marwar; that is, in areas where Rathor control was weak.[35] Unlike the *meṇās*, *bhīls*, and rajputs—all armed groups that raided—the *thorīs* and *bāvrīs* were more scattered and less formidable foes to the state. Most importantly, they also did not control land. Their mobility and association with theft made them enough of an irritant to cause the Rathor state to use their reliance on hunting as an excuse to surveil, disarm, and even expel them. At the same time, the acknowledgment in Rathor orders above of continuing reports of the use of arms by *thorīs* and *bāvrīs* suggests that these groups were able to resist Rathor disciplinary efforts to some degree.

Here we have an example of the limits to the reach of the Rathor state, enabled in this case by ecology: the thorny scrubs and sand dunes of desert tracts and thickly forested woods of the Aravalli Hills. Historians of Rajasthan broadly and its western tracts like Marwar in particular are mindful of the region's ecology, given the particularly arid climate there. Historians of early modern Marwar have read the ecological constraints such as frequent famine and the precarity of agricultural cultivation there as generating protections from excessive taxation and oppression.[36] Tanuja Kothiyal points us to the spatial mobility that the harsh climate of the Thar Desert demanded from all of the region's residents and the disjunctures that emerged between a centralizing state and its rajput subordinates that commanded ecological frontiers.[37]

My findings here about the *thorīs* and *bāvrīs* provide a prehistory for the development in colonial hands of the "criminal tribe" concept. In the nineteenth century, British colonial observers popularized the idea that certain castes, or "tribes," in South Asia were hereditary practitioners of banditry and theft and had been so for centuries. In 1871, the colonial state passed the Criminal Tribes Act, which sought to discipline and redirect toward more respectable professions those members of communities habitually steeped in crime. The Rathor state's attribution of an inherent tendency toward killing animals and its criminalization of the *thorīs* and *bāvrīs* as entire castes offers a precolonial lineage, otherwise glimpsed only in the mediated voices of "native informers" in colonial accounts, of not only the stigmatization and peripheralization in discourse but also the criminalization in practice and state law of certain vagrant castes that were later deemed "criminal tribes."[38]

The manner in which the Rathor state dealt with the *thorīs* and *bāvrīs* reflects its perception and configuration of these groups as inherently criminal, even if this criminality was figured in the era of enforced nonharm as a proclivity for hunting. Some of the state's orders discussed above also betray its perception of *thorīs* and *bāvrīs* as always inclined to steal and to raid villages. Their criminality then was represented as inherent to their caste and it was a threat to both humans and nonhumans. It also was a source of anxiety to Rathor administrators, and this anxiety spilled into the Rathor archive as an excessive concern with *thorī* and *bāvrī* activities. In a limited way then, decades prior to the establishment of colonial rule over Marwar, records indicate that the kernel of an idea of inherently criminal castes came to exist and be deployed in law in precolonial times. Since the ancient period, Sanskrit and Pali texts have reflected a sense of difference and a perception of threat from forest-dwelling peoples.[39] In the early modern period in other parts of South Asia too there is evidence of hill- and forest-dwelling groups being associated with plundering raids and banditry.[40]

In the existing scholarship on banditry in western and north India, however, groups like the *menas*, *mers*, and *bhīls* are simply lumped together as communities whose raiding activities prior to British rule led to their being classified as "criminal tribes." As my discussion above shows, the only groups that the Rathor state declared and treated as inherently and collectively criminal were the *thorīs*, *bāvrīs*, and *sāṃsīs*. The *menas*, *mers*, and *bhīls*, despite being regular and active raiders in eighteenth-century Marwar, were not part of this criminal category in the Rathor state's eyes. The evidence from Marwar then shows that the mere association with hereditary banditry and the use of arms was not sufficient for a caste to be considered innately criminal in precolonial times. Rather, it was a complex of factors—landlessness, poverty, and the resultant martial weakness—in addition to a hereditary association with theft that led to a caste's perception as criminal. In this sense, the "criminal caste" of precolonial times was distinct from the "criminal tribe" as it emerged in the nineteenth century.

MUSLIMS

Muslims received perhaps the harshest punishments among Rathor subjects when they were indicted for animal slaughter. A Muslim (*turak*) killed a goat in the town of Jalor and sold the meat to some shoemakers and *raibārīs* (a pastoralist group) in 1764. At the time that the buyers of the meat were fined, the Muslim escaped unpunished. When administrators in Jodhpur heard of this, they ordered that for the crime of killing the goat the Muslim be immediately banished from the town (*turak bakro mārīyo huvai tiṇ nū saihar bārai kāḍh dejo*).[41] In 1785, a few Muslims (*musalmānāṁ*) killed animals in Jaitaran town for which they were jailed and then released on bail. Soon after, Pancholi Gulalchand ordered their expulsion from the kingdom.[42] Two Shekhanis, members of a Muslim community, served almost three years in jail for repeatedly killing animals.[43] During a review of the inmates in Nagaur's prisons, the crown commanded that these two were now to be released from prison but only to be thrown out of the kingdom. It ordered its subordinates in Nagaur to ensure that the two women were never able to reenter Marwar.[44] In other cases, even as Muslims accused of animal slaughter did not face expulsion from the kingdom, the charge could be used to repeatedly harass members of their entire local caste group. This happened in the case of Julavas (weavers) Mehmud and Asiya, whom the magistracy of Nagaur fined the hefty sum of eighty rupees in connection with the recent discovery of a six-year-old episode of meat eating by two women of their local caste group of weavers. They petitioned the crown for help, saying they had nothing to do with that case.[45]

DIETS AND LIVELIHOODS

This campaign against *jīv haṃsyā* translated into nothing less than an assault upon the dietary preferences and nutritional base, as well as aesthetic and ethical choices, of a swath of Marwar's population. This swath overlapped heavily with all those who had not embraced, or had not been allowed to embrace, sectarian Vaishnavism over the past century or more.

The Rathor crown outlawed the possession of livestock by these now suspect communities, that is, butchers, *thorīs*, *bāvrīs*, and Muslims. Reflecting the attitudes of the king and his advisors, the state saw members of these communities as incapable of resisting the urge or an inducement to kill animals, even after they had been arrested, fined, placed under surveillance, and explicitly prohibited from doing so. Toward this end, the state prohibited the sale of livestock to members of these communities and to those from outside the kingdom. In addition, the state ordered that any livestock already in the possession of these groups were to be forcibly sold off or handed over to members of reliably vegetarian castes.[46]

Singhvi Gyanmal's order from 1785, to be implemented across the kingdom, commands the confiscation and sale of all herds of goats and sheep in the possession of butchers, *thorīs*, and *bāvrīs* (*khaṭīk bāvrī thorīyāṁ rai evaḍ huvai su ṭhīk kar nai sārā bīkāy dejo rākhjo matī*).[47] Singhvi Gyanmal, a mahajan, was a high-ranking officer of the state, and five years after authorizing this command, he became *dīvān* of the kingdom.[48] In the same year, two unnamed *pyād bakhśīs* prohibited "Muslims and other low castes" (*musalmān vagairai nīch jāt*) from keeping herds of goats or sheep.[49] Singhvi Gyanmal ordered a careful watch on Muslims "and others" across all seventeen districts of the kingdom who owned chickens to ensure that they did not kill them. If they did, they were to be rigorously punished.[50] Members of agriculturist communities, especially *jāṭs* and *bishnois*, whose religious convictions upheld a vegetarian diet, were beneficiaries of this policy. They received control over herds of goats and sheep that had earlier belonged to butchers.[51] For instance, in 1776 the crown ordered the distribution of the herds of the butchers of Nagaur among the *jaṭs* of a village.[52] Bishnoi Bala and Jat Sukha were respectively given charge of such herds in Nagaur district.[53]

In all these cases, herds were taken forcibly from the butchers and not purchased from them, as indicated by the concession made to them by the state in allowing them to continue ownership over the wool these animals produced.[54] This was hard to implement, as suggested by a butcher, recognized by the state as poor and in need of funds, having to petition the crown in Jodhpur to receive overdue payments for the wool his sheep had generated. The sheep were in a *jāṭ*'s control.[55] This was a wealth transfer from a subset of the Untouchable castes—butchers and Muslims more generally—to vegetarian peasant castes.

When a *jāṭ* peasant was discovered to have sold some animals to *thorīs*, the crown ordered that both the *jāṭ* and the *thorīs* should be fined if any of those animals were slaughtered.[56] In Koliya district, a moneylender who had seized a *jāṭ's* herd of goats, probably due to the latter's indebtedness to him, sold the herd to a butcher.[57] The *jāṭ* reported this "crime" to the crown.[58] Purohit Kesoram, the *daftar rā darogā* Asopa Surajmal, and Asopa Fatehram, all three brahmans, ruled on this case on behalf of the crown.[59] They demanded an explanation from the mahajan and ordered that any livestock that were in butchers' possession should be sold immediately.[60] The state became so worried about livestock ending up in the wrong hands that it instructed its officers to regularly survey the herds in their domain to ensure that no animals were sold at all.[61]

The crown's targeting of butchers, *thorīs*, *bāvrīs*, and Muslims shrank their respective resource bases and forbade them from practicing animal husbandry. For communities that were already being marginalized, if not expelled, and in the case of the butchers, forced to abandon the occupations in which they were skilled, being prohibited from keeping animals was a severe blow.

All three groups did not control land and so, when pushed out of the trades in which they earned their resources, animal husbandry could have been a viable new source of livelihood. Even if practiced on a small scale, the dairy produced by domesticated animals could have been a valuable source of sustenance for a dispossessed people. Barred from owning pastoral wealth and forced out of the professions in which they were skilled, the butchers in late eighteenth-century Marwar would likely have been reduced to poverty. The crown dismissively recognized this by recommending that if they were worried about earning a living, the erstwhile butchers of Nagaur should become load-carriers.[62] The campaign to stamp out animal slaughter in Marwar was a blow to the livelihoods, nutritional base, and dietary preferences particularly of butchers, Muslims, and *thorīs* and *bāvrīs*. For Muslims, as well as followers of other religious paths such as goddess worship that entailed ritual animal sacrifice, the prohibition restricted their ability to fully practice their faiths.

SURVEILLANCE, INFORMING, AND SOCIAL CONFLICT

As a result of the crown's directive to its officers and to its subjects to keep an eye upon their neighbors from the butcher, *thorī*, and *bāvrī* communities, informers began to present the desired reports to the crown. In 1784, Muhnot Gokul, a mahajan who worked for the governor, spotted meat in some butchers' homes in Parbatsar district.[63] The local authorities failed to carry out a rigorous investigation and could not apprehend the guilty, who had purportedly run away to Malwa, a region in modern-day Punjab and northern Rajasthan that lay to the north of Marwar. The crown reprimanded the local authorities for failing to mount a full-fledged investigation and ordered that the one person who had been caught in connection with the matter should be fully punished.[64]

In another instance, acting on information collected by royal newswriters (*uvākāṁ rī fardāṁ rā samāchār*), the local authorities arrested two women, one of the caste of dyers (*rangrejāṁ*) and the other a blacksmith.[65] In captivity, the two coughed up the names of all the others who had been involved in the meat-eating episode with them. As a result, a drummer in royal employ (*savāī nagārchī*) was caught and he too was pressured to name names. Sensing laxity on the part of district administrators, the *pyād bakhśī* Bhandari Ramchand ordered that all those named in the case should be fined and a search undertaken for the absconding butchers.[66]

The crown's surveillance networks helped to point its energies toward particular individuals suspected of animal slaughter. In 1785, the crown received reports (*samāchār śrī hajūr mālam huvā*) from a village in Nagaur district of the role of a *thorī* in shooting a deer dead, of a *gujjar* (pastoralist) in castrating a bull, and of butchers (*khaṭīks*) regularly slaughtering animals.[67] The crown was informed by its newswriters that the butchers of Bagru village in Sambhar district were freely slaying animals and selling the meat in the towns.[68] Two guards of the local magistracy had been in charge of keeping an eye on the place, and the crown adjudged that it was they who should pay a price for the crime. The crown ordered that the guards be fined in proportion to their means.[69]

An atmosphere of surveillance and informing became palpable in Marwar. For instance, Rathor records reflect the curious phenomenon of meat showing up in the homes of respectable Marwaris without any solicitation of it on their part, or so they claimed. When district authorities fined a woman from the goldsmith caste, Sunari Viri, for eating meat, she appealed to the crown for mercy, arguing that she was innocent.[70] She blamed her Muslim neighbors who, she said, had regularly killed animals and had thrown the animal flesh into her house. The crown responded favorably to her appeal and ordered the local administration to dismiss the case against the *sunārī*, without ordering an inquiry against the Muslim neighbors she had named.[71] The next year, in 1786, the crown summoned a *jāgīrdār* when some of his employees were accused of hunting animals in Desuri district.[72] The *jāgīrdār* defended himself by blaming a *ḍheḍh* (leather-working) woman, who it appears had reported him, for having filed the complaint out of malice toward him. The crown closed the case, concluding that the perpetrator of the crime was a *golā*[73] man from outside the region who had since gotten away.[74] Bhat Harchand's wife and son, all from a caste of hereditary genealogists, were arrested for eating meat, and in their defense, the *bhāṭ* blamed a *khaṭīknī* (a woman of the butcher caste) for bringing meat, without any solicitation, to their home.[75]

Each subject was a potential informer and, given the state's intolerance toward meat eating, many a Marwari seized the opportunity to settle scores by accusing a neighbor, a caste fellow, or a kin for being involved in animal slaughter. Jat Valiya's son, of a peasant caste, unintentionally caused a sheep's death while watching his family's crops. A brahman soon came to their house, asking for alms, and when the *jāṭ* refused to give him any, the brahman created a ruckus. Later, the brahman went to the authorities and accused the *jāṭ* of killing the sheep that had earlier died. As a result, the Daulatpura governor fined the *jāṭ*. It was only after the *jāṭ* managed to relay this account to the crown that the fine against him was dropped and the brahman asked to explain himself.[76] In another episode, someone falsely named *khaṭīkni* Mani, a woman of the butcher caste who earned a living from dying hides, of being involved in animal slaughter.[77]

In a similar case as that of Jat Valiya above, the Brahman Kachro of Parbatsar accused Jat Harko of shirking his duties at the royal temple in Parbatsar district in which they both worked and of eating meat. In his defense, the *jāṭ* argued in 1776 that he reported to work every day and had never been involved in *jīv haṃsyā* (injuring animals). Instead, it was the brahman who disappeared for long intervals to the town due to which prayers were only intermittently held at the temple. The *jāṭ* said it was because he demanded his salary from the brahman that the latter had become incensed and fabricated these baseless allegations against him.[78]

When Mahajans Dunga and Dipa hired an ascetic (*sāmī*, vernacularization of "swami") to revive Dipa's unconscious wife by performing an exorcism (*dīpā rī lugāī ro ḍīl bechāk tho jiṇ su sāmī nu jhāḍā rai vāstai bulāy lyāyā thā*), someone informed the crown that he and his family had consumed meat and alcohol as part of the ritual.[79] As a result, the Desuri magistrate stationed his men at the two merchants' homes. The merchants then asked the crown for help, alleging that someone had concocted the story and that the report was false (*jhūṭī chuglī kīvī*).[80] Another *jāṭ*, Devla, of a village in Nagaur district protested in 1777 his indictment for animal slaughter when he was innocent. He argued that the *jāgīrdār* of his village harbored ill will toward him after the *jāṭ* had demanded repayment of the twenty-five rupees he had loaned to the *jāgīrdār* eight years ago. Out of malice, the *jāgīrdār* teamed up with another *jāṭ* and lodged a complaint of animal slaughter against Jat Devla, taking advantage of the sudden death of one of the goats in his herd. Jat Devla protested against this false report (*jhūthī chuglī*) that resulted in a fine of seventy rupees upon him. In response, Singhvi Tilokmal ordered on behalf of the crown that the governor of Nagaur conduct a hearing of the case that brought the *jāṭ*, the *jāgīrdār*, and all their witnesses to the case face-to-face.[81] Jat Khivla of Nagaur also had to ask the crown in Jodhpur to help when another *jāṭ*, he claimed, falsely reported him to the governor for killing a snake.[82]

An accusation of animal slaughter became a weapon in everyday conflicts, occasionally used even against locally powerful and armed rajput landholders. The landholder of Bhakhri village in Parbatsar informed the crown when the son of the local *jāgīrdār* killed a deer, one that was pregnant.[83] Mahajan Mayachand raised an alarm (*helā kīyā*) when he realized that a *jāgīrdār* was killing animals inside his fortress in Siwana district.[84] In 1789, rajput Hanvantsingh Jivansinghot informed the crown that another rajput, a young man who had been in the state's employ but had been fired for killing an animal, was innocent. He explained that the young rajput used to frequently play with the boys of a local swami settlement.[85] One day, the rajput's retainers beat up the swami boys. Despite the swamis' complaints to him, the rajput failed to upbraid the servants involved. Soon after, a couple of the swamis' goats died due to an infection in the herd. When a third goat died, the seething swamis vented their anger toward the rajput by wringing its neck and complaining to the governor that the rajput had killed it. The rajput was declared guilty and fired from state service, and it was only after a determined campaign by Hanvantsingh that the crown accepted his innocence and ordered his reinstatement.[86]

Even though such informers aided the crown's campaign, these complaints generated fissures in families, caste communities, and local orders. A woman from the trading *mehrā* community petitioned the crown for help, saying that her son-in-law had become hostile toward her and started taunting her because she had reported him for eating meat.[87] Another farmer, Sirvi Birai, was thrown out of his village and threatened with murder after he reported the *jāgīrdārs* of the village to the authorities for killing an animal.[88] Jat Ratansi faced pressure to leave his village after a complaint by him resulted in the other residents of his village being fined by the authorities. When he first set out to present his case before the crown, these villagers intercepted and beat him *en route*.[89] Jat Ratna's wife complained to the governor when some Kyamkhanis in her village killed an animal. The Kyamkhanis were fined and, in revenge, persuaded the village *jāgīrdār* to confiscate all her belongings and throw her out of the village. Despite her procuring two subsequent orders from the crown for her resettlement in the village, she was not allowed back in.[90] In 1791, Jat Natha reported the other *jāṭs* of his village in Siwana district to the local authorities for killing animals.[91] Instead of the meat-eaters being penalized, it was Natha who was beaten up. He then approached the crown for help and managed to elicit a ruling from brahman Asopa Fatehram and the merchant-caste *pyād bakhśī*, Bhandari Balkishan that commanded the punishment of the guilty and of those who beat up Natha.[92] There were other instances too of informers facing retaliation.[93]

The campaign against animal slaughter quickly descended into an impossible tangle of allegations and counter-allegations. A *jāgīrdār* in Nagaur district who was accused of killing a local peasant's ram countered the allegation by naming a Bhati rajput as the person who had committed the crime.[94] Cotton-ginner (*pīñjārā*) Jīva told the governor's office that another cotton-ginner, Inayat, had gone to another village and eaten meat.[95] The governor fined Inayat but he petitioned the crown for a dismissal of the charges, saying that Jiva had made them up.[96]

Elsewhere, Pancholi Maharam came to Jodhpur to petition the crown, pleading the innocence of his son and another *pañcholī* who were behind bars for killing animals. Pancholi Fatehkaran and the *pyād bakhśī*, Mumhta Gopaldas, ordered on behalf of the crown that if no proof was available, the Merta magistracy should release the two men.[97] In another instance, a woman from the *bhāṭ* (bardic) caste got a butcher to secretly deliver some meat to her home.[98] When news of this spread, she and her daughter-in-law fled and hid at a *pañcholī*'s home. They were soon caught by the local authorities and under pressure, named another man, the son of Pancholi Maharam, as being the one for whom she had ordered the meat. *Pyād bakhśī* Mumhta Gopaldas, a mahajan, ordered the arrest of everyone that the *bhāṭ* woman named.[99] Other allegations and charges also elicited contestation. A rajput and his supporters were able to convince the crown that an allegation of animal slaughter against him was entirely false and was born of a servant's anger toward his master, arising from a prior dispute.[100] In Merta, another *pīṇjārā* asserted his innocence, and in a bid to exonerate himself, he accused four other members of his caste of eating meat (*mānṭī khāvaṇ*).[101] Bhat Harchand of Merta blamed a woman of the butcher community for bringing meat to his home without his asking for it.[102]

Reports of animal slaughter, both true and concocted, created fissures in local communities when, for instance, caste fellows turned on one another. Butcher Natha attracted the ire of all the other butchers of Nagaur when he reported their now illegal activities to the crown.[103] Cloth-printer Nathu dutifully reported to the crown the trapping of birds and animals by some *chīḍīmārs* (birdcatchers) and the subsequent sale of this catch to some of his caste fellows.[104] He probably never imagined that this conflict would engulf his own family; soon after, one of his own sons falsely implicated the other for being involved in the purchase of those very trapped creatures.[105] Weavers Bilaval and Nathu, along with some unnamed members of their caste, found themselves facing eviction from their village by their caste fellows for reporting other weavers to the crown for killing animals.[106]

The crown's encouragement of an atmosphere where its subjects became its eyes and ears in the campaign against *jīv haṃsyā* created a mass of judicial complaints to sort through. The ban on animal slaughter became a weapon in the hands of the Rathor state's subjects for the playing out of their grievances against each other. Among castes in which *jīv haṃsyā* was anathema, the membership of someone found guilty of the crime would become a source of intra-caste conflict. An atmosphere of suspicion and mistrust would certainly have resulted from the ever-present possibility of a friend, a neighbor, an employee, a kin, or a caste fellow turning into an informant, not to mention the threat posed by the crown's own network of newswriters.

CASTE AND DIET

The scale of the effort to criminalize meat eating and impose a vegetarian diet that played out in late eighteenth-century Marwar was one that, with our current state of historical knowledge, lacks historical precedent and perhaps also remains without parallel. To that extent, the processes described in this chapter and in chapter 5 are a hitherto unknown episode in the history of South Asia. Reading the mass of state orders pertaining to animal slaughter in the context of the wider changes underway in Marwar makes it possible to draw connections between this seemingly anomalous set of developments and the transformations the region was experiencing in the latter half of the eighteenth century.

The project to build a vegetarian polity was entirely in consonance with Vaishnav and Jain ethics to which much of Marwar's elites subscribed by the late eighteenth century. It served to further stigmatize the *achhep* or "Untouchable" pole against which a Hindu identity was taking shape. Now, to the "lowliness" and "impurity" of the Untouchable was added the moral stain of supposedly being given to taking nonhuman lives. In the hands of the Rathor state and its merchant bureaucrats, the drive to protect animals became an added weapon with which to beat down a subset of the Untouchables that also included Muslims. Along with *thorīs*, *bāvrīs*, and butchers, Muslims saw their livestock transferred and bore the brunt of a ban preventing them from owning any animals. These groups bore an outlawing of their dietary preferences and ritual practices entailing animal slaughter. Most significantly, they bore the brunt of being deemed inherently and collectively criminal.

For most others in Marwar, however, the campaign against animal slaughter created an atmosphere of surveillance and dissolved over the years into a welter of allegations and counter-allegations that were frequently exhausting if not impossible to untangle. The crown's authority still rested in part on that of rajput landlords, many of whom continued to hunt and eat animals, and this curtailed its ability to punish everyone who was guilty. Stray orders indicate that the ban was not easy to execute over a sustained period of time. So a 1795 order noted that butchers were plying their trade across the kingdom, and in the same year, a rajput in Didwana advised the local magistrate to not fine butchers because butchery had resumed even in the capital Jodhpur.[107] This may of course have been a rumor, but it is also possible that the rajput may have been right. Still, an order issued toward the end of this period, in 1801—a missive to the governor of Desuri district—underscored the outlawing of animal slaughter, reminding him to make special arrangements to prevent it.[108] In 1803, an order from Jodhpur issued by a mahajan, Lodha Kisanram, observed that *jīv haṃsyā* had been curtailed in the city of Jalor even as it noted that the state's officers themselves were killing animals within the fort.[109] Despite this continuing concern for an overarching ban on killing animals, in the end, it was the *thorīs*, *bāvrīs*, butchers, and Muslims who bore the greatest burden of the Rathor state's battle for vegetarianism and nonharm.

Whatever its degree of success on the ground, the singling out of vegetarianism as the most significant element of a moral regime of nonharm gave rise to a coercive campaign that forced those deemed "Hindu" to be vegetarian while also constructing those not Hindu, or not allowed to be Hindu, as immutably given toward now-immoral meat eating. The campaign against meat eating in Marwar was an important prong in the forging of an early modern Hindu subject. This process, however, was deeply political, built upon the legislative, punitive, and surveillance capabilities of the crown. Touching the everyday lives of ordinary people in the towns and villages of Marwar, the forging of this new community was premised on the delineation of the Untouchable domain as indelibly marked by qualities of body and mind—an inherent and inescapable tendency toward meat eating—that were incompatible with Hindu-ness. This in turn legitimized oppression through state law and even expulsion of some of those who belonged to the core of the imagined untouchable domain. This effort to protect life overlapped with the Rathor state's effort to outlaw abortion too, discussed in chapter 7, within its domain. Like the Rathor state's interventions in the domains of abortion and illicit sex, drinking, and gambling, the campaign to impose an ethic of nonharm was in principle universally applicable to all subjects. The difference between the other ethical goals and the pursuit of nonharm lay in the latter being pursued with varying degrees of enthusiasm and severities of punishment across the subject body. The former set of laws were in effect applied more rigorously on the kingdom's aspirant elites—the merchants and brahmans. The injunction to cease animal slaughter, however, was enforced on all, with merchant communities policing themselves for conformity but with butchers (Muslims and "low"-caste Hindus), landless vagrants, and Muslims being penalized the most by the state.

The fact that a recent "convert" to Vaishnavism, Maharaja Vijai Singh, was at the helm of affairs no doubt played an important role in the elevation of nonharm into universal law. At the same time, with Vijai Singh being a beleaguered king facing constant challenge from his rajput feudatories, his embrace of and enacting as law the ethical codes of Vaishnavs and Jains could well have also been a strategic move. For mahajans, all Vaishnavs and Jains were a rival power center within the state, one that could help Vijai Singh counter his rebellious rajput nobility.

In this period, an ethic of protection toward nonhuman life forms, particularly its manifestation in a vegetarian diet, came to be associated with elite social rank. This was a process that built on a long history of growing disassociation from animal slaughter within brahmanical thought and practice and the Vaishnav and Jain insistence on nonharm. Yet, it was the particular influence that merchants enjoyed in western Indian polities such as Marwar, particularly from the eighteenth century onward for reasons already delineated, that nonharm and vegetarianism become markers of high caste for all. State power—the enactment and enforcement of a universal ban on animal slaughter—played an important role in the naturalization of the association between ritual purity, high social rank, and an animal protectionist ethos. This process reinforced the move within brahmanical thought and practice that associated ritual purity, and therefore an important determinant of caste rank, with nonharm.

For the merchants, the elevation of their castes' ethical codes to universal law and the commitment to protecting animal life imbued them with an aura of virtue. Not only were they model subjects in dutifully observing noninjury, but as bureaucratic agents of a state working to prevent violence against animals, they were acquiring merit in the spiritual scheme of things. This helped offset their tremendous economic gains, made as much through commissions, brokerage, and deposits as through debt. The mahajans made money from money, and in the eighteenth century they made a lot of it. A campaign to protect helpless animal lives, I suggest, then allowed the mahajans to offset their increasing association with wealth and power with that of committed caregivers to beings that could not advocate for their own interests.

While rajputs in the old order legitimately wielded wealth and power as kings, warriors, and holders of land, merchants' entry into the topmost echelons of the caste order was new and based in large part on their mastery of capital and the interest it could generate. Brahmans, even though they did enjoy a high ritual rank, had not historically commanded wealth or political power in Marwar. Their rise in the region, as leaders of Vaishnav orders and as administrators for the state, was of recent vintage. The inclusion of merchants and brahmans among a newly defined elite then required a transformation of the social order and the ideological basis underpinning it. To be carried through, this change needed the power of virtue.

The ban on the killing of animals was central to the ongoing polarization of Marwari society, a process in which state authority played an indispensible part. Butchers and vagrant hunters such as *bāvrīs* and *thorīs* were marked as suspect and placed under pervasive surveillance. Painted as agents of violence against sentient beings, they were subjected to extreme forms of punishments by the standards of the day. Mass arrest, expulsion from villages, economic dispossession, and surveillance were some of the punishments that the Rathor state awarded to these groups. In all of this, the body emerged as a crucial site for the expression of high caste, "Hindu" status, and the attribution of being "Untouchable." Command over the senses—a rejection of meat eating, drinking, gambling, and "excess" sex—and an ethical embrace of nonharm recast the bodies of elite subjects, lifting them out of base desires into a realm of subtle and "clean" communion. This effort was directed not only at the Other but also simultaneously at the Self.

PART TWO

Self

5

Nonharm

The constitution of the Hindu caste body entailed a reconstitution of the Self through a regime of bodily discipline centered on austerity. This effort to protect nonhuman lives was a crucial part of the eighteenth-century construction not only of the Other, the Untouchable, but also the Hindu. The ethical imperative of nonharm to living beings was a central tenet of both Vaishnav devotion and Jainism. The initiation of Maharaja Vijai Singh into the Vaishnav sect of the Vallabhites in 1765 no doubt played an important role in the imposition across the kingdom of laws banning animal slaughter. At the same time, the role that merchants, both as administrators and as wealthy subjects, played in driving the hard edge of this campaign into the body politic is one that needs greater attention and offers a better explanation of the temporal and kingdom-wide scale of this campaign.

From the 1770s until about 1820, the Rathor state threw the weight of its authority, punitive powers, and means of surveillance into stamping out meat eating. In the same years, as shown in chapters 2 and 3, Vijai Singh and his officers facilitated the expansion of sectarian Vaishnavism in the Rathor domain as well as the crystallization of a self-conscious Hindu community. This helped to elevate the status of groups—particularly merchants—that were seeking to cordon off an exclusive Hindu realm of prestige and privilege. Vaishnavism, from the outset, enshrined nonharm (*ahiṃsā*) in general and vegetarianism in particular as a core value, adherence to which was essential for its followers. Jainism, widely influential among mercantile groups since the medieval period, too held an ethic of nonharm at its core and demanded adherence to a vegetarian diet. The norms enshrined by the sect of which Maharaja Vijai Singh was a part aligned with the ethical values held dear by the Vaishnav-Jain officers, along with brahmans, who manned the Rathor administration. In the same decades that they issued commands decreeing the Hindu to be all who were not leatherworkers, sweepers, landless vagrants, and Muslims, in which they facilitated the separation in everyday life of "high" and Hindu from "low" and Muslim, and in which they worked to discipline their own bodies into a more austere way of life, these merchant and brahman officers participated in a campaign to criminalize injury to animals.

By arrogating for themselves the authority to speak for the voiceless, the merchant-dominated Rathor administration and its merchant-brahman subjects sought to accumulate the moral capital they needed to tighten their grip on power. While some rajput lineages, particularly the more cosmopolitan and elite ones exposed to the world of Mughal *bhakti*, had also joined the vegetarian and Vaishnav fold, other rajputs remained immersed in Shakta-Shaiva and meat-eating practices. This caused conflict, as I will show. Further, for the merchant and brahman elites of the kingdom, the sustained campaign to stigmatize and criminalize meat eating helped to naturalize the correlation between social status and diet, making vegetarianism a hallmark of elite caste status and pushing meat eating firmly into the domain of the "Untouchable."

LAYING DOWN THE LAW

In decrees dispatched to the administrative headquarters of each district, the Rathor administration exhorted its officials to ensure that arrangements to eradicate violence against sentient beings (*jīv haṃsyā*) were made in each town and village within their jurisdiction.[1] An early articulation of this policy was in a stray order issued to the governor of Phalodhi district. It approvingly noted, "Animals and other creatures (*jīv jīnāvar*) are never killed in the villages of the Bishnois and they never cut the *kheḍā*[2] and other trees. Write to the *paṭṭā* holders in the villages that they should not kill animals. It is the order of Śrī Hajūr."[3]

This effort picked up momentum by the late 1770s. The king and his administrators in Jodhpur imposed a total ban on the killing of animals across Marwar, forbidding the slaughter of animals both for sport and for food. These injunctions were often issued as kingdom-wide pronouncements, such as the ones authorized in 1781 by Pancholi Nandram and in 1791 by the *dīvān*, mahajan Bhandari Bhavanidas, and in 1803 by the *dīvān* at that time, mahajan Bhandari Gangaram. The broad injunction to state officers to prohibit violence against animals was accompanied in these kingdom-wide orders by more specific commands, such as the one in figure 6, that brought within the ambit of *jīv haṃsyā* forms of violence against animals that may otherwise go unnoticed. Toward this end, official decrees mandated the use of a sieve to strain water as it was drawn from water tanks and ponds, in order to save the lives of hapless creatures that might otherwise die by drifting into a water vessel.[4] Royal officers were directed to ensure that a sieve was placed for public use at all the major public sources of water supply and to ensure that no one defied the royal order while potting water.[5] If a creature did make its way into a pot, it was to be released back into the water.[6]

The prohibition of *jīv haṃsyā* extended also to a ban on the castration of bulls (*baladh khasī karnā*). In early modern Marwar as in other agrarian societies since ancient times, bulls were castrated in order to render their bodies and

FIGURE 6. JSPB 23, VS 1836/1779 CE, f 355b–356a: Laws to protect nonhuman lives. Image courtesy of the Rajasthan State Archives, Bikaner (RSAB). Do not reuse or reproduce without permission from the RSAB.

temperaments more suitable for work. From the late 1770s onward, Rathor administrators outlawed the castration of bulls, an act that rendered them incapable of reproduction, on the grounds that it was a form of violence against living beings.[7] The Rathor state strove to protect the lives of winged insects that were susceptible to dying by accidentally flying into the flames of lamps.[8] It instructed the officers across the towns in Marwar to ensure that when people lit oil lamps at night, they covered them with shades.[9] The gathering of fresh cow dung into dung cakes to use as fuel was a common practice. Royal orders declared that because tiny insects burrowed in the dung in the rainy season, the rolling of dung cakes during the *chaumāsā* (the four months of the rainy season) was now prohibited in order to save their lives.[10]

The Rathor state's effort to protect the fauna in its domain went so far as to prohibit even the killing of parasites, pests, and venomous creatures. Royal decrees noted that the more ignorant of their subjects tended to deal with lice and spider infestations by eliminating the pests through exposure to high heat or water. This was no longer acceptable.[11] A crop-eating caterpillar (the tiger moth caterpillar or *kātrā*), known to attack the monsoon (*kharīf*) crop, and the Bengal monitor lizard (*goyḍā* or *goyrā* in Rajasthan) were among the other creatures that were blessed with the crown's explicit protection.[12] Jodhpur administrators also forbade the killing of poisonous creatures such as scorpions, snakes, and spiders (*mākaḍ*), even in self-defense.[13]

Many of these injunctions, especially those concerned with the well-being of invisible insects and microbes, echo not just a Vaishnav concern with nonharm but also a recognizably Jain ethos. In comparison with other parts of South Asia, western India, including Marwar, had by the end of the first millennium CE become home to a relatively large Jain population. This Jain population consisted overwhelmingly, if not exclusively, of merchants. The merchants of western India were largely either Vaishnav or Jain, and by the eighteenth century, men from these two communities dominated regional and subcontinental fiscal networks as well as the Rathor administration.[14] Across the Vaishnav-Jain divide was a shared preoccupation with nonharm, an imperative placed not only upon monks and priests but also upon lay practitioners of both creeds. Whether it was Krishna or a *tīrthaṅkar*[15] before whom they bowed, the merchants of western India by the eighteenth century were united by the distinctive cultivation of an ethico-moral stance that valued nonharm, chastity, and personal austerity combined with generous religious gifting.[16] Many Jains also worshipped other brahmanical divinities such as Hanuman, Shakti, and Shiva as Bhairav.[17] Jains celebrated the festival of Diwali, in late October, just like Vaishnavs and other brahmanical sects, although they linked it to the final spiritual liberation of the *tīrthaṅkar* Mahavir. Like Hindus, Jains in western India considered Diwali as the beginning of the new year for ritual and commercial purposes and inaugurated new account books after praying to the goddess of wealth, Lakshmi.

Further, the Vaishnav-Jain boundary, particularly that between Vallabhite Vaishnavs and Jains, was a fluid one, at least among eighteenth-century merchant groups. Mercantile castes, such as the *bhaṇḍārīs* who played such a prominent role in administration, could consist of both Vaishnav and Jain members.[18] Marriages occurred across the line and the two groups collaborated in professional and civic endeavors to further their common economic interest.[19] People too could move across this boundary, as indicated by the early nineteenth-century example of the Marwari Jagat Seth family in Bengal turning Vaishnav, from the Jains they had earlier been, without having to perform any ritual or formal conversion.[20] From the perspective of law and civic participation, the caste category "mahajan" as used from the seventeenth through the nineteenth centuries in Marwar encompassed both Vaishnav and Jain merchants and moneylenders.[21] Scholars have noted the dwindling of Jain mendicant orders in Rajasthan by the mid-nineteenth century, suggesting that the process may have begun in prior decades. It is possible that the Vallabh Sect won over many Shvetambar Jains, causing a shrinkage in the patronage available to support mendicant orders as well as reduced interest in taking initiation into them. Certainly, the Osvāl caste, despite its Jain origins, is noted to have included Vaishnavs in its ranks in the nineteenth and twentieth centuries.

Theologically, as well, the two realms overlapped, with Vaishnavs incorporating the first Jain *tīrthaṅkar* Rishabh as a minor avatar of Vishnu and the Jains absorbing Krishna by claiming the *tīrthaṅkar* Neminath to be his cousin.[22] By this I do not mean to completely collapse Jainism and Vaishnavism together; Jain thinkers maintained opposition to brahmanical thought and practice through the early modern period.[23] From its inception, Jainism was marked by a rejection of the Vedas and of the authority of brahmans. In that sense, it attacked the very foundations of brahmanism. Jain polemicists criticized the Hindu god Shiva and rejected the mythological accounts of the medieval *Purāṇas*. Medieval Jain texts regarded the worship of Hindu deities as inconsistent with the Jain path.[24] Given the tremendous variation in the social and political contexts in which Jains wrote and practiced in two millennia since the emergence of Jainism, considerable variation can be found in their attitudes toward brahmanism.[25] Jain writers were not, for instance, as dismissive of Vishnu as they were of Shiva, even according the former with a degree of respect.[26]

Yet, in practice and in social constitution, Jainism and Vaishnavism overlapped, particularly the Vallabh Sect.[27] The proximity between the two groups by the eighteenth century is indicated by the insistence of some Jains in early British censuses of India to report themselves as "Hindu," leading the census-takers to record them as "Jain-Hindus."[28] Ethnographic studies have pointed to a persisting ambiguity among present-day Jains toward Hindu identity, with some claiming it and others resolutely rejecting it. Still, Jains today worship in Hindu temples and take part in Hindu festivals.[29]

Scholarship on premodern Jainism has tended to remain focused on the enormous intellectual output of Jains, spanning not just issues of debate among Jains regarding theology and orthopraxy but also areas such as philosophy, aesthetics, literature, and the sciences.[30] At the same time, scholarship on Jains in the world makes clear that they forged intimate ties with Muslim kings, participated in lively court, literary, artistic, historiographical, and intellectual cultures in a range of languages, thrived as scribes, accountants, and traders, and adapted in response to the historical changes, even reformulating aspects of their own tradition.[31]

NONHARM AND VEGETARIANISM IN HISTORY

While the extent to which the Rathor state went to impose its ban on animal slaughter is unprecedented in South Asian history, the complicated and often contradictory roots of this development run deep. The Vedas, among the earliest extant texts composed in South Asia and held in brahmanical religious practice as revealed words whose authority cannot be questioned, contain numerous references to the consumption of meat and to animal slaughter for ritual sacrifice. The horse, the sheep, the goat, and even the cow were among the sacrificial offerings to the gods that the Vedas permitted and the consumption of whose meat they condoned. Somewhere in the middle of the first millennium BCE, due to profound changes in social, economic, and political life, emerged new religious ethos that emphasized asceticism. This gave rise to such new religious orders as Buddhism and Jainism, and these new orders in turn may have stimulated a turn in brahmanical practice toward an embrace of *ahiṃsā* or nonharm.[32]

Henk Bodewitz has argued that it is the rise of asceticism as a social and religious practice in the centuries immediately preceding the Common Era to which the origins of the emphasis on nonharm, sometimes also discussed as nonviolence, can be traced.[33] The growing tendency toward asceticism, crystallized especially in Jain and Buddhist practice, challenged brahmanism on a number of counts, prominent among which were the ritual preeminence of the brahman and the violence that the brahmanical ritual performance of animal sacrifice entailed.

Scholars such as Ludwig Alsdorf, David Seyfort Ruegg, and Paul Dundas have argued that an adherence to nonharm need not and did not necessarily equal vegetarianism. For instance, in Jainism, the scope of the potential for violence is understood as so vast, given its concern even for the lives of microbes and insects, that selectively avoiding the consumption of meat while continuing to cause injury or death to other beings would not go far enough in achieving a full adherence to nonharm. Historically, it is only a few centuries after their emergence and their insistence upon nonharm that Jain and Buddhist texts began to prescribe a vegetarian diet. Gautam Buddha is said to have eaten meat.[34] Whether Mahavir ate meat or not has been debated.[35] In both cases, however, the two figures are said to have adhered to the principle of making sure that the animal was not killed for them or before their eyes. While for Jains an explanation is yet to be offered, for Buddhists, Ruegg attributes the move to the rise of a new philosophical approach around the second century BCE that held all sentient beings as holders of the potential to attain enlightenment. To kill or harm a being with such spiritual potential would then be a sin.[36] In brahmanical thought as well, suggests Lance Nelson, two principles aided a growing tendency toward compassion and empathy for nonhuman animals. These were the idea that all beings, human or nonhuman, had qualitatively identical spiritual selves (*ātman*) as well as the belief in rebirth, entailing the possibility that an animal could contain the spirit of a deceased human, including one's own kin.[37]

Rising to the challenge of, or perhaps influenced by, the increasing popularity of Buddhism, Jainism, and renunciant religiosity more generally, brahmanical texts also began to express ambiguity toward animal slaughter and meat eating in the last centuries before the Common Era. Often, the same text would condemn meat eating and animal sacrifice in some verses but condone them in others, as in the *Manusmṛti* circa 100 BCE.[38] The epic *Mahābhārata* contains similar tensions but also includes some of the earliest articulations of the connections among nonharm, vegetarianism, and the growth of Vishnu worship.[39] The condemnation of animal sacrifice and meat eating always stood in a relationship of tension within the brahmanical corpus, since a complete rejection of these practices meant a rejection of the Vedas that prescribed them. Edwin Bryant shows that in the course of the first millennium CE, brahman scholars found ways to reconcile the increasingly uncompromising textual insistence upon vegetarianism and nonharm with Vedic prescriptions of ritual animal slaughter and meat eating.[40]

By the end of the first millennium CE, Vaishnav texts such as the *Bhāgavata Purāṇa* unequivocally demanded an adherence to nonharm and vegetarianism.[41] Histories of vegetarianism in South Asia tend to stop at this point. Studies of Vaishnavism, including those of early modern Krishna-centered devotional groups, recognize the centrality of nonharm and of vegetarianism to it but do not offer a historical account of how this came to be. That said, it is important to note that in premodern South Asian thought, the emphasis upon nonharm could be more focused on the relationship between human and nonhuman beings and not as much on violence between humans.[42] In her study of the third-century BCE emperor Ashoka, for instance, Upinder Singh has noted that his attitude of nonharm, particularly toward animals, did not extend to the people who lived in the forests.[43]

While Buddhism had ceased by the end of the first millennium CE to be influential in most of South Asia, Jainism too found its hold waning despite attracting followers in prior centuries in Odisha, Mathura, Karnataka, and Tamil Nadu. By the twelfth century, Jainism retained a following in large part only among mercantile groups and was largely confined to western India. Even though it began as an ascetic movement, by the thirteenth century a large corpus of Jain literature laid out the duties and obligations of the layperson. Foremost among these was the injunction to try as hard as possible to avoid injury to any life form. This literature proscribed certain occupations that necessarily entailed the performance of violence upon living beings or caused them distress, such as animal husbandry and farming. This restriction, in turn, further helped concentrate Jains in the realm of mercantile activity.

In Marwar, and in western India more broadly, Jainism had come to enjoy by the eighth century CE a stable following among merchant communities. The town of Osian, near Jodhpur, emerged around the eighth century as the locus of an active and prosperous community of the region's Jain merchants.[44] The origin myth of the Jain community in Osian asserted that both the local deity, Sachiya Mata, a goddess requiring blood sacrifice, as well as a population of local rajputs converted to Jainism. Both the deity and the erstwhile warriors embraced the Jain ethic of nonharm, resulting in a cessation of ritual animal slaughter for this goddess. The existence of a stable and lively base of followers in the region meant that Marwar gave rise to major figures in Jain history. Among these was Jinachandrasuri II, the fourth and last of the *Dādāgurus*, a lineage of miracle-working, reformist ascetics who have since themselves become recipients of veneration in the Khartar Gachchh mendicant order of the Shvetambar (White-Clad) Jains.[45] In the eighteenth century, the charismatic Jain reformer and founder of the Terapanth sect among the Shvetambar Jains, Acharya Bhikshu (1726–1803), made Marwar the center of his preaching activity, crisscrossing the region for almost half a century as he amassed followers.[46] Already by the early modern period, sites in Marwar—the village of Osian with its Sachchiya Mata and Mahavir Temples and the town of Bhinmal (earlier known as Shrimal)—were claimed by many diasporic Jain lineages across north India as the place of their origin.[47] As I showed in the first chapter, from around the early sixteenth century, men of mercantile castes, including Jains, rose to the highest positions in the Rathor government in Marwar, whittling away, in concert with successive Rajput kings, the political authority of rajput chiefs.[48] In both a worldly and ritual way, Marwar and developments in it were significant to the history of Jains.

These histories of nonharm and vegetarianism provide a sense of the evolution over time of these values as ideas but do not provide a sense of how and to what extent they were practiced. In particular, studies of shifting textual positions on nonharm and vegetarianism, illustrative as they may be about the intellectual, philosophical, and religious history of these ideas, do not leave us with much of a picture of how it is that their practice became widespread and even normalized. Further, as normative prescriptions, we are left with little sense of whether temporal or ritual authorities enforced an adherence to these values.

Based on the current state of our knowledge it appears that through most of South Asia's past, vegetarianism remained largely limited to textual prescriptions followed by clusters of brahman and Jain communities scattered across the Indian subcontinent. There are a couple of well-known instances of kings embracing religious or ethical codes demanding nonharm or vegetarianism, but none of these kings imposed their beliefs as law upon their subjects. The third century BCE emperor Ashoka, a Buddhist, embraced an ethic of nonharm (*avihiṃsā* or *anālambhā*) to which animals were central.[49] As emperor, Ashoka saw it as his duty to help his subjects do good, attain merit, and progress in their quest for liberation from the cycle of rebirth. He placed rock or pillar edicts at busy crossroads and in the frontier regions of his vast territories, spanning a large swath of the Indian subcontinent. In these edicts, he exhorted his subjects to give up animal slaughter and meat eating but never imposed the policy upon them.

In one of the edicts, recently understood as representing an accommodation to the impossibility of eradicating all violence toward animals, Ashoka sought to at least regulate and reduce the amount of animal slaughter in his domain. At most, he tried to impose vegetarianism on his royal kitchen, but when met with resistance, he was willing to allow some animal slaughter there. Apart from Ashoka's own giving up of hunting and his efforts to adhere to a vegetarian diet, his efforts to protect animal life are thought to have had little direct effect on curbing animal slaughter.[50]

In the early modern period, kings, including Mughal emperors Akbar and Jahangir, embraced vegetarianism to a certain degree in their own personal lives. Akbar, at different points, gave up meat for a day of the week or for a few months at a stretch, aiming to eventually achieve total vegetarianism. He never gave up the hunt, though, and did not succeed in becoming fully vegetarian.[51] Akbar encouraged his nobles too to strive toward a vegetarian diet and, according to court historian Abu'l Fazl, he convinced some of them. Akbar's son and successor Jahangir too gave up meat for a period of four years, and even when he resumed meat eating, would eat only vegetarian food on certain days. He was less successful than Akbar in remaining committed to vegetarianism.[52]

Jain sources take credit for Akbar's interest in vegetarianism, attributing it to the influence of Hiravijaya Suri and Jinachandra Suri II, whom Akbar summoned to his court for a discussion on questions of religion in 1587 and 1591 respectively.[53] Mughal sources attribute it to a mystical vision that Akbar had while hunting in 1578, leading him to release all the animals in the hunting ring (*qamargāh*) before him and to become vegetarian.[54] It is perhaps not a coincidence that Akbar's sympathy for vegetarianism emerged in the very period in which he and his leading nobles were extending generous patronage to the nascent Krishnaite sects in Brindavan. The Mughal-Vaishnav compact, a "Mughal Bhakti" as Jack Hawley calls it, solidified in these very decades. It was perhaps then the influence of Vaishnav nobles, of Vaishnav and Jain financier-bureaucrats, and of the invigorating rise of a new and public form of Krishnaite devotion so closely associated with Mughal authority that pushed Akbar toward vegetarianism. According to Jain sources, Akbar and his son and successor, Jahangir, outlawed animal slaughter during the Jain holy days of *paryūśaṇ* that lasted from eight to twelve days in a lunar calendar year.[55] Still, Akbar did not go so far as to impose vegetarianism on anyone, let alone impose it as a law upon all of his subjects. This is where the case of eighteenth-century Marwar, while demonstrating overlaps and interconnections with wider phenomena in South Asia, remains unique.

SPEAKING FOR THE VOICELESS

The prohibition of violence against living beings and the more extreme interpretations of this law, discussed at the beginning of this chapter, were part of a larger legislative drive by the Rathor state to bring its body politic in line with its ethical beliefs. The declarations against animal slaughter oftentimes also contained rules directed toward other ethical goals of the state. Directives that were listed alongside orders to prevent injury to animals include instructions reflecting concern for the welfare of those infirm with age, placing the onus of their care upon their sons. In such decrees, such as ones issued in 1779, 1782, 1787, and 1797, various officers of the Rathor state and perhaps also the Maharaja himself ordered its district magistracies to ensure that no subject neglected his duty to look after, feed, and clothe his parents.[56] It also ordered its subjects to look after their mentally ill kinsfolk.[57] The state took on the expense of feeding the blind, disabled, and mentally infirm who wandered through Nagaur and Merta towns.[58] The crown observed that greed induced brahmans and mahajans to marry their young daughters to old men (*virāmaṇ mahājan vagairai rupīyā rai lālach buḍhā nū beṭī paraṇāvai hai*).[59] Disapproving of this practice, the crown commanded these subjects to refrain from it and set the age of fifty as the oldest a man could be at the time of engagement.[60]

Noting the incidence of female infanticide in its dominions, the crown outlawed this practice among its subjects,[61] although when read against the one hundred and ninety-odd orders pertaining to violence against nonhumans or *jīv haṃsyā*, the issuing of only three orders prohibiting female infanticide is revealing—saving animal lives was a much higher priority than saving female infants. Veering back to the welfare of its nonhuman subjects, the state ordered the punishment of anyone who failed to feed and take care of aging cattle and directed the local administrations of Nagaur and Merta towns to throw half a *man* (about twenty kilograms) of coarse *roṭīs* (bread) daily to stray dogs and five extra *sers* (almost five kilograms) of seed to pigeons.[62] It discouraged the chopping down of shade-giving trees.[63] Toward the sustenance of those whom it thought needed a helping hand, the crown ordered the daily scattering of grain for birds and ants as well as the distribution of food to mendicants and holy men, singling out members of the Vallabhite order (here, *viṭhalāṁ*) as beneficiaries of its largesse.[64] Of all these constituencies, it was animals who were the beneficiaries of the most zealous protection by the crown. The proclamations prohibiting female infanticide and the marriage of young girls to old men did not generate the mass of judicial and punitive activity that the stipulations about animal slaughter did.

Read in the context of the other laws with which they were laid down, the anti-animal slaughter rulings of the Rathor crown reflect the crown's adoption of the posture of a guardian of the "defenseless"—the elderly, women, animals, mendicants. For the Vaishnav Maharaja Vijai Singh and his largely merchant administrators, this quest to defend the defenseless achieved two goals. First, it idealized the ethical perspective and practices of the religious communities of which they were part—Vaishnav and Jain orders that held noninjury as an inviolable code. The state imposed as law upon all, and without any effort to dress as custom or precedent, merchants' particular caste and sectarian code of adherence to nonharm. Through this elevation to universal law, the effort to claim nonharm as a social ideal and a righteous path gained momentum. Second, as defenders of the defenseless and spokespersons for the voiceless, Vijai Singh, his merchant bureaucracy, and their merchant and brahman social allies earned moral capital. Adopting the role of virtuous protectors of the nonhuman subjects of the Rathor state provided the merchants in particular with the moral capital needed to justify their move from middling to the highest echelons of the region's social order. This moral capital also cut against the ethical stain of amassing wealth through the levying of interest and pushed against the shadows cast by getting rich literally at the expense of others. Central to the pursuit of a vegetarian body politic in Marwar was the overlap between mercantile communities and state power in early modern Marwar.

CASTE AND DIFFERENTIAL PUNISHMENTS

The Rathor state under the leadership of Vijai Singh, his successor Bhim Singh, and their merchant-administrators resolutely implemented its laws against animal slaughter. Yet, the handling of those accused of *jīv haṃsyā* was far from uniform. As also shown in the previous chapter's discussion of the punishments given to *thorīs*, *bāvrīs*, and Muslims, the state's response to the commission of violence against animals depended on the social location and the political clout of the person charged. In addition, district authorities, perhaps due to their ties of caste or acquaintance with the accused, would sometimes be more lax in their punishment of those accused of animal slaughter than the crown in Jodhpur. For instance, local authorities sentenced a brahman who was found guilty of slaying a large number of animals with the very light punishment of distributing fifteen rupees' worth of fodder among cows. When news of this reached the crown, officers Singhvi Motichand and Pancholi Fatehkaran commanded that the magistrate should reprimand those at the *kachaiḍī*, the governor's office, that let off the brahman with such a light fine and that it should impose a higher fine on the brahman.[65] At other times, crown officers too were willing to pardon offenders. Singhvi Tilokmal pardoned Charans Gordhan, Tejsi, and others of a village in Jaitaran for their involvement in a case of animal slaughter after they agreed to being roundly punished if they were ever involved in the crime again.[66] The state dropped allegations of drinking and meat eating (*mand mās vaprāyo*) against Mahajans Dunga and Dipa, discussed earlier, when they argued that the allegations were false and that the magistrate's men stationed at their houses as punishment had become a source of humiliation for them and the rest of the local mahajan community (*īṇ jāb bābat mārai ghare ādmī baiṭhāṇīyo chhai su īṇ bāt su mhā nai nyāt jāt mai chharā lāgai chhai*).[67]

In another episode, local authorities arrested a brahman for killing a snake in self-defense but he was released, at the crown's command, without punishment.[68] When the crown heard that some yogic ascetics (*svāmīs*) near the town of Kotda were continuing to hunt on the revenue-free lands (*sāsan*) that had been granted to them, it ordered an immediate end to this violation of its laws without ordering a punishment.[69] Another *svāmī* was able to convince the crown to order the return of a camel of his that had been confiscated by the governor of Phalodhi for his alleged involvement in animal slaughter.[70]

Mehra Godhu, of a merchant caste, was able to escape punishment for castrating a bull when he argued that the crown's newswriters had falsely implicated him due to the personal malice that they held toward him. In light of his service to the crown, and perhaps due to the doubt cast by his testimony upon the allegations against him, the crown dismissed the case against him.[71] In similar cases, charges were dropped against members of high-ranking or well-to-do communities.[72]

Often the crown's own rajput subordinates refused to comply with its orders outlawing animal slaughter. The state was appalled by the refusal of a *jāgīrdār* of a village in Nagaur to refrain from hunting despite the crown's directives outlawing it. It ordered the district's governor to explain this inaction by having each of his officers submit a separate report on the progress made toward getting the rajput to stop hunting.[73] Despite the crown's efforts to rectify the situation, it is worth noting that it did not explicitly order the *jāgīrdār*'s arrest. In a separate incident, upon discovering that a young rajput, the son of a Rathor, had killed a large number of animals in the countryside, the crown merely reiterated the strict and total application of its prohibition of animal slaughter.[74]

Elsewhere, in Didwana, the governor Pancholi Fatehkaran's son arranged for a fawn to be captured and kept as a pet for his amusement (*tathā itlāk naves ra kāgad su samāchār śrī hajūr mālam huvā hākam beṭā ramāvaṇ nu hīrṇī ro bacho mangāyo tho*). After a while, he grew tired of the fawn and threw it out, leaving the fawn to the fate of being eaten by dogs (*pachhai kiṇī kayo tarai kāḍh dīyo su hej līyo nahīṁ su mar gayo tathā kutai mārīyo*). When Asopa Surajmal, a brahman officer, got wind of this through a newswriter, he asked for a confirmation of whether this had indeed happened.[75] Yet, Asopa Surajmal did not punish the governor or his son for causing the fawn's death.

Faced with the disobedience of its own employees, the crown officers demanded explanations and, in some cases, commanded that they be punished. In Siwana district, the son of Sawaisingh Partapsinghot, a rajput landlord, continued to kill animals, despite a public recognition of the crown's prohibition of the practice. In spite of being repeatedly upbraided, the young rajput could not give up his taste for meat. When the crown discovered that, on the occasion of another rajput's visit, he had recently killed a deer, it ordered the immediate suspension of the payment of his father's salary.[76] In another episode, Bhandari Dayaldas ordered from the capital the immediate fining of four *jāgīrdārs* in Desuri whom the crown's newswriters observed to have hunted animals after the outlawing of animal slaughter.[77] Five years later, in 1782, the crown ordered the heavy fining of those of its *rajput* office-holders who were found to be capturing *raibārī* pastoralists' goats for slaughter.[78]

A *rajput* in Siwana lost his title (*paṭṭā*) to a village and had to pay a fine of a hundred rupees for killing an animal.[79] Other rajputs, this time in Desuri district, were fired from their posts as an inspector of weights and as a watchman, respectively, for killing animals.[80] In other cases, the Rathor crown insisted on fining or upbraiding more seriously rajput landholders whom the governor's office had failed to punish at all for the crime of animal slaughter.[81] The crown rued the lack of inquiry into a rajput's complicity in the killing of a deer in Maroth district, a crime that was discovered when the man charged with delivering the venison to the rajput's father was intercepted by the authorities.[82] Clearly, locally influential and landed rajputs continued to kill animals and eat meat, in spite of the crown's ban. This even included those rajputs who held the state-issued office of *jāgīrdār*.

It is possible that district officers simply hesitated to punish the powerful and the elite with whom they lived in daily proximity and with whom they had to work in order to effectively administer the territory. There are a number of cases, including some mentioned above, that show crown officers' frustration with district authorities' failure to prosecute rajput violators of the ban on animal slaughter. This is illustrated by a 1784 observation by the crown of the failure of local authorities to act on a complaint by the landlord of Bhakhri village in Parbatsar district. In it, the landlord (*bhomia*) of this village notified the governor when the village *jāgīrdār*, also a rajput, killed a pregnant deer (*gyābhṇī hirṇī mārī*) but the local authorities failed to pursue the matter.[83] The *jāgīrdār* of another village in the same district also slaughtered animals and then too, the case was dismissed without an inquiry.[84] In Siwana, when a dependent laborer (*hālī*) from a *jāgīrdār*'s estate killed an animal, the *jāgīrdār* evaded punishment by claiming that the servant had gone off to his natal village and having another rajput vouch for him.[85] The record is rife with other instances of the crown noting the local administration's failure to punish rajputs, including *jāgīrdārs*, for killing animals.[86] At other times, rajputs were able to convince even the crown to drop cases against them or to reduce the punishments.[87]

Other than fear of reprisals by locally powerful groups, local officials who bore the responsibility of implementing the ban on animal slaughter sometimes succumbed to inducements. In one case, a rajput managed to get away with a much lower fine than another rajput of equal standing by being willing to sell his winter and monsoon crops at a discounted rate to all the district officials.[88] Fined for killing an animal, the *jāgīrdār* of a village in Koliya district paid a bribe of twenty-five rupees to local officers and, as a result, was let off with a lower payment of fifteen rupees.[89] Fines in Marwar were decided in proportion to the gravity of the crime and the financial standing of the guilty. By that measure, this was a small amount for a landed person.

On other occasions, the perpetrators of violence against animals were beyond the punitive reach of the state. A rajput in Sojhat raided a village, carrying away forty animals into the fastness and killing eleven.[90] With the rajput raider already beyond its reach, the crown could do no more than issue a directive for the recovery of the raided pastoral wealth and for the punishment of the thieves. From Daulatpura district, a rajput *jāgīrdār* reported a raid on his village in which, apart from the theft of residents' belongings, an animal had been killed and carried off. Despite its desire to catch the killer of the animal, the crown under the circumstances could do no more than order his capture.[91]

Toward people of agriculturist and other middling castes who got caught up in accusations of animal slaughter, too, the local authorities were frequently quite lax in imposing punishment. It was only when the crown got wind of this that strict punishment was ordered. The governor summoned Jats Sukha and Jalap and a few of their caste fellows for castrating bulls, but due to the intervention of the employees of the village *jāgīrdār* in their favor, they were let off without any punishment.[92]

There were a few other cases from different districts in which *jāṭs* accused of *jīv haṃsyā* were not punished by district authorities, leading crown officers such as Pancholi Bansidhar to command immediate punishment of the guilty.[93] In 1784, district officers arrested but soon let off Mali Durga, of a peasant caste, who was involved in hitting a cow so hard that she aborted the fetus she was carrying.[94] In 1801, the governor of Desuri did not charge a *sirvī*, also of a peasant caste, despite his having killed a snake.[95] In all these cases, when crown officers discovered, through their newswriters, the laxity of the local authorities in prosecuting those guilty of hurting animals, they ordered the immediate punishment of all those who had committed the crime. The value of peasants as the agricultural backbone of the economy and the state's fisc likely prevented district administrators, whose offices were also involved in the collection of land revenue, from bearing down too hard on them for injuring animals. In any case, like the mahajans, peasant castes, particularly *jāṭs*, had come under the sway of Vaishnav sects and had largely embraced a vegetarian diet.[96] Most of the cases involving them entailed the injury of animals. In cases in which they were accused of taking animal lives, these appeared to be accidental killings.

In line with the value that the state ascribed to *jāṭs* and other peasant castes, occasionally, in response to petitioners pleading their innocence at the capital, crown officers would order district authorities to waive the fine. This is what happened in the case of Jat Godiya, whom a *ḍom* (drummer) named as being the one who had asked him to kill a goat. The drummer said that the *jāṭ* had commissioned a new drum to celebrate the birth of a son and that he killed the goat in the *jāṭ's* barn. When local authorities got wind of this, they arrested and interrogated the drummer. Since four *jāṭ* families had divided up the slain goat's hide among them, local authorities in Merta had fined them a total of ninety-five rupees. At Godiya's persistent petitioning—he appeared in Jodhpur twice in a span of four months—Muhnot Savairam and Pancholi Parsadiram ruled on behalf of the crown that all the accused were innocent. The goat had died due to the barn's roof collapsing upon it.[97]

The treatment of artisanal castes, those that fell under the ambit of "lowly" as chapter 2 showed, was entirely different. This underscores that the place of artisanal castes was distinct from and "lower" than professionally "peasant" castes such as *jāṭs* and *sirvīs*, even if artisans in the countryside may also have tilled land. The few members of artisanal and service castes who were caught on charges of animal slaughter were always punished. Unlike the many rajputs, brahmans, mahajans, and peasants who were accused of animal slaughter but managed to escape punishment through appeals, local ties, or bribes, the artisanal castes were largely unable to wiggle their way out of punishment. This was true even if the accusations against them stood on shaky ground. In 1782, a keeper of the crown's fodder supply, Charvadar Bakhtiya, falsely accused Nai (barber) Rodiya of having killed an animal as retaliation for the barber's having reported him to the crown for killing an animal. Before releasing him, a local official had the barber hung from a tree and flogged until his skin began to peel off. Meanwhile, the fodder keeper was arrested so that he could be forced to explain his lie, but he managed to sneak past the jail guards and escape from the fortress in which he was imprisoned.[98] Women of the salt-maker (*khārol*) caste, Ajbi and Khetudi of Pachpadra, cloth-printer Maniya of Nagaur, brewer Daliya of Parbatsar, carpenter Lavara of Maroth, oilpresser Kesariya of Sojhat, and a tailor from Sojhat were all fined in different orders for their involvement in injuring animals (*jīv haṃsyā*).[99]

Jagris Jodhiya and Kusyala, of a caste of musicians, were arrested by the Pali magistrate for eating meat at the house of Patar (courtesan) Ramba. The meat had been brought by a rajput, Bhati Bhabhut Singh, of a village in Bikaner. There is no mention of how the rajput was treated, but the Patar's male caste fellows, the *jāgrī* men listed above, found themselves in jail. In response to a petition submitted by another *pātar*, Jiu, the crown's officers ordered the men's release on submitting an undertaking (*muchalkā*) to never eat meat again. Of these, the tailor was fined for selling a herd of goats to a butcher. Some of them petitioned the crown for a reduction of the fine since it was too heavy for them to pay. An exception to this pattern is a single case in which Bhandari Dayaldas and Mumhta Bhavanidas pardoned a group of oilpressers, textile-printers, and cotton-ginners for killing animals, identifying all of these as titleholders of land.[100]

For those who belonged to leatherworking, sweeping, and "*achhep*" castes, an allegation of *jīv haṃsyā* translated automatically into punishment, typically fines but in some instances imprisonment or corporal punishment too. Sometimes, the crown even concluded that the fine originally imposed was insufficient and that it be raised. Even as leatherwork continued due to the availability of skins from animals that died of natural causes or disease, it became fraught with risk due to the looming possibility, especially for skinners, of being accused of having killed the animal whose hide they were treating. The governor of Daulatpura district imprisoned for four months and slapped with a large fine of twenty-five rupees leatherworker Balai Natha and his sister's son, but he only fined and did not imprison the others accused of animal slaughter with them.[101] In another case, the crown demanded a higher fine than the ten *annas* (less than a rupee) each that the governor's men had imposed on the leather-working *meghvāls* of Sojhat for eating meat.[102] It also ordered the punishment of leather-working Balai Dala for hitting a pregnant buffalo so hard that she aborted her fetus.[103] Muhnot Savairam and Pancholi Parsadiram ordered that a *khaṭīk* (butcher) of Didwana be fined for *jīv haṃsyā*.[104]

A *ḍheḍh* (also a leather-working caste) from Maroth killed an animal and ran away for fear of the punishment. The rajput *jāgīrdār* of the village arrested the *ḍheḍh's* son and handed him over to the district governor, using this service to the crown as grounds to demand the canceling of outstanding summons against his subordinates.[105] A *bhaṅgī*, unnamed, of Jodhpur district was arrested and beaten for his involvement in *jīv haṃsyā*.[106] District officers fined a *jhāḍūkas*, another name for the caste of *bhaṅgīs*, twelve rupees for killing an animal.[107] By way of comparison, seven rupees was the monthly salary of a clerk in the magistrate's office. A brahman accused Balai Hira of stabbing his cow, for which Pancholi Fatehkaran and Lakhotiya Suratram, a Maheshwari mahajan, ordered that the leatherworker be properly fined.[108] As the previous chapter showed, for other castes elsewhere deemed "achhep" or Untouchable—*thorīs*, *bāvrīs*, and Muslims—this effort to protect nonhuman lives resulted in banishments, dispossession, and criminalization. In the case of the "Untouchable" then, there were no instances of a reduction of punishment at the hands of the crown, unlike many examples of just such an action for merchants, brahmans, and rajputs.

The ban on animal slaughter was the one ethical pursuit that the Rathor state and its Vaishnav-Jain officers sought to enthusiastically impose upon all. Even as Vijai Singh and his Rathor administrator announced bans on brewing and drinking liquor, gambling, and abortion, those prohibitions were generally imposed most enthusiastically among members of the very castes that made up the leadership of the state. The ban on animal slaughter on the other hand was pursued, this chapter and the previous one have argued, with immense vigor with respect to all subjects. Vijai Singh was not the first king to embrace or prescribe vegetarianism in South Asian history, but he may have been the first one to use the coercive and surveillance powers of his state to ensure adherence to a code of animal protection. In this, his merchant officers were not just passive instruments for the channeling of the top-down ethical vision of the king. Their own ethical codes and ideals emphasized the practice and preaching of nonharm beyond their own sect and caste. As indicated by merchant and brahman communities' policing, through intra-caste mechanisms as well as the state, of their own members' adherence to vegetarianism and nonharm, the merchant and brahman officers of the Rathor state were deeply invested in pursuit of these virtues. Their active role, as state officers, in the imposition of these values upon those whose caste codes did not prescribe vegetarianism or nonharm, can be read as an effort to align their larger ethical vision with the world around them. Rather than reading Vijai Singh's effort to save the lives of moths, snakes, and pests as a curious and anomalous chapter in South Asian history, the role of his merchant officers in the practice and implementation of these laws suggests that these developments were in fact related to a new ethical orientation of the Rathor state. This new ethical orientation in turn was the product of increasing cohesion between courtly rajputs, such as Maharaja Vijai Singh, and the world of merchants.

6

Austerity

The constitution of the Hindu caste body entailed a reconstitution of the self through a regime of bodily discipline centered on austerity. As they accumulated wealth and power, Vaishnav and Jain merchant castes fused their ethical perspectives and bodily practices with currents within brahmanism and popular devotionalism that also celebrated asceticism, including an emphasis on nonviolence. Sectarian Vaishnavism, including that of the Vallabhites, and most Jain orders prescribed an austere life and a lack of attachment to sensory pleasure even as they encouraged large and conspicuous expenditure and lavish worship at temples and religious festivals. In the Jain perspective, at least, to practice its austere codes was in itself a type of war, a war upon one's ego, base desires, and worldly attachments. This is why the figures most revered by the Jains were the *tīrthaṅkars*, who were considered to be victors, commanding effective sovereignty upon their own bodies and inner selves.

The eighteenth-century alignment of historical factors in Marwar—an enthusiastic Vaishnav king and his consort and a body of politically and socially influential Vaishnav-Jain merchants and brahmans—drew the state into generalizing an ethic of austerity and even more so, as chapters 4 and 5 argued, nonviolence upon its subjects. Merchant and brahman castes were the only ones among the Rathor state's subjects to also police themselves in order to effect greater conformity with an ethical code emphasizing vegetarianism, teetotalism, and a "vice"-free life.

Marwar's mahajans converted their position of immense influence in Marwar into local power. As they jockeyed to cement their place among the "old order" elites of Marwar—the rajputs and brahmans, who derived their status from land and ritual power, respectively—they did so while aspiring to a life of austere domesticity. Under Vijai Singh and his successor, Bhim Singh, both Vaishnav kings, Marwar saw the imposition of kingdom-wide, universal bans on injury to nonhumans, brewing and drinking liquor, and gambling. In these same decades, the Rathor state worked to punish those involved in "illicit" sex and one of its consequences, abortion. It attempted to impose a code of chastity, channeling sexual activity into wedlock. With the exception of the ban on animal slaughter, which was imposed with vigor on all subjects, it was members of Vaishnav and Jain merchant communities who received the most attention from state-imposed efforts to cultivate through these laws a virtuous body politic. Vaishnav and Jain merchant state officers perhaps were most invested in disciplining their own caste fellows—men and women—in order to create and preserve distinction from the mass of those below. As they sought to join the old guard of elites and mark off a new elite domain, of the Hindu, of which they were part, they used state machinery to forge a connection between austerity, a denial of sensory pleasure, and virtue on the one hand and being Hindu on the other.

Scriptures of the Shvetambar Jain community, the sect to which the Osvāl Jains belonged, emphasized asceticism not only for monks but also imbued the lay path heavily with ascetic values. By the thirteenth century, an extensive literature laid out the duties and obligations of the Jain layman. The Five Lesser Vows expected of laymen, paralleling the Five Great Vows expected of the Jain ascetic, emphasized nonviolence, honesty, chastity, abstention from stealing, and nonattachment to worldly possessions. Since the measures to which monks went to adhere to values like nonviolence were too much to expect from laity, the expectations of lay followers were lesser. With respect to nonviolence, lay Jains were to avoid all unnecessary destruction of life forms. An important means of achieving this end was the avoidance of those occupations that entailed injury to living beings, such as farming and animal husbandry. Historians frequently cite this as an explanation for why Jains became concentrated in the professions of trade and moneylending.[1]

Vis-à-vis chastity, the norms for lay Jains prescribed restriction of sexual activity to within wedlock and prescribed monogamy.[2] The ideal lay Jain was to curb his sex drive and, if possible, renounce all sexual activity after the birth of a son who could inherit his business.[3] It is important to note here that these were normative prescriptions and also that even at the level of prescription, Jain monastic authors made room for lay followers to adapt to local custom (*deśācāra*). Historical evidence, in manuscript illustrations and inscriptions, often depicts Jain male donors with more than one wife, suggesting that Jain laymen practiced polygyny.[4] This makes the drive among mahajan caste groups in eighteenth-century Marwar to enforce adherence among their members all the more remarkable.

Nonattachment to worldly possessions translated for lay Jains into an exhortation to live simply and expend all surplus wealth in religious and charitable giving.[5] Other prescriptions emphasized fasting on holy days. Monastic preaching and didactic literature circulated these values among lay Jains. Needless to say, then as now, lay Jains may not have adhered strictly to all of these ethical prescriptions. Yet, lay Jains subscribed to these values in principle and strove to enact their "correct ethical dispositions" through such public acts as religious gifting, community participation, and a pursuit of correctness in business and familial affairs.[6]

For Jain and Vaishnav merchants, *ābrū* or reputation had implications not only for their standing within the community of Jains but also their creditworthiness. This reputation was based on correct behavior, or public conformity with expectations of Jain laymen, which in turn was an index of inner piety. Simplicity, strict vegetarianism, temperance, generous gifting for one's religious sect, and carefully regulated marriage alliances were among the behaviors that bestowed a good reputation upon a Jain merchant. Religious giving entailed the construction and maintenance of temples and libraries and the financing of communal festivals.[7] Expenditures in pursuit of the collective goals of one's religious community then helped to transform money into spiritual and social credit.[8] To that extent, the cultivation of virtue was directly related for the Vaishnav and Jain merchant to business success and power within the local community.

Jains were divided by the mendicant lineage to which their caste bore ritual affiliation. These divisions could be deep enough, such as those between Digambars and Shvetambars, to prevent their members from uniting in a single *saṅgh* (assembly). Generally, leadership of a town's Jain *saṅgh* and of mercantile associations such as a *mahājan* in Gujarat was bestowed upon the most prosperous man in their midst. This was because Jains considered business success an index of moral worth. In seventeenth-century Gujarat, the merchant magnate Virji Vora (d. 1675) was also the head of the order of lay Jains (*saṅghpati*) in the port of Surat.[9] Another magnate and a specialist in jewels and moneylending, Shantidas Jhaveri (d. 1660) of Ahmedabad, was very close to Mughal emperors Jahangir and Shahjahan. The wealth, business networks, and political connections he cultivated were eventually inherited by his grandson, Khushalchand. In 1725, the merchants of Ahmedabad bestowed on Khushalchand the hereditary office of *nagarśeṭh* (literally, "Chief of the City") of Ahmedabad in 1725.[10] In their time, both Virji Vora and Shantidas Jhaveri also exercised tremendous influence in the Shvetambar communities that they were part of. As active participants in the world around them and as mobile people, merchants would also have been exposed to Persianate ethics of balance and self-control, which too impinged on the body. In that sense, the investment in the body as a site of ethical cultivation was a marker of elite identity across early modern South Asia.[11] The Jain *saṅgh* and its leaders played an active role in directing their community toward moral uplift, which also could manifest itself in other ways beyond the body, such as saving the lives of animals and other nonhuman creatures.

MERCANTILE ETHICS AND ANIMAL PROTECTION

As wealthy members of society and at the very heart of the administration of the Rathor state, merchants in Marwar were able to elevate into universally applicable law what had until then been their caste *dharma*, as I discussed in greater detail in chapter 4. While the strict requirement to adhere to noninjury in Jainism is known, the association between Vaishnav identity and sworn vegetarianism was also a strict one. The *MVSK*, part of the history of the Rathors commissioned by Maharaja Mansingh in the early nineteenth century, draws a connection between Vijai Singh's shift of allegiance to the Vallabhite order and his outlawing of butchery and alcohol consumption. In the very next statement, mentioned in chapter 1, after noting that in 1765 Vijai Singh "accepted the [Vaishnav] Gusains," the *MVSK* says: "*Kasāīvāḍo mane huvo. Sehar meṁ dārū manē huvo* (Slaughterhouses were forbidden. Alcohol was forbidden in the towns)."[12] Elsewhere too, while praising the prosperity achieved by Vijai Singh, the *MVSK* notes: "*mhārāj to bhagatī rai bas hoy śrījī rī sevā kare su kasāīvāḍo meṭ dīyo* (the Maharaja is serving the Lord under the influence of *bhakti* and has eradicated slaughterhouses)."[13]

In 1786, Singhvi Bhimraj, the Osvāl Jain courtier very close to Maharaja Vijai Singh and his beloved consort, Gulab Rai, who was serving at the time as the *bakhśī* or head of military matters in Marwar, issued a command to the governor of Jodhpur. Apart from demonstrating the hand of a Jain mahajan in guiding the "nonviolent" posture of the crown, the order also shows the naturalized association between Vaishnav affiliation, the protection of animal lives, and vegetarianism:

> A goat died in Rajput Hara's home in Nev village and the family threw the carcass to a camel. A swami used to live on Hara's estate as a *hālī* (a laborer in debt) but the two fell out. The swami came to the *kachaiḍī* (district governor's office) to report that the rajput had killed the goat. In response, the *kachaiḍī* conducted an investigation and the crown issued a *sanad*. Now, the *jāgīrdār* of Nev has appealed to the crown again, vouching for the rajput's innocence and saying, "The swami is lying. The rajput's family have been devotees of Shri Thakurji (Krishna) for two generations. They are Vaishnavs ("*tulchhī*") and have taken a vow to refrain from meat-eating ("*mās ro sūṃs chhai*"). The entire village can testify to this." Dismiss the earlier judgment by the order of Shri Hajur.
>
> —*Duvāyatī* Singhvi Bhimraj[14]

Singhvi Bhimraj's order not only demonstrates that Vaishnav affiliation served as evidence of adherence to vegetarianism but also that even some families of rajput landholders in rural Marwar had started to join Vaishnav sects. In this historical setting—that is, given just how widespread Vaishnav and Jain affiliation was among the region's elites—the pursuit of a vegetarian body politic was not a unilateral imposition by the Vaishnav Maharaja Vijai Singh or his successor Bhim Singh upon their subject body. This policy enjoyed the enthusiastic support of powerful constituents of state and society: merchants and brahmans as already demonstrated and some rajputs too. Manning the highest echelons and the rank and file of the Rathor state, these wealthy and influential sections of the Marwari populace may well have even initiated the strict enforcement of a ban on animal slaughter. For the sections that rallied behind the crown's campaign against animal slaughter were the same groups that were either Vaishnav or Jain. These Vaishnav and Jain merchants and their brahman allies had been driving the Rathor state toward the policing of the boundaries of their Hindu community, as I have shown in chapters 2 and 3. Among the Jains at least, the most prosperous and therefore most honorable merchants in the locality were also holders of moral authority. As leaders of local mercantile caste councils, they were in charge of not only enforcing business norms and regulating relationships but also directing the ethical life of the community.[15]

An indicator of the self-imposed nature of nonviolence and vegetarianism among mahajans and brahmans is that cases of animal slaughter in which they figured drew in not only the state but also played out in their local caste councils. For instance, Mahajan Dipa cited the humiliation caused to his local caste group (*nyāt*) by allegations of eating meat and drinking against him and his family.[16] Put another way, merchant castes were so associated with vegetarianism and teetotalism that if even one of their members violated this code, this would be an aberration that drew attention from the local community. Conformity to these codes became linked with family and caste honor, such that a member of the merchant caste eating meat brought humiliation to the entire community of merchants. No doubt, the merchant community applied social pressure and tools of caste-based discipline to keep their members in line with a life-preserving ethic. In another instance, a mahajan's neighbors started to harass him after two other mahajans accused his wife of regularly being involved in animal slaughter.[17] The accused mahajan woman was put through an ordeal (*dhīj*) and emerged innocent but the district administration still declared her guilty.[18] It was after this that Mahajan Dipa's neighbors started to harass his family by digging a pit next to his front door, to obstruct free passage in and out of the house.[19] When it rained, the pit would collect water, weakening the foundation of the Dipa's house. Helpless, the mahajan finally turned to the crown in Jodhpur for help, winning an order from Singhvi Motichand, Pancholi Fatehkaran, and Asopa Fatehram that commanded the district governor to fill up the pit and punish the officer who had wrongly sentenced the mahajan's wife.[20]

The crown's involvement, however, was insufficient in preventing the local caste group's harassment of Mahajan Dipa and his family. A year later, in 1789, he petitioned the crown once more. Perhaps emboldened by the crown's support, he reported that now officers from the local magistracy—which officer lists reflect at the time as being mostly mahajans—had demolished a platform (*chaukī*) that had always stood before the entrance to his home. They would not let him rebuild it unless he had a deed (*paṭṭā*) for the platform registered in his name. Mahajan Dipa pointed out that there was no custom of requiring a *paṭṭā* for the platform that people often had outside their houses. Once more, the crown, represented by Bhandari Dayaldas and Pancholi Fatehkaran, responded sympathetically, asking for an explanation from the local authorities as to why they had not implemented the earlier order and instructing them to only charge the mahajan for registering the platform to his name if they did so with others' platforms.[21] As with many cases in the *Jodhpur Sanad Parwāna Bahī* records, we do not know how this case was eventually resolved, but regardless of the outcome it is possible to say that for merchants, accusations of animal slaughter were sufficient to merit relentless social pressure, even harassment in some cases, from their caste fellows. Local administrators, many of whom were mahajans themselves, aided mercantile castes' efforts to discipline their members into resolute vegetarianism. The association between merchant caste identity and the practice of nonharm was already in place by the eighteenth century.[22]

A similar pattern can be observed among brahmans too. When Brahman Nihala was accused of killing many animals, his local caste group expelled him in 1786. This punishment exceeded even that imposed by the state, which was the payment of a very small fine to the governor's office, the *kachaiḍī*. Some of his caste fellows made an attempt to reintegrate him into the caste as long as he atoned by making a pilgrimage to the river Ganga, leading other caste fellows to appeal to the crown for an intervention to prevent Brahman Nihala's reintegration into the caste.[23] While neither side disagreed that the killing of animals was a grave crime, they did not see eye-to-eye on whether expiation absolved the guilty brahman of his sins.

Elsewhere, the caste fellows of Brahman Chatra, of Badu village in Parbatsar district, expelled him from their caste for his son's unintentional killing of an animal. In order to engineer a return into the caste fold, the brahman hosted a communal feast (*jīmaṇ*) for all of his caste fellows from twenty-five villages.[24] The issue was a fractious one and not everyone was in the mood to forgive. Caste members from roughly seven villages refused to partake of the feast, thus formally withholding their assent to the effort to reintegrate Chatra into the brahman caste. Under pressure from this faction, the brahman family whose daughter was engaged to Chatra's son broke off the engagement and married the girl to someone else. Chatra was in the midst of a social boycott. Refusing to accept this fate, Chatra petitioned the crown for help, citing an ongoing feud with his brother Jiva as an excuse and saying it was this that led his son to unintentionally kill the animal in the first place.

Pancholi Fatehkaran, on behalf of the Rathor crown, did not adjudicate the dispute but referred it back to the local brahman caste council for resolution. What the council did was to command the holding of an even larger convention of the brahman caste, gathering the heads of brahman castes of fifty-two villages in the area to adjudicate the dispute. The crown declared that it would uphold whatever conclusion this caste convention reached.[25] As is common with cases in the *bahīs*, we do not know how the case played out and what the supra-local caste convention decided, but this episode makes clear that brahmans, like merchants, were on board with a stance of noninjury toward all nonhuman life.

LIQUOR

It was not just meat but alcohol too that was deemed off-limits in late eighteenth-century Marwar. From at least 1770, the Rathor state outlawed the general production and sale of alcohol. Liquor was now only to be consumed with royal permission and there are a few instances of such permission being granted even in this time of general prohibition.[26] The quest for vegetarianism and temperance were intertwined, as reflected in state orders that bundle the two issues together. In 1784, the crown's newswriters informed it that they had found evidence of animal slaughter and the existence of breweries (*dārū rī bhaṭī*) in the vicinity of the border region of Ghanerao.[27] The crown immediately ordered its administrators at the nearest district headquarters, in Desuri, to make special arrangements there to put an end to these practices.[28] Seventeen years later, in 1801, officers in Jodhpur were still dispatching orders to enforce the ban across the kingdom. They sent out a decree to all of Marwar's district headquarters stating:

- There should be no animal slaughter (*jīv haṃsyā*). Prevent the butchers (*kasāīs*) from practicing their trade. Have them sign an undertaking (*muchalkā*).
- Do not allow the sale of alcohol without a permit. Get the brewers (*kalāls*) to sign an undertaking committing to this.

  Enforce this in the towns. For the villages in the district, dispatch *parvānās* (written orders) bearing these commands. These practices should cease everywhere. Whoever continues with them will be punished and fined to ensure that they never repeat these again.[29]

Similarly, in 1793, when the crown received reports that the governor of Didwana had permitted the brewers in his jurisdiction to sell alcohol (*dārū*), it threatened him with severe punishment if such a report ever surfaced again. It ordered him to explain himself in writing and to fine the brewers who had gone ahead with defying the crown's ban on the sale of alcohol.[30]

Articulating a felt connection between the two "crimes," in 1801, an unnamed crown officer reprimanded the subordinates of the governor of Daulatpura district for defying crown orders banning animal slaughter (*jīv haṁsyā*) and drinking. These men—the *kilādār* (fortkeeper) and the *faujdār* (the district's military chief), both rajputs, and a servant (*chākar*) of unidentified caste—had gotten drunk and indulged in revelry (*fitur* and *matvāl*) right in front of the fort's gate.[31] Crown officers heard of this misbehavior directly from their newswriters and demanded an explanation for this open disregard for its laws, that too by its own officers. The crown instructed in the same order that the Daulatpura governor should put an end to the sale of alcohol in the butchers' quarter (*kasāīvāḍā*) in the town, suggesting that at least in Daulatpura at the time, not just meat but also alcohol could be obtained from butchers.[32] When notified of yet another instance of its officers, all nonmahajans, defying the ban on alcohol, the crown bunched its response to the report of drinking with one concerning animal slaughter.[33]

The prohibition of violence upon animals, then, was part of the same moral regime in early modern Marwar that proscribed the consumption of alcohol. In both cases, the state elevated the ethical injunctions embraced by particular castes, in particular, merchants and brahmans, to the status of universal law. That is, the taking of animal lives and the production and consumption of liquor were now banned in the entire kingdom. The expectation of adherence to these laws from all subjects was a departure from the prior practice of upholding custom that varied among castes and localities. At the same time, the implementation of these laws was not uniform. In the case of gambling, drinking, and abortion, the state decreed universal bans but in practice largely pursued adherence from members of mercantile and brahman castes. When it came to protecting animal lives, the state did punish all violators of the ban on animal slaughter. Still, as chapter 4 showed, punishments for animal slaughter varied by caste and some were punished far more harshly than others.

These orders are quite remarkable for a state in which monarchical authority lay with a rajput and in which rajputs remained a powerful force as landed chiefs and military rank holders. This is because rajputs had long been associated with a culture of hunting, meat eating, and liquor consumption. There is plenty of evidence of the rajputs' involvement in hunting from paintings commissioned by kings and nobles. Paintings depicting the rajput noble or king out for a hunt date back to at least the seventeenth century.[34] Such visual depictions continued to be produced in Marwar even in Vijai Singh's reign, that is, in the same decades that the Rathor state was waging a war on animal slaughter. In Vijai Singh's reign, these depictions, however, were generally produced by smaller *ṭhikāṇās* or seats of rajput lords in Marwar rather than by the Rathor ruling family at Jodhpur or the leading lineages at court.[35]

In addition, rajputs had since the medieval period venerated the Devi (Goddess), whether as Durga or in the form of the many female deities associated either with rajput clans (*kul devīs*) or with the land. The worship of these devis involved the ritual slaughter of animals such as goats or buffaloes, sacrifices made as offerings to appease the goddess. At the same time, the ritual practice surrounding many of these goddesses was itself in a process of transition in the course of the early modern period, with a shift away from blood sacrifice and toward the offering of foodstuffs and flowers. At the same time, it is unclear how far along such a shift was in Marwar by the mid-eighteenth century. Evidence from painting suggests that in at least some parts of Marwar, the ritual offering of blood sacrifice to the Goddess remained in practice and that rajput lords remained patrons of this practice.[36] As indicated by an order discussed above—the one centered on a rajput family that claimed Vaishnav affiliation as proof of their innocence when charged with the killing of a goat—this was a time of change even among rajputs as a caste group. That is, many rajputs had become Vaishnav, some taking formal initiation into sects such as the Vallabh Sampraday of which Majaraja Vijai Singh and a large number of the region's merchants were part. It is difficult to say if these Vaishnav rajputs immediately abandoned the killing of animals, whether for food or as ritual sacrifice to deeply revered goddesses. But by taking allegiance as Vaishnavs, they would certainly have sworn to refrain from animal slaughter and meat eating.

Still, it is clear that whether they became Vaishnav or not, rajputs were a wrinkle in the Rathor state's plan to impose vegetarianism and animal protectionism across its domain. From the outset, as demonstrated above in cases involving mostly rajputs, its own district officials defied the crown's attempt to impose prohibition within its domain. Some of these were errant mahajans too. The earliest reference in the *Jodhpur Sanad Parwāna Bahīs* to prohibition in Marwar is from 1771. In that year, the crown's newswriters informed it that at a celebration at the house of the treasurer (*kārkūn*) of Phalodhi district, rajput and *sunār* (goldsmith) women sang songs and, a few days later, drank the alcohol that the *kārkūn* served them in return for their services. The crown demanded that all the local officers send in a report explaining their version of this event.[37]

At other times, it was not district officers but the people in their jurisdiction who violated the ban on drink. In 1772, the crown's newswriters brought reports of the people of Nagaur drinking alcohol while celebrating the spring festival of Holi. The crown asked the administrators of the town to explain why they allowed this violation of the kingdom's laws.[38] Holi clearly occasioned much merriment, and in the same year an armored soldier (*silhaipos*) in another town, Bilada, asked the local governor for some alcohol on the occasion of the festival. Instead of procuring the alcohol under state supervision from the brewers' homes, the soldier had his subordinates bring it directly and drank it. Even as the governor denied granting them the permission to do this, the crown ordered him to investigate how such a flagrant infringement of state laws could occur in his jurisdiction.[39]

In another episode, the crown's newswriters informed it in 1772 of the drunken carousing that the sons of two high-ranking officers in Jalor, along with a *mutsaddi* (clerk), had indulged in while on their way to attend the annual fair of Mahadevji Jalandharji. Jalandharji, or Jalandar Nath, was a legendary figure revered by Jalor-based yogis and their followers. On their way back to Jalor, they invited some courtesans (*pātarīyāṁ*) along and the party entered the town singing. Appalled, the crown asked for a detailed report of the entire matter, trying to ascertain exactly who among the many officers involved was to blame.[40] Once more, records do not reflect how this matter was resolved. Low-ranking state employees too broke the law against drinking and paid a price for it. Barber (*nāī*) Nagla, a soldier in the *darogā*'s troop, molested a woman and struck a leatherworker (*meghvāl*) with a sword after getting drunk. For this he was fired.[41]

Sometimes different wings of district administrations could get caught up in a conflict over implementing the ban on drinking. In 1774, a brewer from a village in Parbatsar faced the wrath of a local rajput landholder for refusing to set up a brewery (*dārū rī bhaṭī*) for him. The brewer was seeking to comply with the royal prohibition (*iṇ bāt rī śrī darbār rī manāī hai*) on producing alcohol. In retaliation, the landlord, a *jāgīrdār* or holder of state-bestowed rights in land, confiscated the brewer's livestock, leading the brewer to turn to the governor for justice. Despite the governor's order commanding the landlord to return the brewer's animals to him, the *jāgīrdār* refused to comply. The brewer then approached the crown for help. In response to his petition, the crown instructed the governor to ensure that the *jāgīrdār* returned the brewer's livestock.[42]

It is unclear if the brewer was able to win his livestock back, but the episode demonstrates the fissures within district and local administrative orders that could arise over the implementation of crown laws. It also shows the recognition by some ordinary subjects of the risks of defying crown laws and, stemming from this, their compliance with these laws even in the face of extreme retaliation by local overlords. That said, the Rathor crown in Jodhpur sought to punish every instance of defiance of the ban on drinking not only by ordinary subjects but also by its officers, most of the defiant ones in the case of liquor being rajputs.

Why did the Rathor state outlaw drinking within its domain? I suggest that the royal position on the issue, emanating from Vijai Singh's effort to craft a new kingly profile as a devout Vaishnav, aligned with the moral preoccupations of the crown's mercantile subjects and officers. Both gambling and drinking had long carried unwholesome connotations, reflected in the prohibitions that various religious codes, including those of Islam, Vaishnavism, Shastric brahmanism, and Jainism, placed upon these "vices." Historically, however, membership of these religious communities did not necessarily translate into a resolute adherence to temperance. Rather, the relationship between ethico-legal injunctions and practice varied tremendously over time and place and from person to person.

Among merchants in eighteenth-century Marwar, both of the religious orders that they were most drawn to, Krishna-centered Vaishnav sects and Jainism, were firmly opposed to drinking. In this, they sharply distinguished themselves from Shaiva and tantric practice, in competition with whom the *bhakti* mode had arisen, whose very ritual entailed the consumption and offering to the deity of alcohol. The declaration and enforcement of a ban on liquor by royal fiat upon an entire society, as it occurred in Marwar, is notable then for its strict imposition of the ethical principles of particular religious communities upon all. It is also significant that this proscription aligned with attitudes toward alcohol that were dominant among particular castes, especially merchants.

Just as with vegetarianism, merchants and brahmans imposed abstinence from alcohol upon their own caste fellows. If members of these communities violated the ban on drinking, it was not just the state but also their own local caste councils that would punish them. In 1786, the community of Shrimali brahmans of a few villages in Siwana became polarized into factions on the question of how to deal with their caste fellow, Anop, a drinker. The dispute escalated all the way to capital, Jodhpur, as we know from this command issued in 1789:

> [To the Siwana governor's office] Sirimali brahmans Sivlal, Devram, Kheta, and Bakhta of Sivanchi village submitted an appeal: "Sirimali Anop drinks alcohol. This caused conflict in our local caste group (*nyāt*). We sent our payment of thirty rupees toward the *mārkhāī* cess with the Chakar Bhaira who works there and had the

> matter addressed. Anop was caught in the act of drinking. Anop's niece, his brother Daulatram's daughter, was about to get married when our caste fellows said we won't let anyone attend the celebratory feast (*jīmaṇ*) the family will host. For two–three days, no one was able to attend. But after that, Anopa and the Sirimalis of the caste sat down together and ate. Now they have expelled us from the caste. This section of the caste has in this way eaten with a fallen (*bīṭalyoḍā*) brahman. This is wrong." The order is: If this is what happened, once it is proven that Anopa drank, then fine him roundly. In future, do as is customary (*sirasto*) in their local caste group. If these brahmans ate with Anopa even after knowing that he had been expelled, then look into this matter. Such a deed should never be done again. If this is not what happened then each of the officers there should separately send in a report.
>
> —By the order of Singhvi Motichand[43]

Four Shrimali brahman men, in their determination to have a caste fellow punished for being a drinker, ganged up, paid thirty rupees of extra tax to win the support of local administrators, and managed to catch him in the act of drinking. They then tried to engineer a boycott of a feast hosted by the accused brahman Anopa's family, an action whose social meaning was the excommunication of Anopa and his family from the caste. The plan backfired and the men found themselves expelled instead. They turned to the crown in Jodhpur, whose officer, of a merchant caste, ruled that if Anopa had indeed drunk then he should have been boycotted, and that if other brahmans failed to boycott him knowing that he was a drinker, they deserved to be investigated. In practice, then, members of brahman communities were not united in a rigid imposition of temperance. Some could be willing to look the other way to a certain extent. The involvement of the state and the introduction and application of a state law banning drink, however, set in motion a new set of dynamics. The state, with its punitive capabilities of fines and arrests, became an added tool in the hands of those seeking a straight and narrow adherence to a "vice"-free life.

In this particular case, local authorities in Siwana next conducted an ordeal to try to resolve the matter but both sides were proven true. Anopa and his family were, as a result of the inconclusive ordeal, reincorporated into the local caste group. Secure in their position, they began to bully one of the men, Kheta, who had originally reported Anopa, disrupting his interactions with other caste fellows. They were so persistent that this bullied brahman approached the crown in 1789, three years after he had first petitioned it regarding the matter.[44] While the petitioner won the crown's sympathy yet again, the case demonstrates that among brahmans, the consumption of alcohol was considered in principle a violation severe enough to result in expulsion from the caste. In Anopa's case, most of his caste fellows decided to let the matter of his drinking pass, but had they all formally accepted his guilt, the norms within their community would have demanded Anopa's expulsion from the caste group. It was not the question of whether alcohol consumption was wrong that divided the Shrimali brahmans of Nagaur, but whether to formally hold Anopa responsible for the lapse.

A similar acquiescence to the outlawing of liquor can be observed among those upwardly mobile communities that sought inclusion in the elite realm of the mahajans and brahmans. In 1776, the local caste group of goldsmiths (*sunārs*) in Phalodhi gathered and decided to fine fifteen of their caste fellows two hundred and twenty-five rupees for drinking. This group punishment was surely meant to set an example. The fifteen men then petitioned the crown for a discount on the fine, citing their inability to pay such a large sum, and managed to have it reduced to seventy-five rupees.[45] The goldsmiths, since at least the mid-eighteenth century, had been making a concerted effort to assert caste parity with the mahajans.[46] They fought for the right of their bridegrooms to lead their wedding processions astride horses, for their women to wear veils, and for their inclusion in communal rituals—all privileges that the mahajans enjoyed but tried to deny to the goldsmiths in order to preserve the exclusivity of the elite caste domain to which they aspired.

Apart from generalizing what had until then been an unevenly followed ethical prescription among some faiths and castes, the Rathor state's ban on liquor was an economic blow to the brewers (*kalāls*) of Marwar. Like butchers, they found their trade outlawed and the craft in which they were skilled no longer permissible. Risking punishment, some continued to brew and sell alcohol on the sly. And for doing so, some of them got caught. In 1786, the crown asked the governor's office in Merta to explain why it had permitted its brewers to resettle in the town when they had been expelled earlier for brewing alcohol (*kalālāṁ dārū kāḍhī thī*). It demanded a list of names of all the brewers involved, likely in order to follow up more effectively on the earlier command to remove them from Merta.[47]

Other brewers were more fortunate, ingeniously building on influential contacts and continued demand. Running a successful brewing business in these times, however, attracted the anger of those brewers who had complied with the law of the land. In 1789, all the brewers of Sojhat formed a delegation and petitioned the crown. They complained that despite the royal ban on alcohol, brewer Jairam had set up many breweries and also imported alcohol for sale in Marwar. All the local authorities in Sojhat had failed to prevent this. "All of us have turned to farming to earn a living. Despite his selling alcohol in a time of prohibition, why hasn't he been fined?" they asked. The crown instructed the governor of Sojhat to explain himself and to fine Jairam.[48]

The prohibition on the production and consumption of liquor in Marwar under Vijai Singh then was implemented in practice through arrests, fines, and banishments. The virtue of temperance was no longer just something to aspire to but rather required from all the residents of Marwar. Of course, even as there was a degree of enforcement of the law, it is likely that the brewing, sale, and consumption of liquor continued in those pockets and regions of Marwar in which the Rathor state's reach was not quite as deep. Compared to the mass of documentation generated by the quest to outlaw animal slaughter, the orders in pursuit of a sober subject body are fewer in number. This suggests that despite the multipronged nature of the quest to recast the markers of elite identity in Marwar, some efforts held higher priority than others. Still, the ban on drinking added to the stigmatization of liquor consumption and made the brewing of liquor, a skill generally commanded by a relatively "low" caste, a particularly risky activity.

GAMBLING

In the same decades, the Rathor crown also criminalized gambling (*juvai ramnā*). Unlike with Rathor efforts to enforce vegetarianism, which enveloped all subjects, it was mahajans who were prominent among those accused of gambling. In 1771, the Rathor crown reiterated to its administrators in Phalodhi an earlier order that banned gambling in all the kingdom's towns. It pressured the governor of Phalodhi to impose higher fines on anyone caught gambling, reprimanding it for lowering fines recently.[49] Mahajans are conspicuous in their centrality to cases of gambling.[50] In 1774, Mahajan Bhikha of Jalor petitioned the crown, saying that while he had been fined four and half rupees upon being caught gambling, the other mahajans who were caught with him were fined only one or two rupees each. Noting the baseless discrepancy, the crown ordered the magistracy in Jalor to give him a discount of two rupees on the fine.[51] The next year two Vaishnav devotees, Bhagats Chainram and Surdas, appealed to the crown for help when the magistracy in Merta fined them for gambling. They said that while they were on their begging rounds, they had merely sat with some mahajan boys who were gambling (*juvai ramtā thā*). The boys were about to give the devotees a few cowries in charity when the local authorities arrested the boys for gambling.

Later, the magistrate's man arrested the *bhagat* devotees too, accusing them of lending money to the mahajan boys so that the latter could gamble on their behalf (*īṇā nu rupīyā udhārā de nai tai juvai ramāyā chhai*). As punishment, the magistracy then canceled a debt of twenty-one rupees that a local mahajan owed the devotees and kept them under arrest for seven days. Sympathetic to the Bhagats' plight, the crown ordered the Merta magistracy to have the money that was due to them returned and to explain why it had treated them so harshly.[52] In other examples of gambling merchants running afoul of the state, in 1788, three mahajans and two brahmans got caught in Sojhat, and in Merta a handful of mahajans ran afoul of a local officer for gambling.[53]

It is noteworthy that the mahajans are predominant among those fined for gambling. In late eighteenth-century Marwar, the mahajans were among the few communities that had the quantum of wealth and skill with handling money to regularly gamble. Entrepreneurship and the handling of capital, that is, the mercantile trade, entailed the regular taking of risk. Investment and gambling then were not too far removed. Strands in mercantile caste cultures of western India may even have encouraged gambling and speculation and presented it as essential to their caste character, as the activities of the diaspora in the 1880s and 1890s indicate.[54] As Ritu Birla notes for the colonial context, the category "gambling" could be wrongly imposed upon forms of speculation and hedging associated with merchants of Marwari origin that had nothing to do with games of chance played for entertainment.[55] Based on the details available about the cases of gambling intercepted by agents of the Rathor state, however, it was not types of speculation, hedging, or betting (*saṭṭā*) that were illegal or unacceptable to this precolonial government. Rather, it was gambling as play (*juvai ramnā*)— keeping in mind that not insignificant sums of money could be at stake during such play—that was troublesome to a courtly elite looking to discipline its fellow "upright" merchants.

Due to the overlaps among entrepreneurship, moneylending, and speculation, merchants may have gambled more than their contemporaries from other walks of life and it is likely that this is why they got caught most often for it. Apart from being invested in disciplining their caste fellows, Rathor administrators may also have disciplined merchants more for the crime of gambling due to their ability to pay larger fines. However, when seen in the context of the larger campaign to target vice and cultivate virtue among mahajans, both self- and state-imposed, it is clear that money was not the main driver for the greater disciplining of merchants.

That the crown was especially concerned with mahajans gambling is shown by its laxer response to the few recorded instances of other communities' gambling. Leatherworker Chokhla, from a village in Nagaur, complained that he was among four men that Jat Naga, a farmer, gave money to gamble on his behalf. From the ones who lost money, Jat Naga extracted debt papers but soon ripped up, for unspecified reasons, these papers for all but the leatherworker. The crown ordered the governor to get the *jāṭ* to cancel the leatherworker's debt too since he had canceled everyone else's.[56] It did not discipline any of the men involved for gambling.

The merchants' wealth was accompanied by their indispensability to the crown's own functioning. They lent money to the crown, and royal indebtedness to individual mahajans quite frequently undercut its effort to penalize them. This happened in the case of Ami Khandelval, whom the governor of Merta fined a hundred and five rupees for gambling. In the span of a few months, Ami succeeded in having the crown instruct the district governor to reimburse the entire sum to him, alluding in the command to the ongoing "give-and-take" (*leṇ deṇ*) that the state had with Ami.[57] In another instance of this, the authorities in Sojhat punished three mahajans and two brahmans that they had caught gambling by confiscating the six rupees, sixty-one-and-a-half *ṭakās*,[58] and a handful of valuable goods that lay on the gambling table. The crown underscored to the governor the importance of making it clear to these men that they were never to gamble again and demanded that the money and goods be immediately dispatched to the central treasury, illustrating its interest in fines upon gambling as a source of income.[59] One of the implicated merchants, however, petitioned the crown for leniency, and within a few weeks the governor's office in Sojhat received an instruction to return all the money and valuables that it had earlier confiscated.[60]

Despite its intention to punish gambling with fines, the crown could also end up reversing district authorities' actions due to the political influence that some merchants could wield upon it. The effort to ban gambling then was an arena in which the dependence of the state upon mercantile capital played out. A shared moral disapproval of gambling gave the crown an opportunity to discipline and fine merchants even as its indebtedness to mercantile capital constrained its ability to effectively enact its punitive authority. Fines for violations of custom or law in Marwar were generally levied in proportion to the payee's economic standing.

Mahajans held sway over district administrative officers, aiding their ability to bypass the law against gambling. In 1788, while on his rounds (*chaukī phirtā*), a guard at the Merta magistracy, Sipahi Nivaj, caught some mahajans in the town gambling on one of the days leading up to the Diwali festival. He confiscated the money they had been gambling with and brought it to the magistracy. To his surprise, the magistrate refused to deposit the money in the magistracy, saying that gambling in the days before Diwali was permissible and that Nivaj had erred in confiscating the money. Nivaj returned the money to all but one of the mahajans since one of them had left by then. Accusing Nivaj of graft, the magistrate fined him a rupee, wrote to the governor's officers to lodge a complaint against him, and even before collecting the fine, fired Nivaj from service.

In his quest for justice, Nivaj petitioned the crown, relaying his side of the story and explaining that he was not at fault (*mho maiṁ chūk nahī*). While the crown ordered him reinstated to the rolls in Merta, it did not waive off his fine nor upbraid or punish the magistrate for his actions. The Merta magistrate's harsh actions against his junior employee on a dubious charge of graft could well have been triggered by Nivaj's temerity in confiscating money from a community as influential as the mahajans. The state's reluctance to disturb this status quo is indicated by the crown's refusal to confirm or deny the Diwali caveat to its ban on gambling that the magistrate may have summarily introduced while trying to protect the mahajans.[61]

Taken in isolation, the Rathor crown's drive against gambling and its particular targeting of men from merchant castes may appear to be a precolonial antecedent of the outlawing of gambling and indigenous forms of speculation witnessed under colonial rule in the late nineteenth and early twentieth centuries. But when read in the context of the wider efforts at producing an ethical body of merchant and brahman subjects, the penalization of gambling in Marwar appears to be a piece of the wider campaign of moral "uplift" that a Vaishnav king and his upwardly mobile Vaishnav-Jain merchant administrators sought to implement across the region.

Ascetic values, emphasizing a denial or limiting of sensory pleasures and the pursuit of a simple life, were what constituted this idea of virtue. This lends nuance to any simple association of Vallabhite practice with "*bhog*" or an indulgence of the senses. Rather, certain kinds of indulgences of the base passions were anathema to the Vaishnav-Jain mercantile milieu. This was not limited to such "illicit" indulgences as liquor, meat, and gambling but also to "excessive" sex, as the next chapter will show. A Vaishnav king and Vaishnav-Jain merchants raised the ethical imperatives of their sects to universal laws applicable to all in the domain. Yet, when it came to laws pertaining to drinking, gambling, and chastity, it was the merchants and brahmans who were the chief targets of the Rathor state's effort to craft a body of ethical subjects. As with meat eating, the adoption into universal law of these ethical codes idealized the caste groups, particularly merchants, that had already embraced them on their own. For religious communities, such as Shaivas and yogis, whose religious practice required the offering of liquor to the deity and its ritual consumption by devotees, these state-led changes restricted their ability to openly practice their faith. These changes also stigmatized the ritual practices of Shaiva, tantric, and devi-worshipping communities.

In their pursuit to move up in the world, it was not the mere emulation of brahmanical strictures of caste and ritual that the merchants brought to the eighteenth-century milieu in Marwar. Missing from a king- and text-centered history of Hindu-ness and of caste is the transformation of "brahmanical orthodoxy" or "brahmanism" itself. It was precisely in these centuries that ritual "purity" in brahmanical terms was recast in various sites to include an emphasis on a strict adherence to vegetarianism and the protection of nonhuman lives. In Marwar, this charge was led not by brahmans but by nonbrahmans, that is, merchants. Brahmans played an important but not leading role.

In addition, the body of documents generated by the effort to end animal slaughter in Marwar helps to fill in a gap in our understanding of legislation and legal culture in early modern South Asia. Farhat Hasan's exploration of the operation of the Mughal state as a legal order on the ground in seventeenth-century Gujarat made clear the involvement of local notables in the resolution of disputes and the practice of state law. Nandita Sahai has pointed to the bonds of dependence that could tie early modern kings to their productive subjects as well as the limits placed on sovereign action by the discourse of custom. By this point in this book, it will be clear that the making of new laws and the resolution of disputes began to be grounded in the eighteenth century in Marwar in the pursuit of particular ethical visions now deemed universal. While we know of laws pronounced by kings and emperors, Vijai Singh's Marwar offers us a detailed look at how the implementation of sovereign laws played out on the ground. What emerges is both a picture of governing through consensus, as with the region's elite, but also one of imposing laws through coercion.

The degree to which the Rathor state intervened in the moral lives of its subjects has few precedents in South Asian history. One of these is the neighboring kingdom of Amer (Jaipur) under Jai Singh II (r. 1699–1743).[62] The Peshwa's government in the western Deccan during the eighteenth century is another example of an interventionist state policing the moral lives of its subjects.[63] Contrary to the dominant idea about premodern South Asian states not being too invested in actively intervening in the "private" lives of their subjects, the material from Marwar when read alongside information about eighteenth-century Jaipur and the Maratha state suggests that in the post-Mughal milieu, a new type of state form had emerged in some parts of South Asia. This type of eighteenth-century state considered the reformation of the moral fiber of its elite subjects to be an important element in the fashioning of its authority. Perhaps it is not a coincidence that all of these kingdoms also made a turn toward a greater concern with regulating caste.

7

Chastity

For women of rajput, brahman, and by the eighteenth century, mahajan groups, sex was only permissible within the one marriage they were allowed in their lifetimes. Chaste, ascetic widowhood was the norm after their husbands died, even if this happened prior to the marriage's consummation or when the woman was very young. The chaste widowhood of their women allowed these castes to maintain social difference from the mass of castes beneath them in the social order, whose lowliness seemed marked by the very prevalence of widow remarriage among them.[1] The Rathor state, staffed as it was by merchant and other elite caste men, intervened in the everyday lives of its subjects to prevent and punish acts that both state and caste authorities deemed deviant. The state strove to uphold caste and family efforts to police women's sexual behavior.

On the ground, this translated into much more of an interest in regulating the moral lives and physical bodies of merchant-caste and brahman women. As merchants strove to be included in the highest echelon of the region's caste order, the codes through which they announced their social "arrival" were centered on the disciplining of their women. To be counted as part of the very Hindu domain that they were redefining, merchants strove to craft the Hindu woman. The sexual ethics of the old-order elites, rajputs, were now implemented by the merchant-manned state as codes by which merchant women were also to live. However, this was not just a wholesale adoption and imitation of rajput sexual mores. Instead, despite their claims to elite status, merchant castes still adhered, unlike rajputs, to the practice of monogamy. To that extent, men too were expected to corral their sexual activity into wedlock even as, unlike women, they could always remarry should their wives die. A prohibited sexual relationship, crossing the boundaries of caste and religion, even if willingly entered into by both parties, drew the ire of the customary keepers of social propriety such as caste councils and family elders.

The state's interest in disciplining "deviant" sexual relationships left its mark on its archival records. In eighteenth-century Marwar, the state's law and order apparatus also intervened in social life to prevent and punish such relationships. This effort to police the sexual lives of subjects generated whole sets of judgments that reflect the creation of a typology of sexual relations ranging from the acceptable to the abhorrent.[2] Sex within marriage to a virgin woman was the most desirable type of sexual relationship. Among all but the most elite castes, marriage to a divorcée or widow (*nātā*) of the same caste was acceptable. Among non-elite castes, living together without formal marriage rituals (*ghar maiṁ ghālnā*, literally, to put in one's home) with a divorcée or widow of the same caste was tolerated but less acceptable than formal marriage.

Firmly on the side of the "illicit" in the eyes of caste and state authorities was *lagvāḍ* (literally, "attachment"), a term used to describe long-term sexual relationships into which both partners willingly entered. *Lagvāḍ* relations were generally between men and women who were not eligible to be married by the customary codes of caste and region. That is, one of them could still be married or they could belong to different castes. A term sometimes used interchangeably with *lagvāḍ* but shot through with the same disapproval was *chāmchorī*. Scholars of eighteenth-century Rajasthan have tended to translate this term as either "rape" or "adultery."[3] Given the absence of the idea of an individual, free-standing, rights-bearing female subject—a product of modernity—an uncritical projection of notions of consent and therefore the violation of consent as "rape" in premodern legal frameworks needs to be abandoned.[4]

Indeed, *chāmchorī* case descriptions and judgments simply were not concerned with whether or not the woman was a willing participant in the sexual act under discussion. Instead, it is the establishment of sexual relations between two people who should not have been having sex under the customary codes of caste and region, just like *lagvāḍ*, that made *chāmchorī* illicit and illegal. The unsanctioned nature of these relations is why, I suggest, historians of eighteenth-century Rajasthan have so far translated *chāmchorī* as both adultery and rape. Rathor records condemn and punish such relations on grounds of their being unacceptable. Consent is immaterial to these records and the legal thinking behind them.

Rather than reading rape into Rathor jurisprudence, the way forward might be to grapple with the property-like status of the female body as suggested by the fact that it is overwhelmingly male partners in *chāmchorī* relations alone who are fined for their participation in these sexual acts.[5] The mahajan and brahman officers of the Rathor state used its punitive strength and surveillance capabilities to prosecute cases of *lagvāḍ* and *chāmchorī*, particularly among members of their own castes.[6] Fines and, occasionally, expulsion from the town were the punishments handed to men for sex deemed "deviant." For instance, a Palliwal brahman, along with seventeen others, from Siwana district authorized the engagement of a caste fellow from Bikaner with a *meghwal* (leatherworking) woman while all of them were in Malwa, a region in Punjab bearing the same name as the more commonly known Malwa in central India. To have the engagement approved, the Palliwal brahman from Bikaner paid his caste fellows five hundred rupees. When news of this reached the Palliwals of Siwana back in Marwar, they expelled one of the authorizing brahmans from their caste. The Rathor state also swung into action, with Pancholi Gulalchand asking that all eighteen men submit bonds (*muchalkā*) committing to better behavior in future.[7]

Women no doubt suffered social censure as punishment for sexual deviance, but Rathor records rarely mention these extra-state forms of discipline. There are some exceptions to this silence such as the occasional mention of rajput women being murdered by their male kin for having a relationship out of wedlock, generally as widows.[8] Rajput women would have to elope with their lovers if they wanted a chance at building a home with them.[9] Ramya Sreenivasan has shown that by the eighteenth century, rajputs had become stricter in the pursuit of caste and lineage purity, particularly by refusing to integrate fully into their caste the offspring of rajput men from their nonrajput concubines. A greater sensitivity to lineage and caste purity as markers of elite status may also have contributed in the latter half of the eighteenth century to the regime of sexual discipline to which noncourtly rajput women too were subjected.

The state's orders pertaining to illicit affairs (*lagvāḍ*) are dominated largely by men and women of the rajput, brahman, and merchant castes.[10] All three of these caste groups had in common the proscription of widow remarriage. At the same time, accusations of "illicit" sex involved not only widows but also unmarried and married women, particularly of merchant and brahman castes. The anxiety of family and caste authorities then found support in the Rathor state, which itself was constituted of rajputs and merchants. Women's chastity, understood as sex only within one marriage, was an index of male honor and the honor of the family and the caste. For merchants, who were in the process of cementing their position at the apex of the caste order alongside rajputs and brahmans, this translated into an urgent need to discipline their women's bodies.

An outcome of illicit sexual relationships, whether consensual or not, was unwanted pregnancy. The costs of having a child out of wedlock can be seen in the choices that people in such a situation made. An extreme case unfolded in 1798, one whose fullest contours will never be known to us. Mahajan Khemo in the town of Sojhat in Marwar killed a brahman widow (*ranḍol*) with whom he had been having an affair because she got pregnant. Whatever the full set of reasons for her murder, her pregnancy certainly was a contributing cause. Once the murder and the underlying pregnancy became known, the governor of Sojhat fined Khemo a hundred and forty-one rupees and closed the case. But news of the murder and pregnancy reached the state's newswriters. In response, the crown promptly dispatched an order to Sojhat's district authorities to extract a much larger fine from the merchant. Khemo was a wealthy man, it noted, and the state stood to earn as much as a thousand rupees by fining him for this crime. The gravity of Khemo's crimes—an illicit affair and a murder—offered the state an opportunity to extract a large sum of money.

In this milieu, a pregnancy (*ādhān rehnā* or *āsā rehnā*) that occurred out of wedlock was irrefutable evidence of "wrongdoing" ("*khoṭo karam*," as one scribe put it[11]). To avoid the social censure upon them and their families that stemmed from unwanted pregnancies, women would seek out abortions. Midwives (*dāīs*) and Jain *yatis* (Shvetambar Jain monks with incomplete initiation into the monastic order) performed abortions, inducing them by administering herbs (*aukhad*).[12] The involvement of learned Jain men, despite their doctrinal commitment to nonviolence, did not attract special comment in these records. Jain *yatis* were associated with training in a range of fields with everyday application, such as magic, astrology, and medicine. It was likely this medical knowledge that drew them into the work of performing abortions.

Under the auspices of the Rathor crown in the late eighteenth century, however, abortion (*adhūrā nākhnā*, *ādhān nākhnā*, or *ṭāb nākhnā*, literally, "to throw away when incomplete," "to discard a pregnancy," or "to throw a child away," respectively) was illegal. "There is much illicit sex in the town [of Nagaur] and abortions are common (*saihar maiṁ ghaṇī chāmchori huvai hai nai adhūrā nakhījai hai*). Keep an eye out especially for this," Pancholi Bansidhar, the officer in charge of nonmilitary personnel (*pyād bakhśī*), instructed the Nagaur magistracy in 1776 on behalf of the crown.[13] In 1784, an unnamed officer of the crown's issued the following order to the Merta magistracy based on the reports that its newswriters carried to it:

> There is a well in front of Sojhatiya Gate in Merta. Children's bodies were thrown deep into the well and have now been extricated from it. Yet, it remains unknown who threw the bodies in. Keep an eye out for news about this.[14]

As with "illicit" sex, the state often received news of abortion through its network of news writers, which I will discuss in greater detail later in this chapter. The Rathor crown would investigate those reports of abortion that reached it and ensure, in most cases, that anyone deemed complicit—the mother-to-be, the father of the unborn child, anyone who aided or enabled the feticide, and anyone who failed to report it—were punished. If reports of a planned abortion or a pregnancy out of wedlock reached the state, it would intervene to prevent the abortion.[15] In this, the Rathor state was not alone. Historical scholarship has noted that other eighteenth-century kingdoms—Jaipur under Maharaja Jai Singh II (r. 1699–1743) and the Peshwas in their capital city Pune in the eighteenth century—had also outlawed abortion and punished those found guilty of involvement in it.[16]

As with many other crimes in eighteenth-century Marwar, the punishment for abortion varied from case to case, depending on the economic, social, and political clout that the accused could marshal in his or her defense. In most cases, district authorities fined those held guilty.[17] These fines, when specified, ranged from fifteen to four hundred and forty-five rupees, assessed on the basis of the perceived gravity of the crime and the payer's economic standing.[18] Expulsion from government employment, where possible, was another means of punishing those deemed complicit in an abortion case. Under pressure from the crown, the governor of Sanchor, Mahajan Mumhta Bhojo, fired Kothari Uda from his service after Uda, also of mercantile caste, impregnated a mahajan's widow (*rānḍol*) who then fled to Gujarat in order to escape the social and legal repercussions of her pregnancy. Kothari Uda had earlier commissioned the mahajan widow to make *roṭīs* (bread) for the governor's camp.[19] In another episode, the magistrate of Merta expelled Solanki Rajputs Sirdar and Hayat from their employment as soldiers in his magistracy for allegedly failing to report an abortion in their local caste group, one that they had been especially instructed to prevent once the widow's pregnancy had become known.[20]

In a few cases, punishments were more extreme, such as banishment from the town and the imposition of a ruinously large fine. The authorities in Didwana affixed the high fine of one hundred and forty-five rupees upon the family of a young man from the weaver (*julāvā*) caste who impregnated a mahajan woman, a widow with whom he had been in a sexual relationship (*lagvāḍ*).[21] In the same decades, cloth-printer (*chhīṁpā*) Ahmad impregnated his caste fellow Isakh's unmarried daughter. The girl aborted the fetus (*ṭāb nai mār nākhīyo*). For this, the crown in Jodhpur ordered Isakh's house to be confiscated and for him to be thrown out of the town, Sojhat, in which he lived. In this case, as with most cases of abortion and unlike those of sexual deviance, the woman too was punished. The crown commanded that the young girl also be expelled from the town.[22]

For being involved in an abortion, the state meted out the harsh punishment of banishment from a town not only to "low"-caste men and women but also to members of the brahman or mahajan communities, even if rarely. For instance, the authorities in Didwana found a brahman woman guilty of aborting a pregnancy that had resulted from an extramarital relationship with a mahajan. She was a married woman and her in-laws reported the matter to the local authorities, who closed the case after levying a small fine on her mahajan partner. It was only after persistent litigation by the girl's father, over a year or more, that the crown slapped a higher fine on the mahajan and ordered him expelled from the town, but it did so while also commanding that the brahman woman be banished.[23]

This woman, Gaud Brahman Mana's daughter, found herself in the state's crosshairs again later that same year. She had been having an affair with another mahajan. She got pregnant and her parents took her out of the kingdom, to a village in Bikaner, where she gave birth to a baby girl. They killed the girl when she was eight days old, poisoning her with opium. Three months later, the parents returned to Nagaur and, using their connections, managed to bring their daughter back in too. A caste fellow of theirs reported the entire matter to the crown and the crown asked its administrators in Nagaur to explain how it was that a woman who had earlier been expelled from the town had been able to make her way back in. The informer from Nagaur had brought reports of many a "misdeed" in the same brahman household, and the crown ordered its officers to keep a close eye on them in future.[24]

For members of these elite castes, then, banishment from a town was not always an irreversible punishment. In 1778, Kiki, a woman from the brahman community of Nandvana Bohras, traders by profession, petitioned the crown to permit her daughter, one of three women expelled from Nagaur for an abortion, to return to the town. She cited her own blindness and ailing health (*monu phoḍā paḍai chhai*, or "I get boils") and mentioned that one of the other exiled women had already made her way back into the town. Bhandari Savantram and Pancholi Fatehkaran, officers ruling on behalf of the Maharaja, responded sympathetically to her appeal, permitting her daughter to return to Nagaur.[25]

Local power relations mediated judicial responses to abortion, resulting in uneven punishments and unexplained exemptions. Quite commonly, district authorities would punish only some of those involved in an abortion case. News of such discrepancies would reach the crown through its surveillance networks or when a petitioner would appeal to it for an intervention. For instance, district administrators in Merta fined Mayaram Daftari, a Jain mahajan[26], fifty-one rupees in 1771 for his daughter's abortion and imprisoned the Jain monk (*jatī*, a vernacularization of "*yati*") who had administered the herbs (*aukhad*) that induced the abortion. These local administrators, however, left the father of the unborn child, Kana Pancholi, a *kāyasth*, untouched. When news of this reached the crown, it ordered the Pancholi arrested for the pregnancy.[27]

In the same year, a Jain devotee in Jalor, a follower (*chelā*) of a local *bhattārak*,[28] impregnated a woman from the butcher caste (*khaṭīknī*), a community that stood firmly within the domain of the "untouchable" in early modern Marwar.[29] Attempting a quiet resolution of the matter, the devotee took her to a remote village in 1772 and had the pregnancy terminated at seven months. Despite multiple newswriters informing the Jalor governor of the episode, he did not pursue the matter. The newswriters then informed the crown, which responded by upbraiding the Jalor governor's office for its failure to follow up on the case.[30] Yet, in this case, the crown did not order the local authorities to punish the guilty—neither the butcher woman nor the Jain devotee who had caused the pregnancy and had then ensured its termination. In yet another case, after cloth-printer Fata's mother managed to prove her innocence in the face of abortion charges from her caste fellows, the crown had to intervene to ensure that the Nagaur magistracy collected the dues owed to it by the men who had made the false allegations.[31] There were numerous such instances in which district authorities failed to impose significant fines, take action against men accused or indicted, or completely failed to investigate reports of abortion.

For instance, in 1793, a *havāldār* (revenue functionary) of a village in Merta district summoned and possibly held captive a brahman woman, Kamvri, whose husband was away. He, along with some *jāṭ* subordinates, a brahman, a rajput, and a butcher (*khaṭīk*), then had sex with her over a period of time, causing her to have two abortions. The crown's newswriters informed it of the entire matter in 1794, noting that she was eight months pregnant. Acting perhaps on the same report, the local authorities in Merta had, of all the men involved in the illicit sex and abortions, arrested only two. Interestingly, these were a *jāṭ* and the butcher's father, that is, both of low caste in comparison with the rajputs and brahmans involved. This, according to Merta officers, was because the *havāldār* had flatly refused to hand over the rest of this associates. The *havāldār* also hid the brahman woman, preventing the authorities from reaching her. Informed of this state of affairs, the crown ordered the immediate arrest of the *havāldār* and all of his other associates involved in having sex with the brahman woman and the imposition of a proper fine.[32] As always, we do not know how this case eventually turned out, but it is possible to read in this case once again a lack of investment in whether or not the sexual relations under scrutiny were consensual. In the details of this case, it is possible to discern that the brahman woman was forced into having sex with the men involved. Yet, the state's judgment does not deem the act worthy of any greater punishment than if the woman was having an affair.

If reports of a planned abortion or a pregnancy out of wedlock reached the state, officers would intervene to prevent the abortion. In 1777, the authorities in Merta placed Solankhi Sardar Hayat in charge of keeping an eye on the widowed daughter of his caste fellow, Sardar Khan, to ensure that she did not abort the fetus she was carrying.[33] A decade later, Sundri, a woman from the Mehra community among the merchants, was carrying mahajan Mumhta Jora's child. The magistracy in Sojhat collected a fine from her, getting her to attest to an undertaking (a written document called a *muchalkā* that specified what punishment the signatory would be awarded upon violation of the terms) committing to not aborting the pregnancy and agreeing to an added fine if she did abort it.[34]

Surveillance and reporting played a central role in the crown's punitive regime against abortion and, in effect, against nonmarital sex. Many reports of abortion, or of district administrators' unsatisfactory handling of cases of abortion, reached the Rathor state through its network of newswriters (*itlāk naves* and *uvākā naves*) who appear to have also worked as intelligence gatherers in the kingdom's localities. If district administrators failed to adequately resolve an abortion case or extract as high a fine as the crown deemed fit, the matter would reach the crown's officers in Jodhpur through its news gatherers' dispatches. Individual subjects would also sometimes take the lead in reporting instances of abortion that had occurred in their families, neighborhoods, or local caste groups.

This fostered an atmosphere in which neighbors, caste fellows, and family members became willing reporters to the crown of each other's activities. To prevent just this, a woman from the brahman community who had an abortion sought to buy the silence of three female acquaintances—two *jāṭs* and a brahman—by paying them a *mohrā* (gold coin) each. Unfortunately for her, news of the abortion and her generous gift to all those who knew of it reached the state.[35] As in the campaign against animal slaughter, the state's implementation of an anti-abortion law offered a fertile ground on which to play out grudges and long-standing feuds. An accusation of abortion would, at the very least, embroil the accused in long and costly legal proceedings, if not lead to their arrest or fining.

The Rathor crown encouraged the reporting of one's neighbors or acquaintances for abortion, punishing those who concealed such information and rewarding those who divulged it. Administrators in Koliya confiscated *vīṇīyāṇī* (*banīyā* or trader woman) Kusli's cow and fined her fifteen rupees for her alleged failure to report her neighbor's plans to abort an unwanted pregnancy to the state.[36] When under fire for impregnating a brahman woman, Jaju Jasa, of the Maheshwari community of merchants, tried to deflect the heat by reporting someone else for having an illicit relationship. He accused a fellow Maheshwari merchant, Baheti Gangavisan, of being in an illicit relationship with someone else's wife, though the allegation was later proved false.[37] Brahman Ramrai's widowed daughter, under arrest for having an abortion, revealed that Vyas (brahman) Nanu's wife too had an abortion four months after she got pregnant while her husband was abroad (*pardes*). When news of this new case reached the crown, it ordered that in recognition of her cooperation, Ramrai's daughter's fine be reduced to a quarter of the original sum.[38]

From a survey of these cases, it appears that mahajans and brahmans played a leading role in reporting abortions, usually making complaints against their own caste fellows. Agarval Naga, a mahajan, reported the district administrators of Pali for their inaction against Patni Karma, a Jain, who had administered three abortions.[39] Bohra Chaina, a brahman, informed the crown of mahajan Hema's daughter's abortion and the local administrators' usurping of the fines collected for it.[40] That mahajans and brahmans usually only reported each other could be a result of the social worlds that they inhabited, marked by intimate social ties foremost with their own caste fellows and with each other. But the fact that reports of abortion to the state were centered largely on merchant and brahman women suggests that the state's seemingly general ban on abortion was directed most zealously upon women of these two caste communities. Once more, Rathor administrators were themselves of these same caste groups, that is, they were in large number mahajans and brahmans.

Investigations could establish the innocence of women who were accused of abortion if the accused woman or her family took on the expense and the effort to wage a legal challenge. Cloth-printer (*chhīṁpā*) Phata's mother managed to prove her innocence (*sāchī kīvī*) by contesting the allegations some of her caste fellows in Merta made against her.[41] Unwanted pregnancies would, in many cases, force women to pursue discreet abortions in far-flung places. Such journeys and abortions would likely have been perilous and expensive undertakings. A mahajan widow, seven months pregnant, left Sanchor for Gujarat in 1775, unaccompanied as she embarked on this difficult journey.[42] In 1801, mahajan Agarvala Ramsukh's wife left Didwana to have an abortion, news of which reached the crown.[43]

For many women burdened by unwanted pregnancies, their natal families emerged as a significant source of material, social, and legal support. In 1776, Jivaniya Majiji accompanied his widowed mother when she left Didwana for the countryside, seeking a low-key abortion for her. He bribed the officers that the Didwana governor had sent after them, fending them off. They managed to terminate the mother's pregnancy while on the run and the family used its local influence to allow them reentry into Didwana.[44] In 1784, mahajan Asava[45] Bagsiram's wife and Jat Syama's daughter moved from their marital homes to their natal villages in order to end their unwanted pregnancies.[46] In 1787, Agarval Sukha, a mahajan, came to the defense of his cousin fourth-removed, successfully appealing to the crown in Jodhpur to intervene in her favor when she was accused in Merta of having an abortion.[47] So pervasive was the association between married women convalescing in their natal homes and secret abortions that a *jāgīrdār* (landlord) in Nagaur district tried to levy a fine on a *jāṭ* peasant in his jurisdiction on grounds that the *jāṭ* had facilitated his married daughter's abortion. The *jāṭ* appealed to the crown for help, arguing that all he had done was tend to his daughter for a few days after she had fainted while away from her marital home.[48] Such support for pregnant women might have been driven not just by affective ties but also in part by the fact that quite often it was the natal family that had to pay the social and legal costs of an illicit pregnancy.[49] The discreet handling of an unwanted pregnancy and the clearing of an accused woman's name was a matter of familial and caste honor.

Still, it is noteworthy that unlike natal kin, members of women's marital homes could well turn upon them if they were discovered to be pregnant with a child fathered by someone from outside their marital home.[50] It was her in-laws who reported brahman Upadhyay Mana's daughter's pregnancy out of wedlock to the magistrate in Nagaur.[51] Even though she was eventually expelled from the town for getting pregnant out of wedlock and then having an abortion, her father's persistence with the magistrate ensured that the wealthy family of the merchant who impregnated her paid her a sum of two hundred rupees.[52]

The state responded a little differently to pregnancies resulting from relationships that were "incestuous" or deemed illicit because they were between two people related by blood or marriage in a manner that made any sexual relationship between them transgressive. The standards for establishing which relationship was incestuous and which was not of course varied among communities and regions. It is worth noting though that in these records there was no distinct term for incest. Still, if a relationship was deemed illicit for being between kin, a pregnancy resulting from it saw the Rathor state adopt a more flexible stance toward abortion. When Mahajan Karma impregnated his brother's wife, the local authorities collected a fine of twenty-five rupees from him and threw the woman out of the village in Merta district in which she lived. Hearing of the incident from its newswriters, Singhvi Chainram ordered on behalf of the crown that five more rupees be collected from the mahajan and that efforts be made to prevent the child from being born (*jāyāṁ huṇ dejo matī*), ostensibly since it was the product of a forbidden intrafamily union.[53] A woman from the goldsmith community named her brother-in-law as the father of the fetus she had aborted. The crown ordered that if this was indeed the case, then the man should be fined.[54] When caught for having an abortion, a rajput woman from Maroth named her husband's grandfather as the man who had impregnated her.[55] In these cases, even if they were reported when the women were pregnant, the crown did not insist upon the prevention of abortion. In cases of pregnancies resulting from forbidden intrafamilial relationships, then, the crown seemed to make an exception to its general insistence upon preventing abortion. This could be due to questions of inheritance and descent generated by the offspring of taboo intrafamilial relationships.

It was women of the merchant and brahman communities who bore the brunt of the imposition of a ban on abortion. Over half of the thirty-three instances of abortion that I found involve women from mercantile or priestly families, and of the remaining cases about half concerned women from elite families whose exact caste identity is unclear.[56] Only four cases of abortion by women of artisanal communities and just one in which an "untouchable" woman was involved reached the crown for adjudication. The "universal" ban upon abortion was, in effect, implemented more rigorously upon members of brahman and mahajan castes. Out of the thirty-three orders pertaining to abortion that I found, fourteen were issued by mahajan officers and four by brahmans.[57] Eleven of the orders did not record who issued them.[58] That is, almost half of the commands about abortion, all of which unequivocally stood by its illegality, were issued by mahajan men. Since we know that merchants and brahmans dominated the Rathor bureaucracy, we may include the unattributed commands to them. If we add brahman-issued orders to the tally, the total number of mahajan- and brahman-issued commands goes up to twenty-nine (of thirty-three), that is, an overwhelming majority. Rather than see these officers as mechanistically implementing moral and legal imperatives of the king or some other superior, it is important to see these men as agents rooted in their own caste cultures and the ethical and political drives of their caste fellows and families. The state's effort to cultivate chastity among its subjects then dovetailed with ongoing changes in local caste orders. In particular, the congealing of a new elite caste identity and the deployment of "Hindu" to name this highest echelon of elite castes that now also included merchants meant that women of merchant families were subjected to far more sexual regulation.

Brahman and mahajan women's special treatment in the implementation of the anti-abortion law was the product of several historical forces. First, the merchant and brahman communities were at the forefront of the effort to define a new community of elites, marked off spatially, ritually, and economically, and also demarcated by the cultural practices of vegetarianism. An ethical insistence upon nonharm became the basis upon which these communities justified and valorized the adherence to vegetarianism and the Rathor state imposed it as law upon the rest of the population. The naturalization of this ethical precept as an attribute of elite caste status fueled the zeal against abortion, being as it was an act of violence upon a living being, among brahman and mahajan communities in particular.

Second, elite status in early modern Marwar correlated with attitudes toward widow remarriage. Among brahmans and mahajans, along with other high-status groups such as the rajputs, a widow could not remarry. Elite-caste widows' abstinence from all bodily pleasure after the death of their husbands was a symbol of their community's high status. Brahman and mahajan widows continued to live as vulnerable dependents in their marital homes and, as the numerous incidents of abortion among them indicate, found themselves in clandestine sexual relationships that, in some cases, may have been against their will.

Third, the social and legal intolerance of abortion served as added pressure upon the men and especially the women of these preeminent castes within the Hindu domain, itself under construction, to refrain from non- or extramarital sexual relationships. Non- or extramarital relationships were largely illicit in the customary caste codes of brahman and mahajan communities by the eighteenth century. This applied especially to the women of these communities, forbidden as they were by custom from having any sexual relationship other than within the one marriage they were permitted in their lifetimes.

The criminalization of abortion in state law then created added pressure toward conformity with a moral code emphasizing sexual abstinence outside of wedlock. Such a life of chastity was in keeping with the more austere way of life that the formation of an elite, Vaishnav-Jain milieu in Marwar expected of its members. Scholars have noted the association of the Vallabh Sampraday, the most influential of the Krishnaite sects in Marwar, with lavish displays of wealth and its rejection of asceticism. Norbert Peabody, in particular, has emphasized the sect's "this-worldly mysticism," equating the concept of *bhog* (enjoyment) in the sect's ritual with the idea that it prescribed to its followers a generalized enjoyment of sensory pleasures.[59]

While the Vallabhites did reject asceticism and criticized yogic techniques of bodily self-discipline, it is important to pay attention to the context in which they prescribed and practiced an indulgence of the senses or a lavishing of wealth: only wealth spent in the "right" manner—that is, on Vallabhite ritual and establishments—had the potential to generate merit. Vallabh's teaching encouraged the pursuit of material well-being and sensory pleasure but only when directed toward the worship of Krishna.[60] Historians have noted an adherence to values of simplicity, restraint, and frugality among Vallabhite merchants in their personal lives.[61] Among Jains too ethical codes prescribed austerity in the conduct of one's everyday life along with a showering of wealth toward ritual and charity. Identifying precisely this tension between the value of simplicity and the desire for lavishness within the merchant community, Christopher Bayly notes that the Vallabhite sanction of lavishness in the ritual context helped its resolution.[62]

Given the close association between merchants on the one hand and Vaishnavism and Jainism on the other, it may well be that the valorization of austerity—that is, outside of the ritual and charitable context—originated in mercantile culture and came to be associated with the religions in which they became dominant forces. This can also be seen in the case of such *nirguṇa* bhakti communities as the Dadupanth and the Niranjani Sampraday, whose monastic centers included sites in Marwar. Both these communities drew merchant followers and towns like Didwana became centers of literary production and gathering. At the same time, both communities preached a message that encouraged the continuing generation of wealth and participation in familial life while cultivating nonattachment to both activities.[63] Within mercantile networks of information, a family firm's creditworthiness was assessed, among other factors, by the degree of its austerity in the domestic context. Household and bodily frugality was a measure of respectability among merchant families.[64] In the emergent Hindu community in the eighteenth century in Marwar, I suggest, the centrality of merchants helped elevate austerity to a desirable trait.

The emphasis upon austerity extended from outward behavior to the regulation of bodily appetites. For the women of "respectable" communities, the process of the demarcation of an early modern Hindu community entailed sexual disciplining. This moral regime of sexual discipline was enforced not only through the societal stigmatization of unwed mothers if they belonged to these groups but also through the implementation of anti-abortion strictures. As bearers of the fruits of illicit sexual relationships, the outlawing of abortion meant that elite—rajput, merchant, and brahman—women also paid a greater price than their male counterparts for nonconformity with this regime of sexual discipline.

The greater regulation of the sexuality of brahman and mahajan women and the correlation between their "virtue" and their community's high status meant that accusations against a mahajan or brahman woman sullied the entire local caste group's social standing. This certainly can be discerned in the Rathor state's treatment of abortion allegations against Agarvala Chimna's wife. Rathor officer Singhvi Motichand, a mahajan, wrote to the Merta magistrate, "She is a mahajan's daughter," in response to abortion allegations against merchant Agarvala Chimna's wife. "To make an issue of this without any basis will not go down well in her caste [*nyāt maiṁ āchho nā lāgai*]." Reiterating her mahajan identity, the officer, Singhvi

Motichand, who was also a mahajan, ordered the magistracy to fine the woman of the barber caste who had supported the woman's accusers.[65]

BODILY SANCTITY AND SELF-HARM

In cases in which the entire local caste group felt its prestige at stake, brahmans too would assert the respect that their caste status entitled them to. Here, once more, it was women's bodies that came to function as a synecdoche for the community. In 1797, Palliwal brahman Naran impregnated his caste fellow Harjida's daughter, a widow. District officers investigating the matter dealt with the Palliwal brahmans in a manner that they found too heavy-handed. In their determination to right this wrong, the Palliwals performed a *juhar* ceremony, one in which they sacrificed an old woman (*ḍokrī*) from their community, burning her alive (*palīvāl bhelā huī juhar kīyo ḍokrī ek bālī*).[66] *Juhar* or *jauhar* denoted an act of self-harm performed in response to rule that is considered unjust.[67] The term has been associated in South Asian history with ritual suicide committed by the women of a defeated rajput king's household in defense of the honor—understood as residing in their sexuality—of their lineage. References such as this one in the *Jodhpur Sanad Parwāna Bahīs*, however, indicate that other communities, those that commanded ritual authority, could also inflict harm upon themselves as a means of exerting moral pressure upon state authorities.

In early modern Marwar, members of the castes that wielded ritual authority, such as charans and brahmans, could mutilate their own bodies in order to place the onus of righting a moral wrong upon the person they held responsible. Self-mutilation and harm to one's own body was a means of demanding rectification of an unacceptable situation presented as a violation of moral and ethical codes. It was a tactic through which the brahman allocated moral responsibility for physical harm to his body, a body the maintenance of whose sanctity was the duty of all, not least of whom was the sovereign.[68] In this case, the brahmans of Phalodhi collectively sacrificed a member of their community, an old woman past reproductive age and possibly too frail to contribute much to household and other economies. The old brahman widow's physical body stood in, just as it did when it came to her sexual relationships, for the communal body and honor of the local brahman caste.

The sacrifice of the brahman widow had the desired outcome. It forced the Rathor crown to swing into action. The state immediately deemed the allegation of abortion false and ordered disciplinary action against the men who had conducted the heavy-handed inquiry among the Palliwals.[69] In this particular case of pregnancy out of wedlock, the brahmans of this village in Phalodhi were able to band together and mobilize their ritual status in order to be treated exceptionally and to have the charges of illicit sex against members of their community dropped.

The women of brahman and mahajan communities were caught in a double bind. Irrefutable evidence of forbidden sexual intercourse, a pregnancy out of wedlock, even one that resulted from what we would today call rape, placed them in the impossible position of choosing between the criminal offense of abortion and giving birth to a child out of wedlock.[70] Having an abortion would attract the state's punishment and held the possible risk of expulsion from the town or village. Not having an abortion and instead bearing a child out of wedlock would bring social censure and possible expulsion from the community.

The Rathor state and local caste councils attempted to limit the women of the mahajan and brahman communities to a sexual life that was firmly contained within the boundary of marriage. Abortion and the nonmarital sexual relationships that caused unwanted pregnancies would surely not have been limited to women of these castes alone. Women of peasant, artisan, and "low" service castes too would certainly have gotten pregnant out of wedlock, whether as a result of willing or unwilling sexual relationships. The *Jodhpur Sanad Parwāna Bahīs*, as records of the state's legislative practice, are reticent on the incidence of abortion among non-elite castes. Yet, as the state worked to strengthen its penetration of early modern Marwari society and as community leaders sought to forge an exclusive elite domain, imposing a regime of sexual discipline upon the women of this elite domain became far more important than policing non-elite women to claims of high status, articulated as they were in moral and ethical terms.[71]

As Marwar, and South Asia more generally, journeyed through the eighteenth century, women's bodies became the tools for the conditioning of a new body social. In zealously pursuing the implementation of laws against alcohol and gambling and in policing nonmarital sexual relationships, the Rathor state and its merchant- and brahman-run apparatus were especially concerned with enforcing probity upon mahajan and brahman communities, the same groups that had coalesced around Vaishnav devotion and Jainism. The surveillance and policing involved served as a means to regulate the sexual and moral lives of an aspirant regional elite, consisting largely of merchants and brahmans and united by shared cultural and devotional practices. State and caste councils combined to enforce at least a formal acquiescence to these moral codes, aiding the process of the demarcation on the grounds of a new transcaste identity—that of the early modern Hindu. Constructing the early modern Hindu then rested also on crafting the early modern Hindu woman, innately an elite-caste woman, chaste of body and mind. The imposition of sexual chastity upon women and, to a lesser extent, men of merchant and brahman castes was an element of a wider effort, particularly among merchant groups, to cultivate virtue and bodily vigor.

EPILOGUE

As the eighteenth century came to a close, circumstances in Marwar changed quite rapidly. The Rathors had suffered a crushing defeat against the Marathas in 1791, bringing new demands for tributary payments. Internal schisms within the polity escalated. These developments took on increasing momentum through the reigns of Vijai Singh's successors, Bhim Singh and Man Singh, lasting well into the first two decades of the nineteenth century. The *Jodhpur Sanad Parwāna Bahīs* become slimmer from the early years of the nineteenth century, containing far fewer orders than before. It appears that Jodhpur was too mired in conflict in the first quarter of the nineteenth century for the central authorities to respond to local cases and individual petitions—or at least to copy and collect them all systematically at the chancery—in the manner that they had managed through most of Vijai Singh and Bhim Singh's reigns. The establishment of English East India Company paramountcy over Jodhpur in 1818 also introduced an entirely different kind of government.[1] It is for all of these reasons that I terminate my study at this point in Marwari history, but the political and ethical shifts that I have traced had consequences far beyond the geographical and temporal limits of eighteenth- and early nineteenth-century Marwar. The activities of Vijai Singh and his merchant and brahman officers and subjects built upon wider changes underway not only in the region but also at transregional and global scales. Yet, at the same time, the developments in Marwar that I have traced in this book are important for a fuller appreciation of the precolonial lineages of the transformations in caste and community and the imaginations of the nation, of the body, and of "Hinduism" in the colonial era.

I have argued that merchants built on the dominance they had gained in the course of the seventeenth and early eighteenth centuries over state and society in Marwar to play a key role in reordering the region's localized caste orders. They worked through the state and its Krishna-devotee king to elevate their caste practices such as Krishna-centric devotion, an adherence to nonharm and vegetarianism, and bodily austerity to be read as markers of high social rank. In this process, ritual, space, diet, and sexuality became sites for the reconfiguration of elite status. The ethical codes of some became normalized through law as virtuous. Merchants, unlike rajputs, could not base their claims to elite rank in the land or in descent. Nor, unlike brahmans, could they turn to brahmanical prescriptions to justify claims to fullest inclusion among the caste elite. What they could wield was an adherence to a "virtuous" life. This became the grounds upon which they claimed inclusion in the latter half of the eighteenth century among the region's elite and engineered the required shift in the regional caste order.

The elite identity that they remade with state help designated itself "Hindu." A key ingredient of this success, also connected to the growing dependence of kings upon moneylenders, was the Vaishnav affiliation of Maharaja Vijai Singh, the king who ruled Marwar through the bulk of the latter half of the eighteenth century. This precolonial Hindu identity that emerged in eighteenth-century Marwar was defined not in opposition to the Muslim alone, as it came to be in the colonial period, but rather against the figure of the Untouchable. The mobilities and interdependencies that the arid ecology of Marwar generated could not completely hold off efforts across its towns and villages to create a more polarized caste order. Nonetheless, the very existence of these records is a testament to the resistance against this effort, whether through petitions, evasion, or noncompliance. Law, an arena of struggle, was both the ground upon and the means through which this shift played out. Ethics and normative values, in turn rooted in the caste and sectarian cultures of the region's elite, displaced the primacy of custom as a guide to administering social life. Instead, the Rathor state passed universal laws, applicable to all subjects, though in practice these remained differentially applied. This quest for a Hindu body politic played out through a legal vocabulary and practice rooted in a long and deep immersion of the Marwar region in Islamic law.

LEGACIES OF THE VAISHNAV PUBLIC

Was the ethical orientation of the Rathor state in the latter half of the eighteenth century a fleeting chapter in the history of Marwar, one with no lasting effect after the death of Bhim Singh in 1803? Did the Vaishnav-Jain ethos that seemed ascendant in the reign of Vijai Singh simply recede into the domestic lives of the castes and families that were Vaishnav or Jain? On the surface, the record might look quite different because the accession of Man Singh to the throne in 1803 appears to mark a rupture from the precedents set by Vijai Singh and continued by Bhim

Singh. Most notably, Man Singh was not a Vaishnav. Instead, he showered the Nath Yogis of Marwar with the state's largesse. His munificence and protection facilitated the proliferation of new and prominent Nath sites, largely temples and monastic complexes across the kingdom.[2] Man Singh is said to have sponsored the construction of around ninety Nath temples in Marwar, with five of these being in the capital Jodhpur alone.[3] He also built a Nath temple within Mehrangarh Fort, bringing the Nath Yogis into the very heart of Rathor power.[4] And yet, even as the Vallabhite order in particular and Vaishnavism more generally became displaced as the primary beneficiaries of the Rathor court's patronage in the nineteenth century, they continued to be powerful loci of religious life in Marwar, retaining their following especially among merchants but also among artisans and peasants. In important ways, the decades of Vijai Singh and Bhim Singh's reigns along with the rise to regional power of the mahajans had reshaped the ethical landscape of Marwar fundamentally despite the royal orientation in the first half of the nineteenth century toward Nath Yogis. Vaishnavism's enduring hold in Marwar was in no small part due to the generosity and care that kings Vijai Singh and Bhim Singh had showered on the religious community of *bhakts* since the mid-eighteenth century.

Maharaja Man Singh also played a part in this, by taking standards set by the elite Vaishnav *bhakti* of Vijai Singh's reign and applying them to the Naths. As soon as Man Singh acceded to the Rathor throne in 1803, prior to the colonial conquest of the region, he began efforts to cleanse the diffuse Nath Yogi community of elements that in his eyes or those of his newly influential Nath mentors were unsavory. Monika Horstmann's study of asceticism in Rajasthan in the early modern period suggests a tension between two tendencies among the region's Nath Yogis. While some adhered to more "transgressive" tantric practices, others preferred to hew closer to the message preached by *bhakti* poets like Kabir, which emphasized vegetarianism and nonharm.[5] Patton Burchett also has shown the many entanglements among *bhakti*, tantra, and Sufism all through the early modern period.[6] What role did fifty years of the elevation of *bhakti* and of Vaishnav-Jain ethics play in changing the interaction within the Nath Yogis between these different orientations toward *bhakti* ethics? In November–December of 1803, the very month Man Singh came to the throne, the crown dispatched an order to all its districts (*bhelā parganā*) commanding that, of the many members of the Kundapanth order of Naths in Marwar, only those who worshipped "with sincerity" (*man chit suṁ karai*) should be allowed to continue their religious practice. The order commanded the governors of all the districts to slowly whittle down the numbers of those Kundapanthis who were behaving in an increasingly "disorderly" way (*badhto phitūr karai*).[7]

Dominique-Sila Khan describes the Kundapanth as a "secret" order whose interpretation of the tantric/yogic path is said to have emphasized sexual intercourse and sexual fluids. It had little regard for caste injunctions and hierarchies

FIGURE 7: Jalandarnath Worship at Mahamandir, by Raso and Shivdas Bhatti, 1812, RJS 2005. ©Mehrangarh Museum Trust, Jodhpur, Rajasthan, India, and His Highness Maharaja Gaj Singh of Jodhpur. Do not reuse or reproduce image without permission from the Mehrangarh Museum Trust.

and rejected social norms. In Rajasthan, these ritual practices were associated by the twentieth century with disciples of localized orders, possibly of a medieval and forgotten Nizari Shi'a origin, that were dominated by "untouchable" communities such as the leatherworking *meghvāls*.[8] Read in the context of the dominant Vaishnav-Jain ethos in Vijai Singh's reign that this book has shown, this order to reshape an "errant" yogic order from Man Singh's reign points to new avenues for research on the role of the Rathor state in reshaping the Nath "family" toward a "Hindu"-ized form, one that was more in consonance with an emerging elite-caste identity steeped in a Vaishnav-Jain ethos that identified as "Hindu."[9]

MARWARIS AND THE HINDU BODY

At the same time, merchants of Marwari origin gained renown for their pivotal role in a number of arenas outside of Marwar, most central of which was the economy. "Marwari" (meaning "of Marwar") came to be used as a label for a transcaste community of merchants outside of Rajasthan, a community that included a number of merchant families that did not trace their roots to places within the boundaries of the Rathor kingdom of Marwar. Anne Hardgrove argues that the "Marwar" evoked by the caste label "Marwari" in places like Calcutta was straightforwardly an imagined one, bearing only an abstract relationship with the Marwar of the Rathor polity. In many senses, this seems true. In geographical terms, as Hardgrove correctly observes, many of the most prominent "Marwaris" of late nineteenth- and twentieth-century India came from places just outside the borders of the Rathor kingdom. Shekhawati, just northeast of but overlapping with Rathor territory, in particular produced a large number of merchants who went on to make massive fortunes in Calcutta, Bombay, and central India, such as the Birlas, the Goenkas, the Singhanias, the Bajajs, the Poddars, and the Dalmias. Shekhawati also gave rise to many men engaged in trade and moneylending who were smaller players in regional and local markets across most of South Asia. The Bikaner and Jaipur regions, contiguous with Rathor territory, also were home to many families who went on to achieve great business success, such as the Mittals and the Pittys, the latter of whom made their fortune as bankers to the Nizams of Hyderabad.[10]

That said, it would be untenable to argue that the "Marwar" conjured by diasporic Marwaris and their interlocutors had so little to do with Rathor territories or the region called Marwar that "there is an imagined Marwar that does not exist."[11] First, Rathor territories were not fixed and kept shifting over time, and the idea of Marwar geographically never was entirely contiguous with Rathor state boundaries. This makes it difficult to draw a hard line separating localities just outside Rathor borders from those within as being in or out of Marwar. Second, Rathor territories also were a source in the early modern and modern periods of business families pursuing trade, brokerage, speculation, banking, and moneylending outside of Marwar. Some, such as the Jagat Seth family originally from Nagaur, the Dadhas of Phalodhi, and the Bangurs of Didwana, built highly successful businesses in places such as Patna, Murshidabad, Madras, and Calcutta.[12] Of these, the Jagat Seth family of bankers, discussed also in chapter 1, are notable for their role as powerful financiers in eighteenth-century Bengal. The Mughal state relied on them since the early eighteenth century for its fiscal operations and they became in the mid-eighteenth century primary brokers for the English East India Company.[13] Third, as Hardgrove herself points out, there is evidence of the appellation "Marwari" being used to denote diasporic trading groups even prior to the nineteenth century.[14] Thus, an association with Marwar did indeed characterize at least some traders active in the Indian subcontinent and beyond in the early modern period and cannot be attributed only to the dynamics triggered by the colonial setting.

Still, what was it that caused the term "Marwari" to have the currency it did in India's colonial economy? One explanation could be the social and religious significance of sites in Rathor Marwar—such as the town of Bhinmal (earlier known as Shrimal) and the village of Osian near Jodhpur—to the larger Jain diaspora that had already spread into the Gangetic plain by the seventeenth century and which was active in banking and trade. The eighteenth-century processes that I have traced in this book, particularly the combination of capital and governmental power that the merchants of Marwar came to enjoy, contributed to their business success outside of Marwar. We know that merchants of Marwari origin strengthened their grasp over local markets in eastern India and expressed their "arrival" by adopting an aristocratic air. They made their way through town in lavish processions that the partisans of the old order saw as a marker of *inqilāb*, or an upturning of the ideal social order.[15]

Back in Rajasthan, porous territorial boundaries meant that bonds of marriage and businesses partnership linked mahajans from Rathor Marwar with their caste fellows from neighboring territories. "Marwari," when applied to the diasporic mercantile community from Rajasthan, did have roots and connections with Rathor Marwar even as the area it denoted exceeded this kingdom. The political and social standing that the mercantile, Vaishnav-Jain castes achieved in the Rathor polity in the decades that I have studied bestowed on the idea of Marwari origin a particular status and honor that were legible to the wider mercantile diaspora from north and western India. Putative Marwari origin—bringing together diasporic traders of mahajan castes from the wider Rajasthan region—aided cohesion and mutual support within this demographic. The geographic associations of "Marwari" came to be shorthand for caste and ethical codes and helped merchants band together in distant lands, even as their wives and children remained back home in Rajasthan. The label may have provided these diasporic men with the resolve and infrastructure needed to maintain the diet and other lifestyle requirements of their caste.

How the historical experiences of mahajans in eighteenth-century Marwar shaped this history is a question that this book opens up. Marwari merchants had been successful in deploying collective power—in the form of their caste groups or working cooperatively across mercantile castes and with brahmans—to win state support for their political struggles within Marwar. They were able, in the eighteenth century, to discipline members of their own caste bodies, to redraw social boundaries to exclude the "lowly" and to distance from "Untouchables," and to have their ethical stances imposed as law on all others. Could this history shed new light on how merchants of Marwari origin who were scattered across South Asia became vectors of the caste "Hindu" ethos that I traced in this book? As they adapted to the plethora of changes in virtually every arena of life unleashed by colonial domination, did these merchants carry with them the drive to work collectively and through the state to enforce their own ethical visions on the wider social order? Did the recent experience and memory of the fruits of mercantile influence in Marwar impart to Marwari origin a certain purchase and a value?

The Marwari diaspora in north Indian towns played an indispensable role in the nineteenth-century construction of Hindi as a language and of the generation of a new Hindi literature, both of which served as vehicles for the construction of a Hindu community.[16] Bharatendu Harishchandra, an Agrawal of the Marwari mercantile diaspora in Banaras, born into a Vallabhite family and later known as the "father of Hindi," led the way in crafting a new genre of theater that drew upon existing popular traditions but excised from them such "debased" features as unchaste female characters and the use of Persian-origin words.[17] The removal of Persian-origin words was part of the ongoing effort by men among whom Harishchandra was a pioneer to create a new language to accompany the reimagination and reinvigoration of a Hindu community, whose emergence required both reform to meet the challenges of modern times and colonial domination as well as a shedding of "extraneous" elements introduced by "Muslim rule."[18]

Notably, Harishchandra's recasting of theater was to limit its performance to a select audience of elite patrons and to direct it toward moral edification.[19] This was very much in line with the delineation of the Hindu domain in eighteenth-century Marwar as one in which only caste elites were welcome. Harishchandra also positioned himself as a "spokesman of the emergent middle class, advocating thrift, caution, and career planning,"[20] reflecting the projection of mercantile caste ethos as a means of upward mobility for all. Marwaris also contributed in other ways to the "flowering" of Hindi. They were patrons and participants in the growing field of Hindi journalism. The oldest Hindi newspaper in India, *Udant Martand*, began publication in Calcutta in 1826 with Marwari support. There were over twenty Hindi newspapers in India financed by Marwari traders by the end of the nineteenth century, including *Marwari Bapari*, *Burra Bazaar Gazette*, *Marwari*, and *Bharat Mitra*, all of which reported on local economic matters and legal developments.[21] If the new Hindi was the vehicle for the imagination of modern India and a Hindu India, Marwaris played a leading role in its birth.

The Marwari mercantile diaspora also played an active role at the forefront of the *sanātan dharma* or "eternal religion" movement, which projected an unchanged spiritual unity, dating back to an ancient past, as underlying the heart of the many *sampradāys* and orders of South Asia. This "revivalist" movement of socially conservative and "high"-caste men confronted the "reformist" agenda of groups such as the Arya Samaj of north India and the Brahmo Samaj of Bengal. On the reformist side, the Arya Samaj rejected the worship of images and the hereditary nature of caste (even as it did not seek to do away with caste entirely). Philip Lutgendorf has argued that the *sanātan dharmīs* tended to define themselves in opposition to "others." For them, reformist projects such as widow remarriage among "high" castes, the initiation of "untouchables" into elite religious orders, and abandonment of image worship were decidedly incompatible with Hindu identity.[22]

At the same time, the *sanātanīs* needed practices and texts to unite them. The text that met this need was the *Ramcharitmānas*, "a *bhakti* work that still preached reverence for cows and Brahmins, claimed to be in accord with a comfortably undefined 'Veda,' offered a satisfying synthesis of Vaishnavism and Shaivism, and in the minds of many devotees, stood at one and the same time for fervent devotional egalitarianism, the maintenance of the social status quo, and even a kind of nationalism in that it countered the British colonial ethos with an idealized vision of a powerful and harmonious Hindu state."[23] The *Rāmcharitmānas* was a vernacular, premodern Hindi rendering of the story of Ram, originally in Sanskrit. The brahman poet Tulsidas (1532–1623) had originally composed it to make the story of the Vaishnav avatar Ram and devotion to him more accessible to women and "low" castes. By the nineteenth century, caste elites, particularly merchants, in the Awadh region had come around to sponsoring recitations and exegesis of this text in private gatherings. The aim was to foster ideals such as virtuous womanhood, ideal kingship, loyal service, and martial glory that were at the heart of the epic of Ram.

To win more followers and unite those already in the fold, the *sanātanī* movement needed funds. Marwari members and sympathizers stepped up. These donors and patrons were galvanized by a sense of belonging to the community of "Marwari" merchants and traders. This Marwari network, in local contexts as well as transregionally, gave generous grants to *sanātanī* initiatives. One important avenue for this support was the Marwari investment in printing presses as a means of spreading their religio-social ideals. For instance, Ganga Vishnu Bajaj and Krishnadas Bajaj of Churu in Bikaner kingdom set up Shri Venkateshwar Printing Press in Bombay in 1871. Beginning with the *Hanumān Chālīsā* and the *Viśṇu Sahasranām*, the press went on to publish thousands of titles spanning religion, spiritualism, philosophy, culture, and history.[24] Marwari businessmen also sponsored the publication of magazines meant to promote internal introspection and moral "uplift" among their own caste fellows. Whether as individuals or through formalized associations, Marwaris brought out journals such as *Marwari Gazette* (1890), *Marwari Sudhar* (1921), and *Marwari Agarwal* (1923) in order to "revitalize" the community.

The journal *Kalyāṇ*, and the creation of the Gita Press in Gorakhpur (modern-day Uttar Pradesh) in 1923 as the publisher of this monthly, were both funded by Marwari money. Hanuman Prasad Poddar of Shekhawati and Jaidayal Goyandka of Churu, both of whom were active in diasporic organizations of Marwaris like the Shri Marwari Agrawal Mahasabha, were leaders of the Gita Press enterprise.[25] The foundation of the Gita Press marked a turning point in the effort to unite and mobilize not only Marwaris but also a larger Hindu nation with Marwari mercantile castes at its forefront.[26] *Kalyāṇ* saw *sanātan dharma*, a return to the imagined ideals of a pure Hindu religion of the ancient past, as the only savior of Marwaris and all other Hindus.[27] Until the early 1970s, according to Paul Arney, it had the highest circulation of any Indian periodical and, until the early 1990s, retained the highest circulation of any Hindi monthly periodical.[28]

Apart from publishing this popular monthly, the Gita Press also played a key role in making the *Rāmcharitmānas* even more accessible to the wider Hindi-reading public. In this, it met with immense success. By 1983, the Gita Press had sold 5.7 million copies of the *Rāmcharitmānas*.[29] Even as the journal *Kalyāṇ* openly supported untouchability, some of its activities made Hindu devotion accessible to all, at least anyone who could afford a copy or buy a printed image of God.[30] To that extent, the steadfast adherence of Marwari merchants to image worship—central to the Vallabh Sampraday of which many of them were part—in the face of Arya Samaj and other reformist calls for a "return" to a Vedic religion devoid of image worship, played a part in creating a new print-based visual culture of devotion.[31]

Another important avenue for the galvanizing of a unified Hindu body that benefitted from Marwari mercantile support was the cow protection movement, particularly from the early twentieth century onward. *Gaurakśiṇī sabhās* or cow-protecting councils began to pop up across the United Provinces and the region's Marwaris funded them.[32] The appearance of these bodies was in an atmosphere of increasingly strained relations in the United Provinces between Hindus and Muslims, with *prabhāt pherīs* (delegations of devotees on early morning rounds) that played loud music in front of mosques and "reconversion" to Hinduism or *śuddhi* ("purification") becoming tools of Hindu community mobilization and expansion against a Muslim "other." The cow-protectionist impulse also singled out leatherworkers, *chamārs*, and landless, vagrant groups such as *naṭs* (entertainers) and *bañjārās* as complicit in the slaughter of cows.[33] The similarity on this point between the protection of nonhuman lives, and not just cows, in general on the one hand and the persecution of Muslims, butchers, and landless vagrants on the other in eighteenth-century Marwar is hard to miss. Since the protection of cows derived from the particularly sacred nature of this animal in Hindu belief and practice across sects and castes, it could appeal across a vast cross-section of castes in regions like the United Provinces where the Vaishnav-Jain ethos of western Indian merchants was not dominant. As in eighteenth-century Marwar with the concern of animal lives, the United Provinces in the late nineteenth century saw the use of "the cow to separate from upper caste culture these low caste 'outsiders.'"[34]

Arney and Akshay Mukul have noted that at moments when tensions between Hindus and Muslims escalated on a national or regional scale, mouthpieces for the *sanātanīs* among Marwaris, such as the Gita Press's *Kalyāṇ*, came down firmly and clearly on the side of the perception that Hindus, particularly Hindu women, were in danger and needed defense from "others."[35] Were these same moments also times when tensions between "high"-caste Hindus and those they deemed peripheral if not external to the caste order escalated? What *sanātanī* politics on the ground made clear was that the "others" who were a threat to Hindu religion also included such "Untouchables" as *chamārs*, *naṭs*, butchers, and *bañjārās*.

As with any other community, the *sanātanī* path was not the only response of Marwaris to colonial modernity. Some were drawn to the Arya Samaj, though despite all the differences between the "revivalists" and the "reformists," there was also much that votaries of these two approaches to Hindu practice agreed and overlapped on. Ritu Birla has shown other convergences between the reformists and traditionalists among the Marwaris, in particular their shared investment in the joint family as a social institution and their opposition as a result to the extension of civil law of contract into marriage.[36] By the twentieth century, some Marwaris questioned the conservatism of their community, with prominent members of the community like Jamnalal Bajaj and G. D. Birla supporting widow remarriage, a raising of the age of consent, and de-emphasizing caste, particularly within the broader Marwari community.[37]

Marwari participation was only one among a whole complex of factors that contributed to the crafting for the first time of "Hinduism" and to visions of a Hindu nation. Still, the role of Marwari leadership in the articulation of the Hindu nation and the proselytization of this idea at the translocal and local levels was significant. Merchants of Marwari origin carried into this vision of the Hindu community and the Hindu nation some of the caste politics and modes of pursuing it that they had developed in eighteenth-century Marwar. To their role as sponsors, leaders, and committed supporters of the conservative vision of the emergent ideal of the Hindu nation and of the "eternal religion" of Hinduism, Marwaris brought not just their financial might but also their precolonial history of effectively organizing under transcaste banners to act as pressure groups upon the authorities.

Unlike in precolonial Marwar, the mercantile diaspora in colonial South Asia found itself shut out of governmental offices. No longer having the option to be part of the state, the Marwari mercantile diaspora reorganized to craft a new public sphere of print, devotional assemblies, and associational politics to mobilize a collective body, create and energize transregional networks, and lobby the government. They pressured the government not only on matters pertaining to business and representation but also in defense of their caste and ethical ideals. The dominant conservative section among the Marwari mercantile community also worked to propagate beyond their own caste and in alliance with other elite castes, particularly brahmans, their vision of what it meant to be "Hindu." The active involvement of the Marwari mercantile community in the Hindu nationalist parties and organizations continues into the present.

But what does the precolonial, eighteenth-century history of Marwar have to do with nineteenth- and twentieth-century Marwari activism in defense of a particular vision of the Hindu community and Hindu ideals? Despite the message of unity, the collaboration on the ground with such "lower" castes as pastoralists, oilpressers, and sweetmakers, and the effort to make Hindu ideology accessible to the "masses" through cheap printed works, the "Hindu" vision of the mercantile diaspora and its elite caste allies ultimately remains unstable into the present. For the elite castes at the helm of the Hindu nationalist project and in control of the bulk of India's resources, caste hierarchy and difference remain core values that are at odds with a message of broad "Hindu" inclusivity.

Going back to the nineteenth century, the Marwari diaspora did indeed cherish a Hindu identity grounded in caste. As I argued in this book, this was an elite caste identity that took on shape in opposition to the specter of the Untouchable, which in turn subsumed the Muslim. Colonial forms of knowledge transformed caste itself into something "far more pervasive, far more totalizing, and far more uniform" than it had ever been and also defined it as an order rooted in religion.[38] The *sanātanī* agenda—against the reform of caste and gender orders and defending practices, ostensibly emerging from "religion," from encroachment by state legislation—then was an expression of the caste anxiety of the Marwari mercantile diaspora, which in turn had only recently made its way into the very highest echelons of the social order. The creation of distance and the articulation of an embodied distinction from the mass below was hard-won by the merchants, the new middle classes of South Asia, and needed to be defended. The diffusion of Marwari merchants across South Asia in the nineteenth century meant that the political strategies and ethical visions that emerged in eighteenth-century Marwar were dispersed throughout the subcontinent.

Rather than being spokespersons for a premade "conservatism," the mercantile diaspora in the nineteenth century promoted the pursuit of a vision of Hindu India that was shot through with caste and in which they sought to enshrine their caste privilege. This was incompatible with electoral politics, success in which demanded the agglomeration of as large a voting bloc as possible. Neither was this vision of Hindu India compatible with a scenario in which the weight of a representative's words depended on the size of their constituency. This tension continues to run through contemporary Indian democracy that pays lip service to the full inclusion of all while refusing to dismantle the structures that underpin caste discrimination and stigma. Coming into the modern, colonial era, one of India's most powerful mercantile communities, the Marwaris, had an investment in the defense of caste hierarchy and markers of caste distinction as a defining traits of Hindu-ness. A recognition of this is essential for a full understanding of South Asia's colonial and postcolonial modernities.

DISGUST AND CASTE ETHICS

The emphasis on bodily austerity, the sublimation of base desires, and the pursuit of temperance, vegetarianism, and chastity that were features of the historical recasting of Hindu-ness in eighteenth-century Marwar only took on momentum, even as they were inflected by colonial modernity, as both Hindu identity and caste were remade in the colonial era. Anthropological studies of untouchability have noted the affective dimension of caste in the form of disgust or *ghṛṇā/ghin* that those higher up in the caste order are socialized to feel in response to the presence of an "Untouchable."[39] Ambedkar too observed "Hindu dispositions toward 'untouchables' as governed by 'odium and avoidance.'"[40] An ethnographic study of the 2002 pogrom in Gujarat, located just south of Marwar, noted:

> The themes of animal sacrifice, butchering, and meat eating continually recurred in the Gujarati discourse on Muslims. They formed an important part of the imaginary grid of the pogrom and allowed for the mobilization of strong collective resentment. Hindu-identified individuals seemed more eager to be explicit in their discussions with me about their quotidian associations and idiomatic expressions concerning meat. Vegetarian arguments emerged when all other arguments for the legitimacy of violence seemed no longer reasonable and the speaker needed to hold on to a distinction in relation to Muslims.[41]

Here too disgust, particularly at the sight and smell of meat and by extension by proximity to those who ate it, played a powerful role in stimulating affective responses among caste Hindus toward Muslims.[42] A notable feature of the posture of aversion toward meat is that the "vice" of meateating generally was bundled alongside other "bad" habits such as drinking, smoking, and illicit sex.[43] The evocation of disgust, its association with excessive bodily appetites for the flesh, whether as meat or as sex, and of a defiling body, reverberates through popular representations of the Muslim as "other" in literature and film into the present.[44] Reinforced through everyday disputes over odor, hygiene, and sensibilities in office dining spaces, school lunch breaks, and residential spaces, the "vegetarian" has become a euphemism for the high-caste Hindu.[45] Caste operates as an embodied form of difference, and it is through these diffuse and everyday practices rooted in somatic and sensory engagements that the difference, hierarchy, and exclusion of caste are produced and reproduced in India today. Even as modernity has caused the visual markers of caste—of dress, of speech, of bodily adornment—that made caste easily legible in the premodern past to be less reliable, one premodern manifestation of caste, food practice, continues to remain a crucial clue in "discreet" forensics of modern-day caste identification.[46]

Balmurli Natarajan argues that in recent decades elite-caste Indians and the Indian diaspora in the West have recast caste as "culture." In this representation of caste, practices that form the grounds for the assertion of distinction and the attribution of marginality appear only as cultural variety and not as hierarchy or discrimination. The "culturization" of caste then allows practices heavily laden with prejudice to be presented as "diversity" and "preference," which in turn is an obstacle to the anticaste project.[47] Vegetarianism, rather than being a matter of cultural or ethical preference alone, is in the South Asian context imbricated with caste ideology and caste practice. This, I have argued, has a deep history dating back to the early modern era.

The project to annihilate caste then demands a recognition of its quotidian forms, of the centrality of touchability/untouchability, and of the deep history that lies behind present-day attachments to bodily ethics that are an expression of caste. Rather than a vague and unhistoricized "tradition" or timeless brahmanical texts, a history of political struggle and of the emergence of new social groups in the early modern age played a significant role in the fusing of vegetarianism with "elite" caste identity beyond solely brahmans. The slow and diffuse birth of a global capitalist order in the course of the early modern period led to a reformulation of caste through nonviolence and vegetarianism as added attributes of caste "purity." The leadership and activity of mercantile groups played a key role in engineering this shift, demonstrating that caste ideology could be reshaped by nonbrahmans too. Even as the early modern age permitted the geographical circulations, flows, and encounters that recent scholarship on the early modern era has highlighted, it also intensified social fixity for those at the receiving end of local power structures.

ACKNOWLEDGMENTS

This book's journey began a long time ago: all the way back in 2006 at Jawaharlal Nehru University (JNU), New Delhi. Discussions about what anticaste politics and scholarship ought to look like, particularly with Prabodhan Pol, were eye-opening. Gopal Guru's lectures on campus and Tanika Sarkar's class in JNU on caste, gender, and labor in colonial South Asia only solidified my interest in the history of caste in the region's precolonial, early modern past. Nandita Prasad Sahai, who advised my MPhil dissertation, and Rajat Datta, who advised a master's research paper—both of whom alas have passed away—helped me find my way in turning my abstract questions into what eventually became my doctoral research. Najaf Haider gave me a rigorous grounding in the history of Mughal India and has remained a valued interlocutor. At Columbia University, my doctoral advisor Nicholas Dirks trained me to think across disciplines and with an eye to the big picture, and he continued as a source of good counsel during my revision of the dissertation into this book. I owe much to the other members of my doctoral committee. Janaki Bakhle has been an astute reader of my work over the years, helping me sharpen my arguments. Partha Chatterjee brought mirth and insightful feedback in equal measure to each meeting that I had with him about this work. Samira Sheikh helped ground the dissertation in the history of early modern western India and of merchant religiosity while also shaping it to speak to the field as a whole. Pamela Smith's comments on the dissertation version of this book were invaluable in giving it rigor and clarity.

This book would have looked very different without the intellectual community at Princeton University. Successive chairs of my department—William Chester Jordan, Keith Wailoo, and Angela Creager, and Michael Gordin as acting chair for a year—provided thoughtful advice and enthusiastic support as I worked on this book. In ways big and small, my colleagues at the History Department have shaped me. Gyan Prakash has been a sounding board and a careful reader of my work. Jeremy Adelman and Shel Garon drew me toward new approaches to global history. Molly Greene guided me through scholarship on the early modern Ottoman Empire. Michael Laffan gave me thoughtful and fine-grained feedback on a draft of this manuscript. My year working with David Bell at the Davis Center led me to think anew about the eighteenth century in South Asian history.

I have benefitted from conversations with Thomas Conlan, Joshua Guild, Hendrik Hartog, Alison Isenberg, Beth Lew-Williams, and Philip Nord. Margot Canaday, Vera Candiani, Janet Chen, Linda Colley, Yaacob Dweck, Joseph Fronczak, Tera Hunter, Matt Karp, Emmanuel Kreike, Regina Kunzel, Rosina Lozano, Federico Marcon, Erika Milam, Sue Naquin, Jack Tannous, and Wendy Warren have been sources of wise counsel. Teas and meals over the years with He Bian, Jacob Dlamini, Eleanor Hubbard, Rob Karl, Isadora Mota, Xin Wen, Peter Wirzbicki, and Natasha Wheatley have helped sustain me through this journey. Judy Hanson kept things on course. Ben Baer, Fauzia Farooqui, Sadaf Jaffar, Robert Phillips, Anu Ramaswami, Dan Sheffield, Tehseen Thaver, and Muhammad Qasim Zaman have helped recreate a little bit of South Asia at Princeton and for this I am grateful. Students, both graduate and undergraduate, at Princeton have inspired me with their energy, perspectives, and hope. Conversations with Adhitya Dhanapal, Saumyashree Ghosh, Hasan Hameed, Manav Kapur, Rini Kujur, Jiya Pandya, Kalyani Ramnath, Tara Suri, Neel Thakkar, and Niharika Yadav have allowed me to return to my own research and writing reenergized.

This book has also benefitted from conversations with other scholarly communities of which I have been lucky to be a part. The Rutgers Center of Historical Analysis at Rutgers–New Brunswick steeped me in a year of reflection on the history of ethics and power. Seth Koven and Judith Surkis were everything that a mind fresh out of a PhD could have asked for. Sabine Cadeau, Chris Finley, and Özge Serin were a source of warmth and support. The fellowship of Zara Anishanslin, Kate Cooper, Thomas Dodman, Sara Kozameh, Durba Mitra, Cristina Soriano, Massimiliano Tomba, and Kirsten Welt, with David Bell at the helm, at Princeton's Davis Center in 2020–21 was immensely generative.

Along the way, many scholars have commented on drafts of all or part of this work. John Cort, Christian Lee Novetzke, John S. Hawley, and Cynthia Talbot kindly participated in a manuscript workshop for this book. When considering this book for publication, Robert P. Goldman closely read three chapters. I am also grateful to Norbert Peabody and the three anonymous reviewers for the press. Others whose feedback on all or parts of this work over the years has been fruitful are Febe Armanios, Anjali Arondekar, Manan Ahmed Asif, Gajendran Ayyathurai, Shahzad Bashir, Guy L. Beck, Debjani Bhattacharyya, Bhawani Buswala, Indrani Chatterjee, Nandini Chatterjee, Vasudha Dalmia, Purnima Dhavan, Boğaç Ergene,

Simon W. Fuchs, Supriya Gandhi, Arunabh Ghosh, Sumit Guha, Usman Hamid, Abhishek Kaicker, Emma Kalb, Christine M. Karwoski, J. Mark Kenoyer, Joel Lee, Elizabeth Lhost, B. Venkat Mani, Sumeet Mhaskar, Anne Murphy, Naveena Naqvi, Bhavani Raman, Dalpat Rajpurohit, Ramnarayan Rawat, Nathaniel Roberts, Adheesh Sathaye, Mitra Sharafi, Hasan Siddiqui, Ramya Sreenivasan, Anand Vivek Taneja, Elizabeth Thelen, Sharika Thiranagama, Rupa Viswanath, and Tyler Williams. Dalpat Rajpurohit patiently answered my questions about particularly thorny Marwari words and translations. I thank Bart Wright for the maps in this book. As it nears publication, I am deeply saddened to not be able to present it to my teachers who shaped it with their care and counsel but who have passed away: Allison Busch, Rajat Datta, and Nandita Prasad Sahai.

Thanks are due to the all the institutions and people who made the research for this book possible. The Director of the Rajasthan State Archives, Bikaner, Dr. Mahendra Khadgawat, aided the securing of image permissions. His tremendous efforts toward digitizing this vast archive have been a blessing for historians of Rajasthan. At this same repository, the late Shri Poonam Chand Joiyya always made time to introduce any interested new researcher, including me, to the scripts and languages of precolonial Rajasthani records. I can never forget the happiness on his face every time I went running to his office with an exciting new find from the *bahīs*. As someone who spent all of his own free time immersed in the records, Shri Joiyya knew just how special that feeling was. I am also grateful to staff at other repositories in Rajasthan and Gujarat for facilitating my research for this book: the Anup Sanskrit Library and Abhay Jain Granthalaya, both in Bikaner, the Rajasthan Oriental Research Institute branches in Bikaner and Jodhpur, the Maharaja Mansingh Pustak Prakash Library in Jodhpur, the Lalbhai Dalpatbhai Museum and Library in Ahmedabad, and the Acharya Shri Kailasasagarsuri Gyanmandir in Koba (near Gandhinagar). In Delhi, I am thankful to staff at the National Archives of India, and in London, to Emma Weech and Edward Stone at the Royal Asiatic Society. Karni Singh Jasol, Director, and Sunayana Rathore, Curator, at the Mehrangarh Museum Trust in Jodhpur were an immense help in gaining image permissions for this book.

A number of institutions supported my research for this book and for its revision. I am grateful to the American Institute of Indian Studies for a Junior Fellowship, to the Charlotte Newcombe Foundation for a Doctoral Dissertation Fellowship, to Columbia University and its History Department for summer research funds, to the Rutgers Center for Historical Analysis at Rutgers–New Brunswick for a postdoctoral research fellowship, and to the office of the Dean of the Faculty, the History Department, and the University Committee on Research in the Humanities and Social Sciences at Princeton University for research support over the years. Thanks are due to Muzaffar Alam, Gauri Viswanathan, and Robert Goldman, co-editors of the *South Asia Across the Disciplines* series, for selecting this manuscript for publication and for their feedback on the manuscript. I am thankful to the American Institute of Indian Studies for awarding this manuscript the 2022 Joseph W. Elder Prize in the Indian Social Sciences. This prize, along with funds from the *South Asia Across the Disciplines* series, at the University of California Press supported the open-access publication of this book. Reed Malcolm, Kim Robinson, LeKeisha Hughes, Enrique Ochoa-Kaup, and Cindy Fulton deftly shepherded my manuscript through editorial and production processes at UC Press. I thank Paul Tyler for copyediting this book and Alexander Trotter for indexing it.

At the research stage, Kailash Rani "Kanchan" Chaudhari offered me a place to stay on one of my early research trips to Bikaner. As a fellow researcher at the Bikaner archives, she was a companion on long days of work in the research room. Savita Choudhary, Julie E. Hughes, and Elizabeth Thelen were other companions at the Rajasthan State Archives. Kanchan Chaudhari's family, Sanjay, Riya, and Karan Saharan brought fun to my initial forays into Bikaner. The Dhussa family and the residents, especially Nirmala Suthar, of the women's hostel that they ran in Bikaner were my anchors for the many months I spent in the town in 2011–12. Gayatri and Rishabdev Singh of Udai Niwas Bed & Breakfast were warm hosts to me and my family in the summer of 2018. At this point, Bikaner feels like a home away from home.

Keeping this ship afloat would have been impossible without the love, support, and humor of friends and family. For making sure that there were good times, thanks are due to: Meghna Agarwala, Anisha Anthinattu, Shiva Bajpai, Dwaipayan Banerjee, Durba Chattaraj, Mario Da Penha, Joanna Dee Das, Sejuti Dasgupta, Arunabh Ghosh, Samira Junaid, Abhishek Kaicker, Joel Lee, James MacDowell, Ajeet Singh Matharu, Thomas Mathew, Aditi Mehra, Taneesha Devi Mohan, Sarika Mishra, Sinjini Mukherjee, Naïma Phillips, Dalpat Rajpurohit, James Reich, Rashmi Sahni, Shivani Satija, Anirvan Sen, Arup Sen, Rafi Sengupta, William Sentell, Joanna Slater, Matt Swagler, Akshaya Tankha, Kanishk Tharoor, Drew Thomases, Alexios Tsigkas, Laurie Vasily, and Tyler Williams. Nathan and Celeste Arrington, Tom Griffiths, Melissa Holt, Melissa Larrazabal, Tania Lombrozo, Ricardo Mallarino, Catalina Perdomo, Jack and Jeannette Tannous, and Lori VerMurlen helped me survive pandemic parenting. Aditi Anand, Swara Bhasker, Katyayani Dalmia, Vijayanka Nair, and Supriya Nayak feel at this point more like sisters than friends. Cousins, aunts, and uncles of the Athithotathil, Chemmarapalli, Kak, and Karihaloo clans have provided a warm support system. My grandmothers Aleyamma John and Sarojini "Chuni Jigri" Kak built the foundation on which I stand. My maternal grandfather, Ram Nath Kak, inculcated in me a love of learning from a very young age, despite my protestations at the time.

My sister, Madhavi Cherian, has been my cheerleader for as long as I remember. My brother-in-law Khushal Chand Thakur and the Nash and Patton families, particularly Kate Nash, Susan Nash, Wade Nash, and Chuck Stepleton, have been sources of encouragement. My late mother-in-law, DJ Nash, was deeply supportive of my work. She would have been proud to see this book out in the world. My daughters, Aranya and Karuna, have sweetly tolerated the time and mind space that this book has taken from me, even as they are starting to question its existence. It takes a village, they say, and I could not have juggled motherhood with research, teaching, and writing if not for Indra Pieris and the teachers at the Rita Gold Early Childhood Center in New York City and at Crossroads Day Nursery and UNOW Daycare in Princeton. My parents raised me to be curious and to think outside the margins. My mother, Shakti Kak, helped me look after my children in their infancy and during my travels for research. She is a role model to me in more ways than I can count. My father, John Cherian, instilled in me a spirit of adventure and a global outlook. Andrew Nash has been a partner in the challenges and chores of parenthood, a loving companion, and a thoughtful interlocutor. He has brought laughter and stability to the vicissitudes that life never ceases to generate. It is to him and my parents that I dedicate this book.

NOTES

INTRODUCTION

1. Aniket Jaaware, *Practicing Caste: On Touching and Not Touching* (New York: Fordham University Press, 2019), 161 (italics in the original).

2. For recent ethnographic studies of the religious practices of Dalits in contemporary India, see Nathaniel Roberts, *To Be Cared For: The Power of Conversion and the Foreignness of Belonging in an Indian Slum* (Oakland: University of California Press, 2016); and Joel Lee, *Deceptive Majority: Dalits, Hinduism, and Underground Religion* (New York: Cambridge University Press, 2021).

3. Rupa Viswanath, *The Pariah Problem: Caste, Religion, and the Social in Modern India* (New York: Columbia University Press, 2014), 8. Ramnarayan Rawat identifies this as the defining trait and scholarly departure made by the nascent field of Dalit Studies—"Dalit" or "the broken" being the name that formerly "untouchable" communities prefer for themselves. Rawat, "Occupation, Dignity, and Space: The Rise of Dalit Studies," *History Compass* 11/12 (2013): 1059–67.

4. Jaaware, *Practicing Caste*, 160–61.

5. Jaaware, *Practicing Caste*, 33, 57, 156–57, 164, 192.

6. Ramnarayan Rawat has argued this on the basis of colonial-era records in *Reconsidering Untouchability: Chamārs and Dalit History in North India* (Bloomington: Indiana University Press, 2011). See also Viswanath, *The Pariah Problem.*

7. Irfan Habib, *The Agrarian System of Mughal India, 1556–1707*, 3rd ed. (New Delhi: Oxford University Press, 2012 [1963]); Frank Perlin, "Proto-Industrialization and Pre-Colonial South Asia," *Past & Present* 98, no. 1 (1983): 30–95; Dirk H. A. Kolff, *Naukar, Rajput, and Sepoy: The Ethnohistory of the Military Labour Market in Hindustan, 1450–1850* (Cambridge: Cambridge University Press, 1990); Nicholas Dirks, *The Hollow Crown: Ethnohistory of an Indian Kingdom* (Ann Arbor: University of Michigan Press, 1993) and *Castes of Mind: Colonialism and the Making of Modern India* (Princeton: Princeton University Press, 2001);

V. Narayan Rao, David Shulman, and Sanjay Subrahmanyam, *Textures of Time: Writing History in South India, 1600–1800* (New York: Other Press, 2003); Sumit Guha, *History and Collective Memory in South Asia, 1200–2000* (Seattle: University of Washington Press, 2019); Manan Ahmed Asif, *The Loss of Hindustan: The Invention of India* (Cambridge, MA: Harvard University Press, 2020).

8. Dirks, *The Hollow Crown* and *Castes of Mind;* Sumit Guha, *Beyond Caste: Identity and Power in South Asia, Past and Present* (Leiden: Brill, 2013). For studies that highlight the role of brahmans or brahmanical values in seventeenth- and eighteenth-century South Asia, see Susan Bayly, *Caste, Society and Politics in India: From the Eighteenth Century to the Modern Age* (New Delhi: Cambridge University Press, 1999), 4–5, 64–96; Rosalind O'Hanlon, Gergely Hidas, and Csaba Kiss, "Discourses of Caste over the Longue Durée: Gopīnātha and Social Classification in India, ca. 1400–1900," *South Asian History and Culture* 6, no. 1 (2015): 117–18; Rosalind O'Hanlon and Christopher Minkowski, "What Makes People Who They Are? Pandit Networks and the Problem of Livelihoods in Early Modern Western India," *Indian Economic and Social History Review* 45, no. 3 (2008): 412.

9. See for instance Markandey Katju, "The Caste System in India: Its History and How It Can Be Defeated," September 4, 2018, https://swarajyamag.com/blogs/is-caste-system-bad-for-india; and Aravindan Neelakandan, "Of India's 'Invention' of the Caste System and Its Constant Battle against It," April 7, 2017, https://swarajyamag.com/ideas/of-indias-invention-of-the-caste-system-and-its-constant-battle-against-it.

10. Ramnarayan Rawat and K. Satyanarayana, introduction to *Dalit Studies* (Durham: Duke University Press, 2016), 9.

11. As most famously argued by Louis Dumont in *Homo Hierarchicus: The Caste System and Its Implications* (Chicago: University of Chicago Press, 1980), 36–39. For a rebuttal of Dumont grounded in history, see Dirks, *Castes of Mind.*

12. For some recent histories of "untouchable" or Dalit communities in modern South Asia, see Gyan Prakash, *Bonded Histories: Genealogies of Labor Servitude in Colonial India* (New York: Cambridge University Press, 1990), 34–82; Saurabh Dube, *Untouchable Pasts: Religion, Community, and Power among a Central Indian Community, 1780–1950* (Buffalo: SUNY Press, 1998); Vijay Prashad, *Untouchable Freedom: A Social History of a Dalit Community* (New York: Oxford University Press, 2000); Anupama Rao, *The Caste Question: Dalits and the Politics of Modern India* (Berkeley: University of California Press, 2009); Rawat, *Reconsidering Untouchability;* Viswanath, *The Pariah Problem;* Chinnaiah Jangam, *Dalits and the Making of Modern India* (New Delhi: Oxford University Press, 2019).

13. Jon Keune, "Pedagogical Otherness: The Use of Muslims and Untouchables in Some Hindu Devotional Literature," *Journal of the American Academy of Religion* 84, no. 3 (2016): 727–49.

14. Dirks, *Hollow Crown*, 78–93, 117–38.

15. Bayly, *Caste, Society and Politics*, 64–97.

16. *Jodhpur Sanad Parwāna Bahī* (henceforth, JSPB) 32, VS 1842/1785 CE, f 293b. These sources have in recent years been digitized by the Rajasthan State Archives, Bikaner, where they are currently located. They can be accessed at http://rsadapp.rajasthan.gov.in/. This particular record can be found in JSPB 32; it is erroneously listed on the website as being from the Vikram Samvat (VS) year 1841, even though it is from VS 1842, as each entry within the *bahī* attests.

17. *Śrī Parameśvar* is one of the "thousand names" of Vishnu. See Frederick W. Bunce, *An Encyclopedia of Hindu Deities: Demi-Gods, Godlings, Demons, and Heroes*, vol. 1 (New Delhi: DK Printworld, 2000), 397.

18. Sitaram Lalas, *Rājasthānī-Hindī Saṅkśipt Śabdkoṣ* [Concise Rajasthani-Hindi Dictionary], vol. 1 (Jodhpur: Rajasthan Oriental Research Institute vol. 1, 2006 [1986]), 29.

19. "*Turk*"/"*turak*" in north Indian vernaculars such as Hindavi and Rajasthani. The term by the eighteenth century was both an ethnic and a religious one, derived from the initial association of Islam in north India with Persianized Turks who set up the first Islamicate polities in the Gangetic Plains starting with the Delhi Sultanate in the twelfth century CE.

20. The *thorīs* and *bāvrīs* were landless groups that manipulated the boundaries between desert scrub and settled cultivation to eke out a living through small-scale theft, employment as armed retainers to local landlords, and as wage-earning agricultural labor.

21. These castes are often described as "sweepers," "manual scavengers," or "sanitation castes" today. In eighteenth-century Marwar, they did the "dirty" work of clearing human waste and animal carcasses from homes and public spaces in urban and rural South Asia.

22. Gopal Guru and Sundar Sarukkai, *Experience, Caste, and the Everyday Social* (New Delhi: Oxford University Press, 2019).

23. Here I draw upon Sanjay Subrahmanyam's call to think beyond Area Studies and nation-state boundaries as well as Sebastian Conrad's methodological interventions on scale. See Sanjay Subrahmanyam, "Connected Histories: Notes towards a Reconfiguration of Early Modern Eurasia," *Modern Asian Studies* 31, no. 3 (1997): 735–62; Sebastian Conrad, *What Is Global History?* (Princeton: Princeton University Press, 2016).

24. Satish Chandra, "Commercial Activities of the Mughal Emperors during the Seventeenth Century," *Bengal Past and Present* 87 (1959): 92–97; Sanjay Subrahmanyam and Christopher A. Bayly, "Portfolio Capitalists and the Political Economy of Early Modern India," *Indian Economic and Social History Review* 25, no. 4 (1988): 414–15.

25. A. I. Chicherov, *India: Economic Development in the 16th–18th Centuries: Outline History of Crafts and Trade* (Moscow: Nauka Publishing House, 1971); Jairus Banaji, *A Brief History of Commercial Capitalism* (Chicago: Haymarket Books, 2020). Perlin criticizes Chicherov's work for its "sloppy" use of evidence and its dated paradigm, but he accepts and seeks to more successfully argue his thesis about India's integration into an emergent, early capitalist order. Perlin, "Proto-Industrialization," 55. While Banaji's account is centered on Europe and to some extent the Middle East, he makes clear that his framework can apply to other parts of the world as well. Banaji, *Commercial Capitalism*, 119.

26. Perlin, "Proto-Industrialization," 92.

27. Perlin, "Proto-Industrialization," 62–63. Africans were also brought over to be sold as slaves in South Asia. For a comparison of the Atlantic and South Asian contexts vis-à-vis slavery, see Sanjay Subrahmanyam, "Between Eastern Africa and Western India, 1500–1650: Slavery, Commerce, and Elite Formation," *Comparative Studies in Society and History* 61, no. 4 (2019): 805–34.

28. Perlin, "Proto-Industrialization"; Banaji, *Commercial Capitalism*, 119.

29. Perlin, "Proto-Industrialization," 98.

30. Perlin, "Proto-Industrialization," 66.

31. In deploying diplomatics or the structural and institutional analysis of the documents I use as sources, I am inspired by Marina Rustow, *The Lost Archive: Traces of a*

Caliphate in a Cairo Synagogue (Princeton: Princeton University Press, 2020), 8–11. For South Asian history, Nandini Chatterjee's recent study of Mughal law has paid close attention to the form and formal conventions of precolonial documents to come upon novel insights. See Nandini Chatterjee, *Negotiating Mughal Law: A Family of Landlords across Three Indian Empires* (New York: Cambridge University Press, 2020).

32. The early-modern Rathor state in Jodhpur thus has a number of *bahī* series: *Byāv Bahīs*, containing details of royal weddings; *Ohdā Bahīs*, containing lists of officers; *Paṭṭā Bahīs*, recording land revenue assignments; and so on.

33. Baki Tezcan, *The Second Ottoman Empire: Political and Social Transformation in the Early Modern World* (New York: Cambridge University Press, 2010).

34. Ali Yaycıoğlu, *Partners of the Empire: The Crisis of the Ottoman Order in the Age of Revolutions* (Stanford: Stanford University Press, 2016), 65–115.

35. Richard John Lufrano, *Honorable Merchants: Commerce and Self-Cultivation in Late Imperial China* (Honolulu: University of Hawai'i Press, 1997).

36. David L. Howell, "Urbanization, Trade, and Merchants," in *Japan Emerging: Premodern History to 1850*, ed. Karl F. Friday (Boulder, CO: Westview Press, 2012), 361-62.

37. Denis Gainty, "The New Warriors: Samurai in Early Modern Japan," in Friday, *Japan Emerging*, 348.

38. Toby Green, *A Fistful of Shells: West Africa from the Rise of the Slave Trade to the Age of Revolution* (Chicago: Chicago University Press, 2019), 401–29.

39. For the role of brahmans in trade and moneylending in the early modern era, see André Wink, *Land and Sovereignty in India: Agrarian Society and Politics under the Eighteenth-Century Maratha Svarājya* (Cambridge: Cambridge University Press, 1986), 331–39; Francesca Trivellato, *The Familiarity of Strangers: The Sephardic Diaspora, Livorno, and Cross-Cultural Trade in the Early Modern Period* (New Haven: Yale University Press, 2009), 177–93; Rosalind O'Hanlon, "Letters Home: Banaras Pandits and the Maratha Regions in Early Modern India," *Modern Asian Studies* 44, no. 2 (2010): 211.

40. See for instance Bhim Rao Ambedkar, *Dr. Babasaheb Ambedkar: Writings and Speeches*, vol. 3, 2nd ed., ed. Hari Narke (New Delhi: Dr. Ambedkar Foundation, 2014), 25–37, 65–66, 87, 106–7, 128.

41. Anand Teltumbde, "Introduction to the Revised Edition," in *Hindutva and Dalits: Perspectives for Understanding Communal Practice*, rev. ed., ed. Anand Teltumbde (New Delhi: Sage, 2020), xxiv. For an explanation of the term "communalism" as a colonialist form of knowledge and its unique meaning in colonial India, see Gyanendra Pandey, Introduction to *The Construction of Communalism in Colonial North India* (New Delhi: Oxford University Press, 1990), 1–22.

42. On the importance of the everyday to precolonial caste and religion, see Christian L. Novetzke, *Quotidian Revolution: Vernacularization, Religion, and the Premodern Public Sphere in India* (New York: Columbia University Press, 2016). For the significance of the separation of "religion" from the everyday in the colonial period, see Dilip M. Menon, "The Blindness of Insight: Why Communalism in India Is about Caste," in *The Blindness of Insight: Essays on Caste in Modern India*, ed. Dilip Menon (New Delhi: Navayana, 2006), 1–32.

43. Unlike the connotation of a dissident group breaking away from an original religious body that the word "sect" bears in relation to Christianity, in the Indic context the term often translated into "sect" in English, *sampradāy* refers to modes of religious practice that generated structures of meaning internally and independent from each other. Elaine

Fisher, *Hindu Pluralism: Religion and the Public Sphere in Early Modern South India* (Oakland: University of California Press, 2017), 13. "Hinduism" as it came to be named in the colonial era was a product of increasing cohesion among some sects rather than being a preexisting entity. See Romila Thapar, "Imagined Religious Communities? Ancient History and the Search for a Hindu Identity," *Modern Asian Studies* 23, no. 2 (1989): 216; Fisher, *Hindu Pluralism*. For further discussion of the scholarly negotiation of the baggage of the terms "sect" and "sectarian," see chapter 1.

44. Wilfred Cantwell Smith, *The Meaning and End of Religion: A Revolutionary Approach to the Great Religious Traditions* (San Francisco: Harper & Row, 1978), 63–66; Thapar, "Imagined Religious Communities?"; Brian K. Smith, "Questioning Authority: Constructions and Deconstructions of Hinduism," *International Journal of Hindu Studies* 2, no. 3 (1998): 313–39; Vasudha Dalmia and Heinrich von Stietencron, eds., *Representing Hinduism: The Construction of Religious Traditions and National Identity* (New Delhi: Sage, 1995); Robert Frykenberg, "The Emergence of Modern 'Hinduism' as a Concept and as an Institution: A Reappraisal with Special Reference to South India," in *Hinduism Reconsidered*, ed. G. D. Sontheimer and H. Kulke (Delhi: Manohar, 1989), 24–29; Fisher, *Hindu Pluralism*.

45. Christopher A. Bayly, "The Pre-History of 'Communalism'? Religious Conflict in India, 1700–1860," *Modern Asian Studies* 19, no. 2 (1985): 177–203; Sheldon Pollock, "Ramayana and Political Imagination in India," *Journal of Asian Studies* 52, no. 2 (1993), 261–97; Cynthia Talbot, "Inscribing the Other, Inscribing the Self: Hindu-Muslim Identities in Pre-Colonial India," *Comparative Studies in Society and History* 37, no. 4 (1995): 704–10; Ramya Sreenivasan, "The Marriage of 'Hindu' and 'Turak': Medieval Rajput Histories of Jalor," *Medieval History Journal* 7, no. 1 (2004): 87–108; David Lorenzen, "Who Invented Hinduism?," in *Who Invented Hinduism? Essays on Religion in History*, ed. David Lorenzen (New Delhi: Yoda Press, 2006), 1–36; Andrew Nicholson, *Unifying Hinduism: Philosophy and Identity in Indian Intellectual History* (Ranikhet: Permanent Black, 2011); Valerie Stoker, *Polemics and Patronage in the City of Victory: Vyasatirtha, Hindu Sectarianism, and the Sixteenth-Century Vijayanagara Court* (Oakland: University of California Press, 2016); Cynthia Talbot, *The Last Hindu Emperor: Prithviraj Chauhan and the Indian Past, 1200–1800* (Cambridge: Cambridge University Press, 2016), 149, 169, 179.

46. Tony Stewart, "Alternate Structures of Authority: Satya Pīr on the Frontiers of Bengal" (21–54); Christopher Shackle, "Beyond Turk and Hindu: Crossing the Boundaries in Indo-Muslim Romance" (55–73); and Vasudha Narayanan, "Religious Vocabulary and Regional Identity: A Study of the Tamil *Cirappuranam*" (74–97), all in David Gilmartin and Bruce Lawrence, eds., *Beyond Turk and Hindu: Rethinking Religious Identities in Islamicate South Asia* (Gainesville: University of Florida Press, 2000); Muzaffar Alam, *The Languages of Political Islam in India* (Chicago: University of Chicago Press, 2004); Samira Sheikh, *Forging a Region: Sultans, Traders and Pilgrims in Gujarat, 1200–1500* (New Delhi: Oxford University Press, 2010); Finbarr Flood, *Objects of Translation: Material Culture and Medieval "Hindu-Muslim" Encounter* (Princeton: Princeton University Press, 2009); Rajeev Kinra, *Writing Self, Writing Empire: Chandar Bhan Brahman and the Cultural World of the Indo-Persian State Secretary* (Oakland: University of California Press, 2015); Audrey Truschke, *Culture of Encounters: Sanskrit at the Mughal Court* (New York: Columbia University Press, 2016); Manan Ahmed Asif, *A Book of Conquest: The* Chachnama *and Muslim Origins in South Asia* (Cambridge, MA: Harvard University Press, 2016) and *Loss of Hindustan;* Patton Burchett, *A Genealogy of Devotion: Bhakti, Tantra, Yoga, and Sufism*

in North India (New York: Columbia University Press, 2019), 276–304. Among progressive intellectuals who are not specialists in premodern South Asian history, the idea has taken root that the term "Hindu" was not used prior to the colonial era by communities we would today call Hindus to name themselves. See for instance this claim in an article in the progressive Indian news magazine *The Caravan:* "Until [the 1850s, 'Hindu'] had been a floating descriptive term for colonial ethnographers. The people designated as 'Hindu' neither used the word for themselves, nor did they consider themselves as adherents of one religion. The limited use of the term was without substantial consequences for the life of the natives." Divya Dwivedi, Shaj Mohan, and J. Reghu, "The Hindu Hoax: How Upper Castes Invented the Hindu Majority," *The Caravan*, December 31, 2020, https://caravanmagazine.in/religion/how-upper-castes-invented-hindu-majority. While it is true that there was no singular Hindu religion in premodern times, there is plenty of scholarship on bhakti poetry and court literature in which the term "Hindu" is used in contradistinction to "Muslim" to denote the self.

47. Veronique Bouillier, "Nath Yogis' Encounters with Islam," *South Asia Multidisciplinary Academic Journal*, free-standing article (2015), 1–15. https://journals.openedition.org/samaj/3878

48. Janaki Bakhle, *Two Men and Music: Nationalism in the Making of an Indian Classical Tradition* (New York: Oxford University Press, 2005), 81–82, 132.

49. For a discussion and rebuttal of colonial and Hindu nationalist accounts of temple desecration by Muslim rulers in South Asia, see Richard Eaton, "Temple Desecration and Indo-Muslim States," in *Beyond Turk and Hindu: Rethinking Religious Identities in Islamicate South Asia*, ed. David Gilmartin and Bruce Lawrence (Gainesville: University of Florida Press, 2000), 246–81. For an effective countering of Hindu nationalist narratives about the spread of Islam in South Asia, see Richard Eaton, *The Rise of Islam and the Bengal Frontier, 1204–1760* (Delhi: Oxford University Press, 1997).

50. Irfan Habib and Tarapada Mukherjee, "Akbar and the Temples of Mathura and Its Environs," in *Proceedings of the Indian History Congress, 48th Session* (Panaji: Goa University, 1988), 234–50; John S. Hawley, *A Storm of Songs: India and the Idea of the Bhakti Movement* (Cambridge, MA: Harvard University Press, 2015), 59–98; Audrey Truschke, *Culture of Encounters* and *Aurangzeb: The Life and Legacy of India's Most Controversial King* (Stanford: Stanford University Press, 2017).

51. Basile Leclère, "Ambivalent Representations of Muslims in Medieval Indian Theatre," *Studies in History* 27, no. 2 (2011): 155–95.

52. Keune, "Pedagogical Otherness," 743–45.

53. See for instance Abhishek Kaicker, *The King and the People: Sovereignty and Popular Politics in Mughal Delhi* (New York: Oxford University Press, 2020), 9.

54. Dirks, *Castes of Mind*; Viswanath, *The Pariah Problem.*

55. See Purnima Dhavan, *When Sparrows Became Hawks: The Making of the Sikh Warrior Tradition, 1699–1799* (New York: Oxford University Press, 2011); Muzaffar Alam, "Introduction to the Second Edition," *The Crisis of Empire in Mughal North India: Awadh and the Punjab, 1707–1748*, 2nd ed. (New Delhi: Oxford University Press, 2013), xlvi–li; Samira Sheikh, "Aurangzeb as Seen from Gujarat: Shi'i and Millenarian Challenges to Mughal Sovereignty," *Journal of the Royal Asiatic Society* 28, no. 3 (2018): 557–81; Kaicker, *The King and the People.*

56. Debra Diamond, "The Politics and Aesthetics of Citation: Nath Painting in Jodhpur, 1803–1843" (PhD diss., Columbia University, 2000), 10–23.

57. Marwar had its own, regional folk deities, known as the Pāñch (or "Five") Pirs. For a discussion of a history of the epics and of contemporary folk practices centered on their worship, see—For Pabuji: Janet Kamphorst, *In Praise of Death: History and Poetry in Medieval Marwar (South Asia)* (Leiden: Leiden University Press, 2008); John D. Smith, *The Epic of Pabuji: A Study, Transcription and Translation* (Cambridge: Cambridge University Press, 1991). For Ramdevji: Dominique-Sila Khan, *Conversions and Shifting Identities: Ramdev Pir and the Ismailis in Rajasthan* (New Delhi: Manohar, 1997); Christopher Pinney, "The Accidental Ramdev: The Spread of a Popular Cult," in *India's Popular Culture: Iconic Spaces and Fluid Images*, ed. Jyotindra Jain (Mumbai: Marg, 2007), 32–45.

58. Parvis Ghassem-Fachandi, *Pogrom in Gujarat: Hindu Nationalism and Anti-Muslim Violence in India* (Princeton: Princeton University Press, 2012).

59. Faisal Chaudhry, "Repossessing Property in South Asia: Land, Rights, and Law across the Early Modern / Modern Divide—Introduction," *Journal of the Economic and Social History of the Orient* 61, no. 5/6 (2018): 780.

60. The rajputs continued to retain strong hereditary claims and rights in land and in a share of the land revenue, even if this was in return for the expectation of loyalty and service to the king. In reality, many rajputs derived their rights in land from their own military conquest and organization of particular parcels of land; or their hold over those parcels of land was through their own mobilization of military and agrarian labor. They were not entirely dependent on the king for their hold over land and claims to land revenue. See B. L. Bhadani, "The Ruler and Nobility in Marwar during the Reign of Jaswant Singh" and "The Allodial Proprietors? The Bhumias of Marwar," in *Economy and Polity of Rajasthan: Study of Kota and Marwar*, ed. Masanori Sato and B. L. Bhadani (Jaipur: Publication Scheme, 1997), 109–47.

61. The term "mahajan" was also used to denote moneylenders in other parts of eighteenth-century South Asia, such as the neighboring kingdoms of Jaipur and Kota as well as much further afield, in Bengal. In Bengal, the trade of moneylending was called "*mahājanī*." See Habib, "Usury in Medieval India," 395. This could well be a reflection of the dominance of western-Indian merchants (mahajans) in the moneylending business.

62. Paul Friedland, "Friends for Dinner: The Early Modern Roots of Modern Carnivorous Sensibilities," *History of the Present* 1, no. 1 (2011): 84–112.

63. Norbert Peabody, *Hindu Kingship and Polity in Precolonial India* (New York: Cambridge University Press, 2003); Madhu Tandon Sethia, *Rajput Polity: Warriors, Peasants, and Merchants, 1700–1800* (Jaipur: Rawat, 2003). Both these studies are on the Hada principality of Kota in southwestern Rajasthan.

64. For studies of literary production at rajput courts in early modern Rajasthan, see Ramya Sreenivasan, *The Many Lives of a Rajput Queen: Heroic Pasts in India, c. 1500–1900* (Seattle: University of Washington Press, 2007); Talbot, *The Last Hindu Emperor*. For examples of existing studies of Marwar that are focused on particular groups, see Nandita Prasad Sahai, *Politics of Patronage and Protest: The State, Society, and Artisans in Early Modern Rajasthan* (New Delhi: Oxford University Press, 2006) (centered on artisans); Tanuja Kothiyal, *Nomadic Narratives: A History of Mobility and Identity in the Great Indian Desert* (Delhi: Cambridge University Press, 2016) (exploring mobile populations).

1. POWER

1. For western India, see Farhat Hasan, *State and Locality in Mughal India: Power Relations in Western India, c. 1572–1730* (New Delhi: Cambridge University Press, 2006).

2. For a discussion of how incorporation into the Mughal Empire as vassals strengthened a drive toward a more monarchical order among rajput polities in western India, see Normal Ziegler, "Some Notes on Rajput Loyalties during the Mughal Period," in *The Mughal State, 1526–1707*, ed. Muzaffar Alam and Sanjay Subrahmanyam (New Delhi: Oxford University Press, 1998), 169–210. For a discussion of *bhāībāṇṭ* (literally, "brother's share"), see G. D. Sharma, *Rājpūt Polity: A Study of Politics and Administration of the State of Marwar, 1638–1749* (New Delhi: Manohar, 1977), 5–8; Bhadani, "The Ruler and Nobility in Marwar," 116–17.

3. *Bhāībandh* translates to "brother-bound." Richard D. Saran and Norman P. Ziegler, *The Meṛtīyo Rāṭhoṛs of Meṛto, Rājasthān: Select Translations Bearing on the History of a Rājpūt Family, 1462–1660*, vol. 2 (Ann Arbor: University of Michigan Press, 2001), 461.

4. The Marathas were an agglomeration of chiefs united under the titular kingship of the descendants of Shivaji Bhonsle (1630–1680) and the de facto leadership of a brahman Prime Minister (the Peshwa) located in Pune in the western Deccan.

5. Mahadji Sindhia is also known as Mahadji Shinde. Records of the Rathor state, such as Maharaja Vijai Singh's diplomatic correspondence with other states, write his name as "Sindhīyā," so I have preferred to go with the common anglicization of his name as Sindhia.

6. The annual tribute that the Marathas imposed on the Rathors was a hundred and fifty thousand (or one and a half lakh) rupees. Vijai Singh did manage briefly to recapture Ajmer from the Marathas, holding on to it only for a few years, in 1787. The amounts demanded as indemnity ranged from three hundred thousand rupees after Vijai Singh's failed 1762 attempt to annex Ajmer to six million rupees after two successive Rathor defeats in the Battles of Patan and of Merta in 1790 and 1791. G. R. Parihar, *Marwar and the Marathas* (1724–1843 AD) (Jodhpur: Hindi Sahitya Mandir, 1968), 89, 96, 130. The affixing of such astronomical demands in eighteenth-century terms does not mean that the Rathors actually paid them. Since the amounts were so large, the Rathors would slack off on their payments, leading to reprisals and threats from the Marathas.

7. I calculated this amount on the basis of payments recorded in Parihar, *Marwar and the Marathas*, 89, 96, 97, 100, 103, 104, 130.

8. For an articulation of such ambitions in the first half of the eighteenth century by Rathor Maharaja Abhai Singh, see Zirwat Chowdhury, "An Imperial Mughal Tent and Mobile Sovereignty in Eighteenth-Century Jodhpur," *Art History* 38, no. 4 (2015): 668–81. On the establishment of new record series and public celebrations in Jodhpur after 1765, see Rameshwar Prasad Bahuguna, "Religious Festivals as Political Rituals: Kingship and Legitimation in Late Pre-Colonial Rajasthan," in *Revisiting the History of Medieval Rajasthan: Essays for Professor Dilbagh Singh*, ed. Suraj Bhan Bharadwaj, Rameshwar Prasad Bahuguna, and Mayank Kumar (New Delhi: Primus, 2017), 84–92.

9. Sharma, *Rājpūt Polity*, 268.

10. Rima Hooja, *A History of Rajasthan* (New Delhi: Rupa, 2006), 715. Ram Singh died in 1772.

11. For instance, Vijai Singh used the solemn occasion of a funeral of his spiritual preceptor at the time, a Guru Atmaram (about whom little is known), to catch the troublesome

rajput chiefs of Pokhran, Ras, and Asop unawares. When they came to the fort for the funeral, he had them captured and thrown in a dungeon where they all died. When their kinsmen, such as the son of the chief of Pokhran, waged an armed resistance, Vijai Singh's troops did not hold back in repressing them.

12. Burton Stein, "State Formation and Economy Reconsidered: Part One," *Modern Asian Studies* 19, no. 3 (1985): 387–413. See Peabody, *Hindu Kingship*, 80–111, for a discussion of military fiscalism in the nearby polity of Kota in the eighteenth century.

13. These coins were known after Vijai Singh as Vijaishāhīs and continued to be minted and in circulation until the late nineteenth century. They are inscribed on both sides with Persian-language text. The gold coins, for instance, said on the obverse, "*sikkā mubārak bādshah ghāzī shāh 'alam*" ("auspicious coin of the victorious Emperor Shah Alam"). See Vishveshvar Nath Reu, *Coins of Marwar* (Jodhpur: Jodhpur Government Press, 1946), iii, 4–5, 11–12.

14. On *muqati* tenure as fixed-rate and on contract by the end of the seventeenth century in western Rajasthan, see G. S. L. Devra, "Land Control and Agrarian Mercantile Classes in Western Rajasthan, c. 1650-1700," *Proceedings of the Indian History Congress*, vol. 58 (1997): 380n26.

15. For a discussion of Krishna's transformation in the course of the first millennium BCE from a local pastoral deity in the Mathura region near Delhi into an avatar of Vishnu with the attributes of both an ideal king at Dvarka and a playful cowherd in Braj, see Charlotte Vaudeville, *Myths, Saints, and Legends in Medieval India*, compiled and introduced by Vasudha Dalmia (Delhi: Oxford University Press, 1996), 23–38. For a history of the Vallabhite order, see Shandip Saha, "Creating a Community of Grace: A History of the *Puṣṭī Mārga* in Northern and Western India (1493–1905)" (PhD diss., University of Ottawa, 2004).

16. For an understanding of the practices and beliefs of the Vallabhites, see Richard Barz, *The Bhakti Sect of Vallabhācārya* (New Delhi: Munshiram Manoharlal, 1992 [1979]). Recent work has suggested that the Vallabhite order took on its distinctive form after the death of Vallabhacharya and that even as he had "serious theological purposes, it is far less clear that he was actively trying to build a *sampradāy* in the institutional sense." Hawley, *Storm of Songs*, 186.

17. Hawley, *Storm of Songs*, 109; Fisher, *Hindu Pluralism*, 6–13. For the history of the production and use of "sectarianism" as a "modernist knowledge" in the Middle East, see Ussama Makdisi, *The Culture of Sectarianism: Community, History and Violence in Nineteenth-Century Ottoman Lebanon* (Berkeley: University of California Press, 2000).

18. See Fisher's discussion of Monier-Williams in *Hindu Pluralism*, 8.

19. Fisher, *Hindu Pluralism*, 12–13.

20. Habib and Mukherjee, "Akbar and the Temples of Mathura," 236–37; Irfan Habib and Tarapada Mukherjee, "Mughal Administration and the Temples of Vrindavan during the Reigns of Jahangir and Shahjahan," *Proceedings of the Indian History Congress*, 49th Sess. (Dharwad: Karnataka University, 1989), 287–300; Hawley, *Storm of Songs*, 74–81, 150–79, 186. To gain a sense of how the Krishnaite orders acquired property rights in the Braj area, see Irfan Habib, "From Ariṭh to Rādhākund: The History of a Braj Village in Mughal Times," *Indian Historical Review* 38, no. 2 (2011): 211–24.

21. Tanuja Kothiyal, "A 'Mughal' Rajput or a 'Rajput' Mughal? Some Reflections on Rajput-Mughal Marriages in the Sixteenth and Seventeenth Centuries," in Bharadwaj et al., *Revisiting the History*, 264–95.

22. Vaudeville, *Myths, Saints, and Legends*, 50; Saha, "Creating a Community," 85–87. For a history of Vaishnav activity at Braj, see Alan Entwistle, *Braj: Centre of Krishna Pilgrimage* (Groningen: Egbert Forsten, 1987).

23. Kumkum Chatterjee, "Cultural Flows and Cosmopolitanism in Mughal India: The Bishnupur Kingdom," *Indian Economic and Social History Review* 46, no. 2 (2009): 147–82. For the medieval emergence of rajputs as a lordly caste group, see Braja Dulal Chattopadhyaya, "Origin of the Rajputs: The Political, Economic and Social Processes in Early Medieval Rajasthan," in *The Making of Early Medieval India*, ed. B. D. Chattopadhyaya (New Delhi: Oxford University Press, 2012), 59-84. For a study of early rajput court culture, see Ramya Sreenivasan, "Warrior-Tales at Hinterland Courts in North India, c. 1370–1550," in *After Timur Left: Culture and Circulation in Fifteenth-Century North India*, ed. Francesca Orsini and Samira Sheikh (Delhi: Oxford University Press, 2014), 243-73.

24. Heidi Pauwels, "The Saint, the Warlord, and the Emperor: Discourses on Braj Bhakti and Bundela Loyalty," *Journal of the Economic and Social History of the Orient* 52, no. 2 (2009): 210–11. On the Bundela chiefs' Vaishnav affiliation and its relationship to their efforts to cement their claims to "raja" status, see Kolff, *Naukar, Rajput and Sepoy*, 120–34.

25. Pika Ghosh, *Temple to Love: Architecture and Devotion in Seventeenth-Century Bengal* (Bloomington: Indiana University Press, 2005); Chatterjee, "Cultural Flows."

26. Prithviraj Rathor, *Veli Krishan Rukamanee Ree*, trans. Rajvi Amar Singh (Bikaner: Rajvi Amar Singh, 1996).

27. For a rich exploration of Nagaridas's oeuvre, set against the historical developments in his time, see Heidi Pauwels, *Mobilizing Krishna's World: The Writings of Prince Sāvant Singh of Kishangarh* (Seattle: University of Washington Press, 2017).

28. Peabody, *Hindu Kingship*, 17.

29. Emilia Bachrach and Heidi Pauwels, "Aurangzeb as Iconoclast? Vaishnav Accounts of the Krishna Images' Exodus from Braj," *Journal of the Royal Asiatic Society* 28, no. 3 (2018): 505–6.

30. During the eighteenth century, *jāṭs* in the Delhi region began to organize more permanently into militarized groupings that resisted the Mughal state's administrative and revenue machinery. The first *jāṭ* kingdom, Bharatpur, arose near Delhi in the early eighteenth century, after the death of Aurangzeb.

31. Pauwels and Bachrach, "Aurangzeb as Iconoclast?"

32. The caretakers of the most significant icon of the Vallabhite order, Shri Nathji, carved out a new ritual headquarter, Nathdvara (or "the Lord's Portal"), in the Udaipur countryside. Kankroli, also in the Udaipur countryside, was another important new ritual center for the Vallabhites in the eighteenth century.

33. Norbert Peabody, "In Whose Turban Does the Lord Reside? The Objectification of Charisma and the Fetishism of Objects in the Hindu Kingdom of Kota," *Comparative Studies in Society and History* 33, no. 4 (1991): 726–54.

34. Gaurishankar Hirachand Ojha, *Jodhpur Rājya kā Itihās*, vol. 2 (Jodhpur: Maharaja Mansingh Pustak Prakash Library, 2010 [1936]), 157.

35. *Mahārājā Śrī Vijaisiṅghjī rī Khyāt*, ed. Brajesh Kumar Singh (Jodhpur: Rajasthan Oriental Research Institute, 1997), 73. This book is an extract from a much longer text, the Rāṭhaurāṁ rī Khyāt. It contains only that section which discusses the reign of Vijai Singh. The longer text, the *Rāṭhaurāṁ rī Khyāt*, records the history of the reigns of all the Rathor

monarchs of Marwar, starting with the thirteenth-century Siha and ending with Man Singh. While a manuscript copy of this text is at the Rajasthan Oriental Research Institute, Jodhpur, it has been published as the three-volume *Rāṭhaurāṁ rī Khyāt: Sīhā se Mahārājā Mānasiṁha, Vi. Sa. 1300–1735/I. 1243–1678*, ed. Hukamsimh Bhati (Chopasni: Itihas Anusandhan Sansthan, 2007). Maharaja Man Singh commissioned this history and scholars believe that the bulk of it was compiled by Aaidan Khidiya, a Charan. A Joshi Sahibram completed it in the 1870s (*Rāṭhaurāṁ rī Khyāt*, 1–3).

36. "Gusain" is a vernacularization of *gosvāmī* ("master of cattle" or "master of the senses").

37. *MVSK*, 73.

38. *MVSK*, 128.

39. I thank Christian Lee Novetzke for pointing me toward this interpretation.

40. I thank John Stratton Hawley for nudging me toward thinking of this possibility.

41. In 1779, the Rathor crown ordered its officers in Didwana to urgently remit through a bill of exchange (*huṇḍī*) to Brindavan a sum of sixteen hundred and twenty-six rupees, making sure to pay the interest and other surcharges upon principal (*hunḍāvaṇ*) separately to the banker, a mahajan named Muhṇot Udairaj (JSPB 23, CS 1836/1779 CE, f 193a). For examples of devotees in Brindavan on the Rathor payroll, see folios 343b to 347b of JSPB 28 (VS 1839/1782 CE), which list orders to issue payments to many *bhagats*, Vaishnavs, and gusains in the town.

42. Giles Tillotson, *Mehrangarh: Jodhpur Fort and Palace Museum* (Jodhpur: Mehrangarh Museum Trust, 2010): 53.

43. See Debra Diamond, "Maharaja Vijai Singh and the Epic Landscape, 1752–93," in *Garden and Cosmos: The Royal Paintings of Jodhpur*, ed. Debra Diamond, Catherine Glynn, and Karni Singh Jasol (Washington, DC: Smithsonian Institution, 2009), 21–30.

44. In two of the paintings, one of which is figure 2 in this book, the Krishna idol is placed in a *jhūlan* or swing, a common practice in Vallabhite ritual settings. For a discussion of Udairam Bhatti and the family of painters from which he descended, see Shailka Mishra, "Painting at the Court of Jodhpur: Patronage and Artists," in *Dakhan 2018: Recent Studies in Indian Painting*, ed. John Seyller (Hyderabad: Jagdish and Kamla Mittal Museum, 2020), 109–33.

45. The third painting is "Maharaja Vijai Singh Worshipping at a Krishna Shrine in a Garden, by Udairam, Jodhpur, c. 1795," in Rosemary Crill, *Marwar Painting: A History of the Jodhpur Style* (Mumbai: India Book House and Mehrangarh Museum Trust, 2000), 74. The late date attributed to this painting might be because Jodhpur royal paintings were often dated to reflect when they were entered into the royal storehouse.

46. Diamond, "Maharaja Vijai Singh," 24–25.

47. Diamond, "Maharaja Vijai Singh," 305n21.

48. Diamond, "Maharaja Vijai Singh," 305n20.

49. Peabody, *Hindu Kingship*, 52.

50. Nandita P. Sahai, "Crafts and Statecraft in Eighteenth-Century Jodhpur," *Modern Asian Studies* 41, no. 4 (2007): 683–722.

51. Manuscript 130 of the Tod Collection at the Royal Asiatic Society, London.

52. See for instance Elizabeth Thelen's discussion of the Rathor state's disbursal of grants to Sufi shrines at Ajmer through Vijai Singh's reign and for the relations that the managers of these Sufi shrines cultivated with, among other patrons, the Rathor crown. Elizabeth

Thelen, "Intersected Communities: Urban Histories of Rajasthan, c. 1500–1800" (PhD diss., University of California, Berkeley, 2018), 52–53. Even so, Thelen notes (67–68) that the number of new charitable grants to the Sufi shrines at Nagaur declined in Vijai Singh's reign in comparison to those made by prior rulers.

53. For the Bhim Singh portrait, see "Maharaja Bhim Singh Venerating Krishna at Shyamji Temple, Jodhpur, 1801–02," in *Peacock in the Desert: The Royal Arts of Jodhpur, India*, ed. Angma D. Jhala (Houston: Museum of Fine Arts, 2018), 150.

54. Her caste origins are unknown, although some historians say that she was from a *jāṭ* family. Ojha, *Jodhpur Rājya kā Itihās II*, 181–82; Hooja, *History of Rajasthan*, 717. She came into Vijai Singh's orbit as a singer and domestic slave in the establishment of a local merchant officer (*MVSK*, 174; "Bhūraṭ" is a *gotra* (paternal lineage) among Osvāl Jains). Gulab Rai very quickly rose up the ranks of the harem to emerge as Vijai Singh's favorite.

55. *MVSK*, 158.

56. Gulab Rai was an important patron for the construction of the Kunjbihari Temple in Jodhpur and a regular donor to the Balkrishnaji Temple, also in the capital. Priyanka Khanna, "The Female Companion in a World of Men: Friendship and Concubinage in Late Eighteenth Century Marwar," *Studies in History* 33, no. 1 (2017): 1–4. Both temples were centered on Krishna. Gulab Rai also built a large public tank, the Gulab Sagar, and a garden around it, both in Jodhpur (*MVSK*, 93). In 1788, she hosted lavish feasts for brahman priests, supposedly showering them with gold and silver. Hukamsimh Bhati, Bhavanisimh Patavat, and Vikramsimh Bhati, eds., *Mārvāṛ rī Khyāt: Josī Tilokchand Kaṁhā Singhvī Gyānmal Likhāī* (Jodhpur: Rajasthani Shodh Samsthan and Maharaja Pustak Prakash Shodh Kendra, 2000), 106. See also forthcoming work by Nandini Thilak, doctoral candidate at Heidelberg University, for more on Gulab Rai.

57. *Māṝvāṛ rī Khyāt*, 75.

58. Khanna, "The Female Companion," and ongoing doctoral research by Nandini Thilak at the University of Heidelberg.

59. An articulation of her love for Vijai Singh survives in the form of an undated letter she wrote to him. For a study of this letter, see Khanna, "The Female Companion."

60. *MVSK* 93, 121, 128, 136, 152–53, 157, 166.

61. Bhim Singh's accession to the throne was far from smooth. His father had nominated another son, Sher Singh, a favorite of Gulab Rai's, as his successor. Yet, Bhim Singh enjoyed the support of the rajput nobles opposed to Gulab Rai and had even attempted a coup in 1791 (*MVSK*, 161–63). Upon Vijai Singh's death, he was able to cobble together a strong enough alliance to quickly take over the throne (*MVSK*, 169–71).

62. See "Maharaja Bhim Singh Venerating Krishna at Shyamji Temple, Jodhpur," 1801–2, Maharaja Mansingh Trust, RJS 2057, in Jhala, *Peacock in the Desert*, 150.

63. See for instance Ojha, *Jodhpur Rājya kā Itihās*, vol. 2, 194.

64. For the popularity of the Vallabhite order among merchants, see Shandip Saha, "The Movement of Bhakti along a North-West Axis: Tracing the History of the *Puṣṭi Mārga* between the Sixteenth and Nineteenth Centuries," *International Journal of Hindu Studies* 11, no. 3 (2007): 304. Merchants in Rajasthan were also drawn to other Vaishnav orders such as the Dadupanthis and the Niranjanis. Merchant participation in and patronage of the Niranjani order in the early modern period caused it to have a robust culture of manuscript production and copying. See Tyler Williams, "Sacred Sounds and Sacred Books: A History of Writing in Hindi" (PhD diss., Columbia University, 2014).

65. Peabody, *Hindu Kingship.*

66. Chatterjee, "Cultural Flows"; Rosalind O'Hanlon, "The Social Worth of Scribes: Brahmins, Kāyasthas, and the Social Order in Early Modern India," *Indian Economic and Social History Review* 47, no. 4 (2010): 563–95; Sumit Guha, "Serving the Barbarian to Preserve the *Dharma:* Scribal Ideology and Training in Peninsular India, c. 1300–1800," *IESHR* 47, no. 4 (2010): 497–525; Kinra, *Writing Self, Writing Empire.*

67. The interlinkages between the title "mahajan" on the one hand and state recognition as a person bearing claims over revenues and having "public" standing on the other may have deeper roots in the medieval past, as indicated by the bestowing of this title upon brahman recipients of *agrahāras* (grants of the revenue of designated villages, accompanied by the right to administer the villages) by the Yadava kingdom in the twelfth and thirteenth centuries in the western Deccan. Novetzke, *The Quotidian Revolution*, 61–62.

68. See the episodes discussed in Thelen, "Intersected Communities."

69. Due to factional politics at the time, Singhvi Bhimraj did not take on the office but had another Osvāl mahajan, Singhvi Fatehchand, appointed *divan*. This is borne out by other Rathor records. Fatehchand would only be *dīvān* in name, with Bhimraj performing the role in practice (*MVSK*, 93). Indeed, *Ohdā Bahī* 1 lists Singhvi Fateh Chand as succeeding Muhnot Surat Ram to the office of the *dīvān* in 1766. R. K. Saxena, *Apparatus of the Rathors (A Study of Marwar): Assignment of Jagirs, Award of Offices, Titles and Honors to the Rathor Nobility (1764–1858 V.S.)*, vol. 1 (Jodhpur: Maharaja Mansingh Pustak Prakash Research Centre, 2006), xlviii. In addition, Singhvi Bhimraj, a favorite of Gulab Rai's, also held the office of *bakhśī* (or chief paymaster of the army).

70. Saxena, *Apparatus of the Rathor*, vol. 1, xxxv–xxxvi.

71. For example, Pancholi Gopaldas served as *dīvān* from 1802–3. See Hukamsimh Bhati, *Mārvāṛ ke Ohdedāroṃ kā Itihās meṁ Yogdān* (Jodhpur: Rajasthani Granthagar, 2013), 23–37. For a description of the *pañcholī* caste in the late nineteenth century, including their identification as Mathur *kāyasths*, see Hardayal Singh, *Riporṭ Mardumśumārī Rāj Mārvāṛ, 1891: Rājasthān kī Jātiyoṁ kā Itihās evam Unke Rīti Rivāj* (Jodhpur: Shri Jagdishsimh Gehlot Shodh Samsthan, 1991), 398–404.

72. Singh, *Riporṭ Mardumśumārī*, 403.

73. Singh, *Riporṭ Mardumśumārī*, 400.

74. *Byāv rī Bahī* 1, VS 1776/1719 CE, f 214.

75. See Jitendrasimh Bhati, *Rājasthān kī Praśāsanik Vyavasthā: Mārvāṛ ke Sandarbh meṁ, 1300–1800 Īsvī* (Jodhpur: Rajasthani Granthagar, 2011), 101–2, for a list of the chiefs of the royal chancery.

76. For instance, Asopa Surajmal is listed as the *duvāyatī* or authorizing officer on a command from 1782, a year when he was the *daroghā* of the chancery (*śrī hajūr rā daftar*). In some commands, the issuer of the order has been identified as "*daftar rā darogā*" (as in JSPB 37, VS 1844/1787 CE, f 239b).

77. JSPB 35, VS 1843/1786 CE, f 49a.

78. Thelen, "Intersected Communities," 15.

79. Rosalind O'Hanlon, "Performance in a World of Paper: Puranic Histories and Social Communication in Early Modern India," *Past & Present* 219, no. 1 (2013): 87–126.

80. In building their state apparatus, Rathor kings were inspired by the polities of the Delhi and Gujarat sultanates and later by Sher Shah Suri and the Mughals. The offices of *potdār* and *mushraf*, listed here, for instance were borrowed from these polities. *Potdār* is a

Marwari vernacularization of *fotedār*, the term for "treasurer" in Mughal administration. *Mushraf* is a vernacularization of *mushrif*, a term for "accountant" in the Delhi Sultanate and later Islamicate polities in South Asia.

81. Bhati, *Mārvāṛ ke Ohdedāroṃ*, 288–378.

82. The *kachaiḍī* was staffed with a *kārkūn* (a treasurer tasked with maintaining and disbursing the district's funds), *navīsadās* (scribes), and *potdārs* (other treasury officers). In addition, for its military work, the *kachaiḍī* had *tābīndārs* (soldiers), *charvādārs* (horse-keepers), and *chopdārs* (peons). News writers, called *itlāk naves* and *uvākā naves*, were also stationed at the *kachaiḍī* and were tasked with dispatching news reports to both the governor and the crown. See Bhati, *Rajasthan ki Praśāsanik Vyavasthā*, 131–33. *Itlāk naves* and *uvākā naves* were vernacularizations of the Mughal administrative terms *wāqi'a navīs* (writer of happenings) and *ittilā' navīs* (writer of information).

83. Bhati, *Mārvāṛ* ke *Ohdedāroṃ*, 182, 185, 195, 196, 197, 221, 246.

84. For Merta and Pali's *sāyars*, see Bhati, *Mārvāṛ ke Ohdedāroṃ*, 196, 221.

85. *Chauntrā* is a Marwari vernacularization of *chabūtarā*, a four-sided platform upon which public matters were often discussed in settlements across north India.

86. Bhati, *Mārvāṛ ke Ohdedāroṃ*, 182, 195.

87. This was particularly on display in the years following the murder of Maharaja Ajit Singh in 1724. Ajit Singh's son and successor, Abhai Singh, had Bhandari Raghunath, a high-ranking administrator, imprisoned and also rounded up a number of other leading Bhandaris. While the others paid sums ranging from twenty-five thousand to a hundred thousand rupees, Bhandari Raghunath could only secure his freedom on the payment of eight hundred thousand rupees. *Rathaurāṁ rī Khyat*, vol. 2, 456, 477. A lakh in the South Asian numbering system is one hundred thousand.

88. Sreenivasan, "The Marriage of 'Hindu' and '*Turak*'," 106.

89. Others, after their release and on the strength of their skills and experience, would make their way back into the good graces of the king and would be hired once again in key positions such as *hākim* and even *dīvān*. Bhati, *Mārvāṛ ke Ohdedāroṁ*, 246–48.

90. I base this on the discussion of the history of imposing heavy fines on administrators that is laid out in Bhati, *Rājasthān kī Praśāsanik Vyavasthā*, 238–45.

91. Bhati, *Rājasthān kī Praśāsanik Vyavasthā*, 102–3.

92. Bhati, *Rājasthān kī Praśāsanik Vyavasthā*, 112–15.

93. JSPB 5, VS 1823/1766 CE, f 66a and JSPB 14, VS 1831/1774 CE, f 146a. An octroi is a tax levied on incoming goods.

94. There is a large literature on *ijāra* or revenue farming in Mughal and post-Mughal polities. See Habib, *Agrarian System of Mughal India*, 230–97; Alam, *The Crisis of Empire*, 39–42, 199–200; Wink, *Land and Sovereignty in India*, 339–75; Subrahmanyam and Bayly, "Portfolio Capitalists," 408–16.

95. JSPB 13, VS 1830/1771 CE, f 383b-384a. The Agarvāl, of a mercantile caste as indicated by his name, paid five hundred rupees up front to the treasury in Jodhpur and agreed to pay the remaining twenty-four hundred in monthly installments in the course of the year. Presumably, this contract entitled him to collect the minting fee that otherwise would have gone to the state.

96. Sheikh, *Forging a Region*, 139–40.

97. Sebastian R. Prange, *Monsoon Islam: Trade and Faith on the Medieval Malabar Coast* (New York: Cambridge University Press, 2018). Prange's book, however, seeks to understand

the history of Islam in the Indian Ocean world, exemplified by the history of Malabar, as shaped by the actions of traders guided foremost by the quest for profit. In the actions of the merchants of Marwar, profit was the foundation of their actions to reshape social life and regional orders, rather than being the goal they were pursuing in making this effort.

98. For Gujarat, see Hasan, *State and Locality in Mughal India*, 34–69. For Awadh, see Christopher A. Bayly, *Rulers, Townsmen and Bazaars: North Indian Society in the Age of British Expansion, 1770–1870* (New Delhi: Oxford University Press, 1993 [1983]).

99. It is important here to bear in mind Muzaffar Alam and Sanjay Subrahmanyam's argument that due to its adaptability to local conditions, the Mughal state was more akin to a patchwork quilt than a wall-to-wall carpet; that is, there were limits to the territorial integration and uniformity of rule that it was able to achieve. Alam and Subrahmanyam, introduction to *The Mughal State, 1526–1750* (New Delhi: Oxford University Press, 2014 [1998]), 57.

100. Om Prakash, "The System of Credit in Mughal India," in *Money and Credit in Indian History: From Early Medieval Times*, ed. Amiya Kumar Bagchi (New Delhi: Tulika and Indian History Congress, 2002), 41, 47. In the Agra region in the seventeenth century, for instance, the trade in indigo was based on advance loans provided by merchants in exchange for a fixed rate at which they would purchase the indigo produced. Irfan Habib, "Usury in Medieval India," *Comparative Studies in Society and History* 6, no. 4 (1964): 395.

101. Habib, "Usury in Medieval India," 397–98, 407–8.

102. Irfan Habib, "Banking in Mughal India," *Contributions to Indian Economic History* 1 (1960): 10–11.

103. See for instance the seventeenth-century Jain merchant Banarsidas's narrative, which points to the employment taken by his kin, originally from Marwar, with Mughal officers in north India and in Bengal. Banarasidas, *Ardhakathānaka: Half a Tale*, trans., annot., and intro. Mukund Lath (Jaipur: Rajasthan Prakrit Bharati Sansthana, 1981).

104. Subrahmanyam and Bayly, "Portfolio Capitalists," 402–23.

105. Alam and Subrahmanyam, introduction to *The Mughal State*, 26–28. See also the involvement of Deccan courtiers in trade in Emma J. Flatt, *The Courts of the Deccan Sultanates: Living Well in the Persian Cosmopolis* (New York: Cambridge University Press, 2019), 120–64.

106. Chandra, "Commercial Activities of the Mughal Emperors"; Shireen Moosvi, "Mughal Shipping at Surat in the First Half of the Seventeenth Century," *Proceedings of the Indian History Congress* 51 (1990): 308–20; Alam and Subrahmanyam, introduction to *The Mughal State*, 26–28; Shireen Moosvi, "A 'State Sector' in Overseas Trade: The Imperial Mughal Shipping Establishment at Surat," *Studies in People's History* 2, no. 1 (2015): 71–75.

107. Habib, "Usury in Medieval India," 408–9.

108. Habib, "Usury in Medieval India," 409.

109. Karen Leonard, "The 'Great Firm' Theory of the Decline of the Mughal Empire," *Comparative Studies in Society and History* 21, no. 2 (1979): 151–67, and "Indigenous Banking Firms in Mughal India: A Reply," *CSSH* 23, no. 2 (1981): 309–13.

110. John F. Richards, "Mughal State Finance and the Premodern World Economy," *Comparative Studies in Society and History* 23, no. 2 (1981): 285–308; Sudev J. Sheth, "Business Households, Financial Capital and Public Authority in India, 1650–1818" (PhD diss., University of Pennsylvania, 2018), 87–149.

111. Irfan Habib, "The System of Bills of Exchange (*Hundis*) in the Mughal Empire," in *Essays in Medieval Indian Economic History*, ed. Satish Chandra (New Delhi: Munshiram Manoharlal, 1987), 211; Najaf Haider, "The Monetary Basis of Credit and Banking Instruments in the Mughal Empire," in *Money and Credit in Indian History: From Early Medieval Times*, ed. Amiya Kumar Bagchi (New Delhi: Tulika Books and Indian History Congress, 2002), 61.

112. Habib, "Usury in Medieval India," 401–6; Irfan Habib, "Merchant Communities in Pre-Colonial India," in *The Rise of Merchant Empires: Long-Distance Trade in the Early Modern World, 1350–1750*, ed. James D Tracy (Cambridge: Cambridge University Press, 1990), 387. The merchant-moneylender Virji Vora is a famous example of an immensely wealthy seventeenth-century banker whose business included lending to the English East India Company. See S. Gopal, "Virji Vora," in *Jains in India: Historical Essays*, ed. S. Gopal (New Delhi: Routledge, New York: 2019). See Haider, "The Monetary Basis of Credit," for an explanation of how money supply and credit were related in Mughal India.

113. On deposit banking, see Habib, "Usury in Medieval India," 412–13; Haider, "Credit and Banking," 67–71. On bottomry ("*avog*" in English records from Gujarat), that is, a loan for a voyage that is secured by the ship itself, see Habib, "Merchant Communities in Pre-Colonial India," 395–96.

114. Thomas A. Timberg, *The Marwaris: From Traders to Industrialists* (New Delhi: Vikas, 1979), 42; Subrahmanyam and Bayly, "Portfolio Capitalists," 414–15. See also the merchant Banarsidas's *Ardhakathanaka*, a seventeenth-century autobiography, for the significant role of family networks and for the constant movement from one city to another, across north India, of members of a single merchant family. Although Banarsidas was born in Rohtak in modern-day Haryana, his ancestors claimed to originate from Bhinmal in Marwar (Banarsidas, *Ardhakathanaka*, 70–71). This may well have been a mythic claim, for certain Jain lineages and subcastes claimed to have descended from a foundational Jain community centered on a particular town.

115. Stephen F. Dale, *Indian Merchants and Eurasian Trade, 1600–1750* (Cambridge: Cambridge University Press, 1994), 60, 105. Dale mentions a prominent eighteenth-century merchant in Astrakhan who has entered the Russian archive as Marwar Bara[ev] (105).

116. Dale, *Indian Merchants*, 45–77.

117. B. S. Mallick, *Money, Banking and Trade in Mughal India: Currency, Indigenous Fiscal Practices and the English Trade in 17th Century Gujarat and Bengal* (New Delhi: Rawat, 1991), 55–56.

118. B. L. Gupta, *Trade and Commerce in Rajasthan during the 18th Century* (Jaipur: Jaipur Publishing House, 1987), 89–90.

119. Timberg, *The Marwaris*, 41–42.

120. For examples of this type of role, see the discussion of the Marwari Jagat Seth family in J. H. Little, *The House of Jagat Seth, with Introduction by Prof. N K Sinha* (Calcutta: Calcutta Historical Society, 1967), and of the "land revenue family firm," in Samira Sheikh, "Jijabhu's Rights to Ghee: Land Control and Vernacular Capitalism in Gujarat, circa 1803–10," *Modern Asian Studies* 51, no. 2 (2017): 350–74.

121. For a history of this firm, see Little, *House of Jagat Seth*.

122. Timberg, *The Marwaris*, 43–46.

123. Lakshmi Subramanian, *Indigenous Capital and Imperial Expansion: Bombay, Surat and the West Coast* (Delhi: Oxford University Press, 1996). For more information on the

operation of bills of exchange in Mughal India, see Habib, "The System of Bills," and Sanjay Subrahmanyam, introduction to *Money and Market in India, 1100–1700*, ed. Sanjay Subrahmanyam (Delhi: Oxford University Press, 1994), 31–35.

124. Timberg, *The Marwaris*, 87.

125. G. D. Sharma, "Urban Social Structure: A Case Study of the Towns of Western Rajasthan during the Seventeenth Century," in *Studies in Urban History*, ed. J. S. Grewal and Indu Banga (Amritsar: Department of History, Guru Nanak Dev University, 1981), 72–73. Nainsi belonged to the Muhṇot lineage, "Muṃhtā," within the wider mahajan category, which was a collection of Osvāl Jain and perhaps also Vaishnav clans associated with service to rajput courts. See also B. L. Bhadani, "Socio-economic Context of Development of Jainism in Rajasthan," in Bharadwaj et al., *Revisiting the History*, 37–38.

126. Sharma, "Urban Social Structure."

127. Dilbagh Singh, "The Role of Mahajans in the Rural Economy in Eastern Rajasthan during the 18th Century," *Social Scientist* 2, no. 10 (1974): 20–31; S. P. Gupta, *The Agrarian System of Eastern Rajasthan (c. 1650-c. 1750)* (Delhi: Manohar, 1986), 142.

128. Madhavi Bajekal, "The State and the Rural Grain Market in Eighteenth Century Eastern Rajashtan," in *Merchants, Markets, and the State in Early Modern India*, ed. Sanjay Subrahmanyam (New Delhi: Oxford University Press, 1990), 107.

129. Devra, "Land Control and Agrarian Mercantile Classes."

130. Denis Vidal, *Violence and Truth: A Rajasthani Kingdom Confronts Colonial Authority* (Delhi: Oxford University Press, 1997), 166–68.

131. Gupta, *Agrarian System*, 93, 100, 105, 114–15, 140–41; Bajekal, "The State and the Rural Grain Market."

132. Mamta, "Petty Moneylending to Ijaradari: Multiple Facets of Indigenous Banking of Rajasthan during Seventeenth and Eighteenth Centuries," in Bharadwaj et al., *Revisiting the History*, 218. For eastern Rajasthan, see Gupta, *Agrarian System*, 141; Mamta Tyagi, "Moneylenders in the Jaipur State during the Pre-Colonial Period," in Bharadwaj et al., *Revisiting the History*, 310–36.

133. Dilbagh Singh, *The State, Landlords and Peasants: Rajasthan in the 18th Century* (Columbia, MO: South Asia Publications), 134.

134. G. D. Sharma, "*Vyaparis* and *Mahajans* in Western Rajasthan during the Eighteenth Century," in *Essays in Medieval Indian Economic History*, ed. Satish Chandra (New Delhi: Munshiram Manoharlal, 1987), 286–89.

135. Singh, "Role of Mahajans," in Singh, *State, Landlords*, 180.

136. In Marwar, this process had already begun by the mid-seventeenth century. See B. L. Bhadani, "Role of Merchants and Markets in Agrarian Trade in Seventeenth-Century Western Rajasthan," in *Economy and Polity of Rajasthan: Study of Kota and Marwar*, ed. Masanori Sato and B. L. Bhadani, 166–80 (Jaipur: Publication Scheme, 1997).

137. Thelen, "Intersected Communities," 118.

138. Sharma, "*Vyaparis* and *Mahajans*," 285.

139. Sharma, "Urban Social Structure"; Sharma "*Vyaparis* and *Mahajans*," 284–86; Sahai, *Politics of Patronage*.

140. Sahai, *Politics of Patronage*, 144–48.

141. Sahai, *Politics of Patronage*, 188–89.

142. Sahai, *Politics of Patronage*, 145, 186–90.

143. Mamta, "Petty Moneylending to Ijaradari," 215–18.

144. Claude Markovits, "Merchant Circulation in South Asia (Eighteenth to Twentieth Centuries): The Rise of Pan-Indian Merchant Networks," in *Society and Circulation: Mobile People and Itinerant Cultures in South Asia, 1750–1950*, ed. Claude Markovits, Jacques Pouchepadass, and Sanjay Subrahmanyam (Delhi: Permanent Black, 2003), 131–61.

2. PURITY

1. JSPB 32, VS 1842/1785 CE, f 162a. *Tathā pālī rā mahājan aṭhai āyā tiṇā śrī hajūr mai araj mālam karāi su īṇ tarai hukam huvo hai talāb bāvḍī pāṇī sārā hī lok ekaṇ ghāṭ bharai hai su judai ghāṭ bharīyāṁ karai to marjād rahai su hamai āgāṁ suṁ brāmaṇ mhājaṇ vagairai utam jāt to ekai ghāṭ bharīyāṁ karai nai achhep jāt dujai ghāṭ pāṇī bharīyā karai.*

2. *Dharma* is one of the most central concepts in several South Asian belief systems, including not just brahmanism but also Buddhism and Jainism. In brahmanical traditions, *dharma* has a range of connotations that have at their core moral and ritual righteousness. Even as some aspects of *dharma* are universal (such as respect for one's parents and truthfulness), the specific rules and expectations prescribed by *dharma* also vary by the concerned person's social station, such as age, caste, and gender. *Dharma* can include aspects of personal life and behavior, such as bathing, diet, and sexual conduct, as well as legal codes, procedures, and penances. See Ingo Strauch, "*Dharma*," in *Brill's Encyclopedia of Hinduism Online*, ed. Knut A. Jacobsen et al., http://dx.doi.org/10.1163/2212-5019_beh_COM_2050090.

3. Nandita P. Sahai, "The 'Other' Culture: Craft Society and Widow Remarriage in Early Modern India," *Journal of Women's History* 19, no. 1 (2007): 36–58.

4. See Sumit Guha, "An Indian Penal Regime: Maharashtra in the Eighteenth Century," *Past & Present* 147 (1995): 102–26; Sahai, "The 'Other' Culture."

5. N. Chatterjee, *Negotiating Mughal Law*, 38–40.

6. Nandita P. Sahai, "Artisans, the State, and the Politics of Wajabi in Eighteenth-Century Jodhpur," *Indian Economic and Social History Review* 42, no. 1(2005): 56.

7. JSPB 8, VS 1825/1768 CE, f 226b.

8. E. P. Thompson, *Customs in Common: Studies in Popular Culture* (New York: W.W. Norton, 1993), 1–6, 97–104, 110, 175; Sumit Guha, "Wrongs and Rights in the Maratha Country: Antiquity, Custom, and Power in Eighteenth-Century India," in *Changing Concepts of Rights and Justice in South India*, ed. M. R. Anderson and Sumit Guha (New Delhi: Oxford University Press, 2000), 14–29; Sumit Guha, "Civilizations, Markets, and Services: Village Servants in India from the Seventeenth to the Twentieth Centuries," *Indian Economic and Social History Review* 41, no. 1 (2002): 79–101.

9. Sahai, *Politics of Patronage*, 223–24.

10. Dirks, *Castes of Mind;* Guha, *Beyond Caste.*

11. JSPB 15, VS 1832/1775 CE, f 85b.

12. JSPB 36, VS 1844/1787 CE, f 80b.

13. JSPB 40, VS 1846/1789 CE, f 26a.

14. JSPB 23, VS 1836/1779 CE, f 131b.

15. JSPB 57, VS 1860/1803 CE, f 185b.

16. JSPB 15, VS 1832/1775 CE, f 85b.

17. JSPB 15, VS 1832/1775 CE, f 322b.

18. Hasan, *State and Locality*, 69.

19. Bayly, *Rulers, Townsmen and Bazaars.*

20. There were rare exceptions to this, such as goldsmiths (*sunārs*) who were seeking to effect an improvement in their caste status at this time by emulating the rituals and behaviors of their social superiors. These efforts met with opposition by local elites, particularly mahajans, and will be discussed further in the chapter. Also see Nandita P. Sahai, "Crossing the Golden Gate? Sunārs, Social Mobility, and Disciplining the Household in Early Modern Rajasthan," in *Looking Within, Looking Without: Exploring Households in the Subcontinent through Time*, ed. Kumkum Roy (New Delhi: Primus Books, 2015), 389–408.

21. Sahai, "Artisans, the State, and the Politics of Wajabi," 688. The lexicographer Sitaram Lalas suggests that *pūṇ*, when describing castes, derived from *pavan* or "wind" but does not explain what connection this has with the castes or their status. Lalas, *Rājasthānī-Hindī Saṃkśipt Śabdakoś*, vol. II, 47, 93.

22. Lalas, *Saṅkśipt Śabdakoś* I, 199. *Kamīnā* is a commonly used term of abuse in Hindi today.

23. JSPB 18, VS 1834/1777 CE, f 87b; JSPB 24, VS 1837/1780 CE, f 77b-78a; and JSPB 30, VS 1841/1784 CE, f 181b.

24. JSPB 30, VS 1841/1784 CE, f 181b.

25. JSPB 30, VS 1841/1784 CE, f 181b.

26. JSPB 39, VS 1845/1788 CE, f 404a.

27. Recent studies of the colonial era such as Rawat, *Reconsidering Untouchability* and Viswanath, *The Pariah Problem*, have pointed out that the "traditional" caste occupations, particularly of "Untouchable" groups, did not entirely correspond with their work. Colonial processes played a role in the collapsing of the labor that castes performed into neat boxes associated with their "traditional" occupations. The acceptance of a total correspondence between a caste's traditional occupation, often reflected in its name, and the labor it performed led to the erasure of the substantial role as agrarian labor that artisanal castes performed. This is an important point and one that the information from eighteenth-century Marwar corresponds with. At the same time, Rathor records designate subjects by their caste names in addition to their given names. To accurately reflect that the caste identity was part of names at least in the state's perspective, I continue to refer to caste groups by their occupationally derived names. For the ease of readers not familiar with north Indian languages and the social landscape of Rajasthan, I often translate these caste names into English. I do so with recognition that caste names did not always reflect the types of work that a caste might perform and would like to advise readers to also bear this mind.

28. Masanori Sato shows through a study of a few villages in Kota that *chamārs* lost control of whatever little property they might have had in the latter half of the eighteenth century. Sato, "The Chamārs of South-Eastern Rajasthan, A.D. 1650–1800," in *Caste System, Untouchability, and the Depressed*, ed. Hiroyuki Kotani (New Delhi: Manohar, 1997), 31–53.

29. JSPB 6, VS 1824/1767 CE, f 180a (in which a rajput from Bikaner claims a leatherworker from Merta district was his *vasī*); JSPB 8, VS 1825/1768 CE, f 19b (the state tries to aid a Rathor landlord's efforts to trace his runaway *vasī*); JSPB 10, VS 1827/1770 CE, f 85b (a leatherworker challenges the claim of *vasīpaṇā* that a rajput was asserting over him); JSPB 18, VS 1834/1777 CE, f 10a (a *meghvāl vasī* of a charan).

30. JSPB 16, VS 1833/1776 CE, f 161b (a leatherworker who is a *vasī* hits his brahman lord's brother with his hookah); JSPB 38, VS 1845/1788 CE, f 239b-240a (a meghwal keeps protesting—in unspecified ways—against a rajput's assertion of *vasī-dom* upon him; the

state ordered that the leatherworker be disciplined); JSPB 45, VS 1850/1793 CE village, f 342b (the state ordered that two *vasīs* of a Jodha rajput who had fled to another village be traced and returned to him).

31. JSPB 1, VS 1821/1764 CE, f 122.

32. JSPB 15, VS 1832/1775 CE, f 85b.

33. JSPB 36, VS 1844/1787 CE, f 80b.

34. JSPB 36, VS 1844/1787 CE, f 80b. Made aware of this history, however, the crown ordered its governor in Merta to make the mahajans and upper peasantry pay market value, instead of the five rupees they paid earlier, to the state's treasury for the land they were taking over from the leatherworkers.

35. JSPB 40, VS 1846/1789 CE, f 26a.

36. JSPB 40, VS 1846/1789 CE, f 26a.

37. JSPB 40, VS 1846/1789 CE, f 26a.

38. JSPB 26, VS 1839/1782 CE, f 36a.

39. JSPB 55, VS 1858/1801 CE, f 124a.

40. JSPB 57, VS 1860/1803 CE, f 181b and f 185b.

41. JSPB 57, VS 1860/1803 CE, f 181b.

42. JSPB 57, VS 1860/1803 CE, f 185b.

43. JSPB 3, VS 1822/1765 CE, f 48b and 49a. The *balāī* caste was associated with leatherwork. The terms *dhedh, balāī, meghvāl*, and *chamār* all designate leatherworking castes and in some records are used interchangeably to name the same person or caste. This suggests that all three names designated the same or overlapping demographic groups.

44. JSPB 3, VS 1822/1765 CE, f 48b and 49a.

45. JSPB 15, VS 1832/1775 CE, f 322b.

46. JSPB 15, VS 1832/1775 CE, f 322b.

47. Control over sources of artificial irrigation, especially in the arid western tracts of Rajasthan, was a source of political and economic power as early as the early medieval period, that is from the seventh to the twelfth centuries CE. B. D. Chattopadhyaya, "Irrigation in Early Medieval Rajasthan," *Journal of the Social and Economic History of the Orient* 16, no. 2/3 (1973): 298–316.

48. For an example of merchants taking on the responsibility of maintaining water bodies, see Kothiyal, *Nomadic Narratives*, 47.

49. Mayank Kumar, *Monsoon Ecologies: Irrigation, Agriculture, and Settlement Patterns in Rajasthan during the Pre-colonial Period* (New Delhi: Manohar, 2013), 230–32, 241–53.

50. JSPB 33, VS 1842/1785 CE, f 46a–b.

51. JSPB 33, VS 1842/1785 CE, f 46a–b.

52. JSPB 33, VS 1842/1785 CE, f 46a–b.

53. JSPB 33, VS 1842/1785 CE, f 46a–b.

54. JSPB 28, VS 1839/1782 CE, f 241a–b.

55. JSPB 28, VS 1839/1782 CE, f 241a–b.

56. *Sant* means a person who knows the Truth (*sat*); it was a title bestowed on poets whose verses inspired others to join the north Indian *bhakti* (loosely, "devotional") path. *Sants* largely came from non-elite, often artisanal castes that were considered lowly. The iconic *sants* of this mode of *bhakti* religiosity are said to have lived between the fifteenth and seventeenth centuries. For a brief introduction to the *sants*, see Winand Callewaert, "Sants," in Knut Jacobsen et al., eds., *Brill's Encyclopedia of Hinduism Online*, 2018.

57. Winand Callewaert and Bart Op de Beek, eds., *Nirguṇ Bhakti Sagar: Devotional Hindi Literature*, vol. 1 (New Delhi: Manohar, 1991), 245–46. I am grateful to Dalpat Rajpurohit for pointing me to this verse as well as for being a sounding board for the discussion of the etymology and meaning of *achhep* and *achhop* that follows.

58. Ramnarayan Rawat, "Genealogies of the Dalit Political: The Transformation of Achhut from 'Untouched' to 'Untouchable' in Early Twentieth-Century North India," *Indian Economic and Social History Review* 52, no. 3 (2015): 338. Rawat points to the Sanskrit *chupta*, meaning "impurity of touch that is polluting," as being the root for the word *chhūt* used in popular speech and verse to name untouchability.

59. The *Hindī śabdsāgar*, a well-regarded Hindi dictionary published in the 1960s and 1970s, gives the example of the Dadu Dayal verse mentioned above to support its explanation of the meanings of *achhop* as lowly (*nīch*), humble (*tuchchh*), and poor (*dīn*). It also traces the etymology of the term to *chhup*, but takes the root as related to the Hindi word *chhupnā*, as in "hiding." *Chupa* in Sanskrit, however, also means "touch," as mentioned above. *Achhop* then may well have derived from *chupa* (Sanskrit) / *chhup* (Hindi). The *a*- prefix negates *chhup* for the compound word to mean "un-touch." See also Ravidas's reference to the *bhakti* poet-*sant* Namdev as *āchhop chhīpā* (*chhīpā* here denoting the association of Namdev with tailoring); Shyamsundar Das, ed., *Hindi Śabdasāgara, arthāt hindī bhāṣā ka ek brhat koś*, vol. 1 (Banaras: Nagaripracarini Sabha, 1965–75), 118, 426. For the Sanskrit meaning of *chupa* as "touch," see for instance H. H. Wilson, *A Dictionary in Sanskrit and English: Translated, Amended, and Enlarged from an Original Compilation* (Calcutta: Education Press, 1832), 336.

60. Simon Charsley, "'Untouchable': What's in a Name?" *Journal of the Royal Anthropological Institute* 2, no. 1 (1996): 1–23.

61. Manuela Ciotti, "'In the Past We Were a Bit "Chamār"': Education as a Self- and Community-Engineering Process in Northern India," *Journal of the Royal Anthropological Institute* 12, no. 4 (2006): 900; Hugo Gorringe, "Dalit Politics: Untouchability, Identity, and Assertion," in *Routledge Handbook of Indian Politics*, ed. Atul Kohli and Prerna Singh (New York: Routledge, 2013), 119; Surinder Jodhka, *Caste in Contemporary India* (New Delhi: Routledge, 2015), 24; Ajay Varghese, *The Colonial Origins of Ethnic Violence in India* (Stanford: Stanford University Press, 2016): 84; Assa Doron and Robin Jeffrey, *Waste of a Nation: Garbage and Growth in India* (Cambridge, MA: Harvard University Press, 2018), 2n5.

62. Rupa Viswanath, *The Pariah Problem*, 251n45.

63. Charsley, "Untouchable," 15.

64. Ramnarayan Rawat, "Genealogies of the Dalit Political: The Transformation of Achhut from 'Untouched' to 'Untouchable' in Early Twentieth-Century North India," *Indian Economic and Social History Review* 52, no. 3 (2015): 338.

65. B. R. Ambedkar, *The Untouchables: Who Were They and Why They Became Untouchables?* (Chennai: Maven, 2018 [1948]).

66. JSPB 32, VS 1842/1785 CE, f 162a.

67. Novetzke, *Quotidian Revolution*, 15, 26, 117.

68. JSPB 17, VS 1833/1776 CE, f 110b; JSPB 27, VS 1839/1782 CE, f 6b; JSPB 28, VS 1839/1782 CE, f 84a-b; JSPB 32, VS 1842/1785 CE, f 162a; JSPB 34, VS 1843/1786 CE, f 57a; JSPB 38, VS 1845/1788 CE, f 240b; JSPB 49, VS 1854/1797 CE, f 198b; and JSPB 55, VS 1858/1801 CE, f 126a.

69. "*Bhāmbhī udīyā nai ghrīt ru. 100 ro svāī tol dīyo tīṇ mai ru. 1 udīyā kanai chhānai liyo ghrīt ser 1.5 udīyā rī parāt mai su judo līyo su bhāmbhī rī parāt maiṁ su ghrīt le nai ghar*

mai rākhīyo husī tathā bechīyo husī su achhep jāt rā vāsaṇ ro ghīrat kāḍh dujā ro dharam kīṇ tarai raih." JSPB 55, VS 1858/1801 CE, f 126a. The *ser* was a unit for measuring weight. As with most other measures in premodern South Asia, it varied from region to region and with time. James Prinsep, writing in the early nineteenth century, noted that under the system of weights prevalent in "central India" (which he defines as including the Ajmer region in Marwar), one *man* or *maund* consisted of twenty *sers* and weighed an equivalent of forty pounds. That would bring the weight of a *ser* in the Rajasthan area to two pounds or a little over 0.9 kilograms. James Prinsep, "British Indian Weights & Measures," in *Essays on Indian Antiquities: Historic, Numismatic, and Palaeographic, of the Late James Prinsep, F.R.S., Secretary of the Asiatic Society of Bengal*, vol. 3, ed. Edward Thomas (London: John Murray, 1858), 111.

70. JSPB 55, VS 1858/1801 CE, f 126a.

71. JSPB 27, VS 1839/1782 CE, f 6b and JSPB 28, VS 1839/1782 CE, f 84a–b.

72. JSPB 28, VS 1839/1782 CE, f 84a–b.

73. JSPB 28, VS 1839/1782 CE, f 84a–b.

74. JSPB 34, VS 1843/1786 CE, f 57a.

75. JSPB 17, VS 1833/1776 CE, f 110b. "*. . . su hukam huvo hai bhomīyāṁ pādrīyāṁ rajpūt mahājan vagairai nu to āgai sadāī kachaiḍī tālkai rākhīyo huvai jiṇ māfak kachaiḍī tālkai hī jābtā su rākhjo nai koī achhep jāt ro khoḍā maiṁ deṇjyū huvai tiṇ nu chauntrai sūṁpṇo.*"

76. JSPB 28, VS 1845/1788 CE, f 240b.

77. As clearly listed in JSPB 32, VS 1842/1785 CE, f 203b, the state order from 1785 with which the first chapter began.

78. JSPB 28, VS 1845/1788 CE, f 240b.

79. JSPB 49, VS 1854/1797 CE, f 198b.

80. JSPB 49, VS 1854/1797 CE, f 198b. The term *bhīṇṭā* derives from *bhīṇṭṇau*, which names the action of coming into contact with a ritually impure object or thing. Lalas, *Saṅkśipt Śabdakoś* II, 281.

81. These studies are based on brahmanical compositions, Buddhist and Jain sources, and foreign travelers' accounts. See for instance B. R. Ambedkar, *Who Were the Shudras? How They Came to Be the Fourth Varna* (Bombay: Thacker, 1946); Ambedkar, *The Untouchables*; George L. Hart, *The Poems of Ancient Tamil: Their Milieu and Their Sanskrit Counterparts* (Berkeley: University of California Press, 1975); Ram Sharan Sharma, *Śudras in Ancient India: A Social History of the Lower Order Down to Circa AD 600* (Delhi: Motilal Banarsidass, 1990 [1958]); Romila Thapar, "Ethics, Religion, and Social Protest in the First Millennium BC in Northern India," *Daedalus* 104, no. 2 (1975): 119–32; Uma Chakravarti, "Conceptualizing Brahmanical Patriarchy in Early India: Gender, Caste, Class, and State," *Economic and Political Weekly* 28, no. 14 (1993): 579–85; Suvira Jaiswal, *Caste: Origins, Functions, and Dimensions of Change* (New Delhi: Manohar, 1998); Michael Aktor, "Untouchability in Brahminical Law Books: Ritual and Economic Control," in *From Stigma to Assertion: Untouchability, Identity, and Politics in Early and Modern India*, ed. Michael Aktor and Robert Deliège (Copenhagen: Museum Tusculanum Press, 2010), 31–63.

82. Winand Callewaert, *The Life and Works of Ravidas* (New Delhi: Manohar, 1992); Eleanor Zelliot, "Chokhamela: Piety and Protest," in *Bhakti Religion in North India: Community Identity and Political Protest*, ed. David Lorenzen (Albany: SUNY Press, 1995); Patton Burchett, "*Bhakti* Rhetoric in the Hagiography of 'Untouchable' Saints: Discerning *Bhakti*'s

Ambivalence on Caste and Brahminhood," *International Journal of Hindu Studies* 13, no. 2 (2009): 115–41; Novetzke, *Quotidian Revolution*; Jon Keune, "Pedagogical Otherness."

83. Hiroshi Fukazawa, *The Medieval Deccan: Peasants, Social Systems, and States, Sixteenth to Eighteenth Centuries* (Delhi: Oxford University Press, 1991); Hiroyuki Kotani, "Ati Śūdra Castes in the Medieval Deccan," and Masanori Sato, "The Chamārs of South-Eastern Rajasthan," in *Caste System, Untouchability, and the Depressed*, ed. Hiroyuki Kotani (New Delhi: Manohar, 1997), 55–75, 31–53.

84. Prakash, *Bonded Histories*, 82–98; Dube, *Untouchable Pasts*, 25–34.

85. Ambedkar, *The Untouchables*, 123–43.

86. Some representative examples are Arjun Appadurai, "Number in the Colonial Imagination," in *Orientalism and the Postcolonial Predicament: Perspectives on South Asia*, ed. Carol A. Breckenridge and Peter van der Veer (Philadelphia: University of Pennsylvania Press, 1993) 314–49; Dirks, *Castes of Mind*; Bernard S. Cohn, "The Census, Social Structure and Objectification in South Asia," in his *An Anthropologist among Historians and Other Essays* (New Delhi: Oxford University Press, 1987), 224–54.

87. JSPB 27, VS 1839/1782 CE, f 6b and JSPB 28, VS 1839/1782 CE, f 84a-b.

88. JSPB 32, VS 1842/1785 CE, f 293b.

89. JSPB 32, VS 1842/1785 CE, f 93a.

90. JSPB 23, VS 1836/1764 CE, f 131b. Dodhidar Khivo issued this ruling. He added that the Shrimalis were to bear the expenses incurred in the *pīṇjārā's* move.

91. JSPB 36, VS 1844/1787 CE, f28a-b. This is the same *jāṭ* woman who asked for an exemption from the local rule against selling land to Muslims, discussed on the next page.

92. JSPB 20, VS 1835/1778 CE, f41b.

93. JSPB 36, VS 1844/1787 CE, f28a–b. The crown expected the brahman to only use the new plot to add to his house and not to sell it to anyone else.

94. Thelen, "Intersected Communities," 125. On *khatrīs* not being considered part of the more prestigious "mahajan" category of merchants and moneylenders, see Singh, *Riporṭ Mardumśumārī*, 404–5.

95. JSPB 36, VS 1844/1787 CE, f28a–b.

96. JSPB 38, VS 1845/1788 CE, f102a; "*īṇ jāygā ro bārṇo turkāṁ ro mhā kani khaṭāvai nahī.*"

97. JSPB 38, VS 1845/1788 CE, f102a.

98. JSPB 38, VS 1845/1788 CE, f153a–154b. The names of the wells reflected the groups to which they were assigned, with the Hindus expected to fill water from Amarsar and Ramsar wells and the Muslims from Mochya-ra and Saidyo wells.

3. HIERARCHY

1. Carl W. Ernst, *Eternal Garden: Mysticism, History, and Politics at a South Asian Sufi Center* (Albany: State University of New York Press, 1992), 21–25.

2. Pollock, "Ramayana and Political Imagination." B. D. Chattopadhyaya has challenged this argument by suggesting that late medieval Indic kings also drew upon other deities and heroes, such as Vishnu's *varaha* (boar) avatar, in order to articulate their identity. Chattopadhyaya, *Representing the Other? Sanskrit Sources and the Muslims (Eighth to Fourteenth Century)* (New Delhi: Manohar, 1998), 98–115.

3. Leclère, "Ambivalent Representations of Muslims." See also Audrey Truschke, *The Language of History: Sanskrit Narratives of Indo-Muslim Rule* (New York: Columbia University Press, 2021), 55–57, 64, for a discussion of a twelfth-century Sanskrit representation of Ghaznavid and Ghurid armies as outsiders and "Others" in caste terms.

4. Aparna Kapadia, *In Praise of Kings: Rajputs, Sultans and Poets in Fifteenth-Century Gujarat* (Cambridge: Cambridge University Press, 2018), 116, 120; Leclère, "Ambivalent Representations," 194.

5. Nicholson, *Unifying Hinduism.*

6. Talbot, "Inscribing the Other," 700; and Phillip B. Wagoner, "Sultan among Hindu Kings: Dress, Titles, and the Islamicization of Hindu Culture at Vijayanagara," *Modern Asian Studies* 55, no. 4 (1996): 853.

7. Cynthia Talbot, "Inscribing the Other," 700–701.

8. André Wink, *Early Medieval India and the Expansion of Islam*, vol. 1 of *Al-Hind: The Making of the Indo-Islamic World* (Delhi: Oxford University Press, 1990), 190.

9. Gopal Narayan Bahura and Chandramani Singh, eds., *Catalogue of Historical Documents in Kapad Dwara*, vol. 1 (Jaipur: Jaigarh Public Charitable Trust, 1988), 182, 184.; V. S. Bhatnagar, "Attempts at Revivalism or Reassertion of Vedic and 'Shastriya' Traditions through Open Debate in the 18th Century," in *Religious Movements in Rajasthan: Ideas and Antiquities*, ed. S. N. Dube (Jaipur: Centre for Rajasthan Studies, 1996), 97–104; James Laine, *Shivaji: Hindu King in Islamic India* (New York: Oxford University Press, 2003), 50–61; Monika Horstmann "Visions of Kingship in the Twilight of Mughal Rule," Thirteenth Gonda Lecture (Amsterdam: Royal Netherlands Academy of Arts and Sciences, 2006); Allison Busch, "Unhitching the Oxcart of Delhi: A Mughal-Period Hindi Account of Political Insurgency," *Journal of the Royal Asiatic Society* 28, no. 3 (2018): 415–39; Stoker, *Polemics and Patronage*; Horstmann, "Theology and Statecraft," 198.

10. Catherine Asher, "Excavating Communalism: Kachhwaha *Rajadharma* and Mughal Sovereignty," in *Rethinking a Millennium: Perspectives on Indian History from the Eighth to the Eighteenth Century*, ed. Rajat Dutta (New Delhi: Aakar, 2008), 222–46; Wagoner, "Sultan among Hindu Kings"; Stoker, *Polemics and Patronage*, 1, 4–7; Pauwels, *Mobilizing Krishna's World*, 157–61.

11. Caleb Simmons, *Devotional Sovereignty: Kingship and Religion in India* (New York: Oxford University Press, 2020), 71–72.

12. To learn how this played out through micropolitics centered on localized temple communities in Marwar, see Divya Cherian, "Fall from Grace?: Caste, Bhakti, and Politics in Late Eighteenth-Century Marwar," in *Bhakti & Power: Debating India's Religion of the Heart*, ed. John S. Hawley, Christian L. Novetzke, and Swapna Sharma (Seattle: University of Washington Press, 2019), 181–91.

13. Hawley, *A Storm of Songs*, 73.

14. For examples of the goddess's demand for the sacrifice of a buffalo, see Harald Tambs-Lyche, "Goddesses of Western India," in *Brill's Encyclopedia of Hinduism Online*, ed. Knut A. Jacobsen et al., http://dx.doi.org/10.1163/2212-5019_BEH_COM_1010073187.

15. Cemal Kafadar, *Between Two Worlds: The Construction of the Ottoman State* (Berkeley: University of California Press, 1995), 62–92. Kafadar's much-cited concept of metadoxy—"a state of being beyond doxies, a combination of being doxy-naïve and not being doxy-minded, as well as the absence of a state that was interested in rigorously defining

and strictly enforcing an orthodoxy"—too seems an apt description of the religious milieu in Marwar between the thirteenth and sixteenth centuries.

16. Shahid Amin, *Conquest and Community: The Afterlives of Warrior Saint Ghazi Miyan* (Chicago: University of Chicago Press, 2016), 86–89.

17. Dominique-Sila Khan attributes some of the features that these folk cults share with Islam to an erased and forgotten history of Shia proselytization in Rajasthan. She suggests that in the medieval period, Shia polities sent *da'was* (proselytizing missions) overland to Rajasthan, but over the centuries these overland connections collapsed. The isolated Shia communities that survived then blended in with local faith practices but kernels of that Shia core are still discernible in their practices. See Dominique-Sila Khan, *Crossing the Threshold: Understanding Religious Identities in South Asia* (London: IB Tauris, 2004). For a history of the transformation in the worship of one of these figures, Gogaji, see Rajshree Dhali, "The Cult of Goga: A Study of the Religious Process of a Popular Folk Deity of Rajasthan," in Bharadwaj et al., *Revisiting the History*, 116–35.

18. Ziegler, "Some Notes on Rajput Loyalties," 181–83; Kolff, *Naukar, Rajput, Sepoy*; Cynthia Talbot, "Becoming Turk the Rajput Way: Conversion and Identity in an Indian Warrior Narrative," *Modern Asian Studies* 43, no. 1 (2009): 211–43.

19. The marriage of rajput princesses into the Mughal royal family from the sixteenth century onward then was not a departure for the rajputs. See Norman P. Ziegler, "Action, Power, and Service in Rajasthani Culture" (PhD diss., University of Chicago, 1973), 61, 168–69, 174. On the history of Mughal-rajput marital alliances, see Frances H. Taft, "Honor and Alliance: Reconsidering Mughal-Rajput Marriages," in *The Idea of Rajasthan: Explorations in Regional Identity*, vol. 2, ed. Karine Schomer et al. (New Delhi: Manohar, 2001), 217–41.

20. Ziegler, "Action, Power," 60.

21. An ahistoric application of the fifteenth-century Timurid title of "Padshah" ("Emperor") to the fourteenth-century Delhi Sultanate king Sultan Alauddin Khilji.

22. Nainsi, *Khyāt*, vol. 1, 219.

23. Nainsi, *Khyāt*, vol. 1, 219.

24. Sreenivasan, "The 'Marriage' of 'Hindu' and 'Turak,'" 97.

25. Talbot, "Inscribing the Other," 697–98.

26. Sreenivasan, "The 'Marriage' of 'Hindu' and 'Turak,'" 105.

27. Talbot, *The Last Hindu Emperor*, 147–48.

28. Talbot, *The Last Hindu Emperor*, 149.

29. Talbot, *The Last Hindu Emperor*, 168–71.

30. Sreenivasan, *Many Lives of a Rajput Queen*, 111.

31. Cynthia Talbot, "A Poetic Record of the Rajput Rebellion, c. 1680," *Journal of the Royal Asiatic Society* 28, no. 3 (2018): 461–83.

32. Talbot, "A Poetic Record."

33. Sreenivasan, *Many Lives of a Rajput Queen*, 101–4.

34. Sreenivasan, *Many Lives of a Rajput Queen*, 104.

35. JSPB 3, VS 1822/1765 CE, f 43a–b.

36. Cherian, "Fall from Grace?"

37. Cherian, "Fall from Grace?" For instance, Dodhidar Khivo ordered that two months' salary should be cut from the pay of a temple functionary who had made the "error" of

passing on the food offerings brought by a tailor (*darjī*) and an oilpresser (*ghānchī*) in these men's own vessels to the Krishna idol at the Gangshyamji Temple in Jodhpur. He was to have transferred the food into ritual vessels first (JSPB 35, VS 1843/1786 CE, f 21b).

38. For a detailed discussion of these episodes, see Cherian, "Fall from Grace?"

39. JSPB 8, VS 1825/1768 CE, f 258b (issued by Dodhidar Bhavanidas).

40. JSPB 10, VS 1827/1770 CE, f 262b–263a; JSPB 11, VS 1828/1771 CE, f 121b; JSPB 12, VS 1829/1772 CE, f 68b and 235a; JSPB 17, VS 1833/1776 CE, f320b–321a; JSPB 35, VS 1843/1786 CE, f 393a; JSPB 37, VS 1844/1787 CE, f 362b–363a.

41. JSPB 23, VS 1836/1779 CE, f 347a–b.

42. JSPB 30, VS 1841/1785 CE, f 243b.

43. JSPB 37, VS 1844/1787 CE, f 195a. The three temples were those of Gokulnathji, Gokulchandramaji, and Madanmohanji.

44. JSPB 2, VS 1822/1765 CE, f 53b.

45. JSPB 30, VS 1841/1784 CE, f 59b.

46. JSPB 34, VS 1843/1786 CE, f 135b.

47. JSPB 36, VS 1844/1787 CE, f 213b.

48. JSPB 37, VS 1844/1787 CE, f 114b.

49. JSPB 41, VS 1846/1789 CE, f 207b.

50. Francesca Orsini, "Inflected *Kathās*: Sufis and Krishna Bhaktas in Awadh," in *Religious Interactions in Mughal India*, ed. Vasudha Dalmia and Munis Faruqui (New Delhi: Oxford University Press, 2014), 95–232.

51. Monika Horstmann, "Sant and Sufi in Sundardas' Poetry," in Dalmia and Faruqui, *Religious Interactions in Mughal India*, 232–63.

52. Hawley, *Storm of Songs*, 69, 74, 81, 89–98.

53. Shandip Saha, "Muslims as Devotees and Outsiders: Attitudes toward Muslims in the Vārtā Literature of the Vallabha Sampradāya," in Dalmia and Faruqui, *Religious Interactions in Mughal India*, 334–35.

54. Vasudha Dalmia, "Hagiography and the 'Other' in the Vallabh *Sampraday*," in Dalmia and Faruqui, *Religious Interactions in Mughal India*, 264–89; Saha, "Muslims as Devotees."

55. Dalmia, "Hagiography and the 'Other'"; Saha, "Muslims as Devotees."

56. Saha, "Muslims as Devotees."

57. Saha, "Muslims as Devotees," 330–32.

58. For both of these episodes, see Saha, "Muslims as Devotees."

59. Dhavan, *When Sparrows Became Hawks*, 69–73.

60. Brendan LaRocque, "Mahamat Prannath and the Pranami Movement: Hinduism and Islam in a Seventeenth-Century Mercantile Sect," in Dalmia and Faruqui, *Religious Interactions in Mughal India*, 372–75.

61. Even as *nāī* is frequently translated as barber (and it is the modern Hindi word for "barber"), what really distinguished this community was their professional use of sharp implements upon the human body. This included the work of a barber, such as shaving and trimming hair, but also encompassed the skill of performing other cosmetic and hygienic procedures upon the body, such as bursting boils and dressing wounds. In addition, *nāīs* performed medical work such as minor surgeries, including circumcision, and dressing wounds. Women of the *nāī* community worked as midwives, a job that involved not just delivering babies but also pre- and postnatal caregiving. *Nāīs* also supplied the domestic

and military labor markets, performing work such as washing dishes and delivering messages. Finally, *nāīs* worked as "agents" of their patrons' houses, customarily tasked with relaying such formal communications as those to do with weddings and funerals.

62. The *bañjārās* traversed long distances, traveling in bands along with pack animals. They played a crucial role in subcontinental commodity networks, transporting grain and other articles from one region to another.

63. JSPB 24, VS 1837/1780 CE, f 193a–b and JSPB 40, VS 1846/1789 CE, 168b.

64. JSPB 24, VS 1837/1780 CE, f77a.

65. JSPB 24, VS 1837/1780 CE, f77a.

66. JSPB 24, VS 1837/1780 CE, f 193a–b. "*tarai surāṇā chainrām rai nāvai si. Bhīvrāj ro kāgad gayo jīṇ mai līkhīyo musalmān huvo tīṇ ro nyāt mai levai jīṇā nu mākul karjo.*"

67. JSPB 24, VS 1837/1780 CE, f 193a–b.

68. JSPB 40, VS 1846/1789 CE, f168b–169a.

69. JSPB 40, VS 1846/1789 CE, f168b–169a.

70. JSPB 16, VS 1833/1776 CE, f77a. Mahajan Singhvi Tilokmal ruled on behalf of the crown that whatever the shoemakers of Merta decided about including or excluding the convert ought to be upheld. It is worth noting that political boundaries between the Rathor and Kachhwaha principalities were not barriers to caste bonds. This reference also suggests that if local caste groups (*nyāts*), usually consisting of all the caste members of a town or cluster of villages, could not resolve intracaste disputes, one avenue available to petitioners was to turn over matters to a "higher" level of authority within their caste. For some castes, caste councils of particular towns or regions held that sort of superior authority to adjudicate disputes and interpret custom. It appears that for the mochis of Merta, the shoemaker caste council in Jaipur, located outside Marwar, held the authority to resolve matters that the shoemakers of Merta could not work out among themselves. At other points, as we know from the debate among the barbers of Maroth over reintegrating a Muslim convert, a caste group preferred to turn to state authorities for resolving those intracaste disputes that they could not work out themselves.

71. See the case of Pandit Hirdairam above, JSPB 39, VS 1845/1788 CE, f118b–119a. In the case of Muslim rajputs as well, it was only the Kyamkhanis who were treated as peers. The other Muslim rajputs were considered "outsiders," ineligible for such marks of inclusion as sharing meals and smoking from the same *hukā* (pipe) by Hindu rajputs.

72. JSPB 41, VS 1846/1789 CE, f291a.

73. JSPB 21, VS 1835/1778 CE, f321a-322b and JSPB 62, VS 1868/1811CE, f113b–114a.

74. JSPB 62, VS 1868/1811 CE, f113b–114a.

75. JSPB 39, VS 1845/1788 CE, f118b–119a.

76. For instance, a Brajbhasha text composed at the Bundela court around 1710 spoke of Aurangzeb in such tones and presented its rajput hero's struggle as one for the "*hindu dharma*." See Busch, "Unhitching the Oxcart of Delhi," 434–39. Also, a Sanskrit text composed at the Kachhwaha court in the mid-eighteenth century portrayed Aurangzeb in a negative light, using him as a foil to cast the Kachhwaha king as a hero. See Monika Horstmann, "Aurangzeb in the Perspective of Kachhwaha Literature," *Journal of the Royal Asiatic Society* 28, no. 3 (2018): 441–59.

77. Bachrach and Pauwels, "Aurangzeb as Iconoclast?"; Veronique Bouillier, "Aurangzeb and the Nāth Yogīs," *Journal of the Royal Asiatic Society* 28, no. 3 (2018): 525–35.

78. JSPB 39, VS 1845/1788 CE, f118b–119a.

79. For a succinct discussion of Nagaur's history, see Thelen, "Intersected Communities," 63–68.

80. Chatterjee, *Negotiating Mughal Law*, 39-40.

81. Chatterjee, *Negotiating Mughal Law*, 33.

82. Wael B. Hallaq, "The 'Qāḍī's Dīwān (Sijill)' before the Ottomans," *Bulletin of the School of Oriental and African Studies* 61, no. 3 (1998): 415–36.

83. Nandini Chatterjee, "Mahzar-namas in the Mughal and British Empires: The Uses of an Indo-Islamic Legal Form," *Comparative Studies in Society and History* 58, no. 2 (2016): 379–406.

84. Hallaq, "The 'Qāḍī's Dīwān (Sijill)'," 432.

85. Hallaq, "The 'Qāḍī's Dīwān (Sijill)'," 432.

86. Tanuja Kothiyal, *Nomadic Narratives*. See also Manan Ahmed Asif, *A Book of Conquest: The* Chachnama *and Muslim Origins in South Asia* (Cambridge, MA: Harvard University Press, 2016), for the political ethics of early Islamic Sindh.

87. Mana Kia, *Persianate Selves: Memories of Place and Origin before Nationalism* (Stanford: Stanford University Press, 2020), 14.

88. JSPB 15, VS 1832/1775 CE, f 293a.

89. JSPB 15, VS 1832/1775 CE, f 293a.

90. JSPB 32, VS 1842/1785 CE, f28b.

91. Singh, *Riporṭ Mardumśumārī*, 73.

92. Singh, *Riporṭ Mardumśumārī*, 76–78. See also Talbot, "Becoming Turk the Rajput Way," for a discussion of the history of the Kyamkhanis and their conversion to Islam. The article is also informative about the conversion, more broadly, of middling rajputs in Rajasthan to Islam during the Sultanate era.

93. Singh, *Riporṭ Mardumśumārī*, 66–73.

94. Singh, *Riporṭ Mardumśumārī*, 66.

95. Singh, *Riporṭ Mardumśumārī*, 66, 73, 77. On the Kyamkhanis prospering under Mughal rule and on their continuing martial employment in the eighteenth century, see Talbot, "Becoming Turk the Rajput Way," 226–29.

96. Singh, *Riporṭ Mardumśumārī*, 73.

97. Thelen, "Intersected Communities," 74–76.

98. For a history of the spread of Islam among artisans in Rajasthan, see S. Inayat A. Zaidi and Sunita Zaidi, "Conversion to Islam and Formation of Castes in Medieval Rajasthan," in *Art and Culture: Felicitation Volume in Honour of Professor S. Nurul Hasan*, ed. Ahsan Jan Qaisar and Som Prakash Verma (Jaipur: Publication Scheme, 1993), 27–42.

99. A very small number of Shia Bohra Muslims were recorded by Marwar's first colonial-era census in the late nineteenth century as residents of Jodhpur town. Since they are noted to have been Gujarati speakers who specialized in selling "English" goods, it is likely that these Bohra Muslims moved to Marwar in the colonial era. Singh, *Riporṭ Mardumśumārī*, 441–42.

4. DISCIPLINE

1. JSPB 53, VS 1856/1799 CE, f 147a.

2. For the identity of the *dīvān* at the time, see Saxena, *Apparatus of the Rathors* 1, xlviii.

3. On nonviolence as a universal, not a caste or Jain-specific, ethic in Jain eyes, see John E. Cort, *Jains in the World: Religious Values and Ideology in India* (New York: Oxford University Press, 2001), 149. I did not come across evidence of the Jain merchants of Marwar escalating their activities to promote nonharm toward animals during *Paryūṣaṇ*.

4. Singh, *Riporṭ Mardumśumārī*, 560.

5. Sandria Freitag, "*Sansiahs* and the State: The Changing Nature of 'Crime' and 'Justice' in Nineteenth-Century British India," in *Changing Concepts of Rights and Justice in South Asia*, ed. Michael Anderson and Sumit Guha (New Delhi: Oxford University Press, 2000), 82–113.

6. JSPB 32, VS 1842/1785 CE, f 293b.

7. JSPB 23, VS 1836/1779 CE, f 338a–339a and 348a–349a

8. JSPB 23, VS 1836/1779 CE, f 338a–339a and 348a–349a.

9. JSPB 23, VS 1836/1779 CE, f 338a–339a.

10. JSPB 23, VS 1836/1779 CE, f 325b–326a.

11. JSPB 23, VS 1836/1779 CE, f 348a–349a and 355b–356a. A *paisā* was a relatively low-value copper coin, also called a *dām*.

12. JSPB 1, VS 1821/1764 CE, f 127a.

13. JSPB 15, VS 1832/1775 CE, f 376b. This may be indicative of the structure of the butchers' corporate organization, that is, their supra-local caste council may have been based in Jaipur. This would make sense since Vijai Singh had recently captured Sambhar from the Kachhwahas, so it is possible that the caste ties of the butchers of Sambhar continued to extend into Jaipur. Occasionally, if a local (village or town) caste council (*nyāt*) could not resolve an intra-caste dispute, a wider, supra-local council would then be convened. Jurisdictions of such regional and supra-local councils may not have coincided with (shifting) political boundaries.

14. JSPB 30, VS 1841/ 1784 CE, 55b–56a.

15. JSPB 30, VS 1841/1784 CE, 55b–56a.

16. JSPB 30, VS 1841/1784 CE, f 51a.

17. JSPB 47, VS 1852/1795 CE, f 409a.

18. JSPB 49, VS 18541797 CE, f 120a.

19. JSPB 57, VS 1860/1803 CE, f 325a–b.

20. JSPB 17, VS 1833/1776 CE, f 43b.

21. JSPB 16, VS 1833/1776 CE, f 35b–36a.

22. JSPB 8, VS 1825/1768 CE, f 283b.

23. Singh, *Riporṭ Mardumśumārī*, 585–89.

24. JSPB 15, VS 1832/1775 CE, f 141a.

25. JSPB 15, VS 1832/1775 CE, f 141a.

26. JSPB 23, VS 1836/1779 CE, f 348a–349b and f 355b–356a. In another episode, the governor of Jaitaran fined all the cultivators of a village in the district when their rajput *jāgīrdār* refused to respond to the summons against him for his son's killing of an animal. Singhvi Bhimraj, responding on behalf of the crown in Jodhpur, had the fine reduced from one thousand rupees to two hundred (JSPB 41, VS 1846/1789 CE, f 213b). He did not, however, waive the fine on the cultivators.

27. JSPB 28, VS 1839/1782 CE, f 383a–384a.

28. JSPB 30, VS 1841/1784 CE, f 379a–b.

29. JSPB 45, VS 1850/1793 CE, f 96b.
30. JSPB 30, VS 1841/1784 CE, f 173a.
31. JSPB 30, VS 1841/1784 CE, f 173a.
32. JSPB 36, VS 1844/1787 CE, f 167a–b.
33. JSPB 23, VS 1836/1779 CE, f 348a–349b.
34. JSPB 28, VS 1839/1782 CE, f 383a–384a.
35. JSPB 30, VS 1841/1784 CE, f 379a–b.
36. Tanuja Kothiyal, *Nomadic Narratives*, 90–97.
37. Sahai, "Crafts and Statecraft"; Sahai, *Politics of Patronage*, 21–22.
38. Kothiyal, *Nomadic Narratives*, 110.
39. Anand A. Yang, "Dangerous Castes and Tribes: The Criminal Tribes Act and the Magahiya Doms of Northeast India," in *Crime and Criminality in British India*, ed. Anand A. Yang (Tucson: University of Arizona Press, 1985), 108–27; Stewart N. Gordon, "Bhils and the Idea of a Criminal Tribe in Nineteenth-Century India," in *Crime and Criminality in British India*, ed. Anand A. Yang (Tucson: University of Arizona Press, 1985), 128–39; Sumit Guha, "Lower Strata, Older Races, and Aboriginal Peoples: Racial Anthropology and Mythical History Past and Present," *Journal of Asian Studies* 57, no. 2 (1998): 423–41; Meena Radhakrishna, *Dishonoured in History: "Criminal Tribes" and British Colonial Policy* (Hyderabad: Orient Longman, 2001); Sanjay Nigam, "Disciplining and Policing the 'Criminals by Birth,' Part 1: The Making of a Colonial Stereotype—the Criminal Tribes and Castes of North India," *Indian Economic and Social History Review* 27, no. 2 (1990): 131–64; Sanjay Nigam, "Disciplining and Policing the 'Criminals by Birth,' Part 2: The Development of a Disciplinary System, 1871–1900," *IESHR* 27, no. 3 (1990): 257–87; Henry Schwartz, *Constructing the Criminal Tribe in Colonial India: Acting Like a Thief* (London: Wiley-Blackwell, 2010).
40. See Upinder Singh, *Political Violence in Ancient India* (Cambridge, MA: Harvard University Press, 2017), 50, 387–88; Anastasia Piliavsky, "The 'Criminal Tribe' in India before the British," *Comparative Studies in Society and History* 57, no. 2 (2015): 329–34, for a survey of Sanskrit and Pali discussions of forest-dwelling people in this vein.
41. See, for instance, Gordon, "Bhils and the Idea of a Criminal Tribe." Piliavsky, "The 'Criminal Tribe'," 334–38, also has a summary of early modern references to hill- and forest-dwelling groups associated with plunder and banditry.
42. JSPB 1, VS 1821/1764 CE, f 67b–68a.
43. JSPB 32, VS 1842/1785 CE, f 152a.
44. JSPB 35, VS 1843/1786 CE, f 140b–141a.
45. JSPB 35, VS 1843/1786 CE, f 140b–141a.
46. Bhandari Savantram and Pancholi Fatehkaran ordered the Nagaur magistracy to resolve the case and report back to Jodhpur. JSPB 20, VS 1837/1780 CE, f 43b.
47. JSPB 32, VS 1842/1785 CE, f 233a.
48. JSPB 32, VS 1842/1785 CE, f 291b.
49. Bhati, *Marvāṛ ke Ohdedrāroṁ*, 27.
50. JSPB 32, VS 1842/1785 CE, f 93a. The complete entry is: "*musalmān vagairai nīch jāt rai evaḍ nahīṁ raihaṇ pāvaṇ rī sanad āyī thī su hanoj pāñch sāt jāygā evaḍ chhai īj su uvākā naves su pūchh jiṇā rai evaḍ batāvai su ṭhīk kar vikāy dejo nai jīv haṃsyā na huvai jiso jābto rākhjo*." The office of *pyād bakhśī*, as already discussed was held through most of its existence by mahajans or brahmans.

51. JSPB 32, VS 1842/1785 CE, f 93a. "*musalmān vagairai kukḍā rākhī hai jiṇā su tākīd kardeṇī su jīv haṃsyā kar sakai nahī nai pher īṇ bāt rī visekh nīghai rākhṇī nai kiṇī jīv haṃsyā kīyā rī jāhar huvai toh purkas sajhā daiṇī.*"

52. JSPB 15, VS 1832/1775 CE, f 42a-b; JSPB 16, VS 1833/1776 CE, f 9a.

53. JSPB 15, VS 1832/1775 CE, f 42a-b; JSPB 16, VS 1833/1776 CE, f 9a.

54. JSPB 16, VS 1833/1776 CE, f 13b and 27a.

55. JSPB 16, VS 1833/1776 CE. f 9a, 13b, and 27a. This policy, however, proved hard to sustain since those given control of the herds refused to bear the expenditure and taxes incurred in managing the livestock without benefitting from the value of the wool produced. In response, the crown agreed to reimburse the taxed amounts or waive future taxes upon the new managers of the livestock.

56. JSPB 18, VS 1834/1777 CE, f 12b. Singhvi Tilokmal and Pancholi Fatehkaran ruled that the governor should ensure that the butcher received the money due to him.

57. JSPB 36, VS 1844/1787 CE, f 32b–33a.

58. JSPB 32, VS 1842/1785 CE, f 233a.

59. JSPB 41, VS 1846/1789 CE, f 317a–b.

60. For the identity of the *daftar rā darogā*, Bhati, *Marvāṛ ke Ohdedāroṁ*, 259.

61. JSPB 32, VS 1842/1785 CE, f 233a.

62. JSPB 37, VS 1844/1787 CE, f 325b–326a.

63. JSPB 71, VS 1876/1819 CE, f 31a.

64. JSPB 30, VS 1841/1784 CE, f 116b–117a.

65. JSPB 30, VS 1841/1784 CE, f 116b–117a.

66. JSPB 30, VS 1841/1784 CE, f 104a.

67. JSPB 30. VS 1841/1784 CE, f 104a. For the *pyād bakhśī*'s identity, see Saxena, *Apparatus of the Rathors* 1, xlix. While Saxena has transcribed the "bhā." abbreviation that was likely affixed before Ramchand's name as the caste "Bhaīyā," I have observed that the standard practice in Rathor records was to use that abbreviation for "Bhaṇḍārī."

68. JSPB 32, VS 1842/1785 CE, f 28a. Pancholi Gulalchand commanded the governor of Nagaur to punish them as stringently as possible.

69. JSPB 41, VS 1846/1789 CE, f 274b.

70. JSPB 41, VS 1846/1789 CE, f 274b.

71. JSPB 32, VS 1842/1785 CE, f 44a.

72. JSPB 32, VS 1842/1785 CE, f 44a.

73. JSPB 35, VS 1843/1786 CE, f 298a.

74. A category of people born of the union of rajput men with concubines.

75. JSPB 35, VS 1843/1786 CE, f 298a.

76. JSPB 38, VS 1845/1788 CE, f 67a. In response, Pancholi Fatehkaran and the *pyād bakhśī* at the time ruled that the *bhāṭ* be let off by the Merta magistracy, without ordering any further investigation of the case or of the butcher woman's involvement in it (JSPB 38, VS 1845/1788 CE, f 67a and f 93a).

77. JSPB 15, VS 1832/1775 CE, f 305a. Singhvi Tilokmal issued the ruling.

78. JSPB 15, VS 1832/1775 CE, f 66a.

79. JSPB 16, VS 1833/1776 CE, f 147a. Singhvi Tilokmal ordered the governor to conduct an investigation, summoning the two men and their witnesses, in order to decide the case.

80. JSPB 16, VS 1833/1776 CE, f 115b.

81. JSPB 16, VS 1833/1776 CE, f 115b.

82. JSPB 18, VS 1834/1777 CE, f 4a.

83. JSPB 39, VS 1843/1786 CE, f 53b.

84. JSPB 30, VS 1841/1784 CE, f 112b–113a.

85. JSPB 32, VS 1842/1785 CE, f 200a.

86. It is unclear which precise order these "*svāmīs*" belonged to, but the title suggests that they were members of an ascetic order.

87. JSPB 41, VS 1846/1789 CE, f 286b.

88. JSPB 36, VS 1844/1787 CE, f 115a.

89. JSPB 34, VS 1843/1786 CE, f 5b.

90. JSPB 34, VS 1843/1786 CE, f 78a. Singhvi Motichand, the crown officer responding to this petition, ordered the governor of Nagaur to make sure that the *jāṭ* was not harassed by his village *jāgīrdār* and other residents, and that if he was beaten, the *jāgīrdār* should be asked to explain.

91. JSPB 36, VS 1844/1787 CE, f 15b–16a. Another similar episode in which a *sirvī* faces retaliation from his village *jāgīrdār* for reporting animal slaughter to the crown can be found in JSPB 34, VS 1843/1786 CE, f 5b.

92. JSPB 40, VS 1848/1791 CE, f 302b. For the *pyād bakhśī*, see Saxena, *Apparatus of the Rathors* 1, xlix.

93. JSPB 33, VS 1842/1785 CE, f 80b–81a (a *svāmī*, or ascetic, facing retaliation from fellow *svāmīs* for having reported them for animal slaughter) and JSPB 35, VS 1843/1786 CE, 298a (a rajput who claimed that he was wrongly accused by a *ḍheḍhnī*).

94. JSPB 36, VS 1844/1787 CE, f 32b–33a.

95. JSPB 38, VS 1845/1788 CE, f 171b.

96. Pancholi Fatehkaran and the *pyād bakhśī* at the time ordered that the governor investigate if Inayat was innocent, and if he was, to take no action against him (JSPB 38, VS 1845/1788 CE, f 171b).

97. JSPB 38, VS 1845/1788 CE, 92b–93a.

98. JSPB 39, VS 1845/1788 CE, f 167a.

99. JSPB 39, VS 1845/1788 CE, f 167a.

100. JSPB 39, VS 1845/1788 CE, f 167a.

101. JSPB 40, VS 1846/1789 CE, f 115b–116a.

102. JSPB 38, VS 1845/1788 CE, f 67a.

103. JSPB 15, VS 1832/1775 CE, f 66a.

104. JSPB 16, VS 1833/1776 CE, f 34b.

105. JSPB 16, VS 1833/1776 CE, f 34b.

106. JSPB 36, VS 1844/1787 CE, f 167a–b.

107. JSPB 47, VS 1852/1795 CE, f 409a; JSPB 49, VS 18541797 CE, f 120a

108. JSPB 55, VS 1858/1803 CE, f 149b.

109. JSPB 57, VS 1860/1803 CE, f 201b.

5. NONHARM

1. The last of these kingdom-wide decrees was issued in 1803 by the *dīvān* in the reign of Vijai Singh's successor, Bhim Singh, JSPB 57, VS 1860/1803 CE, f 335a. The *dīvān* at this time was the Osvāl Mahajan Bhandari Gangaram (Bhati, *Marvāṛ ke Ohdedāroṁ*, 251).

2. This tree is known as *kheḍ* in Hindi today and as *senegalia catechu* in Latin. It is commonly known in English as the black cutch tree.

3. "*Tathā visnoī rahai tiṇā gāṃvā mai tathā sīv mai jīv jīnāvar kadai mārai na hai nai kheḍā vagairai rukh vāṭhai na hai su gāṃvāṁ rā paṭāyatāṁ nuṁ likh dejo su jīnāvar mārai nahī nai rukh bāḍathai nahī śrī hajūr ro hukam chhai.*" JSPB 1, VS 1821/1764 CE, f 89b.

4. JSPB 23, VS 1836/1779 CE, f 325b–326a (issued by Muhnot Gyanmal and Singhvi Khubchand); JSPB 23, VS 1836/1779 CE, f 355b–356a, JSPB 28, VS 1839/1781, 383a–384a (issued by Pancholi Nandram); JSPB 30, VS 1841/1784 CE, f 135b; JSPB 30, VS 1841/1784 CE, f 224b; JSPB 37, VS 1844/1787 CE, f 325b–326a; JSPB 41, VS 1846/1789 CE, f 208a; JSPB 43, VS 1848/1791 CE, f 388b–389a (issued by the *dīvān*, Bhandari Bhavani Das); and JSPB 49, VS 1854/1797 CE, f 246a (by the *dīvān's* office, in *khālisā* at the time, and signed by Muhnot Simbhukaran, an Osvāl mahajan).

5. JSPB 23, VS 1836/1779 CE, f 325b–326a; JSPB 43, VS 1848/1791 CE, f 388b–389a (by *dīvān* Bhandari Bhavani Das).

6. JSPB 49, VS 1854/1797 CE, f 246a (by Osvāl Mahajan Muhnot Simbhukaran, from the *dīvān's* office).

7. JSPB 23, VS 1836/1779 CE, f 325b–326a; JSPB 32, VS 1842/1785 CE, f 28a; JSPB 37, VS 1844/1787 CE, f 325b–326a.

8. JSPB 23, VS 1836/1779 CE, f 355b–356a.

9. JSPB 23, VS 1836/1779 CE, f 348a–349a; JSPB 23, VS 1836/1779 CE, f 355b–356a; JSPB 37, VS 1844/1787 CE, f 325b–326a; JSPB 49, VS 1854/1797 CE, f 246a (by Osvāl Mahajan Muhnot Simbhukaran, from the *dīvān's* office).

10. JSPB 28, VS 1839, 383a–384a (Pancholi Nandram's order) and JSPB 37, VS 1844/1787 CE, f 325b–326a. The *chaumāsā* or *chaturmās* ("four months") is a period of four lunar months, beginning in June–July and ending in October–November, that are inauspicious for ritual activities in both Jain and Vaishnav practice. For Jains, this is a time in which monks and nuns are to cease their otherwise peripatetic lives. Among Vaishnavs, this is a time at which Vishnu is thought to be asleep and so ought not to be disturbed. These months coincide with the monsoon and the heavy rains that it brings.

11. JSPB 23, VS 1836/1779 CE, f 356b–357.

12. JSPB 49, VS 1854/1797 CE, f 246a (by Osvāl Mahajan Muhnot Simbhukaran, from the *dīvān's* office).

13. JSPB 49, VS 1854/1797 CE, f 246a (by Osvāl Mahajan Muhnot Simbhukaran, from the *dīvān's* office). This command was pre-dated by district officers punishing people for killing snakes as early as 1776. So it was that Kakani Savai Ram, a Maheshwari mahajan, hit a snake that had entered his home and found himself in jail at the Nagaur magistracy. The crown heard of this from a news writer, represented by the *pyād bakhśī*, and ordered the Kakani's release (JSPB 17, VS 1833/1776 CE, f 43a).

14. Bayly, *Rulers, Townsmen and Bazaars*; Paul Dundas, *The Jains* (London: Routledge, 1992), 169.

15. Very briefly, a *tīrthaṅkar* (or "maker of a ford" across the worldly ocean of existence) is an extraordinary human who succeeds in conquering all attachments and aversions entirely by his own efforts and who, before attaining liberation, imparts this liberating knowledge to others so that they too might conquer their passions (Babb, *Absent Lord*, 5–6).

16. Dundas, *The Jains*, 197.

17. Singh, *Riporṭ Mardumśumārī*, 415.

18. Singh, *Riport Mardumśumārī*, 412.

19. Dundas, *The Jains*, 170; Cort, *Jains in the World*, 58, 63. Cort observes that in the twentieth century the wife was expected to accept her marital family's tradition but could retain some elements of her natal tradition after marriage (*Jains in the World*, 63). Lawrence Babb notes that it was common even until the twentieth century for some Osvāl Jain families from Jodhpur to be "somewhere on the frontier between Jainism and Vaiṣṇavism." Babb, *Absent Lord*, 146.

20. Bayly, *Rulers, Townsmen and Bazaars*, 390.

21. This was also true in Gujarat, where "mahajan" denoted a civic council representing all the merchants and moneylenders of a town, without distinguishing between Vaishnavs and Jains (Cort, *Jains in the World*, 55).

22. Dundas, *The Jains*, 200.

23. For a discussion of the differences in the relationship between worshipper and the worshipped between Jainism and Vaishnavism, see Babb, *Absent Lord*, 177–81.

24. Phyllis Granoff, "Being in a Minority: Medieval Jain Reactions to Other Religious Groups," in *Jainism and Prakrit in Ancient and Medieval India: Essays for Prof. Jagdish Chandra Jain*, ed. N. N. Bhattacharyya (New Delhi: Manohar, 1994), 241–66.

25. Jains were part, for instance, of a broad current of "mainstream" tantra, shared by Shaiva, Buddhist, and Vaishnava communities, in medieval South Asia. See Burchett, *Genealogy of Devotion*, 40.

26. Dundas, *The Jains*, 233–36.

27. Dundas, *The Jains*, 195–206.

28. Dundas, *The Jains*, 3–6.

29. Babb, *Absent Lord*, 3–4.

30. Dundas, *The Jains*, 10.

31. Shalin Jain, "Piety, Laity, and Royalty: Jains under the Mughals in the First Half of the Seventeenth Century," *Indian Historical Review* 40, no. 1 (2013): 67–92; Audrey Truschke, "Dangerous Debates: Jain Responses to Theological Challenges at the Mughal Court," *Modern Asian Studies* 49, no. 5 (2015): 1311–44; Truschke, *Culture of Encounters* and *The Language of History*; Vose, "The Making of a Medieval Jain Monk"; Steven Vose, "Jain Memory of the Tughluq Sultans: Alternative Sources for the Historiography of Sultanate India," *Journal of the Royal Asiatic Society*, 32, no. 1 (2022): 115–39.

32. "*Jain*" means "follower of a *Jina*," and "*jina*" in turn means "victor" or "conqueror," denoting here the defeat of all attachments and aversions. *Jinas* are also known as *tīrthaṅkars*. Babb, *Absent Lord*, 5.

33. Henk W. Bodewitz, "Hindu *Ahiṃsā* and Its Root," in *Violence Denied: Violence, Non-Violence, and the Rationalization of Violence in South Asia Cultural History*, ed. Jan E. M. Houben and Karel R. Van Kooij (Leiden: Brill, 1999), 17–44.

34. Ludwig Alsdorf, *The History of Vegetarianism and Cow Veneration in India*, trans. Bal Patil, rev. Nichola Hayton, and ed. Willem Bollee (Routledge: New York, 2011), 4–6.

35. For an example of scholarship discussing Mahavir's eating of meat, see Dundas, *The Jains*, 153; Alsdorf, *The History of Vegetarianism*, 11–14. Others argue that this is too literal a reading and that the term translated as "chicken" refers to a fruit. See Padmanabh Jaini, *The Jaina Path of Purification* (Delhi: Motilal Banarsidass, 1998 [1979]), 22–23n56.

36. D. Seyfort Ruegg, "Ahiṃsā and Vegetarianism in the History of Buddhism," in *Buddhist Studies in Honor of Walpola Rahula*, ed. Somaratna Balasooriya et al. (London: Gordon Fraser Gallery, 1980), 236.

37. Lance Nelson, "Cows, Elephants, Dogs, and Other Lesser Embodiments of *Ātman*: Reflections on Hindu Attitudes towards Non-Human Animals," in *A Communion of Subjects: Animals in Religion, Science, and Ethics*, ed. Paul Waldau and Kimberly Patton (New York: Columbia University Press, 2006), 179–93.

38. Alsdorf, *The History of Vegetarianism*; Edwin Bryant, "Strategies of Vedic Subversion: The Emergence of Vegetarianism in Post-Vedic India," in *A Communion of Subjects: Animals in Religion, Science, and* Ethics, ed. Paul Waldau and Kimberly Patton (New York: Columbia University Press, 2006), 196–98; Singh, *Political Violence*, 128, 408–9.

39. Alsdorf, *The History of Vegetarianism*, 41–42; Singh, *Political Violence*, 74.

40. Bryant, "Strategies of Vedic Subversion."

41. Bryant, "Strategies of Vedic Subversion," 201; Alsdorf, *The History of Vegetarianism*.

42. Wendy Doniger, *The Hindus: An Alternative History* (New York: Penguin Press, 2009), 9.

43. Singh, *Political Violence*, 50, 387–88. Singh notes, "Ashoka's dhamma discourses express more sensitivity and compassion towards the animals that inhabit the forest than toward the forest tribals" (387).

44. Osian seems to have held a special place in the social memory of Shvetambar Jains. For instance, the Shvetambar Jains of Gujarat mostly trace their origins to Osian and another town in Marwar, Bhinmal. Cort, *Jains in the World*, 35.

45. Babb, *Absent Lord*, 124–27. For a discussion of the emergence of the Khartar ("Particularly Sharp-Witted") and other *gachchhs* (mendicant orders) within the Shvetambar Jains, see ibid., 119–24.

46. Dundas, *The Jains*, 218–22. The Jains as a whole are divided between two large orders, the Shvetambar (White-Clad) and Digambar (Sky-Clad). Monks of the Digambar order do not wear clothes and over the centuries they became more concentrated in the Deccan and in the towns of North and Central India. Shvetambar Jain monks are expected to wear simple, white clothes, and followers of this order can be found in Gujarat, Rajasthan, and Punjab. The Shvetambars have over the centuries experienced various schisms—particularly on the question of increasing "laxity" in practice and on whether idol worship is permissible. Major mendicant orders that broke off from the main Shvetambar Jain body are the Lonka Gachchh, the Sthanakvasis, and the Terapanthis. Today, the Murtipujak ("idol-worshipping") Tapa Gachchh is the most common mendicant order among Shvetambar Jains in western India. Cort, *Jains in the World*, 40–43.

47. Osian was endowed with a stepwell and several tanks, all associated with the temples built here in the medieval period. In an otherwise arid landscape, this may have served to reinforce Osian's ability to attract more temples and pilgrims. Michael Meister, "Water in a Desert Landscape," in *Desert Temples: Sacred Centers of Rajasthan in Historical, Art-Historical, and Social* Contexts, ed. Lawrence Babb, John Cort, and Michael Meister (New Delhi: Rawat, 2008), 80–83.

48. In Gujarat too merchants were able to leverage their tremendous wealth, acquired through a successful participation in the burgeoning foreign trade of the region's ports, to play a significant role in local administration. The post of nagarsheth, the honorary chief merchant of Ahmedabad, became a powerful position. The Jain merchant Virji Vorah (d. 1675), nagarsheth of Ahmedabad, would formally mediate between the merchants of his town and Mughal authorities. Shantidas Jhaveri (d. 1675), also a Jain, was the head of the merchant guild of Surat. Both men's riches were fabled and both channeled their wealth into gaining a prominent role in local religious life. Dundas, *The Jains*, 168–69. Jhaveri also used

his mercantile prowess to make important political connections in the Mughal administration, including with the emperor himself. Jain, "Piety, Laity, and Royalty," 70.

49. Singh, *Political Violence*, 49.

50. Singh, *Political Violence*, 398.

51. André Wink, *Akbar* (Oxford: Oneworld, 2009), 56–57. Akbar hosted debates among the learned men of different religions at his court. Both Jain and Mughal sources confirm the participation of Jain monks in these debates and the regard in which Akbar held them. Jain sources claim that Jain monks, such as Jinchandrasuri II (1541–1613), performed rituals for the benefit of the Mughals and defeated their rivals, including Muslims, at court both in debate and in miraculous powers. Jinchandrasuri II was born and raised in Marwar and also died there. He belonged to the Khartar Gachchh order of the Shvetambar Jains (Babb, *Absent Lord*, 124–25).

52. Ellison B. Findly, "Jahangir's Vow of Nonviolence," *Journal of the American Oriental Society* 107, no. 2 (1987), 245–56; Wink, *Akbar*, 56.

53. Dundas, *The Jains*, 125–26; Babb, *Absent Lord*, 124. Jinachandra Suri II was a Marwari reformer, discussed above, among the Shvetambar Jains who attracted a large following in the region.

54. Wink, *Akbar*, 56.

55. Jain, "Piety, Laity, and Royalty," 70.

56. JSPB 23, VS 1836/1779 CE, f 328b–330a (issuer of command unnamed); JSPB 28, VS 1839/1782 CE, 383a–384a (issued by Pancholi Nandram); JSPB 37, VS 1844/1787 CE, f 325b–326a and JSPB 49, VS 1854/1797 CE, f 246a (by Osvāl Mahajan Muhnot Simbhukaran, from the *dīvān's* office).

57. JSPB 49, VS 1836/1779 CE, f 246a.

58. JSPB 23, VS 1836/1779 CE, f 328b–330a.

59. JSPB 32, VS 1842/1785 CE, f 291b.

60. JSPB 32, VS 1842/1785 CE, f 291b and JSPB 49, VS 1854/1797 CE, f 246a (by Osvāl Mahajan Muhnot Simbhukaran, from the *dīvān's* office).

61. JSPB 23, VS 1836/1779 CE, f 328b–330a; JSPB 28, VS 1839, 383a–384a (issued by Pancholi Nandram); JSPB 37, VS 1844/1787 CE, f 325b–326a; and JSPB 49, VS 1836/1787 CE, f 246a (by Osvāl Mahajan Muhnot Simbhukaran, from the *dīvān's* office).

62. For the care of old cattle: JSPB 23, VS 1836/1779 CE, f 328b–330; JSPB 37, VS 1844/1787 CE, f 325b–326a and JSPB 49, VS 1836/1787 CE, f 246a (by Osvāl Mahajan Muhnot Simbhukaran, from the *dīvān's* office). For food for pigeons and stray dogs: JSPB 23, VS 1836/1779 CE, f 328b–330. Since the mid-twentieth century, a *man* as a measure of weight has been standardized to forty kilograms and a *ser* to 0.933 kilograms.

63. JSPB 23, VS 1836/1779 CE, f 328b–330; JSPB 28, VS 1839, 383a–384a (Pancholi Nandram's command); and JSPB 37, VS 1844/1787 CE, f 325b–326a.

64. JSPB 23, VS 1836/1779 CE, f 328b–330; JSPB 55, VS 1858/1801 CE, f 74b (issued by the *pyād bakhśī*, at the time brahman Vyās Motiram); and JSPB 62, VS 1867/1810 CE, f 166a. For the identity of the *pyād bakhśī* in 1801, Bhati, *Mārvāṛ ke Ohdedāroṁ*, 265.

65. JSPB 32, VS 1843/1786 CE, f 142b–143a.

66. JSPB 18, VS 1834/1777 CE, f 89a. Charans are a caste of poets, generally associated with patron families of rajputs for whom they maintain genealogies and about whose heroic deeds they compose and sing ballads. Charans were associated with the worship of the

Goddess, whose veneration had historically involved ritual animal sacrifice. Charans could also be ritualists and were considered to wield sacerdotal power.

67. JSPB 16, VS 1833/1776 CE, f 115b.

68. JSPB 17, VS 1833/1776 CE, f 89a.

69. JSPB 23, VS 1836/1779 CE, 172a.

70. JSPB 35, VS 1843/1786 CE, f 325b.

71. JSPB 37, VS 1844/1787 CE, f 142b.

72. JSPB 32, VS 1842/1785 CE, f 49a–b; JSPB 38, VS 1845/1788 CE, f 67a (a *bhāṭ* family); and JSPB 53, VS 1856/1799 CE, f 147a.

73. JSPB 23, VS 1836/ 1779 CE, f 41a.

74. JSPB 23, VS 1836/1779 CE, f 310b.

75. JSPB 28, VS 1839/1782 CE, f 317a. For the identity of the governor, see Bhati, *Mārvāṛ ke Ohdedāroṁ*, 339.

76. JSPB 23, VS 1836/1779 CE, f 175b.

77. JSPB 23, VS 1839/1782 CE, f 255b–256a.

78. JSPB 28, VS 1839/1782 CE, f 267a.

79. JSPB 30, VS 1841/1784 CE, f 277b–278a and 280a.

80. JSPB 30, VS 1841/1784 CE, f 264a.

81. JSPB 32, VS 1842/1785 CE, f 128b; JSPB 32, VS 1842/1785 CE, f 196b and f 197b.

82. JSPB 30, VS 1841/1784 CE, f 138a. The intercepted carrier tried to evade punishment by claiming that he had thrown away the meat to dogs (*keh dīyo su mānṭī to kutāṁ nu nakhāy dīvī*).

83. JSPB 30, VS 1841/1784 CE, f 112b–113a. An unnamed crown officer commanded that the man should be fined.

84. JSPB 30, VS 1841/1784 CE, f 112b–113a.

85. JSPB 32, VS 1842/1785 CE, f 200b.

86. JSPB 39, VS 1845/1788 CE, f 418b and 420a–b; JSPB 52, VS 1855/1798 CE, f 135b (to the Daulatpura governor).

87. JSPB 37, VS 1844/1787 CE, f 258a–b; JSPB 35, VS 1843/1786 CE, f 109b and 116a; and JSPB 32, VS 1842/1785 CE, f 201b.

88. JSPB 30, VS 1841/1784 CE, f 280a. One wonders if these mahajan officials or their families were involved in the grain trade or the business of interfacing between peasants and the state at the time of revenue collection. If so, buying harvested grain at discounted costs would provide a boost to their businesses.

89. JSPB 32, VS 1842/1785 CE, f 233a.

90. JSPB 30, VS 1841/1784 CE, f 138a.

91. JSPB 30, VS 1841/1784 CE, f 138a.

92. JSPB 26, VS 1839/1782 CE, f 52a–b.

93. JSPB 30, VS 1841/1784 CE, f 98a and 141b–142a.

94. JSPB 37, VS 1844/f 239b–240a.

95. JSPB 55, VS 1858/1801 CE, f 147b. Unnamed crown officers ordered that the *sirvī* be fined, reminding the governor that animal slaughter is forbidden ("*jīv haṃsyā rī to manāī hai*").

96. Other peasant castes, such as the *sirvīs*, however continued to eat meat as is indicated by a command in which crown officer Bhandari Dayaldas had them punished for doing so (JSPB 28, VS 1839/1782 CE, f 235a).

97. For the two petitions submitted by Jat Godiya, see JSPB 14, VS 1831/1774 CE, f 76a–b and 86a.

98. JSPB 28, VS 1839/1782 CE, f 273a.

99. JSPB 30, VS 1841/1784 CE, f 47b–48a; JSPB 32, VS 1842/1785 CE, f 24b (issued by Singhvi Gyanmal), 92a, 93a, and 105b–106a; JSPB 37, VS 1844/1787 CE, f 142b; JSPB 41, VS 1846/1789 CE, and f 194b–195a.

100. JSPB 26, VS 1839/1782 CE, f 44a and 47b–48a.

101. JSPB 15, VS 1832/1775 CE, f 309a; JSPB 16, VS 1833/1776 CE, f 133a; JSPB 17, VS 1833/1776 CE, f 127a and 129a.

102. JSPB 28, VS 1839/1782 CE, f 189a. An *anna* was one-sixteenth of a rupee.

103. JSPB 28, VS 1839/1782 CE, f 146b. Mahajan officers Singhvi Chainmal and Bhandari Dayaldas issued the command from Jodhpur.

104. JSPB 30, VS 1841/1784 CE, f 319b.

105. JSPB 30, VS 1841/1784 CE, f 133b. Muhnot Savairam ruled that the summons be cancelled in exchange for the *ḍheḍh* or his son being captured and handed over the governor of Maroth.

106. JSPB 35, VS 1843/1786 CE, f 44a–b.

107. JSPB 39, VS 1845/1788 CE, f 233a.

108. JSBP 40, VS 1846/1789 CE, f 192a–b.

6. AUSTERITY

1. Dundas, *The Jains*, 188–89.

2. Dundas, *The Jains*, 189.

3. See for instance John E. Cort, "Two Ideals of the Śvētāmbar Mūrtipūjak Jain Layman," *Journal of Indian Philosophy* 19, no. 4 (1991): 396.

4. I thank John Cort for the insight on the accommodation in Jain codes to local custom and for guidance on the practice of polygyny among Jains before the eighteenth century. Personal communication via email on August 2, 2020.

5. Dundas, *The Jains*, 189–90.

6. Dundas, *The Jains*, 192.

7. For a discussion of *ābrū* or reputation among the Jains and its importance also among Vaishnavs, see Dundas, *The Jains*, 196–97. The endowment of animal hospitals or *pinjra pols*, an expression of commitment to nonviolence, was yet another aspect of religious giving among Jains but I have yet to come across an example of this in eighteenth-century Marwar. This Jain ethical culture and its emphasis upon religious giving became the foundation for the growth of philanthropy in the colonial era. See also Douglas Haynes, "From Tribute to Philanthropy: The Politics of Gift Giving in a Western Indian City," *Journal of Asian Studies* 46, no. 2 (1987): 339–60; and Cort, "Two Ideals," 406–10.

8. Dundas, *The Jains*, 198.

9. B. G. Gokhale, *Surat in the Seventeenth Century: A Study in Urban History of Pre-Modern India* (Bombay: Popular Prakashan, 1978), 137. On Virji Vora's economic activities also see S. Gopal, "Virji Vora."

10. John E. Cort, "Jain Society: 1800–1947," in *Brill's Encyclopedia of Jainism Online*, ed. John E. Cort et al., http://dx.doi.org/10.1163/2590-2768_BEJO_COM_043936. See also

Dwijendra Tripathi and M. J. Mehta, "The Nagarsheth of Ahmedabad: The History of an Urban Institution in a Gujarati City," *Proceedings of the Indian History Congress* 39 (1978): 481–96.

11. See for instance Rosalind O'Hanlon, "Manliness and Imperial Service in Mughal North India," *Journal of the Economic and Social History of the Orient* 42, no. 1 (1999): 47–93; Flatt, *Courts of the Deccan Sultanate*, 31–72.

12. *MVSK*, 73.

13. *MVSK*, 85.

14. JSPB 35, VS 1843/1786 CE, f 49a. "*Tathā gāṃv nev rai rājpūt harā rai gharai bakrī maut muī su uṇ ūṭ nu dīvī nai īṇ rai bhelo ek sāmī hālī rayo tho tīṇ nu anbaṇat huī tarai kachaiḍī āy nai kayau īṇ jīv haṃsyā kīvī hai jīṇ rī the talab kīvī su īn bābat sanad to āgai huī thī nai hamār pher nevrā rai jāgīrdār araj karai īṇ bāt maiṁ takāvat huvai to taksīrvār chhāṁ sāmī jhūṭh kahai chhai īṇ rājpūt rai gharai to doy pīḍhī su śrī ṭhākur jī rā sevā chhai tulchhī chhai nai mās ro sūṃs chhai īṇ vāt ro sāro gāṃv sāydī chhai su hamai talab ro uṭhantarī kar dejo śrī hajūr ro hukam chhai*." I do not have an explanation for why the goat's carcass could have been given to a camel, as recorded in the command.

15. John Cort, "Defining Jainism: Reform in the Jain Tradition," in *Jain Doctrine and Practice: Academic Perspectives*, ed. Joseph T. O'Connell and Nikhil Wagle (Toronto: University of Toronto Center for South Asian Studies, 2000), 172.

16. JSPB 16, VS 1833/1776 CE, f 115b.

17. JSPB 38, VS 1845/1788 CE, f 179b.

18. Ordeals (*dhīj*) were a common means of resolving disputes, whether civil or criminal in nature, in eighteenth-century Marwar. There are numerous references in the *Jodhpur Sanad Parwāna Bahīs* to the practice of *dhīj*, although the records do not elaborate on exactly how the ordeals were conducted; see also Nandita P. Sahai, "Crafts in Eighteenth-Century Jodhpur: Questions of Caste, Class and Community Identities," *Journal of the Economic and Social History of the Orient* 48, no. 4 (2005): 542, for another mention of the use of ordeals in legal procedure in eighteenth-century Marwar. State records mentioning ordeals at most specified which kind of ordeal had been applied, such as the "'ordeal by water" (*pāṇī rī dhīj*). But records mentioning ordeals do not explain how they were administered and how the "truth" was then established. Studies of legal practice elsewhere in eighteenth-century South Asia also point to the widespread use of ordeals in legal procedure. See (for the western Deccan) Guha, "An Indian Penal Regime," 111; Sumit Guha, "Speaking Historically: The Changing Voices of Historical Narration in Western India, 1400–1900," *American Historical Review* 109, no. 4 (2004): 1100; and (for Jaipur) Dilbagh Singh, "Regulating the Domestic: Notes on the Pre-colonial State and the Family," *Studies in History* 19, no. 1 (2003): 80.

19. JSPB 38, VS 1845/1788 CE, f 179b.

20. JSPB 38, VS 1845/1788 CE, f 179b.

21. JSPB 40, VS 1846/1789 CE, f 227 a–b.

22. Lawrence Babb notes through his ethnographic fieldwork that the identity of Rajasthani traders was rooted much more in the ethic of nonviolence, in structural opposition to the association of violence with rajputs, than with reference to the fourfold *varṇa* order. See Babb, "Mirrored Warriors: On the Cultural Identity of Rajasthani Traders," *International Journal of Hindu Studies* 3, no. 1 (1999): 1–25.

23. JSPB 32, VS 1843/1786 CE, f 142b–143a.

24. JSPB 38, VS 1845/1788 CE, f 123b. The hosting of communal feasts (*mausar*) was an important element in building and maintaining caste ties. Weddings, births, funerals, and atonement for the violation of caste rules were occasions that merited the holding of feasts for the entire caste group. Communal feasts for the local caste group then performed a sociological function in giving meaning to the caste as a social category. Being debarred from a caste feast or boycott of one's feast was tantamount to expulsion from the caste.

25. JSPB 38, VS 1845/1788 CE, f 123b.

26. JSPB 28, VS 1839/1782 CE, f 101b.

27. Situated near Marwar's southeastern border with Udaipur, Ghanerao arose as a vibrant center of painting, fostered by its local rajput lords, in the eighteenth century. Crill, *Marwar Painting*, 81–83. Evidence from these paintings suggests that the rajput lords, a Rathor lineage, of the Ghanerao *ṭhikānā*, unlike the Vaishnav maharaja of the domain, were Shaiva; see "Thakur Padam Singh of Ghanerao with Nobles" and "Thakur Viram Dev of Ghanerao Worshipping at a Shiva Shrine" in Crill, *Marwar Painting*, 82, 83. While the latter painting, from 1745, depicts the Ghanerao lord praying to Shiva, the former, from 1721, clearly displays the Shaiva sectarian *tilak* or forehead marking on the Ghanerao lord. We know from yet another painting produced by the Ghanerao *ṭhikāṇā* that its rajput lords continued to kill animals for meat into the early nineteenth century. See "Figure 101: Thakur Ajit Singh of Ghanerao in Darbar with His Son Kunwar Pratap Singh," in Crill, *Marwar Painting*, 130.

28. JSPB 30, VS 1841/1784 CE, f 258a.

29. JSPB 55, VS 1858/1801 CE, f 201a–b.

30. JSPB 11, VS 1860/1793 CE, f 138b.

31. *Fitūr* derives from the Arabic *futūr* (literally, "languor"), and the JSPB records frequently use this term to designate a drunken stupor. *Matvāl* or *matvālā* means 'intoxicated.'

32. JSPB 55, VS 1858/1801 CE, f 108b–109a.

33. JSPB 37, VS 1844/1787 CE, f 228b–229a.

34. See "MA 3: A Prince Goes Hunting," in Vicky Ducrot, *Four Centuries of Rajput Painting: Mewar, Marwar, and Dhundhar* (Milan: Skira, 2009), 91. This is a late seventeenth-century painting of a prince on a hunt from an illustrated *Bārahmāsā* ("Twelve Seasons") manuscript from western Rajasthan.

35. See paintings MA 10 and MA 11 in Ducrot, "Four Centuries of Rajput Painting" (97–98), for two examples of paintings commissioned by *ṭhikāṇās* during Vijai Singh's reign that depict their patron rajput lords hunting.

36. See for instance a painting commissioned by an unidentified rajput *ṭhikāṇā* around 1760 CE that shows a ritual being performed to the goddess Durga on the occasion of Navratri. The bottom edge of the painting depicts a buffalo and a goat about to be slaughtered as part of the ritual. See "MA 9: Thakur Kesri and His Son Worship the Devi at Navratri" in Ducrot, *Four Centuries of Rajput Painting*, 96.

37. JSPB 11, VS 1828/1771 CE, f 211b.

38. JSPB 12, VS 1829/1772 CE, f 58b.

39. JSPB 14, VS 1831/1774 CE, f 246a–b.

40. JSPB 12, VS 1829/1772 CE, f 114b.

41. JSPB 55, VS 1858/1801 CE, f 151a.

42. JSPB 14, VS 1831/1774 CE, f 246a-b.

43. JSPB 34, VS 1843/1786 CE, f 241a–b.

44. JSPB 40, VS 1846/1789 CE, f 299b–300a.

45. JSPB 34, VS 1833/1776 CE, f 40b.

46. Sahai, "Crossing the Golden Gate?"

47. JSPB 35, VS 1843/1786 CE, f 176b–177a.

48. JSPB 41, VS 1846/1789 CE, f 200a.

49. JSPB 11, VS 1828/1771 CE, f 211b.

50. JSPB 14, VS 1831/1774 CE, f 130a; JSPB 15, VS 1832/1775 CE, f 154b; JSPB 23, VS 1836/1779 CE, f 92a; JSPB 38, VS 1845/1788 CE, f 183b–184a and 184a-b; JSPB 39, VS 1845/1788 CE, f 165b.

51. JSPB 14, VS 1831/1774 CE, f 130a.

52. JSPB 15, VS 1832/1775 CE, f 154b.

53. JSPB 38, VS 1845/1788 CE, f 183b–184a and 184a–b; and JSPB 39, VS 1845/1788 CE, f 165b.

54. Anne Hardgrove, *Community and Public Culture: The Marwaris in Calcutta, c. 1897–1997* (New York: Columbia University Press, 2003), 279.

55. Ritu Birla, *Stages of Capital: Law, Culture, and Market Governance in Colonial India* (Durham: Duke University Press, 2009), 151–60.

56. JSPB 24, VS 1837/1780 CE, f 21b and 98b.

57. JSPB 23, VS 1836/1779 CE, f 92a.

58. *Takā* is a regional vernacularization of *ṭankā*, which was a type of coin introduced by the Delhi Sultans in the twelfth century and later, in other regional sultanates such as that in Bengal. In the centuries following its first introduction, the *tankā* was made of silver and was a relatively heavy coin, around eleven grams in weight. See John S. Deyell, "Cowries and Coins: The Dual Monetary System of the Bengal Sultanate," *Indian Economic and Social History Review* 47, no. 1 (2010): 66; Najaf Haider, "Coinage and the Silver Crisis," in *Economic History of Medieval India*, ed. Irfan Habib (New Delhi: Pearson 2011), 150. By the eighteenth century, however, it is possible that the *ṭakā* coin in Marwar was made not of silver but of the less valuable copper. This is supported by the incidence of copper *ṭakā* production in kingdoms near Marwar, such as in Alwar in the nineteenth century. See Jan Lucassen, "The Logistics of Wage Payments: Changing Patterns in Northern India in the 1840s," in *Wages and Currency: Global Comparisons from Antiquity to the Twentieth Century*, ed. Jan Lucassen (New York: Peter Lang, 2007), 379–80.

59. JSPB 38, VS 1845/1788 CE, f 183b–184a.

60. JSPB 38, VS 1845/1788 CE, f 184a–b. The crown instructed the office to make the men sign an undertaking, pledging to pay twenty-one rupees if they were ever caught gambling again.

61. JSPB 39, VS 1845/1788 CE, f 165b.

62. Fatima A. Imam, "Institutionalizing *Rajdharma:* Strategies of Sovereignty in Eighteenth-Century Jaipur" (PhD diss., University of Toronto, 2008); Imam, "Decoding the Rhetoric"; Kumar, "Crime and Gender"; Singh, "Regulating the Domestic."

63. Uma Chakravarti, "Wifehood, Widowhood, and Adultery: Female Sexuality, Surveillance, and the State in 18th Century Maharashtra," *Contributions to Indian Sociology* 29, no. 1/2 (1995): 3–21; O'Hanlon, "Disciplining the Brahman Household: The Moral Mission of Empire in the 18th Century Maratha State," in *Looking Within, Looking Without: Exploring Households in the Subcontinent through Time*, ed. Nandita Sahai and Kumkum Roy (New Delhi: Primus Books, 2015); N. K. Wagle, "Women in the Kotwāl's Papers, Puṇe, 1767–1791," in *Images of Women in Maharashtrian Society*, ed. Anne Feldhaus, 15–60 (Albany: SUNY Press, 1998).

7. CHASTITY

1. For remarriage among non-elite groups in Marwar, see Sahai, "The 'Other' Culture," 37; Kailash Rani, "Claims and Counter-Claims: Widow Remarriage in Eighteenth-Century Marwar," in Bharadwaj et al., *Revisiting the History*, 296–309. For elite castes, see Chakravarti, "Wifehood, Widowhood and Adultery"; V. S. Kadam, "The Institution of Marriage and the Position of Women in Eighteenth-Century Maharashtra," *Indian Economic and Social History Review* 25, no. 3 (1988): 341–70; O'Hanlon, "Disciplining the Brahman Household," in Sahai and Roy, *Looking Within, Looking Without*, 381–82; and for early colonial Bengal see Radhika Singha, *A Despotism of Law: Crime and Justice in Early Colonial India* (New Delhi: Oxford University Press, 2000), 112–13, 115.

2. For a detailed discussion of this typology and the questions about archives and methods that it raises, see Divya Cherian, "Stolen Skin and Children Thrown: Governing Sex and Abortion in Eighteenth-Century India," *Modern Asian Studies* 55, no. 5 (2021): 1461–509.

3. For Marwar, see Sahai, "Crossing the Golden Gate?" in Sahai and Roy, *Looking Within, Looking Without*, 399. For Jaipur, see Nirmal Kumar, "Crime and Gender in Eighteenth-Century Rajasthan," *Indian Historical Review* 30, no. 1/2 (2003): 40–54; Singh, "Regulating the Domestic," 74; Imam, "Decoding the Rhetoric of Morality," 412–15. A similar problem of distinguishing "rape" from "adultery" can also be discerned in studies based on records from the Peshwa court in Pune. See Wagle, "Women in the Kotwāl's Papers," in Feldhaus, *Images of Women*.

4. Lyndal Roper, "Will and Honor: Sex, Words and Power in Augsburg Criminal Trials," *Radical History Review* 43 (1989): 45–46.

5. Cherian, "Stolen Skin and Children Thrown," 19–31.

6. Cherian, "Stolen Skin and Children Thrown," 19–31.

7. JSPB 33, VS 1842/1785 CE, f 92b–93a.

8. JSPB 30, VS 1841/1784 CE, f 282a–b and JSPB 37, VS 1844/1787 CE, f 275a are two examples of rajput men killing their female relatives for having an illicit sexual relationship.

9. JSPB 41, VS 1846/1789 CE, f 378a–b; and JSPB 52, VS 1855/1798 CE, f 158b.

10. See Ramya Sreenivasan, "Honoring the Family: Narratives and Politics of Kinship in Pre-Colonial Rajasthan," in *Unfamiliar Relations: Family and History in South* Asia, ed. Indrani Chatterjee (New Delhi: Permanent Black, 2004), 60–62; Sreenivasan, "Drudges, Dancing Girls, and Concubines: Female Slaves in Rajput Polity, 1500–1850," in *Slavery and South Asian History*, ed. Indrani Chatterjee and Richard Eaton (Bloomington: Indiana University Press, 2004), 154.

11. JSPB 18, VS 1834/1777 CE, f 114b.

12. For an instance of the role of Jain *yatis*: JSPB 11, VS 1828/1771 CE, f 137b. JSPB 37, VS 1844/1787 CE, f 231a also mentions the role of a *pātnī*, a member of the Jain community, in executing multiple abortions in Pali. Mentions of the role of professional midwives: JSPB 12, VS 1829/1772 CE, f 113b; JSPB 18, VS 1834/1777 CE, f 53a–b; and JSPB 30, VS 1841/1784 CE, f 55b. References to the use of herbs to induce abortion: JSPB 11, VS 1828/1771 CE, f 137b; JSPB 18, VS 1834/1777 CE, f 53a–b; and JSPB 30, VS 1841/1784 CE, f 55b. *Yatis*, or *jatīs* in the JSPBs, emerged in the medieval era and were a more domesticated sort of ascetic than Jain monks. Even as they took initiation into the monastic community, they did not take the Five Great Vows (essential for monks) in full-fledged form. Still, they earned deference from lay Jains and others due to their command of ritual as well as worldly knowledge.

Unlike monks, they tended to remain in one place and followed a more lax daily regimen. In the nineteenth century, as the Shvetambar Jain community went through a reform effort, it worked to eradicate the *yati* institution, which it now saw as a symbol of laxity. See Cort, *Jains in the World*, 42–46.

13. JSPB 17, VS 1833/1776 CE, f 43a.

14. JSPB 32, VS 1841/1784, f 79a.

15. JSPB 18, VS 1834/1777 CE, f 53a–b and JSPB 37, VS 1844/1787 CE, f 144a–b.

16. See Imam, "Decoding the Rhetoric of Morality," 409; Kumar, "Crime and Gender," 47, 50–51; Wagle, "Women in the Kotwāl's Papers," in Feldhaus, *Images of Women*, 42–51.

17. JSPB 11, VS 1828/1771 CE, f 137b; JSPB 15, VS 1832/1775 CE, f 309b; JSPB 18, VS 1834/1777 CE, f 114b; JSPB 28, VS 1839/1782 CE, f 76a, 78a, 80a–b and 103a; JSPB 30, VS 1841/1784 CE, f 55b; JSPB 32, VS 1842/1785 CE, 82a and 133b; JSPB 33, VS 1842/1785 CE, f 11a; JSPB 35, VS 1843/1786 CE, f 57b–58a, 218a, and 243b; JSPB 37, VS 1844/1787 CE, f 144a–b; JSPB 39, VS 1845/1788 CE, f 168b and 169a; JSPB 45, VS 1850/1793 CE, f 521a–b; JSPB 46, VS 1851/1794 CE, f 86b–87a; JSPB 49, VS 1854/1797 CE, f 98b–99a; and JSPB 55, VS 1858/1801 CE, f 101a.

18. JSPB 39, VS 1845/1788 CE, f 169a.

19. JSPB 17, VS 1832/1775 CE, f 214b; Saxena, *Apparatus of the Rathors* 1, l.

20. JSPB 18, VS 1833/1776 CE, f 53a–b.

21. "*Laḍhā sarūpā rī baū ranḍol*" (JSPB 18, VS 1834/ 1777 CE, f 114b). *Laḍhās* are a lineage among *māheśvarīs*, a community of merchants.

22. JSPB 5, VS 1823/1766 CE, f 164a.

23. JSPB 28, 1839/1782 CE, 76a, 78a, and 80a–b.

24. JSPB 28, VS 1839/1782 CE, f 82b.

25. JSPB 20, 1835/1778 CE, f 42b.

26. The Daftaris are a lineage among the Osvāl Jains of Marwar.

27. JSPB 11, VS 1828/1771 CE, f 137b.

28. A *bhaṭṭārak* is a spiritual leader of localized Digambara Jain communities.

29. As we know from the Rathor order discussed in the introduction that listed all the castes to be counted as *achhep* or "untouchable" in Marwar.

30. JSPB 12, VS 1829/1772 CE, f 113b.

31. JSPB 20, VS 1835/1778 CE, f 105a.

32. JSPB 46, VS 1851/1794 CE, f 86b–87a.

33. JSPB 18, VS 1834/1777 CE, f 53a–b.

34. JSPB 37, VS 1844/1787 CE, f 144a–b. The document records the father's caste with the abbreviated "Mu.," which I have taken as a shorthand for Muṃhtā, a caste grouping within the Osvāl Jains of Marwar.

35. JSPB 45, VS 1850/1793 CE, f 521a–b.

36. JSPB 15, VS 1832/1775 CE, f 309b.

37. JSPB 28, VS 1839/1782 CE, f 76a.

38. JSPB 49, VS 1854/1797 CE, f 98b–99a.

39. JSPB 37, VS 1844/1787 CE, f 231a.

40. JSPB 39, VS 1845/1788 CE, f 22b.

41. JSPB 24, VS 1837/1780 CE, f 105a.

42. JSPB 17, VS 1833/1776 CE, f 214b.

43. JSPB 55, VS 1958/1801 CE, f 101a.

44. JSPB 17, VS 1833/1776 CE, f 126a–b.

45. The Asāvās are a subset of the Maheshwari community of merchants.

46. JSPB 30, VS 1841/1784 CE, f 55b.

47. JSPB 36, VS 1844/1787 CE, f 123b.

48. JSPB 22, VS 1842/1785 CE, f 11a.

49. As in the case of Mayaram Daftari, who had to pay a fine for his daughter's abortion (JSPB 11, VS 1828/1771 CE, f 137b).

50. JSPB 28, VS 1839/1782 CE, f 76a.

51. JSPB 28, VS 1839/1782 CE, f 76a.

52. JSPB 28, VS 1839/1782 CE, 80a–b.

53. JSPB 28, VS 1839/1782 CE, f 103a.

54. JSPB 32, VS 1842/1785 CE, f 82a.

55. JSPB 35, VS 1843/1786 CE, f 218b.

56. The caste affiliation of some of these women is unclear from the available information. For instance, it remains unclear which caste the Majījī or Daftarī families belonged to. While the Majījīs wielded enough influence to convince the local authorities of Didwana to drop the proceedings against them, the Daftarī family's title indicates that they were associated with clerical practice and thus were at least of fair socioeconomic standing. In addition, the Daftarīs are a lineage among the Shvetambar Jains of Marwar and it is possible that this particular Daftarī family was part to the largely mercantile community of Jains.

57. As discussed above, while some orders name only the office whose occupant issued the command, others name the issuing officer. I was often able to identify the occupant of a particular office in a given year by checking Rathor officer lists.

58. One order was issued by a *pañcholī* and one by a rajput. Still others bear names whose caste identity I could not identify, such as Firayat Manakchand.

59. Peabody, *Hindu Kingship*, 105–8.

60. Saha, "Creating a Community of Grace," 115–16.

61. Saha, "Creating a Community of Grace," 114, 218, 470.

62. Bayly, *Rulers, Townsmen and Bazaars*, 470.

63. Tyler Williams, "The Ties That Bind: Individual, Family, and Community in Northwestern Bhakti," in *Bhakti and Power: Debating India's Religion of the Heart*, ed. John S. Hawley, Christian L. Novetzke, and Swapna Sharma (Seattle: University of Washington Press, 2019), 194–95.

64. Bayly, *Rulers, Townsmen and Bazaars*, 218, 464.

65. JSPB 36, VS 1844/1787 CE, f 123b.

66. JSPB 49, VS 1854/1797 CE, f 208b. For the meaning of "*juhār*," see Lalas, 1: 481.

67. Lalas, *Rājasthānī-Hindī* I: 481. The term has been associated in South Asian history with the ritual suicide committed by the women of a defeated rajput king's household in defense of the honor of their lineage. References such as this one in the *Jodhpur Sanad Parwāna Bahīs*, however, indicate that other communities, those that commanded ritual authority, could also inflict harm upon themselves as a means of exerting moral pressure upon state authorities. Records point to charans (bards, genealogists, and ritual specialists) as well as brahmans deploying this strategy; for charans, see James Tod, *Annals and Antiquities of Rajast'han or, the Central and Western Rajpoot States of India*, vol. 2 (New Delhi: Rupa, 1997 [1832]), 500.

68. In addition to James Tod observing this for charans in Rajasthan, early colonial observers also noticed it among the brahmans of Kashmir. Mridu Rai, *Hindi Rulers, Muslim Subjects: Islam, Rights, and the History of Kashmir* (Princeton: Princeton University Press, 2004), 104.

69. Rai, *Hindu Rulers, Muslim Subjects*, 104.

70. Cherian, "Stolen Skin and Children Thrown."

71. In the eighteenth-century Maratha kingdom as well, the Peshwa state was far more focused on regulating the sexuality of its elite women, of the brahman caste, than that of women of other caste groups. As in Marwar, surveillance by kinsfolk, the community, and the state contributed to the smooth working of the legal apparatus that the Peshwa regime constructed to impose moral rectitude upon women, especially those of the locally dominant brahman community. Chakravarti, "Wifehood, Widowhood and Adultery."

EPILOGUE

1. The *Jodhpur Sanad Parwāna Bahīs*, however, start to thicken again as the nineteenth century progresses, so that they are quite large by the mid-nineteenth century. To my knowledge, this later body of records has not received much scholarly attention. It is a promising site for the exploration of a range of questions about how colonial rule played out on the ground in a Princely State like Jodhpur.

2. For instance, the Naths' grand Mahamandir (or "Great Temple") built in the early nineteenth century at the capital, Jodhpur. The Rathor crown ordered a dispatch of ritual offerings for the occasion of Nath Panchami (observed on the fifth day of the bright half of the lunar month of Ashvin or Asoj, that is, September–October by the solar calendar) in 1807 (JSPB 59, VS 1864/1807 CE, f 55a). In 1809, it ordered a gift of four hundred and eighty-five rupees to four Nath temples in Jalor (JSPB 61, VS 1866/1809 CE, f 48a–50a.

3. Diamond, "Politics and Aesthetics of Citation," 17.

4. JSPB 61, VS 1866/1809 CE, f 11 a–b.

5. Monika Horstmann, *Bhakti and Yoga: A Discourse in Seventeenth-Century Codices* (Delhi: Primus, 2021), 8.

6. Burchett, *Genealogy of Devotion*.

7. JSPB 57, VS 1860/1803 CE, f 327a. *Ruko mai likhyo tathā hamār kūṇḍāpanth ghaṇo basīyo hai su koī śrī mātā jī rī pūjan man chit suṁ karai su to bhalāī karo paṇ kūṇḍāpanthī huvai nai badhto phitūr karai su na karaṇ deṇo sanai sanai ghaṭāvaṇo śrī hajūr ro hukam chhai.*

8. Dominique-Sila Khan, *Crossing the Threshold: Understanding Religious Identities in South Asia* (London: IB Tauris, 2004), 130–32.

9. Even so, the Naths' embrace of brahmanical values did not entail an embrace of brahmans as well. This is suggested by a couple of state orders in which the main priest of a Nath temple is changed from a brahman to an *āyas* or a Nath monk (JSPB 61, VS 1866/1809 CE, f 75a–76a and JSPB 62, 1867/1810 CE, f 84b). For a history of the early modern openness of the Nath Yogis of Gorakhpur for instance to Islam, see Bouillier, "Nath Yogis' Encounters with Islam."

10. Timberg, *The Marwaris*, 36.

11. Hardgrove, *Community and Public Culture*, 93.

12. Timberg, *The Marwaris*, 36, 67.

13. Sushil Chaudhury, "Merchants, Companies, and Rulers: Bengal in the Eighteenth Century," *Journal of the Economic and Social History of the Orient* 31, no. 1 (1988): 80.

14. Hardgrove, *Community and Public Culture*, 106.

15. Kumkum Chatterjee, *Merchants, Politics and Society in Early Modern India: Bihar, 1733–1820* (Leiden: Brill, 1996), 225. See also Chatterjee's larger discussion on *inqilāb*, 222–30.

16. For a fuller discussion of the role of the Marwari diaspora in supporting the birth of modern Hindi in the nineteenth century, see Rahul B. Parson, "The Bazaar and the Bari: Calcutta, Marwaris, and the World of Hindi Letters" (PhD diss., University of California, Berkeley, 2012), 36–49.

17. Kathryn Hansen, "The Birth of Hindi Drama in Banaras," in *Culture and Power in Banaras: Community, Performance, and Environment*, ed. Sandria Freitag (Berkeley: University of California Press, 1989), 88. See Vasudha Dalmia, *The Nationalization of Hindu Traditions: Bhāratendu Hariścandra and Nineteenth-Century Banaras* (New Delhi: Oxford University Press, 1997), 126, 351–54, for Harishchandra's association with the Vallabhites and for a history of the significance of merchants in shaping Hindi language and the Hindu nation.

18. Dalmia, *The Nationalization of Hindu Traditions*.

19. Kathryn Hansen, "The Birth of Hindi Drama," 84, 88.

20. Dalmia, *Nationalization of Hindu Traditions*, 142.

21. Hardgrove, *Community and Public Culture*, 111

22. Philip Lutgendorf, "Ram's Story in Shiva's City: Public Arenas and Private Patronage," in *Culture and Power in Banaras: Community, Performance, and Environment*, ed. Sandria Freitag (Berkeley: University of California Press, 1989), 46–47.

23. Lutgendorf, "Ram's Story," 47.

24. Akshaya Mukul, *Gita Press and the Making of Hindu India* (New Delhi: HarperCollins), 11.

25. Paul Arney, "The 'Mouth' of Sanatana Dharma: The Role of Gita Press in Spreading the Word," paper presented at the American Academy of Religion Annual Conference, November 21, 1993, 7–11. Goyandka was born into a devout Vaishnav family of Agrawal mahajans in Churu, which was then in the kingdom of Bikaner. Arney argues elsewhere that he may have represented, to his peers and to succeeding generations of Marwaris, an ideal for all Marwari men.

26. Mukul, *Gita Press*. It ought to be noted that the journal *Kalyān* also published pieces by authors who were not *sanātanīs* and even those who were not Hindu. Yet, this did not "dilute the soul of Gita Press's belief system" (209).

27. Mukul, *Gita Press*, 13.

28. Arney, "The 'Mouth' of Sanatana Dharma," 2. I thank Paul Arney for sharing a copy of this paper with me and Jack Hawley for connecting me to Paul.

29. Mukul, *Gita Press*, 19. On the role of the Gita Press in popularizing the *Rāmcharitmānas*, see Lutgendorf, "Ram's Story," 48.

30. Mukul, *Gita Press*, 140–41.

31. For a discussion of the role of Vaishnav merchants and their capital in the print iconography of an emergent Hinduism in modern India, see Kajri Jain, *Gods in the Bazaar: The Economies of Indian Calendar Art* (Durham: Duke University Press, 2007), particularly 217–67.

32. Sandria Freitag, "Sacred Symbol as Mobilizing Ideology: The North Indian Search for a "Hindu" Community," *Comparative Studies in Society and History* 22, no. 4 (1980): 609n50; Anand A. Yang, "Sacred Symbol and Sacred Space in Rural India: Community Mobilization in the 'Anti-Cow Killing' Riot of 1893," *CSSH* 22, no. 4 (1980): 586–88; Mukul, *Gita Press*, 10.

33. Sandria Freitag, "Sacred Symbol," 622; Mukul, *Gita Press*, 111. Cow-protectionist impulses also helped to galvanize a perceived "Hindu" body against the British. Yang, "Sacred Symbol," 596.

34. Freitag, "Sacred Symbol," 622.

35. Paul Arney, "The 'Mouth'," 13–16; Mukul, *Gita Press*, 209.

36. Birla, *Stages of Capital*, 199–231. Birla argues that this defense of the joint family as "private" was among the ways that the Marwari community protected the patriarchal kinship ties in which their market practices were embedded and, in the twentieth century, dealt with the colonial division of "public" from "private" and, hence, of "commerce" from "kinship" (even as the two domains continued to shape each other in mercantile activity).

37. Organizations such as the Vaishya Sabha and the All India Agarwal Mahasabha were formed to resist the conservative Marwari Association and to push for causes like widow remarriage among the Marwaris. Hardgrove, *Community and Public Culture*, 297, 314.

38. Dirks, *Castes of Mind*, 13. See also Cohn, "The Census"; Arjun Appadurai, "Number in the Colonial Imagination"; Guha, *Beyond Caste*, 164–74. For an argument for a further transformation of caste in colonial South Asia such that English colonial rulers created for themselves "a bounded ruling caste," see Guha, *Beyond Caste*, 176–83.

39. Ghassem-Fachandi, *Pogrom in Gujarat*, 143; Joel Lee, "Disgust and Untouchability: Towards an Affective Theory of Caste," *South Asian History and Culture* 12, no. 2/3 (2021): 1–18.

40. Tanweer Fazal, "Scheduled Castes, Reservations, and Religion: Revisiting a Juridical Debate," *Contributions to Indian Sociology* 51, no. 1 (2017): 6n4, cited in Lee, "Disgust and Untouchability," 15.

41. Ghassem-Fachandi, *Pogrom in Gujarat*, 143.

42. Ghassem-Fachandi, *Pogrom in Gujarat*, 150, 151, 179, 183.

43. Ghassem-Fachandi, *Pogrom in Gujarat*, 177.

44. See for instance the representation of Alauddin Khilji in the immensely successful 2018 Hindi film, *Padmaavat*. For elite nineteenth-century representations, ostensibly grounded in folklore, of the "defiling" touch of Muslims, see Shahid Amin, "Representing the Musalman: Then and Now, Now and Then," in *Muslims, Dalits and the Fabrications of History*, ed. Shail Mayaram, M. S. S. Pandian, and Ajay Skaria (New York: Seagull Books, 2006), 20–23.

45. On vegetarian-only office dining spaces: Hugo Gorringe and D. Karthikeyan, "The Hidden Politics of Vegetarianism: Caste and 'The Hindu' Canteen," *Economic and Political Weekly* 49, no. 20 (2014): 20–22; https://scroll.in/article/662132/liberal-hindu-newspaper-reiterates-no-meat-policy-in-office-sparks-debate-on-vegetarian-fundamentalism. On vegetarian-only residential complexes: http://edition.cnn.com/2005/WORLD/asiapcf/09/16/india.eye.vegetarian/; https://www.business-standard.com/article/current-affairs/housing-societies-deny-flat-to-non-vegetarians-in-mumbai-alleges-mns-117042900295_1.html. On the proscription of meat in children's school lunches: https://www.thenews

minute.com/article/no-eggs-rice-meat-or-noodles-hyd-school-bans-kids-bringing-these-items-lunch-84704; https://www.npr.org/sections/goatsandsoda/2015/07/08/419569772/indian-governor-to-schoolkids-no-eggs-for-you.

46. Jaaware, *Practicing Caste*, 128.

47. Balmurli Natarajan, *The Culturization of Caste in India* (London: Routledge, 2012).

BIBLIOGRAPHY

PRIMARY

Unpublished

Byāv rī Bahī, vol. 1, Rajasthan State Archives, Bikaner (online).

Jodhpur Sanad Parwāna Bahīs, vols. 1–71, Rajasthan State Archives, Bikaner.

Ohdā Bahī, vol. 1, Rajasthan State Archives, Bikaner (online).

Vijay Vilās, Manuscript 130, Tod Collection, Royal Asiatic Society, London.

Published

Banarasidas. *Ardhakathānaka: Half a Tale*. Translated, annotated, and introduced by Mukund Lath. Jaipur: Rajasthan Prakrit Bharati Samsthan, 1981.

Mahārājā Śrī Vijaisiṅghjī rī Khyāt, edited by Brajesh Kumar Singh. Jodhpur: Rajasthan Oriental Research Institute, 1997.

Mārvāṛ rī Khyāt: Josī Tilokchand Kanha Singhvī Gyānmal Likhāī, edited by Hukamsimh Bhati, Bhavanisimh Patavat, and Vikramsimh Bhati. Jodhpur: Rajasthani Shodh Samsthan and Maharaja Mansingh Pustak Prakash Shodh Kendra, 2000.

Mumhta Nainsi. *Muṁhtā naiṇsī rī likhī mārvāṛ rā parganāṃ rī vigat*, vols. I–III. Edited by Narayansimh Bhati. Jodhpur: Rajasthan Oriental Research Institute, 1968–74.

———. *Muṁhtā Naiṇsī rī Khyāt*, vols. I–IV. Edited by Badriprasad Sakariya. Jodhpur: Rajasthan Oriental Research Institute, 1984–2006.

Rāṭhaurāṁ rī Khyāt: Sīhā se Mahārājā Mānasiṁha, Vi. Sa. 1300–1735/Ī. 1243–1678. Edited by Hukamsimh Bhati. Chopasni: Itihas Anusandhan Sansthan, 2007.

Singh, Hardayal. *Riporṭ Mardumśumārī Rāj Mārvāṛ, 1891: Rājasthān kī Jātiyoṁ kā Itihās evam Unke Rīti Rivāj*. Jodhpur: Shri Jagdishsimh Gehlot Shodh Samsthan, 1991.

SECONDARY

Adams, Archibald. *The Western Rajputana States: A Medico-Topographical and General Account of Marwar, Sirohi, Jaisalmir*. London: Junior Army & Navy Stores, 1899.

Aktor, Michael. "Untouchability in Brahminical Law Books: Ritual and Economic Control." In *From Stigma to Assertion: Untouchability, Identity, and Politics in Early and Modern India*, edited by Michael Aktor and Robert Deliège, 31–63. Copenhagen: Museum Tusculanum Press, 2010.

Alam, Muzaffar. *The Languages of Political Islam in India*. Chicago: University of Chicago Press, 2004.

———. *The Crisis of Empire in Mughal North India: Awadh and the Punjab, 1707–48*, 2nd ed. New Delhi: Oxford University Press, 2013 [1986].

Alam, Muzaffar, and Sanjay Subrahmanyam. "The Making of a Munshi." *Comparative Studies in South Asia, Africa, and the Middle East* 24, no. 2 (2004): 61–72.

———. Introduction to *The Mughal State, 1526–1750*, edited by Muzaffar Alam and Sanjay Subrahmanyam, 1–71. New Delhi: Oxford University Press, 2014 [1998].

Alpers, Edward A. "Gujarat and the Trade of East Africa, c. 1500–1800." *International Journal of African Historical Studies* 9, no. 1 (1976): 22–44.

Alsdorf, Ludwig. *The History of Vegetarianism and Cow Veneration in India*. Translated by Bal Patil, revised by Nichola Hayton, and edited by Willem Bollee. Routledge: New York, 2011.

Alter, Joseph. *Gandhi's Body: Sex, Diet, and the Politics of Nationalism*. Philadelphia: University of Pennsylvania Press, 2000.

Ambedkar, Bhim Rao. *Who Were the Shudras? How They Came to Be the Fourth Varna*. Bombay: Thacker, 1946.

———. *Dr. Babasaheb Ambedkar: Writings and Speeches*, vol. 3 (2nd ed.), edited by Hari Narke. New Delhi: Dr. Ambedkar Foundation, 2014.

———. *The Untouchables: Who Were They and Why They Became Untouchables?* Chennai: Maven, 2018 [1948].

Amin, Shahid. "Representing the Musalman: Then and Now, Now and Then." In *Muslims, Dalits and the Fabrications of History*, edited by Shail Mayaram, M. S. S. Pandian, and Ajay Skaria, 1–35. New York: Seagull Books, 2006.

———. *Conquest and Community: The Afterlives of Warrior Saint Ghazi Miyan*. Chicago: University of Chicago Press, 2016.

Appadurai, Arjun. "Number in the Colonial Imagination." In *Orientalism and the Postcolonial Predicament: Perspectives on South Asia*, edited by Carol A. Breckenridge and Peter van der Veer, 314–49. Philadelphia: University of Pennsylvania Press, 1993.

Arney, Paul. "The 'Mouth' of Sanatana Dharma: The Role of Gita Press in Spreading the Word." Paper presented at the American Academy of Religion Annual Conference, November 21, 1993.

Asher, Catherine. "Excavating Communalism: Kachhwaha *Rajadharma* and Mughal Sovereignty." In *Rethinking a Millennium: Perspectives on Indian History from the Eighth to the Eighteenth Century*, edited by Rajat Dutta, 222–46. New Delhi: Aakar, 2008.

Asif, Manan Ahmed. *A Book of Conquest: The* Chachnama *and Muslim Origins in South Asia*. Cambridge, MA: Harvard University Press, 2016.

———. *The Loss of Hindustan: The Invention of India*. Cambridge, MA: Harvard University Press, 2020.

Babb, Lawrence. *Absent Lord: Ascetics and Kings in a Jain Ritual Culture*. Berkeley: University of California Press, 1996.

———. "Mirrored Warriors: On the Cultural Identity of Rajasthani Traders." *International Journal of Hindu Studies* 3, no. 1 (1999): 1–25.

Bachrach, Emilia, and Heidi Pauwels. "Aurangzeb as Iconoclast? Vaishnav Accounts of the Krishna Images' Exodus from Braj." *Journal of the Royal Asiatic Society* 28, no. 3 (2018): 485–508.

Bahuguna, Rameshwar Prasad. "Religious Festivals as Political Rituals: Kingship and Legitimation in Late Pre-colonial Rajasthan." In *Revisiting the History of Medieval Rajasthan: Essays for Professor Dilbagh Singh*, edited by Suraj Bhan Bharadwaj, Rameshwar Prasad Bahuguna, and Mayank Kumar, 84–92. New Delhi: Primus, 2017.

Bahura, Gopal Narayan, and Chandramani Singh, eds. *Catalogue of Historical Documents in Kapad Dwara*, vol. 1. Jaipur: Jaigarh Public Charitable Trust, 1988.

Bajekal, Madhavi. "The State and the Rural Grain Market in Eighteenth-Century Eastern Rajasthan." In *Merchants, Markets, and the State in Early Modern India*, edited by Sanjay Subrahmanyam, 90–120. New Delhi: Oxford University Press, 1990.

Bakhle, Janaki. *Two Men and Music: Nationalism in the Making of an Indian Classical Tradition*. Oxford University Press: New York, 2005.

Banaji, Jairus. *A Brief History of Commercial Capitalism*. Chicago: Haymarket Books, 2020.

Barz, Richard. *The Bhakti Sect of Vallabhācārya*. New Delhi: Munshiram Manoharlal, 1992 [1979].

Bayly, Christopher A. "The Pre-history of 'Communalism'? Religious Conflict in India, 1700–1860." *Modern Asian Studies* 19, no. 2 (1985): 177–203.

———. *Rulers, Townsmen and Bazaars: North Indian Society in the Age of British Expansion, 1770–1870*. New Delhi: Oxford University Press, 1993 [1983].

Bayly, Susan. *Caste, Society and Politics in India: From the Eighteenth Century to the Modern Age*. New Delhi: Cambridge University Press, 1999.

Bhadani, B. L. "The Ruler and Nobility in Marwar during the Reign of Jaswant Singh." In *Economy and Polity of Rajasthan: Study of Kota and Marwar*, edited by Masanori Sato and B. L. Bhadani, 109–25. Jaipur: Publication Scheme, 1997.

———. "The Allodial Proprietors? The Bhumias of Marwar." In *Economy and Polity of Rajasthan: Study of Kota and Marwar*, edited by Masanori Sato and B. L. Bhadani, 127–47. Jaipur: Publication Scheme, 1997.

———. "Role of Merchants and Markets in Agrarian Trade in Seventeenth-Century Western Rajasthan." In *Economy and Polity of Rajasthan: Study of Kota and Marwar*, edited by Masanori Sato and B. L. Bhadani, 166–80. Jaipur: Publication Scheme, 1997.

———. *Peasants, Artisans and Entrepreneurs: The Economy of Marwar in the Seventeenth Century*. Jaipur: Rawat, 1999.

———. "Socio-economic Context of Development of Jainism in Rajasthan." In *Revisiting the History of Medieval Rajasthan: Essays for Professor Dilbagh Singh*, edited by Suraj Bhan Bharadwaj, Rameshwar Prasad Bahuguna, and Mayank Kumar, 36–43. New Delhi: Primus, 2017.

Bharadwaj, Suraj Bhan, Rameshwar Prasad Bahuguna, and Mayank Kumar, eds. *Revisiting the History of Medieval Rajasthan: Essays for Professor Dilbagh Singh*. New Delhi: Primus, 2017.

Bhati, Hukamsimh. *Mārvāṛ ke Ohdedāroṃ kā Itihās meṁ Yogdān*. Jodhpur: Rajasthani Granthagar, 2013.

Bhati, Jitendrasimh. *Rājasthān kī Praśāsanik Vyavasthā: Mārvār ke Sandarbh Meṃ, 1300–1800 Īsvī*. Jodhpur: Rajasthani Granthagar, 2011.

Bhatnagar, V. S. "Attempts at Revivalism or Reassertion of Vedic and 'Shastriya' Traditions through Open Debate in the 18th Century." In *Religious Movements in Rajasthan: Ideas and Antiquities*, edited by S.N. Dube, 97–104. Jaipur: Centre for Rajasthan Studies, 1999.

Birla, Ritu. *Stages of Capital: Law, Culture, and Market Governance in Colonial India*. Durham: Duke University Press, 2009.

Blake, Stephen. "Contributors to the Urban Landscape: Women Builders in Safavid Isfahan and Mughal Shahjahanabad." In *Women in the Medieval Islamic World: Power, Patronage, and Piety*, edited by Gavin Hambly, 407–28. New York: St. Martin's Press, 1998.

Bodewitz, Henk W. "Hindu *Ahiṁsā* and Its Roots." In *Violence Denied: Violence, Non-Violence, and the Rationalization of Violence in South Asia Cultural History*, edited by Jan E. M. Houben and Karel R. Van Kooij, 17–44. Leiden: Brill, 1999.

Bouillier, Veronique. "Nath Yogis' Encounters with Islam." *South Asia Multidisciplinary Academic Journal*, free-standing article (2015), 1–15. https://journals.openedition.org/samaj/3878.

———. "Aurangzeb and the Nāth Yogīs." *Journal of the Royal Asiatic Society* 28, no. 3 (2018): 525–35.

Bryant, Edwin. "Strategies of Vedic Subversion: The Emergence of Vegetarianism in Post-Vedic India." In *A Communion of Subjects: Animals in Religion, Science, and* Ethics, edited by Paul Waldau and Kimberly Patton, 194–203. New York: Columbia University Press, 2006.

Bunce, Frederick W. *An Encyclopedia of Hindu Deities, Demi-Gods, Godlings, Demons, and Heroes*, vol. 1. New Delhi: DK Printworld, 2000.

Burchett, Patton E. "*Bhakti* Rhetoric in the Hagiography of 'Untouchable' Saints: Discerning *Bhakti*'s Ambivalence on Caste and Brahminhood." *International Journal of Hindu Studies* 13, no. 2 (2009): 115–41.

———. *A Genealogy of Devotion: Bhakti, Tantra, Yoga, and Sufism in North India*. New York: Columbia University Press, 2019.

Busch, Allison. "Hidden in Plain View: Brajbhasha Poets at the Mughal Court." *Modern Asian Studies* 44, no. 2 (2010): 267–309.

———. "Unhitching the Oxcart of Delhi: A Mughal-Period Hindi Account of Political Insurgency." *Journal of the Royal Asiatic Society* 28, no. 3 (2018): 415–39.

Callewaert, Winand. *The Life and Works of Ravidas*. New Delhi: Manohar, 1992.

———. "Sants." In Knut Jacobsen et al., eds., *Brill's Encyclopedia of Hinduism Online*, 2018.

Callewaert, Winand, and Bart Op de Beek, eds. *Nirguṇ Bhakti Sagar: Devotional Hindi Literature*, vol. 1. New Delhi: Manohar, 1991.

Chakravarti, Uma. "Conceptualizing Brahmanical Patriarchy in Early India: Gender, Caste, Class, and State." *Economic and Political Weekly* 28, no. 14 (1993): 579–85.

———. "Wifehood, Widowhood, and Adultery: Female Sexuality, Surveillance, and the State in 18th Century Maharashtra." *Contributions to Indian Sociology* 29, no. 1/2 (1995): 3–21.

Chandra, Satish. "Commercial Activities of the Mughal Emperors during the Seventeenth Century." *Bengal Past and Present* 87 (1959): 92–97.

Charsley, Simon. "'Untouchable': What's in a Name?" *Journal of the Royal Anthropological Institute* 2, no. 1 (1996): 1–23.

Chatterjee, Indrani. “Women, Monastic Commerce, and Coverture in Eastern India circa 1600–1800 CE.” *Modern Asian Studies* 50, no. 1 (2016): 175–216.

Chatterjee, Kumkum. *Merchants, Politics and Society in Early Modern India: Bihar, 1733–1820*. Leiden: Brill, 1996.

———. “Cultural Flows and Cosmopolitanism in Mughal India: The Bishnupur Kingdom.” *Indian Economic and Social History Review* 46, no. 2 (2009): 147–82.

———. “Scribal Elites in Sultanate and Mughal Period Bengal.” *Indian Economic and Social History Review* 47, no. 4 (2010): 445–72.

Chatterjee, Nandini. “Mahzar-namas in the Mughal and British Empires: The Uses of an Indo-Islamic Legal Form.” *Comparative Studies in Society and History* 58, no. 2 (2016): 379–406.

———. *Negotiating Mughal Law: A Family of Landlords across Three Indian Empires*. New York: Cambridge University Press, 2020.

Chattopadhyaya, Braja Dulal. “Irrigation in Early Medieval Rajasthan.” *Journal of the Economic and Social History of the Orient* 16, no. 2/3 (1973): 298–316.

———. *Representing the Other? Sanskrit Sources and the Muslims (Eighth to Fourteenth Century)*. Delhi: Manohar, 1998.

———. “Origin of the Rajputs: The Political, Economic and Social Processes in Early Medieval Rajasthan.” In *The Making of Early Medieval India*, edited by B. D. Chattopadhyaya, 59–84. New Delhi: Oxford University Press, 2012.

Chaudhry, Faisal. “Repossessing Property in South Asia: Land, Rights, and Law across the Early Modern / Modern Divide—Introduction.” *Journal of the Economic and Social History of the Orient* 61, no. 5/6 (2018): 759–802.

Chaudhury, Sushil. “Merchants, Companies, and Rulers: Bengal in the Eighteenth Century.” *Journal of the Economic and Social History of the Orient* 31, no. 1 (1988): 74–109.

Cherian, Divya. “Fall from Grace?: Caste, Bhakti, and Politics in Late Eighteenth-Century Marwar.” In *Bhakti & Power: Debating India’s Religion of the Heart*, edited by John S. Hawley, Christian L. Novetzke, and Swapna Sharma, 181–91. Seattle: University of Washington Press, 2019.

———. “Stolen Skin and Children Thrown: Governing Sex and Abortion in Early Modern South Asia.” *Modern Asian Studies* 55, no. 5 (2021): 1461–509.

Chicherov, A. I. *India: Economic Development in the 16th-18th Centuries: Outline History of Crafts and Trade*. Moscow: Nauka Publishing House, 1971.

Chowdhury, Zirwat. “An Imperial Mughal Tent and Mobile Sovereignty in Eighteenth-Century Jodhpur.” *Art History* 38, no. 4 (2015): 668–81.

Ciotti, Manuela. “‘In the Past We Were a Bit “Chamar”’: Education as a Self- and Community-Engineering Process in Northern India.” *Journal of the Royal Anthropological Institute* 12, no. 4 (2006): 899–916.

Cohn, Bernard S. “The Census, Social Structure and Objectification in South Asia.” In *An Anthropologist among Historians and Other Essays*, edited by Bernard Cohn, 224–54. New Delhi: Oxford University Press, 1987.

Conrad, Sebastian. *What Is Global History?* Princeton, NJ: Princeton University Press, 2016.

Cort, John E. “Two Ideals of the Śvētāmbar Mūrtipūjak Jain Layman.” *Journal of Indian Philosophy* 19, no. 4 (1991): 391–420.

———. "Defining Jainism: Reform in the Jain Tradition." In *Jain Doctrine and Practice: Academic Perspectives*, edited by Joseph T. O'Connell and Nikhil Wagle, 165–91. Toronto: University of Toronto Center for South Asian Studies, 2000.

_____. *Jains in the World: Religious Values and Ideology in India*. New York: Oxford University Press, 2001.

———. "Bhakti in the Early Jain Tradition: Understanding Devotional Religion in South Asia.," *History of Religions* 42, no. 1 (2002): 59–86.

———. "Bhakti as Elite Cultural Practice: Digambar Jain Bhakti in Early Modern India.," Iin *Bhakti & Power: Debating India's Religion of the Heart*, e. Edited by John S. Hawley, Christian L. Novetzke, and& Swapna Sharma, 95–104. Seattle: University of Washington Press, 2019.

———. "Jain Society: 1800–1947." In *Brill's Encyclopedia of Jainism Online*, edited by John E. Cort et al. http://dx.doi.org/10.1163/2590-2768_BEJO_COM_043936.

Crill, Rosemary. *Marwar Painting: A History of the Jodhpur Style*. Mumbai: India Book House and Mehrangarh Museum Trust, 2000.

Dale, Stephen F. *Indian Merchants and Eurasian Trade, 1600–1750*. Cambridge: Cambridge University Press, 1994.

Dalmia, Vasudha. *The Nationalization of Hindu Traditions: Bhāratendu Hariścandra and Nineteenth-Century Banaras*. New Delhi: Oxford University Press, 1997.

———. "Hagiography and the 'Other' in the Vallabh *Sampraday*." In *Religious Interactions in Mughal India*, edited by Vasudha Dalmia and Munis Faruqui, 264–89. New Delhi: Oxford University Press, 2014.

Dalmia, Vasudha, and Heinrich von Stietencron, eds. *Representing Hinduism: The Construction of Religious Traditions and National Identity*. New Delhi: Sage, 1995.

Das, Shyamsundar, ed. *Hindi Śabdasāgara, arthāt hindī bhāṣā ka ek brhat koś*, vol. 1. Banaras: Nagaripracarini Sabha, 1965–75.

Devra, G. S. L. "Land Control and Agrarian Mercantile Classes in Western Rajasthan, c. 1650–1700." *Proceedings of the Indian History Congress* 58 (1997): 371-81.

Deyell, John S. "Cowries and Coins: The Dual Monetary System of the Bengal Sultanate." *Indian Economic and Social History Review* 47, no. 1 (2010): 63–106.

Dhali, Rajshree. "The Cult of Goga: A Study of the Religious Process of a Popular Folk Deity of Rajasthan." In *Revisiting the History of Medieval Rajasthan: Essays for Professor Dilbagh Singh*, edited by Suraj Bhan Bharadwaj, Rameshwar Prasad Bahuguna, and Mayank Kumar, 116–35. New Delhi: Primus, 2017.

Dhavan, Purnima. *When Sparrows Became Hawks: The Making of the Sikh Warrior Tradition, 1699–1799*. New York: Oxford University Press, 2011.

Diamond, Debra. "The Politics and Aesthetics of Citation: Nath Painting in Jodhpur, 1803–1843." PhD diss., Columbia University, 2000.

———. "Maharaja Vijai Singh and the Epic Landscape, 1752–93." In *Garden and Cosmos: The Royal Paintings of Jodhpur*, edited by Debra Diamond, Catherine Glynn, and Karni Singh Jasol, 21–30. Washington, DC: Smithsonian Institution, 2009.

Diamond, Debra, et al. *Garden & Cosmos: The Royal Paintings of Jodhpur*. Washington, DC: Smithsonian Institution, 2009.

Digby, Simon. "The Sufi Shaikh as a Source of Authority in Medieval India,." In *Sufism and Society in Medieval India*, edited by Raziuddin Aquil. New Delhi: Oxford University Press, 2010.

Dirks, Nicholas. *The Hollow Crown: Ethnohistory of an Indian Kingdom*. Ann Arbor: University of Michigan Press, 1993.

———. *Castes of Mind: Colonialism and the Making of Modern India*. Princeton: Princeton University Press, 2001.

Doniger, Wendy. "Hinduism by Any Other Name." *Wilson Quarterly* 15, no. 1 (1991): 35–41.

———. *The Hindus: An Alternative History*. New York: Penguin Press, 2009.

Doron, Assa, and Robin Jeffrey. *Waste of a Nation: Garbage and Growth in India*. Cambridge, MA: Harvard University Press, 2018.

Dube, Saurabh. *Untouchable Pasts: Religion, Community, and Power among a Central Indian Community, 1780–1950*. Buffalo: SUNY Press, 1998.

Ducrot, Vicky, Daljeet, and Rosa Maria Cimino, eds. *Four Centuries of Rajput Painting: Mewar, Marwar and Dhundhar Miniatures from the Collection of Isabella and Vicky Ducrot*. Milan: Skira, 2009.

Dumont, Louis. *Homo Hierarchicus: The Caste System and Its Implications*. Translated by Mark Sainsbury et al. Chicago: University of Chicago Press, 1980 [1970].

Dundas, Paul. *The Jains*. London: Routledge, 1992.

Eaton, Richard M. *The Rise of Islam and the Bengal Frontier, 1204–1760*. Delhi: Oxford University Press, 1997.

———. "Temple Desecration and Indo-Muslim States." In idem, *Essays on Islam and Indian History*, 94–112. New Delhi: Oxford University Press, 2002.

Entwistle, Alan. *Braj: Centre of Krishna Pilgrimage*. Groningen: Egbert Forsten, 1987.

Ernst, Carl W. *Eternal Garden: Mysticism, History, and Politics at a South Asian Sufi Center*. Albany: State University of New York Press, 1992.

Fazal, Tanweer. "Scheduled Castes, Reservations, and Religion: Revisiting a Juridical Debate." *Contributions to Indian Sociology* 51, no. 1 (2017): 1–24.

Findly, Ellison B. "Jahangir's Vow of Nonviolence." *Journal of the American Oriental Society* 107, no. 2 (1987): 245–56.

Fisher, Elaine. *Hindu Pluralism: Religion and the Public Sphere in Early Modern South India*. Oakland: University of California Press, 2017.

Flatt, Emma J. *The Courts of the Deccan Sultanates: Living Well in the Persian Cosmopolis*. New York: Cambridge University Press, 2019.

Flood, Finbarr. *Objects of Translation: Material Culture and Medieval "Hindu-Muslim" Encounter*. Princeton: Princeton University Press, 2009.

Freitag, Sandria. "Sacred Symbol as Mobilizing Ideology: The North Indian Search for a 'Hindu' Community." *Comparative Studies in Society and History* 22, no. 4 (1980): 597–625.

———. "*Sansiahs* and the State: The Changing Nature of 'Crime' and 'Justice' in Nineteenth-Century British India." In *Changing Concepts of Rights and Justice in South Asia*, edited by Michael Anderson and Sumit Guha, 82–113. New Delhi: Oxford University Press, 2000.

Friedland, Paul. "Friends for Dinner: The Early Modern Roots of Modern Carnivorous Sensibilities." *History of the Present* 1, no. 1 (2011): 84–112.

Frykenberg, Robert. "The Emergence of Modern 'Hinduism' as a Concept and as an Institution: A Reappraisal with Special Reference to South India." In *Hinduism Reconsidered*, edited by G. D. Sontheimer and H. Kulke, 29–49. Delhi: Manohar, 1989.

Fukazawa, Hiroshi. *The Medieval Deccan: Peasants, Social Systems, and States, Sixteenth to Eighteenth Centuries*. Delhi: Oxford University Press, 1991.

Fuller, C. J. "Misconceiving the Grain Heap: A Critique of the Concept of the Indian Jajmani System." In *Money and the Morality of Exchange*, edited by J. Parry and M. Bloch. Cambridge: Cambridge University Press, 1989.

Ghassem-Fachandi, Parvis. *Pogrom in Gujarat: Hindu Nationalism and Anti-Muslim Violence in India*. Princeton: Princeton University Press, 2012.

Ghosh, Pika. *Temple to Love: Architecture and Devotion in Seventeenth-Century Bengal*. Bloomington: Indiana University Press, 2005.

Gokhale, B. G. *Surat in the Seventeenth Century: A Study in Urban History of Pre-modern India*. Bombay: Popular Prakashan, 1978.

Gopal, S. "Virji Vora." In *Jains in India: Historical Essays*, edited by S. Gopal. New Delhi: Routledge, New York, 2019.

Gordon, Stewart N. "Bhils and the Idea of a Criminal Tribe in Nineteenth-Century India." In *Crime and Criminality in British India*, edited by Anand A. Yang, 128–39. Tucson: University of Arizona Press, 1985.

Gorringe, Hugo. "Dalit Politics: Untouchability, Identity, and Assertion." In *Routledge Handbook of Indian Politics*, edited by Atul Kohli and Prerna Singh, 119–28. New York: Routledge, 2013.

Gorringe, Hugo, and D. Karthikeyan. "The Hidden Politics of Vegetarianism: Caste and 'The Hindu' Canteen." *Economic and Political Weekly* 49, no. 20 (2014): 20–22.

Granoff, Phyllis. "Tales of Broken Limbs and Bleeding Wounds: Responses to Muslim Iconoclasm in Medieval India." *East and West* 41, no. 1/4 (1991): 189–203.

———. "Jinaprabhasūri and Jinadattasūri: Two Studies from the Śvetāmbara Jain Tradition." In *Speaking of Monks: Religious Biography in India and China*, edited by Phyllis Granoff and Koichi Shinohara, 1–96. Oakville, ON: Mosaic Press, 1992.

———. "Being in a Minority: Medieval Jain Reactions to Other Religious Groups." In *Jainism and Prakrit in Ancient and Medieval India: Essays for Prof. Jagdish Chandra Jain*, edited by N. N. Bhattacharyya, 241–66. New Delhi: Manohar, 1994.

Green, Toby. *A Fistful of Shells: West Africa from the Rise of the Slave Trade to the Age of Revolution*. Chicago: University of Chicago Press, 2019.

Guha, Sumit. "An Indian Penal Regime: Maharashtra in the Eighteenth Century." *Past and Present* 147 (May 1995): 102–26.

———. "Lower Strata, Older Races, and Aboriginal Peoples: Racial Anthropology and Mythical History Past and Present." *Journal of Asian Studies* 57, no. 2 (1998): 423–41.

———. "Wrongs and Rights in the Maratha Country: Antiquity, Custom, and Power in Eighteenth-Century India." In *Changing Concepts of Rights and Justice in South India*, edited by M. R. Anderson and Sumit Guha, 14–29. New Delhi: Oxford University Press, 2000.

———. "Civilizations, Markets, and Services: Village Servants in India from the Seventeenth to the Twentieth Centuries." *Indian Economic and Social History Review* 41, no. 1 (2002).

———. "The Politics of Identity and Enumeration in India, c. 1600–1990." *Comparative Studies in Society and History* 45, no. 1 (2003): 148–67.

———. "Speaking Historically: The Changing Voices of Historical Narration in Western India, 1400–1900." *American Historical Review* 109, no. 4 (2004): 1084–103.

———. "The Frontiers of Memory: What the Marathas Remembered of Vijayanagara." *Modern Asian Studies* 43, no. 1 (2009): 269–88.

———. "Serving the Barbarian to Preserve the *Dharma:* Scribal Ideology and Training in Peninsular India, c. 1300–1800." *Indian Economic and Social History Review* 47, no. 4 (2010): 497–525.

———. *Beyond Caste: Identity and Power in South Asia, Past and Present.* Leiden: Brill, 2013.

———. *History and Collective Memory in South Asia, 1200–2000.* Seattle: University of Washington Press, 2019.

Gupta, B. L. *Trade and Commerce in Rajasthan during the 18th Century.* Jaipur: Jaipur Publishing House, 1987.

Gupta, Satya Prakash. *The Agrarian System of Eastern Rajasthan (c. 1650–c. 1750).* Delhi: Manohar, 1986.

Guru, Gopal, and Sundar Sarukkai. *Experience, Caste, and the Everyday Social.* New Delhi: Oxford University Press, 2019.

Habib, Irfan. "Banking in Mughal India." *Contributions to Indian Economic History* 1 (1960): 1–20.

———. *The Agrarian System of Mughal India, 1556–1707.* New York: Asian Publication House, 1963.

———. "Usury in Medieval India." *Comparative Studies in Society and History* 6, no. 4 (1964): 393–419.

———. "Presidential Address." *Proceedings of the Indian History Congress* 31 (1969): 139–61.

———. "The System of Bills of Exchange (*Hundis*) in the Mughal Empire." In *Essays in Medieval Indian Economic History*, edited by Satish Chandra, 207–21. New Delhi: Munshiram Manoharlal, 1987.

———. "From Ariṭh to Rādhākund: The History of a Braj Village in Mughal Times." *Indian Historical Review* 38, no. 2 (2011): 211–24.

Habib, Irfan, and Tarapada Mukherjee. "Akbar and the Temples of Mathura and Its Environs." In *Proceedings of the Indian History Congress*, 48th Session, 234–50. Panaji: Goa University, 1988.

———. "The Mughal Administration and the Temples of Vrindavan During the Reigns of Jahangir and Shahjahan." In *Proceedings of the Indian History Congress*, 49th Session, 287–300. Dharwad: Karnataka University, 1989.

———. "Land Rights in the Reign of Akbar: The Evidence of the Sale-Deeds of Vrindaban and Aritha." In *Proceedings of the Indian History Congress*, 50th Session, 236–55. Gorakhpur: Gorakhpur University, 1990.

———. "Merchant Communities in Pre-colonial India." In *The Rise of Merchant Empires: Long-Distance Trade in the Early Modern World, 1350–1750*, edited by James D. Tracy, 371–99. New York: Cambridge University Press, 1990.

———. "Medieval Popular Monotheism and Its Humanism: The Historical Setting." *Social Scientist* 21, no. 3/4 (1993): 78–88.

Haider, Najaf. "The Monetary Basis of Credit and Banking Instruments in the Mughal Empire." In *Money and Credit in Indian History: From Early Medieval Times*, edited by Amiya Kumar Bagchi, 58–83. New Delhi: Tulika Books and Indian History Congress, 2002.

———. "Coinage and the Silver Crisis." In *Economic History of Medieval India*, edited by Irfan Habib, 149–62. New Delhi: Pearson, 2011.

Hallaq, Wael B. "The 'Qāḍī's Dīwān (Sijill)' before the Ottomans." *Bulletin of the School of Oriental and African Studies* 61, no. 3 (1998): 415–36.

Hansen, Kathryn. "The Birth of Hindi Drama in Banaras." In *Culture and Power in Banaras: Community, Performance, and Environment*, edited by Sandria Freitag, 62–92. Berkeley: University of California Press, 1989.

Hardgrove, Anne. *Community and Public Culture: The Marwaris in Calcutta, c. 1897–1997*. New York: Columbia University Press, 2003.

Hart, George L. *The Poems of Ancient Tamil: Their Milieu and Their Sanskrit Counterparts*. Berkeley: University of California Press, 1975.

Hasan, Farhat. *State and Locality in Mughal India, c. 1572–1730*. New Delhi: Cambridge University Press, 2006.

Hawley, John S. "Naming Hinduism." *Wilson Quarterly* 15, no. 3 (1991): 20–34.

———. *A Storm of Songs: India and the Idea of the Bhakti Movement*. Cambridge, MA: Harvard University Press, 2015.

Haynes, Douglas. "From Tribute to Philanthropy: The Politics of Gift Giving in a Western Indian City." *Journal of Asian Studies* 46, no. 2 (1987): 339–60.

Hooja, Rima. *A History of Rajasthan*. New Delhi: Rupa, 2006.

Horstmann, Monika. *In Favour of Govinddevjī: Historical Documents Relating to a Deity of Vrindaban and Eastern Rajasthan*. New Delhi: Indira Gandhi National Center for the Arts and Manohar, 1999.

———. "Visions of Kingship in the Twilight of Mughal Rule." Thirteenth Gonda Lecture. Amsterdam: Royal Netherlands Academy of Arts and Sciences, 2006.

———. "Theology and Statecraft." *South Asian History and Culture* 2, no. 2 (2011): 184–204.

———. "Sant and Sufi in Sundardas' Poetry." In *Religious Interactions in Mughal India*, edited by Vasudha Dalmia and Munis Faruqui, 232–63. New Delhi: Oxford University Press, 2014.

———. "Aurangzeb in the Perspective of Kachhwaha Literature." *Journal of the Royal Asiatic Society* 28, no. 3 (2018): 441–59.

———. *Bhakti and Yoga: A Discourse in Seventeenth-Century Codices*. Delhi: Primus, 2021.

Imam, Fatima A. "Institutionalizing *Rajdharma:* Strategies of Sovereignty in Eighteenth-Century Jaipur." PhD diss., University of Toronto, 2008.

———. "Decoding the Rhetoric of Morality in Eighteenth-Century India: The Interventionist Nature of the Jaipur State." *Indian Journal of Gender Studies* 21 (2014): 401–19.

Jaaware, Aniket. *Practicing Caste: On Touching and Not Touching*. New York: Fordham University Press, 2019.

Jain, Kajri. *Gods in the Bazaar: The Economies of Indian Calendar Art*. Durham, NC: Duke University Press, 2007.

Jain, Shalin. "Piety, Laity, and Royalty: Jains under the Mughals in the First Half of the Seventeenth Century." *Indian Historical Review* 40, no. 1 (2013): 67–92.

Jaini, Padmanabh. *The Jaina Path of Purification*. Delhi: Motilal Banarsidass, 1998 [1979].

Jaiswal, Suvira. *Caste: Origin, Functions, and Dimensions of Change*. New Delhi: Manohar, 1998.

Jangam, Chinnaiah. *Dalits and the Making of Modern India*. New Delhi: Oxford University Press, 2019.

Jhala, Angma D., ed. *Peacock in the Desert: The Royal Arts of Jodhpur, India*. Houston: Museum of Fine Arts, 2018.

Jodhka, Surinder. *Caste in Contemporary India*. New Delhi: Routledge, 2015.

Johnson-Roehr, Susan. "The Spatialization of Knowledge and Power at the Astronomical Observatories of Sawai Jai Singh II, c. 1721–1743 CE." PhD diss., University of Virginia, 2012.

Kadam, V. S. "The Institution of Marriage and the Position of Women in Eighteenth-Century Maharashtra." *Indian Economic and Social History Review* 25, no. 3 (1988): 341–70.

Kafadar, Çemal. *Between Two Worlds: The Construction of the Ottoman State*. Berkeley: University of California Press, 1995.

Kaicker, Abhishek. *The King and the People: Sovereignty and Popular Politics in Mughal Delhi*. New York: Oxford University Press, 2020.

Kamphorst, Janet. *In Praise of Death: History and Poetry in Medieval Marwar (South Asia)*. Leiden: Leiden University Press, 2008.

Kapadia, Aparna. *In Praise of Kings: Rajputs, Sultans and Poets in Fifteenth-Century Gujarat*. Cambridge: Cambridge University Press, 2018.

Keune, Jon. "Pedagogical Otherness: The Use of Muslims and Untouchables in Some Hindu Devotional Literature." *Journal of the American Academy of Religion* 84, no. 3 (2016): 727–49.

Khan, Dominique-Sila. *Conversions and Shifting Identities: Ramdev Pir and the Ismailis in Rajasthan*. New Delhi: Manohar, 1997.

———. *Crossing the Threshold: Understanding Religious Identities in South Asia*. London: IB Tauris, 2004.

Khanna, Priyanka. "The Female Companion in a World of Men: Friendship and Concubinage in Late Eighteenth Century Marwar." *Studies in History* 33, no. 1 (2017): 98–116.

Kia, Mana. *Persianate Selves: Memories of Place and Origin before Nationalism*. Stanford: Stanford University Press, 2020.

Kinra, Rajeev. *Writing Self, Writing Empire: Chandar Bhan Brahman and the Cultural World of the Indo-Persian State Secretary*. Oakland: University of California Press, 2015.

Kolff, Dirk H. A. *Naukar, Rajput and Sepoy: The Ethnohistory of the Military Labour Market in Hindustan, 1450–1850*. Cambridge: Cambridge University Press, 1990.

Kotani, Hiroyuki. "Ati Śūdra Castes in the Medieval Deccan." In *Caste System, Untouchability, and the Depressed*, edited by Hiroyuki Kotani, 31–53. New Delhi: Manohar, 1997.

Kothiyal, Tanuja. *Nomadic Narratives: A History of Mobility and Identity in the Great Indian Desert*. New Delhi: Cambridge University Press, 2016.

———. "A 'Mughal' Rajput or a 'Rajput' Mughal? Some Reflections on Rajput-Mughal Marriages in the Sixteenth and Seventeenth Centuries." In *Revisiting the History of Medieval Rajasthan: Essays for Professor Dilbagh Singh*, edited by Suraj Bhan Bharadwaj, Rameshwar Prasad Bahuguna, and Mayank Kumar, 264–95. New Delhi: Primus, 2017.

Kozlowski, Gregory. "Private Lives and Public Piety: Women and the Practice of Islam in Mughal India." In *Women in the Medieval Islamic World: Power, Patronage, and Piety*, edited by Gavin Hambly. New York: St. Martin's Press, 1998.

Kumar, Mayank. *Monsoon Ecologies: Irrigation, Agriculture, and Settlement Patterns in Rajasthan during the Pre-colonial Period*. New Delhi: Manohar, 2013.

Kumar, Nirmal. "Crime and Gender in Eighteenth-Century Rajasthan." *Indian Historical Review* 30, no. 1/2 (2003): 40–54.

Laine, James. *Shivaji: Hindu King in Islamic India*. New York: Oxford University Press, 2003.

Lalas, Sitaram. *Rājasthānī-Hindī Saṃkśipt Śabdkoṣ*. 2 volumes. Jodhpur: Rajasthan Oriental Research Institute, 2006 [1986].

———. "Madhyakālīn Rājasthānī Gadya Sāhitya." *Paramparā* 15–16 (1963).

Lamb, Ramdas. *Rapt in the Name: The Ramnamis, Ramnam, and the Untouchable Religion in Central India*. Albany: SUNY Press, 2002.

LaRocque, Brendan. "Trade, State and Religion in Early Modern India: Devotionalism and the Market Economy in the Mughal Empire." PhD diss., University of Wisconsin, Madison, 2004.

———. "Mahamat Prannath and the Pranami Movement: Hinduism and Islam in a Seventeenth-Century Mercantile Sect." In *Religious Interactions in Mughal India*, edited by Vasudha Dalmia and Munis Faruqui, 342–78. New Delhi: Oxford University Press, 2014.

Leclère, Basile. "Ambivalent Representations of Muslims in Medieval Indian Theatre." *Studies in History* 27, no. 2 (2011): 155–95.

Lee, Joel. *Deceptions of the Majority: Hinduism, Dalit Religion, and the Semiotics of the Oppressed*. New York: Cambridge University Press, 2021.

———. "Disgust and Untouchability: Towards an Affective Theory of Caste." *South Asian History and Culture* 12, no. 2/3 (2021): 1–18.

Leonard, Karen. "The 'Great Firm' Theory of the Decline of the Mughal Empire." *Comparative Studies in Society and History* 21, no. 2 (1979): 151–67.

———. "Indigenous Banking Firms in Mughal India: A Reply." *Comparative Studies in Society and History* 23, no. 2 (1981): 309–13.

Little, J. H. *The House of Jagat Seth*. Calcutta: Calcutta Historical Society, 1967.

Lorenzen, David. "Who Invented Hinduism?" *Comparative Studies in Society and History* 41, no. 4 (1999): 630–59.

Lucassen, Jan. "The Logistics of Wage Payments: Changing Patterns in Northern India in the 1840s." In *Wages and Currency: Global Comparisons from Antiquity to the Twentieth Century*, edited by Jan Lucassen, 349–90. New York: Peter Lang, 2007.

Lufrano, Richard John. *Honorable Merchants: Commerce and Self-Cultivation in Late Imperial China*. Honolulu: University of Hawai'i Press, 1997.

Lutgendorf, Philip. "Ram's Story in Shiva's City: Public Arenas and Private Patronage." In *Culture and Power in Banaras: Community, Performance, and Environment*, edited by Sandria Freitag, 34–61. Berkeley: University of California Press, 1989.

Makdisi, Ussama. *The Culture of Sectarianism: Community, History and Violence in Nineteenth-Century Ottoman Lebanon*. Berkeley: University of California Press, 2000.

Mallick, B. S. *Money, Banking and Trade in Mughal India: Currency, Indigenous Fiscal Practices and the English Trade in 17th Century Gujarat and Bengal*. New Delhi: Rawat, 1991.

Mamta. "Petty Moneylending to Ijaradari: Multiple Facets of Indigenous Banking of Rajasthan during Seventeenth and Eighteenth Centuries." In *Revisiting the History of Medieval Rajasthan: Essays for Professor Dilbagh Singh*, edited by Suraj Bhan Bharadwaj, Rameshwar Prasad Bahuguna, and Mayank Kumar, 197–239. New Delhi: Primus, 2017.

Markovits, Claude. "Merchant Circulation in South Asia (Eighteenth to Twentieth Centuries): The Rise of Pan-Indian Merchant Networks." In *Society and Circulation: Mobile People and Itinerant Cultures in South Asia, 1750–1950*, edited by Claude Markovits, Jacques Pouchepadass, and Sanjay Subrahmanyam, 131–61. Delhi: Permanent Black, 2003.

Meister, Michael. "Sweetmeats or Corpses? Community, Conversion, and Sacred Places." In *Open Boundaries: Jain Communities and Cultures in Indian History*, edited by John Cort, 111–38. Albany: SUNY Press, 1998.

———. "Water in a Desert Landscape." In *Desert Temples: Sacred Centers of Rajasthan in Historical, Art-Historical, and Social Contexts*, edited by Lawrence Babb, John Cort, and Michael Meister, 80–83. New Delhi: Rawat, 2008.

Menon, Dilip. "The Blindness of Insight: Why Communalism in India Is about Caste." In *The Blindness of Insight: Essays on Caste in Modern India*, edited by Dilip Menon, 1–32. New Delhi: Navayana, 2006.

Mishra, Shailka. "Painting at the Court of Jodhpur: Patronage and Artists." In *Dakhan 2018: Recent Studies in Indian Painting*, edited by John Seyller, 109–33. Hyderabad: Jagdish and Kamla Mittal Museum, 2020.

Moin, A. Azfar. *The Millennial Sovereign: Sacred Kinship and Sainthood in Islam*. New York: Columbia University Press, 2012.

Moosvi, Shireen. "Mughal Shipping at Surat in the First Half of the Seventeenth Century." *Proceedings of the Indian History Congress*, 51st Session (Calcutta, 1990): 308–20.

______. "A 'State Sector' in Overseas Trade: The Imperial Mughal Shipping Establishment at Surat." *Studies in People's History* 2, no. 1 (2015): 71–75.

Mukul, Akshaya. *Gita Press and the Making of Hindu India*. New Delhi: Harper Collins, 2015.

Narayanan, Vasudha. "Religious Vocabulary and Regional Identity: A Study of the Tamil *Cirappuranam*." In *Beyond Turk and Hindu: Rethinking Religious Identities in Islamicate South Asia*, edited by David Gilmartin and Bruce Lawrence, 74–97. Gainesville: University of Florida Press, 2000.

Natarajan, Balmurli. *The Culturization of Caste in India*. London: Routledge, 2012.

Nelson, Lance. "Cows, Elephants, Dogs, and Other Lesser Embodiments of Ātman: Reflections on Hindu Attitudes towards Non-human Animals." In *A Communion of Subjects: Animals in Religion, Science, and* Ethics, edited by Paul Waldau and Kimberly Patton, 179–93. New York: Columbia University Press, 2006.

Nicholson, Andrew J. *Unifying Hinduism: Philosophy and Identity in Indian Intellectual History*. New Delhi: Permanent Black, 2011.

Nigam, Sanjay. "Disciplining and Policing the 'Criminals by Birth,' Part 1: The Making of a Colonial Stereotype—the Criminal Tribes and Castes of North India." *Indian Economic and Social History Review* 27, no. 2 (1990): 131–64.

———. "Disciplining and Policing the 'Criminals by Birth,' Part 2: The Development of a Disciplinary System, 1871–1900." *Indian Economic and Social History Review* 27, no. 3 (1990): 257–87.

Novetzke, Christian L. *The Quotidian Revolution: Vernacularization, Religion, and the Premodern Public Sphere in India*. New York: Columbia University Press, 2016.

Ojha, Gaurishankar Hirachand. *Jodhpur Rājya kā Itihās*, vol. 2. Jodhpur: Maharaja Mansingh Pustak Prakash Library, 2010 [1936].

O'Hanlon, Rosalind. "Manliness and Imperial Service in Mughal North India." *Journal of the Economic and Social History of the Orient* 42, no. 1 (1999): 47–93.

———. "Letters Home: Banaras Pandits and the Maratha Regions in Early Modern India." *Modern Asian Studies* 44, no. 2 (2010): 201–40.

———. "The Social Worth of Scribes: Brahmins, Kāyasthas, and the Social Order in Early Modern India." *Indian Economic and Social History Review* 47, no. 4 (2010): 563–95.

———. "Performance in a World of Paper: Puranic Histories and Social Communication in Early Modern India." *Past & Present* 219, no. 1 (2013): 87–126.

———. "Disciplining the Brahman Household: The Moral Mission of Empire in the 18th Century Maratha State." In *Looking Within, Looking Without: Exploring Households in the Subcontinent through Time*, edited by Nandita Sahai and Kumkum Roy. New Delhi: Primus Books, 2015.

O'Hanlon, Rosalind, and Christopher Minkowski. "What Makes People Who They Are? Pandit Networks and the Problem of Livelihoods in Early Modern Western India." *Indian Economic and Social History Review* 45, no. 3 (2008): 381–416.

O'Hanlon, Rosalind, Gergely Hidas, and Csaba Kiss. "Discourses of Caste over the Longue Durée: Gopīnātha and Social Classification in India, ca. 1400–1900." *South Asian History and Culture* 6, no. 1 (2015): 117–18.

Olivelle, Patrick. "Hair and Society: Social Significance of Hair in South Asian Traditions." In *Language, Texts, and Society: Explorations in Ancient Indian Culture and Religion*, edited by Patrick Olivelle, 327–34. New York: Anthem Press, 2011.

Orsini, Francesca. "Inflected *Kathās*: Sufis and Krishna Bhaktas in Awadh." In *Religious Interactions in Mughal India*, edited by Vasudha Dalmia and Munis Faruqui, 95–232. New Delhi: Oxford University Press, 2014.

Pandey, Gyanendra. Introduction to *The Construction of Communalism in Colonial North India*. New Delhi: Oxford University Press, 1990.

Parihar, G. R. *Marwar and the Marathas* (1724–1843 AD). Jodhpur: Hindi Sahitya Mandir, 1968.

Parson, Rahul B. "The Bazaar and the Bari: Calcutta, Marwaris, and the World of Hindi Letters." PhD diss., University of California, Berkeley, 2012.

Pauwels, Heidi. "Romancing Rādhā: Nāgarīdās' Royal Appropriations of *Bhakti* Themes." *South Asia Research* 25, no. 1 (2005): 55–78.

———. "The Saint, the Warlord, and the Emperor: Discourses on Braj Bhakti and Bundela Loyalty." *Journal of the Economic and Social History of the Orient* 52, no. 2 (2009): 187–228.

———. "Diatribes against Śāktas in Banarasi Bazaars and Rural Rajasthan: Kabīr and His Rāmānandī Hagiographers." In *Religious Interactions in Mughal India*, edited by Vasudha Dalmia and Munis Faruqui, 290–318. New Delhi: Oxford University Press, 2014.

———. *Mobilizing Krishna's World: The Writings of Prince Sāvant Singh of Kishangarh*. Seattle: University of Washington Press, 2017.

Peabody, Norbert. "In Whose Turban Does the Lord Reside?: The Objectification of Charisma and the Fetishism of Objects in the Hindu Kingdom of Kota." *Comparative Studies in Society and History* 33, no. 4 (1991): 726–54.

———. "Cents, Sense, Census: Human Inventories in Late Precolonial and Early Colonial India." *Comparative Studies in Society and History* 43, no. 4 (2001): 819–50.

———. *Hindu Kingship and Polity in Precolonial India*. New York: Cambridge University Press, 2003.

Perlin, Frank. "Of White Whale and Countrymen in the Eighteenth-Century Maratha Deccan: Extended Class Relations, Rights, and the Problem of Rural Autonomy under the Old Regime." *Journal of Peasant Studies* 5, no. 2 (1978): 172–237.

———. "Proto-Industrialization and Pre-colonial South Asia." *Past & Present* 98, no. 1 (1983): 30–95.

Piliavsky, Anastasia. "The 'Criminal Tribe' in India before the British." *Comparative Studies in Society and History* 57, no. 2 (2015): 323–54.

Pinney, Christopher. "The Accidental Ramdev: The Spread of a Popular Cult." In *India's Popular Culture: Iconic Spaces and Fluid Images*, edited by Jyotindra Jain, 32–45. Mumbai: Marg, 2007.

Pollock, Sheldon. "Ramayana and Political Imagination in India." *Journal of Asian Studies* 52, no. 2 (1993): 261–97.

Prakash, Gyan. *Bonded Histories: Genealogies of Labor Servitude in Colonial India*. Cambridge: Cambridge University Press, 1990.

Prakash, Om. "The System of Credit in Mughal India." In *Money and Credit in Indian History: From Early Medieval Times*, edited by Amiya Kumar Bagchi. New Delhi: Tulika and Indian History Congress, 2002.

Prange, Sebastian R. *Monsoon Islam: Trade and Faith on the Medieval Malabar Coast*. New York: Cambridge University Press, 2018.

Prashad, Vijay. *Untouchable Freedom: A Social History of a Dalit Community*. New York: Oxford University Press, 2000.

Prinsep, James. "British Indian Weights & Measures." In *Essays on Indian Antiquities: Historic, Numismatic, and Palaeographic, of the Late James Prinsep, F.R.S., Secretary of the Asiatic Society of Bengal*, vol. 3, edited by Edward Thomas, 95–129. London: John Murray, 1858.

Qanungo, Kalika Ranjan. *History of the Jats*. New Delhi: DK, 2003 [1925].

Radhakrishna, Meena. *Dishonoured in History: "Criminal Tribes" and British Colonial Policy*. Hyderabad: Orient Longman, 2001.

Rai, Mridu. *Hindu Rulers, Muslim Subjects: Islam, Rights, and the History of Kashmir*. Princeton: Princeton University Press, 2004.

Rani, Kailash. "Claims and Counter-Claims: Widow Remarriage in Eighteenth-Century Marwar." In *Revisiting the History of Medieval Rajasthan: Essays for Professor Dilbagh Singh*, edited by Suraj Bhan Bharadwaj, Rameshwar Prasad Bahuguna, and Mayank Kumar, 296–309. New Delhi: Primus, 2017.

Rao, Anupama. *The Caste Question: Dalits and the Politics of Modern India*. Berkeley: University of California Press, 2009.

Rao, Velcheru Narayana, and Sanjay Subrahmanyam. "Notes on Political Thought in Medieval and Early Modern South India." *Modern Asian Studies* 43, no. 1 (2009): 175–210.

Rao, V. Narayan, David Shulman, and Sanjay Subrahmanyam. *Textures of Time: Writing History in South India, 1600–1800*. New York: Other Press, 2003.

Rathor, Prithviraj. *Veli Krishan Rukamanee Ree*. Translated by Rajvi Amar Singh. Bikaner: Rajvi Amar Singh, 1996.

Rawat, Ramnarayan S. *Reconsidering Untouchability: Chamars and Dalit History in North India*. Bloomington: Indiana University Press, 2011.

———. "Occupation, Dignity, and Space: The Rise of Dalit Studies." *History Compass* 11/12 (2013): 1059–67.

———. "Genealogies of the Dalit Political: The Transformation of Achhut from 'Untouched' to 'Untouchable' in Early Twentieth-Century North India." *Indian Economic and Social History Review* 52, no. 3 (2015): 335–55.

Rawat, Ramnarayan, and K. Satyanarayana. Introduction to *Dalit* Studies, edited by Ramnarayan Rawat and K. Satyanarayana, 1–30. Durham, NC: Duke University Press, 2016.

Reu, Vishveshvar Nath. *Marvāḍ kā Itihās*, vol. 1. Jodhpur: Maharaja Mansingh Pustak Prakash, 1999 [1940].

———. *Coins of Marwar*. Jodhpur: Jodhpur Government Press, 1946.

Richards, John F. "Mughal State Finance and the Premodern World Economy." *Comparative Studies in Society and History* 23, no. 2 (1981): 285–308.

———. "The Formulation of Imperial Authority under Akbar and Jahangir." In *Kingship and Authority in South Asia*, edited by J. F. Richards. New Delhi: Oxford University Press, 1998.

Roberts, Nathaniel. *To Be Cared For: The Power of Conversion and the Foreignness of Belonging in an Indian Slum*. Oakland: University of California Press, 2016.

Roper, Lyndal. "Will and Honor: Sex, Words and Power in Augsburg Criminal Trials." *Radical History Review* 43 (1989): 45–71.

Ruegg, D. Seyfort. "Ahiṃsā and Vegetarianism in the History of Buddhism." In *Buddhist Studies in Honor of Walpola Rahula*, edited by Somaratna Balasooriya et al., 234–41. London: Gordon Fraser Gallery, 1980.

Rustow, Marina. *The Lost Archive: Traces of a Caliphate in a Cairo Synagogue*. Princeton, NJ: Princeton University Press, 2020.

Saha, Shandip. "Creating a Community of Grace: A History of the *Puṣṭi Mārga* in Northern and Western India (1493–1905)." PhD diss., University of Ottawa, 2004.

———. "The Movement of Bhakti along a North-West Axis: Tracing the History of the Puṣṭīmarg between the Sixteenth and Nineteenth Centuries." *International Journal of Hindu Studies* 11, no. 3 (2007): 299–318.

———. "Muslims as Devotees and Outsiders: Attitudes toward Muslims in the Vārtā Literature of the Vallabha Sampradāya." In *Religious Interactions in Mughal India*, edited by Vasudha Dalmia and Munis Faruqui, 319–41. New Delhi: Oxford University Press, 2014.

Sahai, Nandita Prasad. "Collaboration and Conflict: Artisanal Jati Panchayats and the Eighteenth Century Jodhpur State." *Medieval History Journal* 5, no. 1 (2002): 77–101.

———. "Artisans, the State, and the Politics of Wajabi in Eighteenth Century Jodhpur." *Indian Economic and Social History Review* 42, no. 1 (2005): 41–68.

———. "Crafts in Eighteenth-Century Jodhpur: Questions of Caste, Class and Community Identities." *Journal of the Economic History of the Orient* 48, no. 4 (2005): 524–51.

———. *Politics of Patronage and Protest: The State, Society, and Artisans in Early Modern Rajasthan*. New Delhi: Oxford University Press, 2006.

———. "Crafts and Statecraft in Eighteenth-Century Jodhpur." *Modern Asian Studies* 41, no. 4 (2007): 683–722.

———. "The 'Other' Culture: Craft Society and Widow Remarriage in Early Modern India." *Journal of Women's History* 19, no. 1 (2007): 36–58.

———. "Crossing the Golden Gate? Sunars, Social Mobility, and Disciplining the Household in Early Modern Rajasthan." In *Looking Within, Looking Without: Exploring Households in the Subcontinent through Time*, edited by Nandita Sahai and Kumkum Roy, 389–408. New Delhi: Primus Books, 2015.

Saran, Richard D. "Conquest and Colonization: Rajputs and Vasis in Middle Period Marvar." PhD diss., University of Michigan, 1978.

Saran, Richard D., and Norman P. Ziegler. *The Meṛtīyo Rāṭhoṛs of Meṛto, Rājasthān: Select Translations Bearing on the History of a Rājpūt Family, 1462–1660*, vol. 2. Ann Arbor: University of Michigan Press, 2001.

Sato, Masanori. "Ati Śūdras in the Medieval Deccan." In *Caste System, Untouchability, and the Depressed*, edited by Hiroyuki Kotani, 55–75. New Delhi: Manohar, 1997.

———. "The Chamārs of South-Eastern Rajasthan, A.D. 1650–1800." In *Caste System, Untouchability, and the Depressed*, edited by Hiroyuki Kotani, 31–53. New Delhi: Manohar, 1997.

Saxena, R. K. *Apparatus of the Rathors (A Study of Marwar): Assignment of Jagirs, Award of Offices, Titles and Honors to the Rathor Nobility (1764–1858 V. S.)*, vol. 1. Jodhpur: Maharaja Mansingh Pustak Prakash Research Centre, 2006.

Schwartz, Henry. *Constructing the Criminal Tribe in Colonial India: Acting Like a Thief.* London: Wiley-Blackwell, 2010.

Sethia, Madhu Tandon. *Rajput Polity: Warriors, Peasants, and Merchants (1700–1900).* New Delhi: Rawat, 2003.

Shackle, Christopher. "Beyond Turk and Hindu: Crossing the Boundaries in Indo-Muslim Romance." In *Beyond Turk and Hindu: Rethinking Religious Identities in Islamicate South Asia*, edited by David Gilmartin and Bruce Lawrence, 55–73. Gainesville: University of Florida Press, 2000.

Sharma, G. D. *Rajput Polity: A Study of Politics and Administration of the State of Marwar, 1638–1749.* New Delhi: Manohar, 1977.

———. "Urban Social Structure: A Case Study of the Towns of Western Rajasthan during the Seventeenth Century." In *Studies in Urban History*, edited by J. S. Grewal and Indu Banga, 70–79. Amritsar: Department of History, Guru Nanak Dev University, 1981.

———. "*Vyaparis* and *Mahajans* in Western Rajasthan during the Eighteenth Century." In *Essays in Medieval Indian Economic History*, edited by Satish Chandra, 284–91. New Delhi: Munshiram Manoharlal, 1987.

Sharma, Ram Sharan. Śudras in Ancient India: A Social History of the Lower Order *Down to Circa AD 600.* Delhi: Motilal Banarsidass, 1990 [1958].

Sheikh, Samira. *Forging a Region: Sultans, Traders and Pilgrims in Gujarat, 1200–1500.* New Delhi: Oxford University Press, 2010.

———. "Jijabhu's Rights to Ghee: Land Control and Vernacular Capitalism in Gujarat, circa 1803–10." *Modern Asian Studies* 51, no. 2 (2017): 350–74.

———. "Aurangzeb as Seen from Gujarat: Shi'i and Millenarian Challenges to Mughal Sovereignty." *Journal of the Royal Asiatic Society* 28, no. 3 (2018): 557–81.

Sheth, Sudev J. "Business Households, Financial Capital and Public Authority in India, 1650–1818." PhD diss., University of Pennsylvania, 2018.

Simmons, Caleb. *Devotional Sovereignty: Kingship and Religion in India.* New York: Oxford University Press, 2020.

Singh, Dilbagh. "The Role of Mahajans in the Rural Economy in Eastern Rajasthan during the 18th Century." *Social Scientist* 2, no. 10 (1974): 20–31.

———. *The State, Landlords and Peasants: Rajasthan in the 18th Century.* Columbia, MO: South Asia Publications, 1990.

———. "Regulating the Domestic: Notes on the Pre-colonial State and the Family." *Studies in History* 19, no. 1 (2003): 69–86.

Singh, Upinder. *Political Violence in Ancient India.* Cambridge, MA: Harvard University Press, 2017.

Singha, Radhika. *A Despotism of Law: Crime and Justice in Early Colonial India.* New Delhi: Oxford University Press, 2000.

Sinha, Surajit. "State Formation and Rajput Myth in Tribal Central India." *Man in India* 42, no. 1 (1962): 35–80.

Smith, Brian K. "Questioning Authority: Constructions and Deconstructions of Hinduism." *International Journal of Hindu Studies* 2, no. 3 (1998): 313–39.

Smith, John D. *The Epic of Pabuji: A Study, Transcription and Translation.* Cambridge: Cambridge University Press, 1991.

Smith, Wilfred Cantwell. *The Meaning and End of Religion: A Revolutionary Approach to the Great Religious Traditions.* San Francisco: Harper & Row, 1978.

Sreenivasan, Ramya. "Honoring the Family: Narratives and Politics of Kingship in Pre-colonial Rajasthan." In *Unfamiliar Relations: Family and History in South Asia*, edited by Indrani Chatterjee. New Brunswick, NJ: Rutgers University Press, 2004.

———. "The Marriage of 'Hindu' and '*Turak*': Medieval Rajput Histories of Jalor." *Medieval History Journal* 7, no. 1 (2004): 87–108.

———. "Drudges, Dancing Girls, Concubines: Female Slaves in Rajput Polity, 1500–1850." In *Slavery and South Asian History*, edited by Indrani Chatterjee and Richard Eaton, 136–61. Bloomington: Indian University Press, 2006.

———. *The Many Lives of a Rajput Queen: Heroic Lives in India, c. 1500–1900*. Seattle: University of Washington Press, 2007.

———. "Warrior-Tales at Hinterland Courts in North India, c. 1370–1550." In *After Timur Left: Culture and Circulation in Fifteenth-Century North India*, edited by Francesca Orsini and Samira Sheikh, 243–73. Delhi: Oxford University Press, 2014.

———. "Faith and Allegiance in the Mughal Era: Perspectives from Rajasthan." In *Religious Interactions in Mughal India*, edited by Vasudha Dalmia and Munis Faruqui, 159–191. New Delhi: Oxford University Press, 2014.

———. "Rethinking Kingship and Authority in South Asia: Amber (Rajasthan), ca. 1560–1615." *Journal of the Economic and Social History of the Orient* 57, no. 4 (2014): 576–79.

Stein, Burton. "State Formation and Economy Reconsidered: Part One." *Modern Asian Studies* 19, no. 3 (1985): 387–413.

Stewart, Tony. "Alternate Structures of Authority: Satya Pīr on the Frontiers of Bengal." In *Beyond Turk and Hindu: Rethinking Religious Identities in Islamicate South Asia*, edited by David Gilmartin and Bruce Lawrence, 21–54. Gainesville: University of Florida Press, 2000.

Stoker, Valerie. *Polemics and Patronage in the City of Victory: Vyasatirtha, Hindu Sectarianism, and the Sixteenth-Century Vijayanagara Court*. Oakland: University of California Press, 2016.

Strauch, Ingo. "Dharma." *Brill's Encyclopedia of Hinduism Online*, edited by Knut A. Jacobsen et al. http://dx.doi.org/10.1163/2212-5019_beh_COM_2050090.

Subrahmanyam, Sanjay. Introduction to *Money and Market in India, 1100–1700*, edited by Sanjay Subrahmanyam, 1–56. Delhi: Oxford University Press, 1994.

———. "Iranians Abroad: Intra-Asian Elite Migration and State Formation." *Journal of Asian Studies* 51, no. 2 (1992): 340–63.

———. "Connected Histories: Notes towards a Reconfiguration of Early Modern Eurasia." *Modern Asian Studies* 31, no. 3 (1997): 735–62.

———. *Explorations in Connected History: From the Tagus to the Ganges*. New Delhi: Oxford University Press, 2005.

———. *Three Ways to Be Alien: Travails and Encounters in the Early Modern World*. Waltham, MA: Brandeis University Press / Historical Society of Israel, 2011.

———. "Between Eastern Africa and Western India, 1500–1650: Slavery, Commerce, and Elite Formation." *Comparative Studies in Society and History* 61, no. 4 (2019): 805–34.

Subrahmanyam, Sanjay, and Christopher A. Bayly. "Portfolio Capitalists and the Political Economy of Early Modern India." *Indian Economic and Social History Review* 25, no. 4 (1988): 401–23.

Subramanian, Lakshmi. *Indigenous Capital and Imperial Expansion: Bombay, Surat and the West Coast*. Delhi: Oxford University Press, 1996.

Taft, Frances H. "Honor and Alliance: Reconsidering Mughal-Rajput Marriages.' In *The Idea of Rajasthan: Explorations in Regional Identity*, vol. 2, edited by Karine Schomer et al., 217–41. New Delhi: Manohar, 2001.

Talbot, Cynthia. "Inscribing the Other, Inscribing the Self: Hindu-Muslim Identities in Pre-colonial India." *Comparative Studies in Society and History* 37, no. 4 (1995): 692–722.

———. *Pre-colonial India in Practice: Society, Region and Identity in Medieval Andhra*. New York: Oxford University Press, 2001.

———. "Becoming Turk the Rajput Way: Conversion and Identity in an Indian Warrior Narrative." *Modern Asian Studies* 43, no. 1 (2009): 211–43.

———. *The Last Hindu Emperor: Prithviraj Chauhan and the Indian Past, 1200–1800*. Cambridge: Cambridge University Press, 2016.

Tambs-Lyche, Harald. "Goddesses of Western India." In *Brill's Encyclopedia of Hinduism Online*, edited by Knut A. Jacobsen et al. http://dx.doi.org/10.1163/2212-5019_BEH_COM_1010073187.

Teltumbde, Anand. "Introduction to the Revised Edition." In *Hindutva and Dalits: Perspectives for Understanding Communal Practice*, rev. ed., edited by Anand Teltumbde. New Delhi: Sage, 2020.

Tezcan, Baki. *The Second Ottoman Empire: Political and Social Transformation in the Early Modern World*. New York: Cambridge University Press, 2010.

Thapar, Romila. "Ethics, Religion, and Social Protest in the First Millennium BC in Northern India." *Daedalus* 104, no. 2 (1975): 119–32.

———. "Imagined Religious Communities? Ancient History and the Search for a Hindu Identity." *Modern Asian Studies* 23, no. 2 (1989): 209–31.

Thelen, Elizabeth. "Intersected Communities: Urban Histories of Rajasthan, c. 1500–1800." PhD diss., University of California, Berkeley, 2018.

Thompson, E. P. *Customs in Common: Studies in Popular Culture*. New York: W. W. Norton, 1993.

Tillotson, Giles. *Mehrangarh: Jodhpur Fort and Palace Museum*. Jodhpur: Mehrangarh Museum Trust, 2010.

Timberg, Thomas A. *The Marwaris: From Traders to Industrialists*. New Delhi: Vikas, 1979.

Tod, James. *Annals and Antiquities of Rajast'han or, the Central and Western Rajpoot States of India*, vol. 2. New Delhi: Rupa, 1997 [1832].

Tripathi, Dwijendra, and M. J. Mehta. "The Nagarsheth of Ahmedabad: The History of an Urban Institution in a Gujarati City." *Proceedings of the Indian History Congress* 39 (1978): 481–96.

Trivellato, Francesca. *The Familiarity of Strangers: The Sephardic Diaspora, Livorno, and Cross-Cultural Trade in the Early Modern Period*. New Haven, CT: Yale University Press, 2009.

Truschke, Audrey. "Setting the Record Wrong: A Sanskrit Vision of Mughal Conquests." *South Asian History and Culture* 3, no. 3 (2012): 373–96.

———. "Dangerous Debates: Jain Responses to Theological Challenges at the Mughal Court." *Modern Asian Studies* 49, no. 5 (2015): 1311–44.

———. *Culture of Encounters: Sanskrit at the Mughal Court*. New York: Columbia University Press, 2016.

———. *Aurangzeb: The Life and Legacy of India's Most Controversial King*. Stanford, CA: Stanford University Press, 2017.

———. *The Language of History: Sanskrit Narratives of Indo-Muslim Rule*. New York: Columbia University Press, 2021.

Tyagi, Mamta. "Moneylenders in the Jaipur State during the Pre-colonial Period." In *Revisiting the History of Medieval Rajasthan: Essays for Professor Dilbagh Singh*, edited by Suraj Bhan Bharadwaj, Rameshwar Prasad Bahuguna, and Mayank Kumar, 310–36. New Delhi: Primus, 2017.

Varghese, Ajay. *The Colonial Origins of Ethnic Violence in India*. Stanford: Stanford University Press, 2016.

Vaudeville, Charlotte. *Myths, Saints, and Legends in Medieval India*. Compiled and introduced by Vasudha Dalmia. Delhi: Oxford University Press, 1996.

Venkatkrishnan, Anand. "Mīmāṃsā, Vedānta, and the Bhakti Movement." PhD diss., Columbia University, 2015.

Vidal, Denis. *Violence and Truth: A Rajasthani Kingdom Confronts Colonial Authority*. Delhi: Oxford University Press, 1997.

Viswanath, Rupa. *The Pariah Problem: Caste, Religion, and the Social in Modern India*. New York: Columbia University Press, 2014.

von Stietencron, Heinrich. 1995. "Religious Configurations in Pre-Muslim India and the Modern Concept of Hinduism." In *Representing Hinduism: The Construction of Religious Traditions and National Identity*, edited by V. Dalmia and H. von Stietencron. New Delhi: Sage, 51–81.

Vose, Steven. "The Making of a Medieval Jain Monk: Language, Power, and Authority in the Works of Jinaprabhasūri (c. 1261–1333)." PhD diss., University of Pennsylvania, 2013.

———. "Jain Memory of the Tughluq Sultans: Alternative Sources for the Historiography of Sultanate India." *Journal of the Royal Asiatic Society* 32, no. 1 (2022): 115–39.

Wagle, N. K. "Women in the Kotwāl's Papers, Pune, 1767–1791." In *Images of Women in Maharashtrian Society*, edited by Anne Feldhaus, 15–60. Albany: SUNY Press, 1998.

Wagoner, Phillip B. "'Sultan among Hindu Kings': Dress, Titles, and the Islamicization of Hindu Culture at Vijayanagara." *Modern Asian Studies* 55, no. 4 (1996): 851–80.

Williams, Tyler. "Sacred Sounds and Sacred Books: A History of Writing in Hindi." PhD diss., Columbia University, 2014.

———. "The Ties That Bind: Individual, Family, and Community in Northwestern Bhakti." In *Bhakti and Power: Debating India's Religion of the Heart*, edited by John S. Hawley, Christian L. Novetzke, and Swapna Sharma, 192–202. Seattle: University of Washington Press, 2019.

Wilson, Horace H. *A Dictionary in Sanskrit and English: Translated, Amended, and Enlarged from an Original Compilation*. Calcutta: Education Press, 1832.

Wink, André. *Land and Sovereignty in India: Agrarian Society and Politics under the Eighteenth-Century Maratha Svarājya*. Cambridge: Cambridge University Press, 1986.

———. *Early Medieval India and the Expansion of Islam*, vol. 1 of *Al-Hind: The Making of the Indo-Islamic World*. Delhi: Oxford University Press, 1990.

———. *Akbar*. Oxford: Oneworld, 2009.

Yang, Anand A. "Sacred Symbol and Sacred Space in Rural India: Community Mobilization in the 'Anti-Cow Killing' Riot of 1893." *Comparative Studies in Society and History* 22, no. 4 (1980): 576–96.

———. "Dangerous Castes and Tribes: The Criminal Tribes Act and the Magahiya Doms of Northeast India." In *Crime and Criminality in British India*, edited by Anand A. Yang, 108–27. Tucson: University of Arizona Press, 1985.

Yaycıoğlu, Ali. *Partners of the Empire: The Crisis of the Ottoman Order in the Age of Revolutions*. Stanford: Stanford University Press, 2016.

Zaidi, S. Inayat A., and Sunita Zaidi. "Conversion to Islam and Formation of Castes in Medieval Rajasthan." In *Art and Culture: Felicitation Volume in Honour of Professor S. Nurul Hasan*, edited by Ahsan Jan Qaisar and Som Prakash Verma, 27–42. Jaipur: Publication Scheme, 1993.

Zelliot, Eleanor. "Chokhamela: Piety and Protest." In *Bhakti Religion in North India: Community Identity and Political Protest*, edited by David Lorenzen. Albany: SUNY Press, 1995.

Ziegler, Norman P. "Action, Power, and Service in Rajasthani Culture." PhD diss., University of Chicago, 1973.

———. "Marvari Historical Chronicles: Sources for the Social and Cultural History of Rajasthan." *Indian Economic and Social History Review* 13, no. 2 (1976): 219–50.

———. "Some Notes on Rajput Loyalties during the Mughal Period." In *The Mughal State, 1526–1707*, edited by Muzaffar Alam and Sanjay Subrahmanyam, 169–210. New Delhi: Oxford University Press, 1998.

INDEX

Abhai Singh, 188n87
abortion (*adhūrā nākhnā, ādhān nākhnā,* or *tāb nākhnā*) 14, 15, 103, 122, 131; differential punishments by caste for, 144–47, 150–51, 152–53, 154; "incestuous" relationships and, 149–50; performed by Jain monks or *yatis*, 144, 146, 216–17n12; surveillance and informing in policing of, 147–48
Abu'l Fazl, 115
achhep (untouchable), 4, 5, 56, 73, 86; defined and separated from "Hindu," 61*fig.*; Hindu identity defined against, 102; as legal category, 53, 57; used in administrative documents, 59. *See also* untouchability and "the Untouchable"
Africa, 6, 8
Agarwal caste, 28, 33
Agarval/Agarvala caste-name: Chimna, 152; Naga, 148; Sukha, 149
Ajit Singh, Maharaja, 18, 80, 188n87
Akbar (Mughal emperor), 20, 75, 115, 210n51
Alam, Muzaffar, 189n99
alcohol consumption bans, 14, 15, 29, 30, 104, 122; animal slaughter prohibition linked with, 130–32; drinking during Holi festival, 132; enforcement of, 133, 134, 135–36; "high" castes as main target of, 131, 139, 154; social polarization generated by, 133–35; state employees as violators of, 132; universal applicability in principle, 103, 124; vegetarianism linked with, 129–30
All India Agarwal Mahasabha, 221n37
Alsdorf, Ludwig, 112
Ambedkar, B. R., 8, 55, 59, 166
Amin, Shahid, 68
animal slaughter prohibition, 12, 13, 64, 90, 107, 203n26; differential punishments by caste, 86, 131; effect on diets and livelihoods of Marwar population, 96–97; in historical perspective, 115; mercantile ethics and, 126–29; ordeal (*dhīj*) from accusations, 128; punishment for animal slaughter, 92, 104; social polarization generated by, 100–101, 104; surveillance and informers in enforcement of, 97–101, 102
Arabic language/literature, 44, 65–66
Ardhakathanka (Banarsidas autobiography), 190n114
artisans, 38, 44, 49, 72, 121
Arya Samaj (Hindu reform movement), 162, 163
asceticism, 73, 112, 124, 137–38, 157
Ashoka, emperor, 113, 115, 209n43
Asiya, 95
Asopa, Fatehram, 73, 97, 100, 128; Surajmal, 73, 97, 118, 187n76
Atmaram, Guru, 22
Aurangzeb (Mughal emperor), 28, 79, 80, 201n76; death of, 18, 184n30; moneylenders and, 34
austerity, bodily, 8, 15, 46, 124–26, 166; as marker of high social rank, 156; reconstitution of the Self and, 107; religious gifting/charity and, 110, 152
Awadh, 33, 47, 70

SERIES LIST

South Asia Across the Disciplines is a series devoted to publishing across a wide range of South Asian studies, including art, history, philology or textual studies, philosophy, religion, and the interpretive social sciences. Series authors all share the goal of opening up new archives and suggesting new methods and approaches, while demonstrating that South Asian scholarship can be at once deep in expertise and broad in appeal.

Extreme Poetry: The South Asian Movement of Simultaneous Narration, by Yigal Bronner (Columbia)

The Social Space of Language: Vernacular Culture in British Colonial Punjab, by Farina Mir (UC Press)

Unifying Hinduism: Philosophy and Identity in Indian Intellectual History, by Andrew J. Nicholson (Columbia)

The Powerful Ephemeral: Everyday Healing in an Ambiguously Islamic Place, by Carla Bellamy (UC Press)

Secularizing Islamists? Jama'at-e-Islami and Jama'at-ud-Da'wa in Urban Pakistan, by Humeira Iqtidar (Chicago)

Islam Translated: Literature, Conversion, and the Arabic Cosmopolis of South and Southeast Asia, by Ronit Ricci (Chicago)

Conjugations: Marriage and Form in New Bollywood Cinema, by Sangita Gopal (Chicago)

Unfinished Gestures: Devadāsīs, Memory, and Modernity in South India, by Davesh Soneji (Chicago)

Document Raj: Writing and Scribes in Early Colonial South India, by Bhavani Raman (Chicago)

The Millennial Sovereign: Sacred Kingship and Sainthood in Islam, by A. Azfar Moin (Columbia)

Making Sense of Tantric Buddhism: History, Semiology, and Transgression in the Indian Traditions, by Christian K. Wedemeyer (Columbia)

The Yogin and the Madman: Reading the Biographical Corpus of Tibet's Great Saint Milarepa, by Andrew Quintman (Columbia)

Body of Victim, Body of Warrior: Refugee Families and the Making of Kashmiri Jihadists, by Cabeiri deBergh Robinson (UC Press)

Receptacle of the Sacred: Illustrated Manuscripts and the Buddhist Book Cult in South Asia, by Jinah Kim (UC Press)

Cut-Pieces: Celluloid Obscenity and Popular Cinema in Bangladesh, by Lotte Hoek (Columbia)

From Text to Tradition: The Naisadhīyacarita and Literary Community in South Asia, by Deven M. Patel (Columbia)

Democracy against Development: Lower Caste Politics and Political Modernity in Postcolonial India, by Jeffrey Witsoe (Chicago)

Into the Twilight of Sanskrit Poetry: The Sena Salon of Bengal and Beyond, by Jesse Ross Knutson (UC Press)

Voicing Subjects: Public Intimacy and Mediation in Kathmandu, by Laura Kunreuther (UC Press)

Writing Resistance: The Rhetorical Imagination of Hindi Dalit Literature, by Laura R. Brueck (Columbia)

Wombs in Labor: Transnational Commercial Surrogacy in India, by Amrita Pande (Columbia)

I Too Have Some Dreams: N.M. Rashed and Modernism in Urdu Poetry, by A. Sean Pue (UC Press)

The Place of Devotion: Siting and Experiencing Divinity in Bengal-Vaishnavism, by Sukanya Sarbadhikary (UC Press)

We Were Adivasis: Aspiration in an Indian Scheduled Tribe, by Megan Moodie (Chicago)

Writing Self, Writing Empire: Chandar Bhan Brahman and the Cultural World of the Indo-Persian State Secretary, by Rajeev Kinra (UC Press)

Landscapes of Accumulation: Real Estate and the Neoliberal Imagination in Contemporary India, by Llerena Searle (Chicago)

Polemics and Patronage in the City of Victory: Vyasatirtha, Hindu Sectarianism, and the Sixteenth-Century Vijayanagara Court, by Valerie Stoker (UC Press)

Hindu Pluralism: Religion and the Public Sphere in Early Modern South India, by Elaine M. Fisher (UC Press)

Negotiating Languages: Urdu, Hindi, and the Definition of Modern South Asia, by Walter N. Hakala (Columbia)

Building Histories: The Archival and Affective Lives of Five Monuments in Modern Delhi, by Mrinalini Rajagopalan (Chicago)

Reading the Mahavamsa: The Literary Aims of a Theravada Buddhist History, by Kristin Scheible (Columbia)

Modernizing Composition: Sinhala Song, Poetry, and Politics in Twentieth-Century Sri Lanka, by Garrett Field (UC Press)

Language of the Snakes: Prakrit, Sanskrit, and the Language Order of Premodern India, by Andrew Ollett (UC Press)

The Hegemony of Heritage: Ritual and the Record in Stone, by Deborah L. Stein (UC Press)

The Monastery Rules: Buddhist Monastic Organization in Pre-Modern Tibet, by Berthe Jansen (UC Press)

Merchants of Virtue: Hindus, Muslims, and Untouchables in Eighteenth-Century South Asia, by Divya Cherian (UC Press)